KANSAS SCHOOL OF RELIGION

W9-AGX-948

LAWRENCE, KANSAS

NICOLAS ZERNOV

is Spalding Lecturer in Eastern Orthodox
Culture in the University of Oxford. Born
in Moscow in 1898, he graduated in
Theology from Belgrade University. For
some time he worked as general secretary
of the Russian Student Movement in exile,
with its headquarters in Paris. Later he
moved to England and became the secretary of the Fellowship of St Alban and
St Sergius and honorary lecturer at the
School of Slavonic Studies in London
University.

Dr Zernov has held a number of academic appointments. He was the Principal of the Catholicate College of Pathan-
amthitta in South India, and visiting
Professor of Ecumenical Theology at Drew
University, New Jersey, USA.

HISTORY OF RELIGION

Eastern Christendom

Eastern Christendom

*A Study of the Origin and Development of the Eastern
Orthodox Church*

NICOLAS ZERNOV

*Spalding Lecturer in Eastern Orthodox Culture,
University of Oxford*

WEIDENFELD AND NICOLSON
20 NEW BOND STREET LONDON WI

© 1961 by Nicolas Zernov

SET IN 11-ON-13 POINT BASKERVILLE AND
PRINTED IN GREAT BRITAIN BY THE SHENVAL PRESS
LONDON, HERTFORD AND HARLOW
17/6905

CONTENTS

5

incorporation of the Ukraine into Moscow Tsardom and the Council of 1666–67—Archpriest Avvacam (1620–82)—The Russian Church on the eve of the reforms of Peter the Great (1668–98)—Peter the Great (1682–1725) and the abolition of the Moscow Patriarchate—The Nonjurors and the Orthodox Church—The St Petersburg Empire and the Russian Church in the eighteenth century—St Tikhon of Zadonsk and Paisy Velichkovsky—Western ascendancy over the Christian East—The Church of St Thomas in South India—The Church of Ethiopia—The Nestorian Church of the East—The Church of the Armenians—The Coptic Church—The Jacobites—Balkan Christians in the seventeenth and eighteenth centuries—The Eastern Orthodox under the Hapsburg rule—The Christian East at the time of its decline (fifteenth–eighteenth centuries)

CONTENTS

LIST OF ILLUSTRATIONS

This book is dedicated to the memory of
H. N. Spalding, 1877–1953
and of his wife
Nellie Spalding, 1876–1957
whose vision and generosity endowed the study of Eastern Christianity
in the University of Oxford

PREFACE

CHRISTENDOM has been identified with Europe for more than a millennium. In the eyes of Asiatic and African people Christianity is the religion of Western man and is closely linked with the scientific and technical civilization which has originated in Western Europe. This generally accepted picture, however, misses an important fact; at least a third of all contemporary Christians do not consider themselves Western, but describe their Church as Eastern Orthodox.

If one could take in all Europe at a glance from some central point such as Switzerland one would be struck by a great division in the architecture of the churches. In the West the churches have steeples, spires and square towers rising above the ordinary dwellings. In the East, by contrast, domes and cupolas replace the spires, and the further East one looks the more complete is the transformation. Moreover the interior of the Eastern churches reveals an even greater difference. A solid screen separates the eastern end from the rest of the building and conceals the altar from the congregation, except when the central door in it is opened. These round churches with cupolas, richly decorated with sacred pictures, mark the Eastern half of Christendom.

Greece, the Balkans, the Caucasus, Western Asia, Egypt and Ethiopia are the traditional home of the Orthodox Churches. Russia and Siberia were added to them later. The lands of the Eastern Christians at present form geographically a huge triangle separating the Christian West from the non-Christian Oriental world. Its base is 12,000 miles long, stretching across the Russo-Siberian plain from Petzamo in the West on the Arctic Ocean where the Russian and Finnish frontiers meet, to Alaska in the East where the Indians were Christianized by the Russian missionaries in the nineteenth century. The western side of the triangle cuts across Finland, Estonia and Latvia, moves south towards Galicia and the Carpathian Mountains, splits Jugoslavia in two halves, touches Albania and reaches the Southern apex of the triangle in Egypt. The eastern side runs through Ethiopia, passes across Palestine, Syria and Iraq, and from there reaches Turkestan, Manchuria, North China, Japan and Korea. The great majority of Eastern Christians now live within this triangle.

One isolated outpost of Eastern Christianity is to be found in South

15

India, where the Orthodox Church has survived in Travancore until the present day, the remnant of the previously widespread Nestorian Church of the Persian Empire. Communities of Eastern Orthodox can also be found all over Western Europe, especially in France and Belgium. They are also scattered throughout Great Britain and her Dominions. Africa has many Orthodox Christians, mostly Greeks and Syrians, and there is a native African Orthodox Church in Uganda. Australia too has many Russian and Greek parishes. The largest number of Orthodox in the West live in the United States of America, which has three million Orthodox drawn from almost every nation of the Christian East.

The geographical position of the Eastern Christians explains their history. Placed between the Christian West and Islam, the Eastern Christians had to face pressure from both sides, and this led to their defeat and to the loss of their political freedom. All Eastern Christians have experienced the bitterness of the yoke of hostile neighbours at some period of their history, but most have eventually regained their independence, although at the cost of part of their former territory and some of their co-religionists. This has meant that the Eastern Christians situated on the fringe of the triangle have been divided and partially absorbed into communities foreign to them. This has happened all along the Eastern frontier where the Eastern Christians have lived for centuries subjected to their Islamic conquerors: in Egypt, Syria and Iraq the Christians are now only a minority, whereas in the past these countries were the strongholds of Eastern Orthodoxy. On the Western frontier the picture is the same. The Albanians and Jugoslavs are divided by their ecclesiastical allegiance; some are Latins, others Orthodox. A similar situation exists in the frontier countries of Czechoslovakia, Latvia, Estonia and Finland. The people of all these lands belong partly to Eastern and partly to Western traditions, while the nations inside the triangle, the Greeks, Serbians, Bulgarians, Rumanians, Russians and Georgians, are solidly Orthodox.

Christianity is essentially a universal religion not confined to any one region or nation, and yet its concrete manifestations are strongly coloured by language, temperament and the local customs of its adherents.

The present work is concerned mainly with the Eastern part of Christendom to whose history, teaching, worship and art it is intended as a general introduction. But although the Christian East and West have lived a separate existence for the last five hundred years, and at times have almost lost sight of each other, they cannot be studied in isolation. Their similarity and contrast, their attraction and repulsion form a central theme of Church history, and their relations are therefore referred to on many pages of this book.

Those readers who desire more detailed knowledge of the Eastern Church will find some additional material in the notes and classified bibliography.

The seventy-one illustrations cover both the architecture of Eastern Churches and also mosaics, frescoes and ikons which have a prominent place in the life and worship of the Orthodox. Some of them show the religious ceremonies and customs of the Christian East.

In producing this book I have been assisted by several people to whom I owe much gratitude. To Mrs Arthur Ward for typing my manuscript, to the Reverend Patrick Thompson, and Mrs Essex-Lewis for reading it and making valuable suggestions, to Professor T. Talbot Rice for his comments on the chapter on the Sacred Art, to Miss Vanessa Jebb and Mrs Robin Porteous for their help in selecting the illustrations. My special thanks are due to Professor E. O. James for his advice and encouragement, and to Miss Mary Bromley who read the first draft of this work and helped me to put into its final shape.

Oxford   N. ZERNOV

CHAPTER ONE

THE CHURCH IN THE EAST DURING
THE STRUGGLE FOR SURVIVAL
(I–IV CENTURIES)

The Church and Judaism—The split of the Church from Israel—The Church and Hellenism—The Church and the Roman State—The persecution: its origin and nature—The causes of the Christian victory—Early sects and heresies—Writers and teachers of the Eastern Church in the second and third centuries

The Church and Judaism

THE CHRISTIAN community came into being on the Feast of Pentecost, when a small group of Galileans 'were all filled with the Holy Ghost, and began to speak with other tongues, as the Spirit gave them utterance'.[1] This event took place in Jerusalem, a frontier city of the Roman Empire, facing the unconquered Orient. It opened a new era in the spiritual evolution of mankind. The new religion spread rapidly along the lines of communication within the Jewish Diaspora. During the lifetime of the Apostles this expansion reached Spain and probably India; Rome, Alexandria, Antioch and other great cities became centres of Christian activities.

The history of the Church presents a picture of continual adaptation to an ever-changing environment. It consists of advances and retreats, victories and defeats; but in spite of all these changes it reveals such a tenacity of purpose, such a unity of faith, that the Christian Church is distinguished from all other religions.

The first problem which confronted the followers of the Messiah was adjustment to the Jewish community within which their religion was born. The Jews occupied a unique place in the Roman multinational State. Racially akin to the other inhabitants of Syria and Arabia, they yet formed a closely knit group, fiercely resisting fusion with their neighbours. This stubborn aloofness was an outcome of their religious history, for the Jews not only professed an uncompromising monotheism, sharply opposed to the predominant polytheism of other nations, but also believed that God had entered into a personal covenant with Israel, had ordered His chosen people to obey His law, and had promised to redeem them from sin and oppression. The books of the Old Testament contain the story of a long process of education and purification, in the course of which Israel, sometimes obedient, sometimes rebellious, had brought

19

a new race into being, capable of fulfilling the task assigned to it by Yahweh. Faith in the humanly impossible, readiness to suffer for the sake of the covenant, a heightened self-awareness and a profound realization that holiness and trust were indispensable conditions for communion with the Lord of Hosts became some of the striking characteristics of the chosen people.

The ardent expectation of deliverance from all their afflictions which would be linked with the coming of a special divine messenger reached its height in the century which saw the birth of the Church. After a period of political independence under the Maccabees (168–63 BC) which had intensified Jewish national and religious aspirations, Palestine became incorporated in the Roman state and was increasingly exposed to enforced hellenization. Under Herod the Great (37–4 BC), who ruled over Judaea, Samaria and Galilee as a King appointed by the Roman senate, and under his successors, pagan cities were founded in Palestine where hellenized foreigners worshipped their many gods. Temples were erected to Augustus, and the land inhabited by a people who abhorred any graven image was polluted by triumphant paganism. Under the impact of this defeat and humiliation a number of Jews began to mix with Gentiles and to give up their religious and national exclusiveness. But this apostasy only increased the zeal of the rest, who with renewed vigour asserted their unshaken confidence in the promised deliverance and reduced to a minimum all contacts with the outside world. Such conduct led inevitably to constant clashes with the Roman authorities. Hardly a year passed without a local revolt or a major rebellion. Some historians consider that no fewer than 250,000 Jews perished during the century preceding the destruction of Jerusalem in 70 AD. These figures represent a heavy toll on a small population which probably did not surpass a million people. In that atmosphere of acute suffering an apocalyptic literature flourished and any rebel who claimed to be the Messiah easily gathered fanatical supporters.

The struggle in Palestine had important repercussions elsewhere. Most Jews in the first century belonged, not to Palestine, but to the Diaspora. Their colonies could be found in all the important seaports and prosperous commercial centres of the Empire, and even far outside its borders, in India, Ceylon and Ethiopia. This Diaspora, which contained five times more Jews than the Holy Land, presented the same picture of tension and exclusiveness, but without that constant bloodshed which was such a tragic feature of Israel's history in its native territory. The Jews in the Diaspora were obliged to have more contacts with the surrounding population, and some mingling with Gentiles could not be entirely avoided. The Old Testament was translated into Greek in Alexandria in the second century BC. There were also some converts to Judaism who acted as intermediaries and helped the first Christians to penetrate into the gentile community.

The message of the Gospel was at first addressed exclusively to that hard pressed and yet undefeated nation, which was so acutely aware of the gulf that separated it from the rest of mankind. The response was a mixed one; some Jews were converted, but the majority refused to accept Jesus Christ as the promised Messiah. The crucified Galilean clashed too sharply with the conventional figure of a national liberator associated in their minds with the coming of the Redeemer. The infant Church broke out almost at once from the confines of orthodox Judaism. The fearless witnesses to the Risen Christ could soon be seen mixing with the Gentile crowds 'ostracized by the Jews.

The split of the Church from Israel
The crucial decision to separate from Israel was made by the Christians when they realized the universality of their religion and decided to incorporate the converts from paganism on equal terms into their society. This step was truly revolutionary for there existed in the first century the strongest possible contrast between Israel and the Hellenistic world. The pagans were disillusioned, submitting to blind fate as the force that governed both gods and men; the universe as they saw it had many divinities but no real master, no guiding principle and no rational purpose, whilst Jews were certain of their privileged position and full of hope. Yet the Christian message was accepted by some members of both societies and it was their close collaboration which built up the strong yet flexible framework of the Church, and made its teaching sufficiently universal to escape confinement to one ethnic or cultural group.

Judaism provided Christianity with its basic assertion that the God of Israel chose this stubborn and vital race for the special purpose of the reconciliation with mankind, and that Jesus Christ was the promised Messiah, who offered deliverance from the power of ignorance and sin to all those who believed in him. Israel also supplied the Church with the Holy Scriptures, and with the rites of initiation and covenant, which in a modified form became the foundation stones of Christian worship and organization. From Judaism the infant Church learned to gather its members to regular weekly services at which the scriptures were read, instruction given, and the divine presence made real by the corporate encounter, at the Eucharistic meal, with the founder of the Church.

From the same source the Church inherited the sense of being a separate community, radically different from those who did not acknowledge the one true God, and instead of Him, worshipped as it affirmed man-made idols. The chosen people also showed an example of complete dedication to the sacred cause and of courage in asserting their uncompromising standpoint. The Jews taught the Church that God is Holy and that His servants must be ready to be tested by fire.

The Church and Hellenism

God is love, but the burning flame of divine compassion consumes all that is impure. This and other fundamental convictions borrowed from the Jews gave the Church its stability and enormous power of resistance. But its ability to expand, to penetrate into new fields, to meet the variety of human needs, and to satisfy very different requirements and aspirations the Christians learned through their contacts with the Hellenistic world. The greatest of its contributions was the Greek language. It is of the utmost importance in the history of the Church that, though its founder spoke in Aramaic, his voice reached the wider circle of mankind in Greek, for in that tongue the books of the New Testament and many of the Patristic commentaries on them were written. No other language could have served this purpose so well, for it was able to express philosophical concepts with a vigour and subtlety unattainable elsewhere, and at the same time to convey the profoundest religious feelings with poetry and grace. The Hellenized world also helped the Church to see the unity of mankind, and the fundamental similarity of men's intellectual and spiritual problems. From the Greek philosophers and writers the Church learned the art of logical thinking and scientific speculation. The Greek was not only a worshipping creature, like the Jew; he was also a thinker and an artist, and the Christian Church found an honoured place for these types of human activity. The Greeks provided the Church with its theologians, with men who critically examined the text of the Holy Scriptures, who interpreted it in the light of contemporary thought, and formulated its main doctrines with the help of philosophical terms. Thus the Church was fertilized by two Eastern traditions, Judaism and Hellenism, the latter of which had already combined Greek philosophy with Oriental mystic religions.

The Church and the Roman State

The material foundation for the rapid expansion of Christianity was provided by a third partner however, this time of Western origin. This was the Roman Empire, with its political and legal institutions. The genius of the Latin mind conceived and realized in the first centuries of the Christian era a multi-national State, with a strong centralized authority vested in the Emperor, but so organized as to enjoy municipal autonomy. Such a policy guaranteed the unity of the realm, security of communication, easy exchange of goods and ideas, and at the same time encouraged local initiative and welcomed regional developments. The Roman Empire was an impressive achievement; the urban population was proud of the title of Roman citizen. Tenure of property was defended by law, the duties and responsibilities of citizens were clearly defined, elections of municipal officers were regularly held, and the benevolent rule of a single monarch offered legal protection to all free inhabitants.

The missionary work of the Church was undertaken in this universal state: the preachers of the Gospel travelled along routes made safe by well-disciplined legions; the Christian communities, accepting the Roman idea of law and order, were organized as self-supporting units, governed by democratically elected officers; the example of a single earthly ruler administering impartial justice facilitated the spread of the Gospel teaching that almighty God is the sole master of all men and yet respects human freedom.

The Church encountered the most favourable conditions where these three major influences were at work. The Latin, Hellenic and Jewish elements of civilization were best represented in the main cities of the Eastern or Greek-speaking half of the Empire, and it was there that the new religion secured its chief strongholds during the first three centuries. The Christian communities consisted mostly of the urban proletariat, although a certain number of people of culture and high social rank joined the Church from time to time. Each community was a self-governing unit, led by a bishop, assisted by presbyters, deacons and deaconesses. A bishop's duties included presiding over the Eucharistic meal, the central act of Christian worship; instruction and baptism of converts; and maintenance of discipline. Presbyters and deacons cared for widows and orphans, for the sick and destitute. The churches were in regular communication with their neighbours; alms were collected and sent to communities in distress; hospitality was willingly afforded to travellers. There was no central authority, but the Churches founded by the Apostles and situated in important centres enjoyed prestige, and their leadership was willingly accepted, the most prominent among them being the Churches of Rome, Alexandria and Antioch. The exchange of opinions and news was maintained. Gaul corresponded with Syria; North Africa with Asia Minor; Rome with Alexandria; Greece with Spain.

At first the Church appeared to the Roman authorities to be another Jewish sect; but the distinction between the New and the Old Israel was soon made clear, and for Christians this began three hundred years of persecution, which shaped the Church into a force capable of defeating the Empire. The second problem that confronted the Christians was how to survive in a hostile Roman world.

The Persecution: Its Origin and Nature

Judaism, Hellenism and the Roman State were not only the cradle of the Church but also the powers that tried to stifle it. The most bitter and persistent enemy was Judaism, its next of kin. The destruction of Jerusalem in 70 AD, when the Christians left the doomed city and retired to Pella, put the final seal on the separation between the two communities. To the Jews, the Christians had accepted an impostor as the true Messiah, who, being man, claimed to be one with the Heavenly Father, and who, as proof of his unique position, pardoned sins and released His followers from the yoke of the law. Jesus Christ was proclaimed in the synagogues to be a destroyer of the Covenant between Yahweh and Israel.

If the leaders of Judaism had had a free hand in dealing with the Christians, they would have tried to annihilate them altogether. But the fall of Jerusalem and the rapid spread of the Church outside the borders of Palestine placed the Christians beyond the reach of their most determined antagonists.

Opposition on the part of Hellenistic society was also widespread but differed from the enmity of the Jews. The Gentiles attacked the Christians on two different levels. The lower classes feared and hated them as an irritating and incomprehensible minority; the upper classes despised them as narrow-minded and bigoted. The cosmopolitan urban population of the Eastern provinces of the Empire was used to a multiplicity of cults and mystery religions. Some of these sects had their own places of worship to which no strangers were admitted, but even those who regarded Mithras, or the Great Mother of Phrygia as their particular protectors also frequented other temples, took part in popular festivals and did not differ from others in their conduct. The Christians were quite unlike other devotees: they were not a separate race like the Jews, but were drawn from all classes and nations; yet they behaved in striking contrast to their own relatives and former friends. They refused to offer sacrifices to the gods and they abstained also from the gladiatorial

24

games and other popular entertainments. All these unaccountable features made them highly suspect in the eyes of the common people. The Christians were accused of being godless, of dabbling in dangerous magic, and their presence was treated as an offence to the recognized deities.

Whenever any calamity occurred, earthquake, fire or epidemic, these disasters were explained as being the vengeance of the gods outraged by the impiety of the Christians. The city mob was always ready to assault them, to drag them to the courts and clamour for their destruction. The hostility of the plebeians was paralleled by the disdain of the cultured and sophisticated. Steeped in classical literature, fascinated by poetry and rhetoric, enlightened by the writings of the great philosophers, educated Romans looked down on the Christians as uncouth and ignorant outcasts, sunk in superstition and worshipping an obscure Galilean crucified by order of the Imperial government. The upper classes did not fear the Christians and thought they deserved punishment, not because they were godless, but because they challenged the supreme authority of the State and spread ideas likely to undermine the political and social order.

Hellenistic society was much less determined in its hostility than the Jews. The city mob was dangerous when excited, but its zeal for persecution often subsided as quickly as it arose. The upper classes were in most cases too sceptical themselves to take Christianity seriously and were more contemptuous than antagonistic.

The third enemy of the Church was the Empire itself and it alone had the necessary means to destroy the new religion. The Roman State was on principle tolerant of the beliefs of its subjects. Many diverse cults were practised in the capital and in the provinces; temples dedicated to foreign gods stood side by side with those honouring the traditional deities of the Latin people. Even the Jews obtained concessions and were allowed to follow their customs, being exempt from observances which clashed with their convictions. Christianity, however, was not included among the tolerated religions. On several occasions the Emperors made determined attempts to eradicate it. At first these persecutions were casual and lacked consistency; gradually, however, they became better planned and wider in range. The greatest number of victims was claimed by the last and fiercest of all the persecutions, that of Diocletian and his co-rulers in the fourth century.

The first assault on Christians was made by Nero (57–68) who commanded their mass execution in Rome in order to appease the popular discontent caused by the great fire which destroyed a large part of the capital. The Apostles Peter and Paul, with a number of their followers, were put to death, but no attempt was made to extend persecution to other parts of the realm or to justify it on any other grounds than an ill-founded charge of incendiarism. Nero's successors did not at first adopt a uniform policy towards the Christians whom they treated however as adherents of an illicit religion, liable at any time to be arrested, deported or executed and to have their property confiscated. For a long time no special legislation was enacted against them. Persecution was therefore severe under some Emperors like Domitian (81–96), and slackened under others like Commodus (180–192). Some of the Caesars were even favourably disposed, like Alexander Severus (222–235) or Philip the Arab (244–49). The intensity of persecution varied also from province to province and often depended on the zeal of local officials.

The exchange of letters between Pliny the Younger, governor of Bithynia (111–113), and the Emperor Trajan (98–117) one of the most humane and enlightened rulers of the Empire, throws some light upon the reasons for this hesitant policy. Pliny found a large number of Christians in his province. He believed them to be undesirable and punished those who fell into his hands, but he did not think that they presented such a serious danger as to deserve wholesale destruction, so he addressed a letter to the Emperor asking for instructions. The Emperor's reply expressed approval of Pliny's moderate policy. Trajan wrote:

'My worthy Pliny, you have followed the correct line of conduct in dealing with those who were brought before you as Christians. They must not be hunted down; if they are denounced and convicted they must be punished but with the reservation that anyone who denies being a Christian and actively proves it by adoring our gods must be forgiven on the ground of his repentance no matter how suspect his past. Nor may anonymous accusations be taken into consideration on any charge; this would set a bad example and would not be in keeping with the spirit of our time.'[2]

Trajan was hesitant and so were many of his predecessors and successors. It was difficult to be precise about the offence committed by Christians, and yet it was generally realized that the Church was a subversive society the very existence of which challenged the claims of the Roman state to be obeyed in all matters civil and religious.

Such was also the opinion of Marcus Aurelius (161–180), the enlightened philosopher on the Imperial throne who condemned

Christians as dangerous and obdurate fanatics.[3] Only when the Emperors realized at last the true character of the Christian opposition did they inaugurate an anti-Christian campaign which aimed at the total extermination of this dangerous religion. The test became the willingness of a citizen to offer sacrifice to gods approved by the Empire. For the first time the limits of the State's power over the individual were delineated and the line of conduct taken by the martyrs led to the foundation of a new society in which freemen could breathe and live. Decius (249–51) was the first ruler who made it obligatory for all to conform to the cult of the Emperor, and who ordered a systematic search for Christians. All those who disobeyed were condemned to death or deportation. His policy was followed by several other Emperors, by Gallus (251–53), Valerian (253–59) and Aurelian (270–75). Its culminating point was reached under the great reforming autocrat Diocletian (284–305), who undertook the last and the best planned attack.

Diocletian, though a mere soldier, was a born statesman. He succeeded in restoring order in the decaying Empire, though at the price of making it a totalitarian state. Local autonomy was curtailed to meet the increasing dangers of internal unrest and foreign invasions. The provinces were reshaped, finance reorganized, the whole economy regulated. Diocletian created a powerful bureaucracy and surrounded himself with an elaborate ritual. For the first time jewels appeared on the garments and shoes of a Roman Emperor, and he demanded worship of his sacred person like an Oriental monarch. Such a ruler, seriously believing in his divine attributes, was bound to come into conflict with the Church, which had meanwhile greatly increased in numbers. Diocletian made careful preparations for a final decisive assault on the unsuspecting Christians. He consulted the oracle of Apollo at Didyma and having found an auspicious date issued a decree in March 303 ordering the systematic destruction of every Christian building. He saw, from his palace in Nicomedia, the burning of the main Church of that city. A series of Imperial edicts followed this first injunction. Christians were expelled from all government offices, deprived of their rank, left without state protection and without right of appeal against any offender, but liable themselves to be tortured and executed without regard for their previous status. The ageing Emperor, who had started his campaign against the Church in association with his son-in-law and co-ruler Galerius (293–311) in the nineteenth year of his reign, wanted to avoid a general massacre of Christians. His main intention was to deprive the members of the Church of their buildings and sacred scriptures, to destroy their organization and to frighten the bulk of them into submission. Only the leaders of the community were expected to offer serious resistance; but once the persecution was launched, the original intentions were soon forgotten and all over the Empire innumerable victims were put to torture and death. The only exceptions were the prefectures of Gaul and Britain ruled by Constantius Chlorus (293–306), one of Diocletian's subordinates with the title of Caesar.

It remains a riddle why Diocletian postponed his contest with the Church till the end of his reign and why he suddenly abdicated on May 1, 305, at the height of his anti-Christian campaign. Galerius and Constantius were proclaimed his successors. This change brought the persecution of Christians to an end in the entire Western half of the Empire allotted to Constantius, but Galerius persisted in his attempts to stamp out the Church in his Eastern domain. He died in 311 from some unidentified, disfiguring and painful disease. On his deathbed he recalled the edict against the Christians and the agony he suffered was interpreted by his contemporaries as a sign of the defeat of this most bitter enemy of the Church. The loss of human life during this last persecution surpassed all previous records. Equally overwhelming was the destruction of Church buildings, libraries and documents. The Church suffered severely; while many Christians showed firmness and were martyred, many others collapsed and surrendered to their persecutors. But the Church was not annihilated and the Empire gained nothing; rather, the authority of its rulers was compromised.

The causes of the Christian victory
The Mediterranean world during the first centuries of the Christian era enjoyed a political, economic and social unity unsurpassed in its history. However, these remarkable achievements emphasized an inner despondency and discord. Pessimism and a sense of impending doom were widespread; time was seen as self-repeating without beginning or end; history moved in endless cycles; the gods were immortal but neither better nor wiser than men, and like men, ultimately helpless. Popular mythology represented the divinities as frivolous and irresponsible, incapable in their multiplicity of satisfying man's quest for communion with the divine. The mystery religions, either orgiastic or magical, failed to meet the needs of more sober minds; while the noble ideals of self-control preached by the stoics seemed to be beyond the reach of ordinary men.

Classical civilization was confused in its ideas of good and evil; it offered no promise of a better future and the secret of happiness had been lost. When men are deprived of joy and hope they and their society become cruel. The gladiatorial games excited the populace by the sight of bloodshed and torture; the poor were oppressed; orphans and widows were sold into slavery; the sick were abandoned to die of hunger and thirst. *Homo homini lupus est,* as the popular Roman proverb bluntly put it.

Christianity broke into this world of pessimism and frustration with a cry of victory. Men saw the face of the Creator, learned the purpose of life and breathed the intoxicating air of hope and freedom.

There are several testimonials dating from the transitional period which describe this inner change in the converts. One of the most eloquent is that of St Cyprian, the bishop martyr of Carthage (*d.* 258). He was a distinguished lawyer, a man of wealth and culture, versed in classical poetry and philosophy. Here is his description of the effect his baptism produced upon him:

'When I was still in darkness, uncertain of my wandering steps, knowing nothing of my real self and remote from truth and light, I used to think it impossible that a man could retain all his bodily structure and yet be transformed in heart and soul.'[4]

'But now, by the help of the water of new birth the stain of former years has been washed away and a light from above, serene and pure, has been infused into my reconciled heart, and a second birth has made me a new man.'[5]

This experience was not merely a passing emotion, it enabled him to lead a new life. The same St Cyprian relates certain episodes which occurred in his native city during the epidemic which broke out at the end of the Decian persecution (251). All who could, fled the towns, leaving behind the sick and dying. All rules of decency were forgotten, everyone tried merely to save his own life. But the Christians alone were unafraid, they preserved their inner peace and self-control and looked after the sick and dead. The most astonishing feature of their conduct was that they nursed even their enemies who had persecuted them. There was something revolutionary and unaccountable in Christian mentality and behaviour, something that staggered and frightened the heathen world by its contrast with accepted standards. This regeneration of the converts proclaimed the dawn of a new epoch.

It is impossible to explain the victory of the Church without recognizing that a previously unknown force had entered into history. A world-wide Community was born whose members were not frightened by death and preserved their unity without the use of fear and compulsion. The message of the Gospel surpassed the ideas preached by the Gentiles and by the Jews: it revealed God not only as omnipotent, but as loving; not only as just, but as merciful. The Christians had a sense of purpose, of belonging, combined with fortitude, charity and humility and this enabled them to become the builders of a better social order. The source of their inspiration was not a novel doctrine, but the personal encounter with that enigmatic Galilean, who promised to his followers his continuous assistance and a degree of love and unity hitherto unobtainable by men. The striking feature of the new religion was the fulfilment of this daring pledge.

Early sects and heresies
During the centuries of suffering and persecution the Christians maintained their unity in a remarkable way, yet various dissenting groups arose in their midst from time to time and separated themselves from the main body, either on account of their special discipline (sectarians) or of their defective teaching (heretics).

The point of dispute usually centered on the manner and degree of Church adaptation to the non-Christian environment. Some of these sects wanted to combine Christianity with observance of the Mosaic Law, and in this way to avoid a final rupture with Judaism. These Christians were repudiated by the Jews and criticized by the Christians and they gradually disappeared as a result of the widening gulf between the Church and the Synagogue. More persistent were the attempts to build a bridge between Christianity and Hellenism. This movement is known under the name of *gnosis*. The history of the Church in the second and the third centuries was profoundly disturbed by the activities of several Gnostic teachers like Basilides, Valentinus and Marcion. There were even instances of entire local Christian communities embracing gnosticism as their creed. In spite of considerable variety in detail the Gnostics displayed an essential similarity. They all considered this world to be the creation of an inferior deity who was responsible for the unfortunate mixture in man of immortal spirit and unclean matter. Many Gnostics thought that God, as revealed in the Old Testament, was this demiurge opposed to the good God whom Jesus Christ called His Father. The Gnostics were syncretists who tried to reconcile the current religious ideas of the Hellenistic world that the cosmos was a divine emanation with the teaching of the Gospel. The word 'gnosis' implied possession of secret and superior knowledge concerning the mystery of

life and death withheld from others. The extravagance of their speculations and disagreement among themselves were their main weaknesses; their strength lay in their theology according with the temper of the
age, for they spoke a language that appealed to a sophisticated audience.
The Gnostics formed their own conclaves and attacked the Catholics
from outside, treating them as inferiors in wisdom and education.

In striking opposition to this syncretism was the sect called the
Montanists. Its adherents tried to undermine the allegiance of Christians
to the Catholic Church from within. Their founder, Montanus, was a
Phrygian who lived in the middle of the second century. He claimed to
be a prophet and shared his authority with two remarkable women,
Priscilla and Maximilla, who were both revered by their followers as
possessing the gifts of the Holy Spirit, such as prophesy, speaking with
tongues and healing. The sect imposed a rigorous asceticism upon its
adherents and aroused unrestrained enthusiasm in them. One theme in
their preaching was the imminence of the second coming. The Montanists had many of the characteristics common today among the
Pentecostals and other revivalist sects. They made a number of converts
all over the Empire, including the gifted North African writer and
apologist, Tertullian (150–222), who later, however, seceded and formed
his own sect.

The Montanists stressed the prophetic element in the life of the Church
at the expense of regular discipline and sound learning. They were
strongly anti-pagan and many were martyred. Their austerity did not
appeal to all Christians, some of whom were tempted to embrace a life
of ease and wealth whenever persecution abated. The best known
example of such worldliness was Paul of Samosata, bishop of Antioch,
who was expelled from his see by the synod in 268 for the pomp and
extravagance of his conduct.

These deviations were resisted by the main body of Christians who
adhered to the Apostolic tradition incorporated in the books of the New
Testament. During these formative centuries a selection was made of
those writings which were to be recognized as authentic, while others
were repudiated as inconsistent with the original message. The first
enumeration of the books of the New Testament dates from the beginning of the third century (Muratori's fragment). This separation of
original from interpolated writings was a gradual process which ended
in unanimous acceptance of the present canon.

The important factor in this struggle of the Church against its internal
and external adversaries was the Apostolic succession of its bishops. No
one could become head of a local church unless he was approved and

consecrated by the neighbouring bishops. This rule checked the influence of extremists and maintained unity among the Christians. Fellowship and intercourse with the older churches founded by the Apostles helped smaller and less instructed communities to preserve their orthodoxy and to combat heresy and schism.

Writers and teachers of the Eastern Church in the second and third centuries
Two types of Church leaders are known to us from the early centuries: martyrs, who bore witness to the truth of their religion by suffering; and apologists, who wrote in defence of their beliefs.

Among the martyrs, St Ignatius of Antioch (died between 107–117) is the most vivid figure. Little is known about his origins, his conversion, or even of the circumstances which led to his arrest and condemnation, but we can still hear his voice rejoicing at the approach of martyrdom and we possess in his writings a unique revelation of the martyr's state of mind. The aged bishop wrote seven epistles during his slow and painful journey in chains from Antioch, the place of his birth in Christ, to Rome, the scene of his death. He addressed his letters to different Christian communities, urging them to remain faithful to the Gospel and to obey and venerate their teachers and pastors. In his Epistle to Rome he said:

'I write to all the Churches and make known to all as my last wish, that I desire freely to die for God, at least if you do not prevent it. I beseech you, show no misplaced sympathy on my account. Let me be a bait for the wild beasts, so that I may be found as pure bread of Christ, or rather coax the wild beasts that they may become my tomb, leaving nothing of my body to be a burden to anyone after my death. Then shall I be a disciple of Jesus Christ in the true sense of the word, when the world sees even my body no more. Pray for me to Christ, that by these instruments I may be found a fitting sacrifice to God.'[6]

In the latter part of the same epistle he wrote:

'From Syria to Rome I fight with wild beasts by land and sea, by night and day, being bound to ten leopards, I mean to a band of soldiers who, though treated with friendliness, become only the more cruel. Yet through these injuries I am growing into true discipleship. May nothing visible or invisible prevent me from attaining to Jesus Christ. Come fire, cross, grappling with wild beasts, cutting and mangling, wrenching of bones, hacking of limbs, crushing of my whole body;

come all the wicked torments of the devil upon me, only let me reach the presence of Christ.'

The Epistle of an eyewitness, describing the martyrdom of St Ignatius's younger contemporary, St Polycarp, Bishop of Smyrna (*d.* 156), and some of his companions, gives a similar picture of exultation and fortitude. The anonymous author wrote:

'Who can choose but admire their nobility and endurance and love for the Master. I speak of the men who were so tortured with whipping that their bodies were laid open to their veins and arteries, yet they endured it, so that all who saw them pitied and lamented their fate. Not one of them sighed or groaned, for the Lord stood by them and consoled them.'[7]

These contemporary documents reveal the dilemma confronting the Roman authorities who desired to discredit Christianity, and to assert the right of the State to control the beliefs of its citizens, but had no intention of making heroes and martyrs. On many occasions persecution produced the opposite results by raising the prestige of the new religion and by attracting the attention to it of wider circles.

The contest between heathen and Christian was not confined however to the realm where the executioner and gaoler had the last word. The antagonists also met on the level of intellectual argument. Several Christian writers tried to explain to the learned heathen the foundation of their belief in the Incarnation. Among these defenders of Christianity the most prominent were Clement of Alexandria (150–215) and Origen (185–253).

The latter part of the second century and the first half of the third were times of a powerful revival in Hellenistic philosophy. Its temper had changed, however, for it had acquired a distinct religious bias, and even its greatest representative, Plotinus (*d.* 270), regarded himself as a religious teacher. At the same time Oriental mysticism captured some of the best minds. India attracted special curiosity and many seekers expected to find illumination in the land of Brahmins and Fakirs.

The questions with which these intellectuals were preoccupied were centred upon the nature of God, the purpose of the physical universe and its relation to the unchanging spiritual world. Their attention was also drawn to the problem of the origin of evil and the destiny of the immortal soul after its separation from the mortal body. Syncretism was popular and many writers tried to reconcile the Old Testament with the writings of Plato and Aristotle. A popular author of that time, Numenius, described Plato as 'Moses speaking in Greek'.[8]

This religious and philosophical revival strengthened pagan opposition to the Church. A number of writers such as Celsus, Philostrates, Numenius and especially Plotinus and his disciple Porphyry attacked the Christians on the grounds of their departure from the sound foundation laid down by the Greek philosophers and of their preference for the writings of obscure Hebrew prophets and teachers. The third century saw the last determined intellectual assault of classical culture on Christianity. In this difficult period the Church found a number of eloquent champions who not only defended the teachings of the Gospel with success but also counter-attacked with vigour and conviction. The pagan enemies of Christianity were confident of their superiority, for they based their arguments on contemporary philosophical and scientific ideas. The Christian apologists seemed out of date, but their independence from current thought proved to be an asset on many occasions. For instance, Plotinus derided them for denying that the sun and the stars had a higher intelligence than men; such an attitude seemed to him an obvious absurdity.[9] His defence of polytheism against monotheism used arguments which likewise soon lost their appeal.[10]

The main encounter between the Christian philosophers and their pagan rivals took place in Alexandria, the most cultured city of the Empire. Its academies and schools, the Museum, the Serapeum, the Sebastion attracted students from all parts of the world where Greek rhetoric and philosophy were studied and admired. It had also long been a centre of Jewish learning. Philo (20 BC–50 AD) and Josephus (37–100 AD) worked there and the Greek translation of the Old Testament, the Septuagint, had been made in Alexandria. The Christians, following the example of the Greeks and Jews, founded their best known Catechetical School in the same famous city. A number of outstanding teachers, Pantaenus (200), Heracleus (247), Denys (265), Theognostus (280), Pierius (310), Peter (311), Didymas the blind (398) and Rhodon maintained a high standard of instruction for more than two hundred years. But Clement and Origen were the greatest of these teachers.

It is probable that Clement was born about 150 AD in Athens, where he was brought up a devout pagan and received an excellent education. There is some evidence that he was connected with the Imperial family, to which his full name Titus Flavius Clemens bears witness. He moved to Alexandria at the age of thirty, and there started his brilliant career as a leading apologist and head of the Catechetical School some time after 190.

The persecution begun in 202 by Septimus Severus (193–211) forced him to leave Egypt. In 211 he appeared as a much venerated teacher in Cappadocia, where one of his former pupils, Alexander, was bishop; he died there about 215.

Clement was an accomplished writer, poetically gifted with an exceptional intellectual grasp. He did not know Latin but his Greek was immaculate. Though most of his books are lost or survive in small fragments, three of his major works are complete and help us to understand the philosophical climate of Alexandria and the way in which Clement presented Christianity to his sophisticated listeners. In the first of these books, the *Protrepticos* (exhortation), he exposes the inconsistency of pagan mythology, and calls his readers to listen to the living God speaking through the prophets and revealing himself in the Incarnate Logos. The second book, *Paidagogos* (the instructor), introduces readers to Christian doctrine. The third, *Stromateis* (a miscellany), initiates inquirers into the mysteries of the New Revelation.

Clement loved and respected Greek philosophy, considered Plato a precursor of Christ, quoted Socrates and Pythagoras in support of the truth of Christian teaching, and regarded the history of the Oriental Empires as a providential preparation for the coming of the Messiah. But he was convinced that the questions raised by the philosophers of antiquity could find their true answers only in the message of the gospel, and that the old myths and legends of Greece had been made obsolete by Christian revelation. 'Now the fables have grown old', wrote Clement, 'and Zeus is no longer a serpent, no longer a swan, nor an eagle, nor a furious lover. He no longer flies, nor loves boys, nor kisses, nor acts with violence.'[11] Traditional paganism was still alive, it fiercely resisted the Christian advance, but its vitality was sapped, for the moral frivolity and inconsistency of its myths deprived it of dignity, authority and power.

Clement saw in Christianity the fulfilment of all that was best in the Hellenistic world; he regarded man as the most perfect being created by God. He wrote:

'A noble hymn to God is man, immortal, founded upon righteousness. The oracles of truth are engraved upon him; for where else save in the wise soul can truth be written, or love, or reverence, or gentleness? Those who have had these divine characters inscribed and sealed upon their souls deem such wisdom a fair port of departure on whatever journey their course is set and this wisdom is also a haven of peace and promise of a safe return.'[12]

Clement treated 'life as a holy festival'[13] and this can be taken as the epitome of his outlook. It is remarkable that this optimistic and courageous note was sounded at the time when martyrdom confronted Christians all over the Empire.

Clement laid the foundation of Christian apologetics, but their most complete system was produced by Origen, his successor at the Catechetical School. Origen was born in Alexandria, in 185. His father, Leonidas, was a Greek, a man of wealth and learning. His mother was a native of Egypt, and both parents were convinced Christians. The family possessed a large library which introduced the young Origen to the world of Classical culture. As a boy, he impressed everyone with his unusual intellectual powers, the maturity of his judgment and his insatiable desire for information. At the age of seventeen, he faced the great crisis of his life when his father was arrested and martyred, the magnificent library confiscated, the family ruined. Origen longed to share his father's crown of martydom, but his life was spared. He started teaching both pagan philosophy and Christian doctrine and in spite of his youth soon acquired a reputation as an able instructor. He continued his own studies and joined the school of Ammonius Sacas, formerly a docker in Alexandria, later a convert to Christianity, although ending his career as a Neoplatonist in opposition to the Church. Ammonius has left no writings, but his excellence as a teacher is proved by the fact that two of the greatest religious thinkers of the century, Origen and Plotinus, were taught and trained in his school and owed much to him.

Origen's growing popularity provoked local jealousies and forced him to leave Alexandria in 231. He transferred his school to Caesarea, where he continued to teach for another nine years. In 240 he was thrown into prison and savagely tortured. The end of persecution released him but his health was ruined and he died in 253 at the age of 68, in Tyre.

Origen was a man of astounding industry. He spent all his nights writing, and his days lecturing. He wrote more than 6,000 books(!), mostly commentaries on the Holy Scriptures. He was the first Biblical scholar, and for twenty-eight years he worked steadily on a critical examination of the Old Testament. This assiduity resulted in the fifty volumes of his *Hexapla* which contained six parallel texts of the Old Testament in Hebrew and in Greek translations.

His curiosity knew no limits. He was interested in every aspect of life and in every philosophical problem. He combined fearless intellectual honesty with complete dedication to Christianity. His ardent nature pushed him to extremes of self-mortification; on a sudden impulse he castrated himself whilst still in the flower of his youth, an act which he regretted later in life and which was used against him by his critics.

Origen was an original and powerful thinker and could argue against the enemies of Christianity with the full knowledge of Greek philosophy and science. He was also an outstanding teacher who not only instructed, but also formed the personalities of his pupils. One of the most illustrious of these, St Gregory Thaumaturgus Bishop of Neocaesarea (213–70), described the years he spent in the school of his beloved master, with deep gratitude and warm affection. He wrote:

'Origen collected for our benefit all that each philosopher had to offer in truth and usefulness for the edification of mankind. But he did not want us to become attached to any one teacher, however wise he was considered by other men. Origen taught us to venerate only God and His Holy prophets.'[14]

In a passage of the panegyric dedicated to Origen, St Gregory dealt with the inspired quality of his teacher's interpretation of the Holy Scriptures:

'The Universal Ruler, who speaks through the prophets, beloved of God, and who inspires all prophetic works, all mystical and divine discourse, honoured Origen as His friend and established him as the master. Those things that God conveyed through others in an enigmatic way, Origen revealed in a clear and intelligible manner. Origen's interpretations of the Scriptures were inspired by the Holy Spirit, for no one can fully understand the prophetic voice, unless he is guided and helped by the same Spirit that spoke through the Prophet.'[15]

For his defence of Christianity Origen used much that he found in Greek philosophy, and incorporated in his system certain ideas which have remained outside the main tradition of the Church, such as the pre-existence of all souls, which he believed were created at the same time equal and eternal. Origen looked upon man's earthly life as a period of purification and testing for those celestial spirits which failed to make a clear choice between good and evil; he also hazarded the opinion that all human beings will eventually be saved.

Origen's unparalleled knowledge of classical philosophy provoked

37

attacks on him from two sides. Pagan opponents of Christianity such as Porphyry were indignant that Origen, a man of such learning, was a Christian. Porphyry wrote: 'Origen lived as a Christian but thought as a Greek and he applied the Greek arts to an alien belief.'[16] His Christian critics objected that he, being a Christian, borrowed too much from pagan philosophy. Yet Origen was able to combine, in a truly creative way, his Christian faith and his classical education.

One of his best known books was the reply to Celsus (*c.* 180), a distinguished Roman and a determined critic of the Christians. Celsus was an educated man, who had studied Christian literature. He raised a number of objections to the veracity of the gospels which were repeated by many later opponents of Christianity. Celsus deplored the spread of the new religion: according to him, it had undermined the foundations of the Roman Empire. He ridiculed the Old Testament as full of incredible miracles and fables. He denied the Virgin birth of the Messiah and insisted that the story of the resurrection was invented by hysterical women and skilfully used by the Apostles. Celsus represented the Christians as crafty, subversive agents, who penetrated into wealthy houses and seduced women and children to their perverted faith when the master of the house was away from home.

Origen's reply to these accusations has become a classic. He asked Celsus whether men who deliberately deceived others would be willing to die as martyrs in witness of their own lie, and also how a lie could alter people's lives and uplift them morally and intellectually to a level previously inaccessible. Celsus had ended his treatise with an appeal addressed to Christians to give up their religion and become loyal citizens of the Empire. Origen's concluding words express a hope that the rulers of the Roman state will be converted and recognize the supremacy of the divine Law revealed by Christ; this wish was realized some seventy years later.

The Christian community in the East matured intellectually under Origen's inspiring tuition. More than any other, he prepared its members for the new and more complex tasks which confronted them after recognition of the Church by the Empire.

CHAPTER TWO

THE ECUMENICAL COUNCILS AND THE ORIENTAL SCHISM

(IV–VIII CENTURIES)

Constantine the Great (306–337)—The Emperor and the Ecumenical Council—Arianism—The consequences of Nicaea—The victory of Nicene Orthodoxy—The second Ecumenical Council and the Emperor Theodosius (379–395)—The mass conversion of the Empire and its effect upon the Church—St John Chrysostom (347–407)—The Nestorian schism—The Second Council of Ephesus (449)—The Fourth Ecumenical Council (451)—The Chalcedonian Schism—Justinian I and his ecclesiastical policy (527–565)—The Chalcedonian definition and the separation of the Oriental Churches—Christianity and Nationalism—Christianity outside the Byzantine Empire—Rome and the Christian East—Eastern monasticism

Constantine the Great (306–337)

AT THE TIME when Diocletian's persecution had shaken the Church and unbalanced the Empire, Constantine, the son of Constantius Chlorus, and a young lieutenant of the dreaded old Emperor, created an entirely unforseen situation by establishing co-operation between the Church and the Roman state. Among the Eastern Christians he is revered as a saint and styled 'Equal to the Apostles'. Few men have had such influence upon the destiny of mankind as this brilliant soldier who altered the course of history by making the Church and the Empire partners for the next seventeen hundred years. He also extended the life of his realm for another twelve hundred years by transferring its capital to the shores of the Bosphorus. For several centuries to come Constantinople was to remain the centre of an original and vigorous Christian culture.

Constantine was a genius, great in every sense, a tall, impetuous man, always victorious, a ruler of vision and a practised administrator. Only a man of Constantine's imagination could have conceived so daring a plan as that of uniting the opposites: the Church and the Empire; only a man of his statesmanship and wisdom could have made it so lasting an alliance. There are conflicting interpretations of his motives. Some historians consider him a sceptic, skilfully using the growing power of the Church against his political opponents,* but this ignores the universal belief of his time in the intervention of benevolent and malignant spirits in public and private affairs; it ill-accords with Constantine's own statements and is also inconsistent with his acceptance as a Christian by

* Among whom are Gibbon, Burckhardt, Schwartz, and Harnack.

39

contemporary leaders of the Church.

The story of his conversion by the vision of the cross on the eve of one of the most decisive military engagements of his reign, the battle of the Milvian Bridge in 312, is reported by two Christian historians, Lactantius and Eusebius. After his spectacular victory, Constantine met, in Milan, his Eastern Co-Emperor, Licinius (312–324). As a result, Licinius issued in 313 the famous edict of religious toleration known as the *Edict of Milan*. It was published in Nicomedia and mainly affected the Eastern half of the Empire, for the West already enjoyed religious peace. The proclamation ran:

'When I, Constantine Augustus, and I, Licinius Augustus, came under favourable auspices to Milan and took into consideration all that pertained to the common prosperity . . . we resolved to grant to Christians and to all men freedom to follow the religion they chose, that whatever heavenly deity exists may be propitious to us and to all who live under our government.'[1]

This decree established equality between Christian and heathen; but after his victory over Licinius in 324, Constantine began to stress still more his leaning towards Christianity by his active interest in Church affairs. He convoked and presided over the Councils and systematically altered the legislation of the Empire in accordance with the teaching of the gospels. The new laws penalized certain sexual offenders (fornicators for instance),[2] removed penalties previously imposed upon celibates, made divorce more difficult,[3] facilitated the liberation of slaves, protected prisoners, widows and orphans and gave bishops certain magisterial powers.[4] Yet Constantine was not baptized until the end of his life and never relinquished the pagan title of *Pontifex Maximus*. His conduct was not inconsistent. Constantine called himself the bishop of those outside the Church,[5] his role being to attract converts by offering Christians every opportunity to exercise their benevolent influence on heathen society. He believed that their community, kept together by voluntary consent, could teach the lesson of unity to the rest of his people.

The Emperor and the Ecumenical Council

In 324 Constantine became sole ruler of the Empire. The period of civil wars and political rivalries over, he hoped to enjoy undisturbed tranquillity and was therefore particularly sensitive to any disturbance, especially among the Christians whom two disagreements troubled at

that time. The first concerned the date when Easter should be celebrated; the second, a quarrel between Alexander, Bishop of Alexandria
(312–327), and his learned and eloquent presbyter, Arius (d. 336).

To bring these two conflicts to a speedy end and to show his special
benevolence to the Church, Constantine convoked a council of bishops
from all parts of his domain, and even from outside its borders. The idea
of the council was probably suggested to him by Hosius, Bishop of
Cordoba (265–358), who acted as his adviser on ecclesiastical matters
and took a leading part in the Council's proceedings. Constantine delegated Hosius to make preliminary investigations into the origin of the
Alexandrian dispute, and his firm stand against Arius influenced Constantine's own early policy in this theological controversy.

The custom of deciding important matters at gatherings of Church
leaders dated from Apostolic times.[6] Under the persecution, the
Christians had continued to hold similar consultations when possible
and their decisions were morally binding on the Churches represented.
North Africa and Rome had held such councils at regular intervals; they
were less frequent in the East. The council convened by the Emperor,
however, was different from its predecessors in being empowered to
legislate both for Church and Empire, for its decrees were recognized as
laws.

The First Ecumenical Council is one of the great landmarks in the
history of the Church. At the Emperor's orders and at the expense of the
state several hundred bishops gathered in Nicaea, a small town near
Nicomedia, then the capital. Most of the bishops came from Asia Minor,
Palestine, Syria and Egypt. Two presbyters represented Sylvester
(314–335), the aged bishop of Rome; North Africa also sent delegates,
and four or five bishops came from outside the Empire. It was an impressive assembly: Some of its participants were renowned for learning;
others for holiness; others bore the marks of torture suffered during the
recent persecution. Constantine showed these last special signs of respect.
The personality of the Emperor dominated the synod, which lasted
from May to June, 325. Constantine was fifty-one, and at the height of
his glory and power. His solemn entrance so much impressed the bishops
that Eusebius compared him to an angel of God.[7] Clothed in purple
raiment, adorned with gold and precious stones, he addressed the
representatives of the Church as their friend and fellow believer:

'It was for some time my chief desire to enjoy the spectacle of your
united presence, and now that this wish is fulfilled I feel myself bound
to render thanks to God the Universal King. . . . Delay not, dear

friends, delay not, ye ministers of God and faithful servants of Him who is our common Lord and Saviour: begin to discard the causes of that disunion which exists among you and remove the perplexity of controversy by embracing the principles of peace. . . . By such conduct you will please the Supreme God and confer an exceeding favour on me, your fellow servant.'[8]

This friendly harangue, accompanied by the presents he lavished on the bishops, could not but produce an overwhelming impact upon men who had recently been exposed to the fury of persecution. Eusebius went so far as to describe the Imperial banquet, to which the bishops were invited before their dismissal, as 'a picture of Christ's Kingdom, a dream rather than a reality'.[9]

The Emperor was an astute statesman with a sure grasp of the essential difference between the Empire and the Church. He was resolved to control them but he realized that the same policy would not do for both. He was an autocratic but not a lawless monarch. He governed a legally organized state with a Senate that codified Imperial decrees and was responsible for their orderly application. Constantine built his relations with the Church on a familiar legal basis. The Episcopal Councils, in Constantine's view, had to perform the same function as the Roman Senate and their proceedings were similar: the bishops, like Senators, sat in a circle round the Emperor's seat, formulated answers to questions raised by the Sovereign and, if he approved, these decisions became law. There was one essential difference: the Senators acted in their own right, and their resolutions were carried by a majority-vote; the bishops' verdict was only valid if inspired by the Holy Spirit, of which the sign was unanimity. On this point Constantine departed from senatorial practice and so made it possible for the Church to retain its proper character. The bishops at the Ecumenical Councils were therefore able to repeat the words which prefaced the resolution of the first Christian council gathered in Jerusalem in 52. The Apostles and the representatives of the local Church had then boldly declared: 'It pleased the Holy Spirit and us.'[10] They were confident that they were guided and inspired because they spoke with one heart and one mind. The same formula was used by the Ecumenical Councils. The Emperor's role was only to sanction decrees passed by the synod and to back them with State power. Such was the plan of ecclesiastical administration conceived by Constantine and it was a remarkable achievement which made possible the close collaboration between the Byzantine, and later the Russian, Empires and their Churches.

The first question, the date of Easter, was easily resolved at Nicaea; but the second problem, Alexander's dispute with Arius, proved difficult. Most of the bishops found Arius's teaching defective, for it suggested that Jesus Christ the Incarnate Logos was inferior to God the Father, but a number of the Council's members also criticized Alexander's excommunication of Arius as harsh and precipitate, and were therefore unwilling to condemn outright this heretic. After long debate, in which the deacon Athanasius (293–373), one of Alexander's chief supporters, revealed his theological insight and ardour for orthodoxy, the vast majority accepted a new formula prepared by Hosius and supported by Athanasius. It defined more exactly than hitherto the equality of the Father and the Son. The Greek word *homoousios* (of the same substance) was introduced into the creed and sanctioned by the Council.

Only two bishops refused to sign. Their stubborn opposition raised the crucial question: could so small a minority be disregarded and the Inspiration of the Holy Spirit claimed, or should the Council disperse without reaching any binding decision? We do not know what alternatives were suggested to the Emperor. Nor do we know who had the final word in this matter, but we know what Constantine did in the end, and his action had far-reaching consequences for the whole history of the Church. He ordered the removal of the two dissenters; whereupon the remaining bishops unanimously promulgated their decrees in the name of the Holy Ghost. The refractory bishops were not molested, and no protest against this intervention has been recorded. It probably seemed at the time that Constantine had found a simple and practical way out of a hopeless dilemma, but in reality he had established a dangerous precedent of compulsion and intimidation. Once force had been accepted as legitimate, further acts of cruelty and persecution might be committed thereafter in the name of the Prince of Peace.

Constantine, elated by his victory, despatched the bishops to their dioceses. In his letter addressed to all the Churches, he praised the achievements of the synod and commanded Christians to receive its decrees 'with all willingness as truly divine injunctions and to regard them as a gift of God. For whatever is determined in the holy assembly of the bishops is to be treated as indicative of the divine Will.'[11] Constantine trusted that the 'unanimity' achieved at Nicaea would end the harmful dispute; but events soon dissipated this optimism. The Nicene Council, instead of securing the tranquillity within the Church, provoked an outburst of unprecedented theological hostilities which kept the Eastern Christians in a state of feverish activity for more than half a century and disturbed the West for another two hundred years.

Arianism

The dispute that began in 319 between bishop Alexander and his leading presbyter Arius, then aged sixty-three, was at first local, only affecting the Church of Alexandria, but it spread fast all over the East and became one of the major doctrinal conflicts of the fourth century.

Arius, with his pale face and long hair of an ascetic, with his poetical imagination and commanding voice and stature, was an impressive personality. He had a large and devoted following and had many admirers especially among the influential body of dedicated virgins. He was a devout and learned man, a disciple of a much revered martyr, Lucius (*d.* 312) Bishop of Antioch. Arius wanted to explain the mystery of the Incarnation in terms of contemporary Hellenistic philosophy and in doing so he distorted the Apostolic tradition and fell into heresy. He taught that if the Father begat the Son then one had to envisage a time when the Son did not exist and thus he placed Christ in an intermediate position between the Creator and the creation.

Arius believed in Jesus Christ devotionally as the Saviour of mankind but theologically he subordinated the Son to the Father. He quoted several texts of the Gospels in support of his contention that the Second Person of the Holy Trinity, the Incarnate Logos, was unequal to God the Creator whom Jesus Christ referred to as His Father.[12] Arianism stood in open contradiction to the fundamental assertion of the Catholic faith that the reconciliation between God and mankind and the redemption of the world was accomplished neither by a messenger sent from above, nor by a holy man or prophet uplifted to a higher sphere when his task fulfilled, but by the Almighty Author of the Universe Himself who was the unique and undivided source of all beings.

The Church from Apostolic times was resolutely opposed to any idea of demiurges or divinities subordinate to the supreme God, the doctrine common to the Gnostic sects. The Gospel teaching that God is love is based on the belief that in the person of Jesus Christ, who was born, crucified and has risen, the triune God Himself suffered the agony of death as known to men. Perfect love does not shrink from any sacrifice or humiliation. Only if Jesus Christ shared the same nature with His Father could the Christian conviction that God has become known to mankind and offered His fellowship to His creation be justified. Arius, teaching of an inferior Christ, shrouded the Creator of the universe in impenetrable mystery, and deprived the members of the Church of that certainty that God truly loved and cared for men, which was essential to the Orthodox doctrine.

Arius called attention to the central problems of Christian theology, and its discussion required all the wisdom and learning available among leaders of the Church; but from the first the dispute he provoked acquired the character of personal rivalry with Alexander, and this encouraged the stubborn presbyter to maintain an extreme position and engendered bitter animosity.* When Arius started composing popular songs incorporating his ideas, Alexander expelled him from the ranks of the clergy and forced him to leave Alexandria. Arius migrated to Palestine and later to Nicomedia where he found many sympathizers, not necessarily as the propagator of heretical tenets but as the victim of autocratic treatment.†

At the Nicene Council the majority of bishops repudiated Arianism as false, but only a few liked the word *homoousios* which was associated in their minds with the previously condemned teaching of Paul of Samosata (*d. c.* 270), who had obliterated distinction between the Father and the Son. Constantine's personal intervention in support of this controversial theological expression, however, carried it through the uneasy assembly. As soon as the bishops returned home many of them began to regret their decision, for they had to face the difficult task of explaining to their people the reason for the acceptance of a creed containing a word which had no biblical authority behind it, a word which had first been introduced by heretics.

Besides this difficulty there was another one connected with the wording of the Nicene Creed. Hitherto the Christian used only baptismal creeds which, in positive terms, affirmed their belief in the Holy Trinity and Jesus Christ as their Saviour. The Nicene Creed introduced new and speculative elements which were the matter of controversy among the theologians. It contained, for instance, the following references to the Incarnate Logos:

'And those who say that once He was not, or that before His generation He was not, and that He came into being out of nothing, or those who claim that the Son of God is of other substance or essence or created, or alterable, or mutable; the catholic Church anathematizes.'

These indictments reflected theological debates in the Council, and

* The Church historian Socrates described the beginning of the Arian dispute in the following way: 'One day Alexander attempted in the presence of the presbyters to explain with a perhaps too philosophical minuteness that great theological mystery, the unity of the Holy Trinity. Arius, imagining that the bishop was subtly teaching as Sabellius the Lybian, from love of controversy took the opposite side.' (Socrates, *Hist. Ecc.*, 1, 5.)

† Sozomen, another Church historian, says: 'Many of the people sided with Arius and his partisans, as frequently happens in similar cases, because they believed them to have been ill-treated and unjustly excommunicated.' (*Hist. Ecc.*, 1, 15.)

many Christians could not grasp their importance. Most of the bishops tried therefore to shelve the new creed and adhere to their own traditional local confessions of faith. A few openly repudiated the Nicene formula and these Constantine banished and replaced by men who would obey the council. This action set the Church on fire. Hostility burst out among the bishops, who accused each other of heresies. These incriminations led their victims into disgrace and exile. In self-defence the expelled clergy appealed to the Emperor, pleading their orthodoxy and denouncing their rivals.

Theological parties were formed, and they clashed at numerous episcopal gatherings, convoked to restore peace. The main point of contention was the term *homoousios*. Resistance was psychologically explicable, for this word was prematurely imposed upon the East, but theologically the term expressed the traditional faith and therefore its defenders refused any concession, and even such an alternative as *homiousios* (of like substance), suggested as a compromise, was rejected by the upholders of the Nicene Council. Many bishops preferred exile to the changing of a single vowel.

Constantine, realizing the futility of compulsion, recalled the banished bishops and used every means to restore peace in the Church; but he failed, for dissension was rife. His sons were even less successful; lacking his magnanimity and vision, and behaving like petty tyrants, they supported their favourite bishops and persecuted those they disliked. Some of these Emperors were Orthodox, and some Arian, while others vacillated and favoured doctrinal compromise. During this period of theological battles and confusion, the central figure was St Athanasius the Great, Patriarch of Alexandria (327–373), who occupied St Mark's Chair for forty-six years. Though physically almost a dwarf he was an intellectual giant, a man of indomitable courage, with a burning zeal for orthodoxy. He combated Arianism without mercy. He became Bishop of Alexandria at the age of thirty-six and at once began campaigning in defence of the Nicene theology. He composed books and pamphlets and appealed in person and in writing to the Emperors, asking them to defend the orthodox and punish heretics. He fought the battle in Egypt and outside its borders, creating enemies and attracting admirers. He was four times exiled by Imperial edicts, spent almost fifteen years in foreign lands or in hiding, but he outlived his enemies, including sixteen Emperors, with most of whom he was in continuous conflict.

Athanasius was a new kind of Christian leader. He was a dignitary who commanded obedience and whose influence rivalled that of the civil governors. He was belligerent and as unlike his humble predecessors as the post-Nicene Church was unlike the Christian community under persecution. Athanasius has often been represented as a saviour of Orthodoxy who rescued the Church from Arianism single-handed. Such a description of his role is hardly justified, for at no time did the majority depart from their traditional faith. The disturbance that followed the Council was caused not so much by doctrinal apostasy, but more by the introduction of compulsion into the Christian community. Athanasius himself was largely responsible for it. He was therefore attacked, not only by those who criticized his theology, but also by those who objected to his interference in the life of other communities and who disliked his use of force and his aggressiveness.

The consequences of Nicaea

At first glance the contrast between the Church before and after Nicaea seems bewildering. During the first three centuries of its existence the Christian community had displayed the power of unity and concord and had won the battle against the Empire. In the middle of the fourth century the same Church suddenly lost its inner harmony and was split into hostile factions. Christians who had refused to obey Imperial orders now invoked the secular arm to close down rival places of worship and arrest their clergy. The main cause of this transformation was the abrupt fusion of Church and Empire. The life of the Christian community before Nicaea had been based on freedom, membership of the Church involved sacrifice. Nicaea altered these fundamental conditions: the Church became a privileged body. The State undertook the protection of its unity and orthodoxy. Those who infringed its rules were to be punished like civil offenders. The confession of faith, which until this time had been a secret revealed only to initiates* became not only public, but so vigorously defended that any cleric who dared deviate from it was liable to severe penalties. The Church leaders, who until then had enjoyed purely moral authority, saw themselves transformed into Imperial officials with powers of coercion that to some were irresistible. The less scrupulous behaved like tyrants. Bishop George, for instance, who was sent to Alexandria in 357 to replace Athanasius,

---

* St Hilary (d. 367), one of the most learned bishops of the West, writing in 356 from his exile in the East to his own Church in Gaul, explained to his flock that the creed which hitherto had been kept secret had now become the subject of public debate and that the local confessions of faith were to be replaced by the Nicene Creed, which he himself had never used till he was expelled from his diocese for his defence of Orthodoxy against Arianism. (*Hilary, de Synod* 91.) St Cyril of Jerusalem (315–86) in his catechetical letters also disapproved of written creeds. He writes: 'I wish you to commit to memory when I recite the Creed; not writing it out on paper . . . taking care while you rehearse it that no catechumen chances to overhear it.' V, 12. The same attitude is shared by Sozomen, I, 20.

treated those who refused to recognize him so cruelly that his own flock drove him from the city. But even the best men, like St Athanasius, had frequent recourse to force. The aged Sylvester, the Pope of Rome, the cautious Hosius, the ardent Athanasius, the learned Eusebius, all gave up the freedom of the Church in exchange for the protection of the Empire.

This surprising surrender was linked with growing emotional tension, centred in Egypt, and especially in Alexandria. That great city of extremes was always ready to support some new cause with wild enthusiasm. In the fourth century it swung into fierce reaction against the sexual licence previously prevalent among its inhabitants. The most austere forms of self-mortification excited general admiration; sex was regarded as degrading; virginity was praised as the chief Christian virtue. A large number of men and women embraced a life of dedicated celibacy. The emotional strain under which many of them lived is well reflected in the life of St Antony (251–356), whose temptations, described by St Athanasius, greatly impressed Christians all over the world.

This stress on virginity became so unbalanced that it provided a favourable ground for the passionate outbreak of the cult of the leader, which has always been one of the characteristics of Egyptian mentality. The head of the Christian community in the Nile Valley acquired a unique position: he was not only regarded as superior to all other local bishops, but became an object of devotion unknown in other parts of the Church. He was the popular hero of Egyptian Christians, their divine oracle and the champion of their awakening nationalism.

In this atmosphere doctrinal disputes also became passionate. Theological issues were debated in the streets and markets with an enthusiasm usually reserved for sport or politics. The supporters of one school of theology abused their opponents and praised their own leaders, as inspired by God and infallible. This verbal hostility, once accepted as compatible with Christianity, easily led to deeds of violence. Tolerance and moderation were branded as a betrayal of truth. Dogmatic zeal exempted Christians from charity and forgiveness. State intervention was welcomed by the contesting parties. As far as the East was concerned, Egypt played a fatal role in opening the gates of the Church to the use of secular force. The Church which excelled all others in the exercise of asceticism and in the cult of the leader was also the first to surrender its freedom. It is therefore significant that the same African soil became the scene of two disastrous schisms in the early Church: the Donatist schism, which eventually extinguished Christianity in North Africa, and the Monophysite schism, which delivered the major part of the Christian East into the hands of Islam.

The victory of Nicene Orthodoxy

Unrest within the Church caused by the Nicene Council coincided with a period of troubles for the Roman Empire. Constantine's sons, Constantius (337–361), Constantine II (337–340) and Constans (340–350), fought each other and weakened the Empire at a time when it needed all its strength to resist the barbarians' increasing pressure. Their nephew and successor, Julian the Apostate (361–363), having unsuccessfully tried to revive paganism, perished when leading his army against the Persians. Valens (364–378) was an active supporter of the Arians and his attempts to fill the leading sees with heretics led to further confusion. He was killed during a campaign against the Goths.

His successor, Theodosius I (379–395), restored at last the peace of the Church and revived the political might of the Empire. He convoked a synod in Constantinople in 381 (the Second Ecumenical Council) which proclaimed that only Nicene Theology was Orthodox, and thereby ended, as far as the East was concerned, the disputes caused by the First Ecumenical Council. This victory was not only due to Imperial support; it was also the result of serious theological thinking by three outstanding men known to us as the Cappadocian Fathers (Plate 31): St Basil the Great (329–379), St Gregory Nazianzen (330–389) and St Gregory of Nyssa (335–396). These new leaders of the Eastern Church ensured the triumph of the Apostolic tradition. Their opponents were ready to shape their theology to suit current philosophical idioms, and so win Court approval. The Cappadocian Fathers, men of integrity and courage, did not seek Imperial favours. They were firm without being pugnacious, ascetics yet free from fanaticism, Orthodox but desiring the restoration of peace in the Church. They worked to reconcile the Nicene party and the Conservative majority of the Eastern Christians. They achieved their aim by justifying doctrinally the contested term *homoousios*, and by resisting any State intervention in doctrinal disputes. They were men of deep learning and culture who heroically defended the freedom of the Church and the dignity of its pastors. They upheld the Nicene formulation because they believed it expressed the traditional faith of the Church and not because it had been sanctioned by the Emperor.

Their great achievement was to have clarified theological terms. They coined a new vocabulary capable of expressing the Christian vision of God. The language of Greek philosophy had been unequal to this task and helped to cause the confusion and bitterness of the post-Nicene disputes. The contemporary Church historian Socrates (379–445) was right when he compared the bishops in their endless disputes to men fighting each other in the dark, not knowing with any precision the doctrinal position of their adversaries and attributing heresies and errors to them which they repudiated.[13] The Cappadocians brought light into this chaos and at the same time purified the moral atmosphere among the leaders of the Church by their freedom from personal ambitions and by their genuine concern for the welfare of the whole community.

St Basil was born in 329 in Caesarea, the capital of Cappadocia, and an important commercial centre on the crossroads which linked the Euphrates with the Black Sea, and Constantinople with the Persian Empire. His father was a wealthy lawyer and a devout Christian; his mother Emilia was renowned for her beauty and piety. His parents had ten children, and three of their sons and one of their daughters are numbered among the Saints of the Church. Basil was educated in Constantinople and in Athens, where he met his lifelong friend, Gregory Nazianzen. Another of his fellow students was Julian, the future Emperor. On his return to his native city, Basil intended to follow his father's profession, but the sudden death of his brother, Nancratius, and the example of his sister, St Macrina, turned his mind to religion. Macrina was a remarkable woman who exercised a powerful influence upon all who came in contact with her. She formed a religious community for women and her charity and wisdom made her famous all over Pontus and Cappadocia.*

St Basil followed Macrina's advice and retired to his father's estate where he gathered like-minded young men round him; and founded a small community which played a significant role in the evolution of Eastern monasticism. He was convinced that a well organized monastery directed by a wise and experienced teacher was of greater benefit than a lonely life in the desert, for those who wanted to dedicate themselves to the worship of God. He himself renounced the world, not because he despised it, but because his love for God called him to give up all other loyalties and attractions. The rules he composed showed, however, that love for God can never be separated from love for men.

Basil was too remarkable a leader to remain for long in the seclusion of monasticism. The Church needed his services. In 358, Eusebius, bishop of Caesaria, ordained him presbyter against his will. In 370, after Eusebius's death, Basil was elected his successor. It was a hard time for the Church. The Emperor Valens was supporting the different ramifications of Arianism; the Orthodox were not only oppressed but also divided, for they had no recognized leader. Athanasius was getting

* St Gregory of Nyssa has left a moving description of his beloved sister (*Vita St Macrinae*).

old, and his influence was in any case confined to Egypt. The Pope of Rome was orthodox, but he was far away and unable to assist the defenders of the traditional faith in the East. At this moment Basil assumed the role of leader and brilliantly performed his task of uniting the Church under the banner of the Nicene theology. He was weak in health, peace loving and genuinely humble, but he had rare firmness of character. He combined tolerance and patience with an uncompromising stand for orthodoxy. Once, cross-examined by the much dreaded prefect Modestus, Basil provoked him into shouting 'No one ever dared to speak to me in this manner!' Basil's reply was: 'Probably you have never met a bishop.' He used another language when he tried to persuade Church leaders. As a theologian he vindicated the term *homoousios* in the eyes of the conservative Eastern bishops. As an ecclesiastical statesman he laboured to restore communion between East and West, employing the pre-Nicene method of inter-church correspondence and objecting to all forms of compulsion. In this he differed from St Athanasius who was often ready to use the secular arm in defence of orthodoxy.

The chief obstacle to reconciliation at that time was the existence of dissident groups in Antioch and Constantinople which were in communion with Rome and Alexandria, and claimed to be the sole representatives of orthodoxy in the East. In order to maintain their position they misrepresented the doctrinal stand of St Basil and of other conservative theologians in the Asiatic provinces. Basil's main object was to persuade the militant supporters of the Nicene Council that most Eastern bishops who objected to the term *homoousios* were nonetheless genuinely Orthodox.

Basil spared no efforts to remove the misunderstanding created by the pro-Nicene extremists. He wrote letters, sent emissaries, invited Western bishops to come to the East and meet him and his friends; though often rebuffed, he persevered. He died in 379 without seeing the reconciliation completed, but he had the satisfaction of observing many signs that the Churches were moving in the right direction and that concord would soon be restored.

In all his labours Basil was greatly helped by his friend and disciple St Gregory Nazianzen, son of a poor cleric of a small sect later reconciled to the Church. His mother Nonna, a stern and ascetic woman, dedicated her only child to the service of God and brought him up in the spirit of orthodoxy. Gregory was small of stature, red haired, always in bad health, but like Basil, fearless and uncompromising. A gifted poet, a writer of excellent prose, he would have preferred a quiet literary life, but circumstances forced him to take an active, and at times decisive part, in the defence of Orthodoxy. He was ordained presbyter, like Basil against his will, and was later forced by Basil himself to become bishop of the forlorn township of Sasima. Basil needed his support in the campaign against the Arians, but Gregory for a long time resented this violation of his privacy by his best friend. He felt himself unworthy of his sacerdotal duties and longed for his austere solitude on his father's estate.

In the year of St Basil's death, Gregory suddenly appeared in Constantinople. The Capital was at that time a stronghold of the anti-Nicene party and the supporters of the *homoousios* had not a single Church at their disposal. St Gregory began celebrating and teaching in a room in a private house. He soon became the most popular preacher in the capital and it was probably at that time that he delivered his five famous orations on the Holy Trinity. They represent one of the highest achievements in theology of the Eastern church.

St Gregory penetrated deeper than any other divine into the mystery of the Triune God, whose inner life of love is the timeless intercourse of three distinct persons who are but one being. God is one in three and three in one, was the refrain that accompanied St Gregory's sermons. In his teaching on the Incarnation St Gregory emphasized the all-important doctrine that only because one of the Holy Trinity became a real man, can men ascend to union with the Godhead. The birth of Christ created a situation which was logically contradictory, for the Incarnate Logos being both God and man retained the characteristics of his two natures and at the same time remained one person, a proof that man can be united with God without being deprived of his personality. Gregory wrote:

'Christ was born, but he was already begotten; he issued from woman, but she was a Virgin. He was baptized, but he remitted sins as God. He thirsted, but he said "If any one thirst let him come unto me and drink". He prayed, but he hears prayers. He asked where Lazarus was laid, for he was a man; and he raised Lazarus, for he is God. He dies, but he gives life. He is buried, but he rises again. He descends into hell, but he saves the damned.'[14]

St Gregory's writings are full of imagery and poetical beauty; at the same time they are doctrinally precise for he avoids arbitrary speculations and adheres to the original apostolic tradition of the Church.

When Valens died in 378, Theodosius, his successor, came to Constantinople; being a staunch upholder of Nicene Orthodoxy he at once ordered the transfer of all Churches to the pro-Nicene clergy. The Arian bishop of the capital was expelled and Gregory was elevated to the leading see, by public acclamation. He who had complained that supervising the ecclesiastical affairs of a small township in Cappadocia was an unbearable burden, accepted with fortitude the administration of the Church of the capital. His success surprised even his friends and admirers, but it also provoked animosity in those who objected to his rapid rise to power.

In 381, when Theodosius convoked a Council of Eastern bishops in Constantinople to confirm the victory of the Nicene Orthodoxy, the Patriarch of Alexandria questioned Gregory's right to occupy his chair, for he was originally elected bishop of Sasima and such a transfer was contrary to ecclesiastical rules. Gregory refused to fight for his position. He left the capital and returned to his father's estate in Ariansus, where he died in 389.

In his farewell oration he painted a striking picture of the new type of wealthy prelate in whose company he felt himself a stranger.

'No one told me that I was to compete with Consuls and Prefects and illustrious Generals. No one told me I was expected to place the treasuries of the Church at the service of gluttony and the Poor Boxes at the service of luxury. No one told me I must be equipped with superb horses and ride in expensive chariots or that everyone must make way for the Patriarch, as though he were some kind of wild beast.'[15]

St Gregory, shrunken, poorly dressed, but with his fiery imagination and biting tongue, stood in sharp contrast with the opulent bishops who behaved and lived like State officials. Gregory's dismissal opened the long rivalry between Alexandria and Constantinople, which ended by pushing the presiding bishops of those two cities into separate ecclesiastical camps.

The third great Cappadocian was St Gregory of Nyssa. This younger brother of St Basil the Great had nothing of St Basil's commanding personality. He was not an ecclesiastical leader but a creative and original thinker. St Gregory was a married man. His beautiful wife, Theosebeia, became a deaconess. Both are revered as saints by Eastern Christians. He, like Gregory Nazianzen, was compelled by St Basil to accept episcopal orders, but his gentle and poetical nature was ill-suited to ecclesiastical warfare. His theological writings breathe a joyful optimism, inspired by the victory achieved by Christ's resurrection. St

Gregory believed that human nature would be restored to its original glory and beauty, for man is created in the living image of God and is blessed by his maker with immortality. According to St Gregory, man's fall only temporarily deprived him of righteousness given to him in Paradise, and again to be bestowed on him at the end of history.

St Gregory took part in the work of the Second Ecumenical Council in 381 and was greeted there as a pillar of Nicene Orthodoxy. The Emperor Theodosius respected his judgment and he was sent as Imperial legate to investigate the state of the Churches in Arabia and Babylon. But he was not at ease as Caesar's envoy and preferred working in Nyssa, where he ended his life in peace in 396. In many respects he is, both as theologian and as writer, the nearest to our time and mentality. Gregory loved nature, he loved the earth and all that belonged to it, and in this he was an exception in his own generation which seemed so absorbed in the contemplation of eternal life that it lost interest in earthly joys and responsibilities. St Gregory's greatness as an original thinker was acknowledged in 787 by the Seventh Ecumenical Council which gave him the remarkable title of 'Father of the Fathers of the Church'.

The Second Ecumenical Council and the Emperor Theodosius (379–395)

The Second Ecumenical Council convoked by the Emperor Theodosius in 381 in Constantinople was restricted, due to political troubles, to the bishops of the Eastern part of the Empire. It was a much smaller gathering than the First, for only 150 members attended, but it left as deep a mark upon the development of the Church. The confession of faith it sanctioned was an adaptation of a local baptismal creed, probably that of Jerusalem, but it became the creed of the whole Church, the bond of unity among all Eastern Christians and an important link between them and the Christian West. This creed, now usually known as the Nicene Creed, although it belongs to the Second Council, incorporated the word *homoousios* from the original Nicene creed. The four Canons adopted by the Second Council defined the ecclesiastical provinces and forbade their leaders to interfere with affairs outside their frontiers. This prohibition was directed mainly at Alexandria whose Popes had acquired the habit of behaving as supreme heads of Christendom. The Bishop of Constantinople was raised to the dignity of Patriarch and was assigned to the second place of honour after Rome, Alexandria taking only third place. This greatly wounded the Egyptian prelates' pride.

When Council members had finished their work they sent a letter to the Emperor informing him of their decisions. Theodosius in response ordered that Church property all over the Empire should be handed over to those bishops who were in communion with Nectarius of Constantinople, Timothy of Alexandria, Diodorus of Tarsus, and Optimus of Antioch.

Constantine made the bishops solely responsible for the formulation of doctrines and for the discipline of the Church. Theodosius himself decided which theological school was right. In 383, he convoked a conference of the heads of the diverse Christian sects, and when they presented to him their various confessions of faith he chose the one embodying the Nicene Orthodoxy and ordered the rest to be publicly burned. He published a law forbidding all Christians who rejected the Nicene Council to hold prayer meetings.[16] The Anti-Nicene opposition collapsed everywhere in the East with surprising speed. Its leaders were too much compromised by their previous reliance on State support to offer serious resistance to the Emperor's new policy. Besides, they were divided, and many of them recognized the soundness of *homoousios* as interpreted by the Cappadocian Fathers. Imperial protection was welcomed by the Orthodox party, few members of which counted the price the Church had to pay for the Emperor's right to choose a school of theology and make it the criterion of Catholicism in the Empire.

The mass conversion of the Empire and its effects upon the Church
In the course of the fourth century the life of the inhabitants of the Eastern half of the Mediterranean world, of Egypt, Syria and Asia Minor, experienced a spiritual transformation which had far reaching repercussions in the secular sphere. The Christian faith, hitherto professed by a minority, replaced the ancient religions; ascetic ideals in an extreme form captured the imagination of the masses; and theological problems evoked widespread interest, unparalleled in the history of the Church. St Gregory of Nyssa graphically described this absorption with religious speculation when he said of the shopkeepers of Constantinople:

'If you ask a man to change a piece of silver, he informs you that the Son differs from the Father; if you ask the price of a loaf, you are told in reply that the Son is inferior to the Father; and if you inquire whether the bath is ready, you are solemnly informed that the Son was made of nothing.'[17]

The inrush of converts altered the composition of the Christian community. The characteristic noise and excitement of the Oriental market penetrated the peaceful precincts of the Christian temple. The long and careful preparation previously required for baptism was relinquished; discipline was relaxed, with the result that the barriers between Christians and the rest of the population were considerably lowered. What the Church lost in purity, the Empire gained in the better treatment of its citizens. Under Christian influence, mercy to criminals, help for the poor and the sick, and the prohibition of cruel and immoral entertainments were all recognized as the duty of the State. The greatest change, however, affected the Emperor. He was seen as a human being, subject to the same rules of conduct as other Christians; no longer elevated above moral control, but called upon to show mercy and forgiveness, and at the Last Judgment to give an account of all his private and public deeds.

This sudden change of the hostile Empire into a friend and even protector of the Church stimulated the many sided growth of the Christian community which was particularly spectacular in the East. In spite of intense doctrinal disputes its history in the fourth and fifth centuries is one of the most glorious in its annals. Membership rapidly increased; theological thought matured and deepened, art flourished, and philanthropic institutions greatly improved the life of the underprivileged. The Church became a great power, with the result that considerable wealth was put at the disposal of its leading bishops, causing a moral deterioration of some of them. Several personal conflicts arose, the most tragic being concerned with St John Chrysostom (the Golden Mouthed), the greatest preacher of this period, and an intrepid social reformer.

St John Chrysostom (347–407)

In 387, during local riots in Antioch, the statues of Theodosius I and his family were smashed by the mob. This act of defiance was regarded as one of the most serious political crimes at that time, and harsh retaliations were expected, including executions and mass deportations. The city was seized with panic and the frightened populace implored the Patriarch to plead with the Emperor for mercy and forgiveness.

The aged Flavianus (d. 404) set out at once on a difficult journey to the capital, braving the winter storms and the frozen snow-covered mountain passes. His mission was crowned with success. Theodosius as a Christian monarch pardoned the city. The bearer of ultimate political power recognized in the Church a higher moral authority than his own, and obeyed it.

The troubles in Antioch brought to the fore John, one of the city presbyters (Plate 31). During the weeks when the citizens had lived in a state of anxiety and suspense, awaiting the news from the capital, he delivered daily sermons in which he contrasted the vices of the opulent city with the precepts of the Gospel, and called his hearers to amendment of their lives. These discourses have been preserved and they provide a vivid picture of the state of contemporary Christianity and of the outstanding quality of the famous preacher.

The good news of Imperial pardon deeply moved the citizens. The moral atmosphere of Antioch was transformed and John acquired a wide popularity as a fearless and dedicated pastor and reformer. It was natural therefore that when in 398 the Patriarchal throne of Constantinople fell vacant, the Emperor Arcadius (395–408) was advised to entrust the Church of his capital to the zealous priest. St John was unwilling to accept this elevation, but was eventually forced to submit to the Imperial pressure. Theophilus, the Pope of Alexandria (d. 412), an ambitious prelate, was nominated by the Emperor to be St John's consecrator, and from that day the enmity arose between Theophilus who lived as a great magnate, and St John, an ascetic whose main concern was social justice and charity to the poor. From the first, St John encountered strong opposition to his campaign for the evangelization of the city. The clergy of the capital were worldly and negligent of their duties; the rich were sunk in luxury; the poor were ignorant and corrupt. St John relentlessly attacked all these evils, and was soon surrounded by determined enemies, who resented the presence of a man of pure life and uncompromising zeal. His greatest opponent, however, was Theophilus, who was jealous of the popularity of his rival and of the priority of honour enjoyed by the see of Constantinople.

The Empress Eudoxia at first admired St John, but later she too became his foe. At her invitation Theophilus came to Constantinople in 403 and assembled a synod of bishops in the palace of the Oak Tree, in a suburb of Chalcedon. He brought twenty-nine of the thirty-six members from Egypt. None had any right to interfere in Church administration in the capital, according to the rule passed by the Second Ecumenical Council of 381. Nevertheless, this illegal assembly summoned St John to appear before it, and in his absence condemned him on various false charges. He protested against this violation of law and justice, but did not want to fight in his own defence, and surrendered to the Imperial bodyguard. As soon as he was carried away from Constantinople an earthquake shook the city, and the terrified Eudoxia begged John to return to his flock.

Theophilus meanwhile fled to Egypt, fearing that the indignant populace would assault him and his supporters. St John's return still further enraged his opponents. Eudoxia resumed her campaign against him, the police arrested and deported many of his friends, while the Emperor was too weak to defend the man whom he had brought to Constantinople.

In 404, when St John was again arrested, a disastrous fire destroyed the Senate House and the Cathedral which Constantine had built. Nevertheless, this time the Patriarch was sent to Cucusus, a remote outpost of the Empire, where he soon became a centre of attraction. It was said that Antioch was deserted, and that its most prominent citizens had moved to that obscure village in order to benefit from his teaching. This popularity intensified hostility among those responsible for his exile. In spite of failing health, he was ordered to move further north, to Pityas in the Caucasus, but he died on the way on 14th September, 407. His last words were: 'Glory be to God for everything.'

In 438 his relics were transferred to Constantinople, and the reigning Emperor Theodosius II (408–50), together with his three sisters, knelt beside the coffin, imploring the Saint to pardon their father and mother for all the evils they had done to him. His exile, like that of St Gregory of Nazianzen, showed how difficult it was for a zealous Christian to remain in charge of the Church in Constantinople, and how dangerous for the future of Christianity was the determined hostility of the Popes of Alexandria. But this tragic story also indicates the moral ascendency of men of strong faith and pure life. St John became a hero of his Church, an example and inspiration, which deepened the spiritual life of the entire Christian community.

The Nestorian schism

During this painful conflict the Roman Church stood firmly on the side of the unjustly condemned Patriarch, and this uncompromising defence of the great saint helped the rehabilitation of his name. The temporary schism in the ranks of the Eastern Christians caused by the exile of John Chrysostom was soon healed, and was followed by an interval of peace in the first quarter of the fifth century. This did not last long, however, for the right claimed by the State to arrest and exile any prelate accused or even suspected of heresy provided too many opportunities for intrigues and plots among the less scrupulous hierarchs.

The new conflict was started by another priest from Antioch, the learned monk Nestorius, who was made Patriarch of Constantinople in 427. Nestorius was the opposite to John Chrysostom; his main concern was the suppression of dissident groups, instead of improving the moral life of his own flock. With the aid of the police he undertook an energetic campaign against heretics, during which he closed places of unauthorised worship. He also attempted to define with greater precision than hitherto the distinction between God and man in Christ, thus bringing his own orthodoxy into question by his opponents. The traditional belief in Jesus Christ as the promised Messiah implied that He was both true God and real man, yet also one person, not two beings operating in the same body. This paradoxical assertion of unity and distinction could be interpreted in two different ways. One school of thought, associated with Alexandria, saw Jesus Christ primarily as the Incarnate Logos, and stressed the divinity of the Saviour. The Antiochian school emphasized Christ's manhood, and dwelt on all those aspects of the Incarnation that revealed Jesus as having the experiences and limitations of ordinary men, with the exception of their sins and inward divisions. Both interpretations were within the orthodox tradition and were complementary.

Nestorius was a militant representative of the Antiochian school; he offended his audiences in Constantinople by stressing the distinction between the divine and human natures in Christ, even objecting to the traditional title of Theotokos (God-Bearer) given to the mother of Jesus whom he preferred to call 'Christ-Bearer'. The doctrinal dispute started by Nestorius in Constantinople soon attracted the attention of St Cyril (412–444), the nephew of Theophilus, the newly-elected Pope of Alexandria. Cyril was a brilliant theologian and a born leader of the nascent nationalism of Egypt. He commanded the blind allegiance of many thousands of monks and consecrated virgins, and was an uncrowned king of his people. His zeal for Orthodoxy was not accompanied by charity to his rivals and from the first his rule was marked by the acts of violence of his fanatical followers. The Jews and heathens were the first to suffer; his doctrinal opponents fared no better. Even Orestus the Prefect of the city was in danger of his life at the hands of the infuriated mob when he dared to oppose the patriarch.

Cyril's appearance on the scene of the controversy raised by Nestorius's sermons predicted an impending storm. Disagreement was aggravated by the active interest of Rome, which sided decisively with Cyril against Nestorius. To prevent trouble the Emperor Theodosius II announced the convocation of an Ecumenical Council at Ephesus. Without waiting for the Council Cyril issued twelve anathemata against Nestorius. He enumerated a series of errors that precluded membership in the Church which included several propositions taught in Antioch.

Nestorius and others of the Antiochian school counter-attacked, accusing Cyril of heresy.

The Ecumenical Council of Ephesus met in 431. Passion and animosity prevailed; Cyril and his supporters in alliance with the local bishop acted as if the Council had no other business than to confirm the anathemata. Nestorius's supporters, the Oriental bishops led by John, Patriarch of Antioch (*d.* 422), were delayed on their way to the Council, and Cyril used this opportunity to summon his followers and solemnly excommunicate Nestorius before John's arrival. When John and his party at last reached Ephesus and heard of this, they in turn excommunicated Cyril and his ally Memnon, Archbishop of Ephesus. The dismayed Emperor confirmed both excommunications and ordered Nestorius, Cyril and Memnon out of office.

Nestorius alone obeyed the Imperial command and was banished. He died in exile in 452. Cyril fled to Egypt and continued the battle from his stronghold. After prolonged and intricate negotiations a peace by compromise was concluded in 433 between Cyril and John of Antioch. Cyril retained his patriarchate but withdrew his anathemata. The Oriental bishops sacrificed Nestorius and subscribed to his deposition. Both parties, however, were dissatisfied for they were convinced that their opponents' teaching was erroneous and should be suppressed.

The point of contention was no longer *homoousios*, but *physis*—the nature of Christ. The Oriental spoke of two natures in Christ, divine and human—Duophysitism. The Alexandrians insisted upon one nature—Monophysitism—saying that the Saviour, being one Person, has but one nature, at once divine and human. This difference in expression was so subtle that both formulae could be accepted, yet this was not the opinion of the ardent partisans of each school of thought. They read into their opponents' expression a dangerous deviation from the truth. The difficulty of disentangling this confusion was further aggravated by conflicting interpretations of the terms involved. Such Greek words as *hypostasis* could be understood both as person and substance, and the word *physis* (nature) was used both as an abstract and a concrete term and sometimes was also identified with substance. Both parties recognized God and man in Jesus Christ and therefore it was possible for them to reach agreement; but the patience and forbearance which this required were absent. The label 'heretic', once attached to an opponent, excluded further conversation with him, and any subsequent attempt to achieve mutual understanding was branded as a betrayal of truth. After an Imperial decree had declared Nestorius to be a traitor and Judas all contact with him became a criminal offence.

Nestorius himself repudiated the opinions attributed to him by his adversaries, and his own writings do not show him to be an extremist. The school of Antioch was never convinced that he deserved the treatment he received at Ephesus. Cyril's supporters were equally angered at the shelving of his anathemata, which they considered the best test of Orthodoxy.

The Second Council of Ephesus (449)

The doctrinal truce concluded between Cyril and the Asian bishops was maintained for fifteen years in spite of opposition by the extremists. Cyril himself was increasingly moderate towards the end of his life. Unfortunately his successor Dioscorus (444–51), also a dominating character, revived the struggle by resuming his attacks on the Patriarch of Constantinople, for which an opportunity was provided by a much revered old monk Eutychius, abbot of a monastery in the capital. He was a well-known ascetic with admirers in high quarters, and a persuasive exponent of Alexandrian theology. In his sermons and instructions he tended to treat the human side of Jesus Christ as nearly assimilated to His divinity.

In 448 at the local council of bishops presided over by Flavianus, Patriarch of Constantinople (446–49), one member drew attention to the dangers of such teaching. Eutychius, summoned before the synod, defended his position; the bishops condemned him and deprived him of his orders. This harsh treatment shocked the admirers of Eutychius, among whom was the eunuch Chrysaphius, the Emperor's favourite. Under his influence Theodosius II decided to vindicate Eutychius by convoking another Ecumenical Council.

The second synod of Ephesus, known as the Robber Council, met in August 449. Its misdeeds offered glaring proof of the ever-increasing subjection of the Church to Imperial control which had begun at Nicaea. Not only was the programme of the Council arranged by the Court, but even membership of the synod was restricted to those who could be depended on to comply with the Imperial plans. So, for instance, Theodoret, bishop of Cyrus, the most learned spokesman of the school of Antioch, was not only expelled from his see on the eve of the Council, but forbidden by the Emperor to attend, even if invited by its members.

Other Imperial letters appointed the Archimandrite Barsumas, an ardent supporter of Eutychius, to represent the Syrian monks. Dioscorus, together with his doctrinal allies, Juvenalius of Jerusalem and Thalassius of Caesarea, were nominated Chairmen of the Council. In violence and irregularity its proceedings surpassed other Ecumenical synods, and demonstrated the moral deterioration of the Eastern clergy, especially of the ascetics under Dioscorus's direction. The Council proclaimed its belief that after the Incarnation Christ had one nature which was both divine and human. This was a confirmation of Cyril's theological formula, but this doctrinal victory so easily obtained did not satisfy Dioscorus and his party. The old rivalry between Alexandria and Constantinople once more flared up. As the First Council of Ephesus was the scene of Cyril's triumph over Nestorius, so the Second Council of Ephesus saw Dioscorus trampling on Flavianus. But there was a difference between these two victories. Nestorius was a militant anti-Alexandrian, who had offended many Christians by his refusal to call the Virgin Mary Theotokos. Flavianus was not a belligerent theologian, but merely president of the synod that had degraded Eutychius. Disregarding these facts, Dioscorus declared Flavianus a heretic and without giving him any chance of self-defence forced the Council to approve this arbitrary decision. As soon as this had been done, the crowd of monks and sailors from Alexandria, whom Dioscorus had brought to Ephesus, invaded the Church where the sessions of the synod were held. The Patriarch tried in vain to save his life by clinging to the altar. He was dragged away by the excited Egyptians and so severely manhandled that he died after three days. The public murder of an innocent prelate, with the connivance of rival bishops, was the price paid by the episcopate for failure to protest against the deportation of the two bishops who had disagreed with the majority at Nicaea in 325.

This Second Council of Ephesus ended with a solemn declaration that the Nicene orthodoxy was the only true rule of faith and that all who dared deviate from it deserved severest punishment. The closing scenes of the Council manifested the joy of the victors who shouted enthusiastically, 'Those who contradict Dioscorus blaspheme against God. God has spoken through our Patriarch; the Holy Spirit has inspired him. All who keep silence are heretics.'[18] Flavianus was not the only victim; other representatives of the school of Antioch, including Dominus, the Patriarch of that city, were also deprived of their offices and exiled.

The violence displayed at Ephesus and Flavianus's death at the hands of Dioscorus's followers stirred all Christians. They were used to the punishment of heretics, but not to the murder of Patriarchs at episcopal assemblies. Nevertheless, as long as Theodosius reigned, no opposition to the Council was raised. In 450 Theodosius died and was succeeded by his sister, Pulcheria, who reversed his ecclesiastical policy. Chrysaphius was executed and the convocation of another council was ordered, with the purpose of revising the irregular proceedings of its predecessor.

The Fourth Ecumenical Council (451)

Originally planned for Nicaea, the new synod met in October 451 at Chalcedon, a suburb of Constantinople. Its leaders were the papal legates, who brought with them *The Tome*, a letter composed by Pope Leo The Great (441–61) and addressed to Flavianus. This epoch-making document defined Christ as one person having two natures, a formula explicitly repudiated by Dioscorus and his followers. Leo's *Tome* incorporated the current theology of the Western Church. Its terminology was more precise, for the words used by Latin Christians, *persona, substantia, natura*, were lacking in the complexity and richness of meaning of the Greek equivalents, *prosopon, hypostasis, ousia, physics*.

The Council of Chalcedon reversed the decisions made at Ephesus: Dioscorus was degraded; Theodoret, together with other members of the Antiochean school, was vindicated on condition however that they condemned Nestorius. The members of the Council declared that St Peter spoke through Leo, and that they all agreed with his teaching. More than 500 bishops were present and the Fourth Council was the largest of all the Ecumenical synods. The Eastern Episcopate did not intend to go farther than to redress the wrongs committed at Ephesus, but the Imperial representatives urged them to draw up a doctrinal statement which once and for all would end the dispute concerning one or two natures in Christ. There was little enthusiasm among the bishops for fulfilling this request, but under strong government pressure a commission was set up which produced the famous Chalcedonian definition. It aimed at safeguarding the mystery of the Incarnation by four negatives without attempting to explain it in a rational way. It states that the two natures in Christ are united without absorption, without admixture, without division and without separation. This formula was a compromise in face of three distinct types of terminology, in use in Rome, Alexandria and Antioch. The Chalcedonian formula may be described as expressing the Greek tradition which kept the balance between the extremes of the Western and Oriental interpretations of the Incarnation. The Council ended in universal jubilation and loud declarations of achieved unanimity. But there were signs of another storm in the encounter between the bishops and the Syrian monks, led by the ascetic, Barsumas. Angry words and wild accusations were exchanged and some bishops shouted at the monks, 'Down with Bar-sumas, the murderer. Let him be taken to the amphitheatre, and thrown to the beasts.' The cries which had accompanied the martyrdom of so many Christians were now raised by Christians against their co-religionists for no other reason, than that they preferred one theological expression to another.

As soon as the Chalcedonian Council ended, the Emperor Marcian (450–457), the nominal husband of the aged Pulcheria, issued a stern order, addressed to all Christians, to accept the synod's decision and to stop debating on the controversial issues. The Empire hoped to secure peace within the Church by making the Chalcedonian definition obligatory. This premature attempt at compulsory uniformity was grossly ill-timed. Christians were not yet ready to accept one theological expression as universally valid: passions ran too high. It would have been wiser to postpone imposition of the Chalcedonian formula, but once the Council had sanctioned it the State felt obliged to press it upon all Christians, with tragic consequences for the Oriental Churches.

The Chalcedonian schism

In response to this Imperial command to submit to Chalcedon the Syrian monks in Jerusalem started a rebellion led by the ascetic Theodosius. Murder and arson accompanied this protest. Only after a regular battle with the armed monks did the Imperial troops restore order in Palestine. Similar bloody revolts occurred elsewhere, worst of all in Egypt. The Popes of Alexandria had long been regarded by the inhabitants of the Nile Valley as their monarchs, in favourable contrast with Imperial authority represented by the civil governors sent from Constantinople. Dioscorus's exile was seen as a national humiliation and with singular unanimity the entire country rejected Chalcedon, declaring its adherence to the formula of 'one nature' associated with the name of St Cyril and sanctioned by the Second Council of Ephesus.

The Christological dispute acquired a new colour. The defence of Monophysitism became linked in Egypt with opposition to foreign rule. 'One nature' was accepted as the national creed, in token of Egypt's resistance to Imperial oppression. The civil authorities saw the danger and tried to lower tension by appointing as Patriarch, Proterius (452–57), who belonged to Dioscorus's school. But even he was rejected by the populace as an Imperial nominee. In 457 the Emperor Marcion died; his death was the signal for a general uprising in Alexandria. Proterius was expelled and Timothy, surnamed the Cat (Aelure, 457–77), was elected and consecrated Patriarch. He was far from being an extremist in theology for he repudiated Eutychius. Nevertheless, he represented the Church of Egypt, which was Monophysite, and his first act was to repudiate Chalcedon and to excommunicate Leo of Rome and Anatolius of Constantinople.

In spite of this challenging action he retained his see, for the Imperial government was frustrated by the stubborn opposition of the Egyptians, and Marcion's successors gave up for the time being their attempts to impose the Chalcedonian definition by force upon Oriental Christians. They searched for a compromise; a most ingenious scheme was sponsored by the Emperor Zeno (476–91) who, on the advice of his energetic Patriarch Acacius (471–89), proposed a general appeasement by eliminating the explosive term 'nature' from the theological debates. Zeno issued a document called *Henoticon* or *Instrument of Union* (482). Its doctrinal content was orthodox, but it did not mention Chalcedon. At the same time it repudiated both extreme wings of the contending parties by condemning Eutychius and Nestorius. The majority of Eastern bishops felt satisfied by this temporary solution and signed the *Henoticon*. Even the Monophysite Patriarch of Alexandria, Peter Mongas (The Stammerer) (477–90), accepted it. This peace was ended, however, by Pope Felix III (483–92) who, in 484, excommunicated Acacius for his attempt to avoid the use of the Chalcedonian definition. This action encouraged all opponents of reconciliation and *Henoticon* was eventually repudiated with equal ardour by both adherents and critics of the Fourth Council. Whenever the central party represented by Constantinople met the demands of the Monophysites, it incurred excommunications from Rome; whenever it made peace with the West it was violently attacked by the Egyptians. Such was the dilemma confronting the outstanding ruler of this period, Justinian I, who spared no effort to solve the Monophysite dispute.

Justinian I and his ecclesiastical policy (527–65)
Justinian was one of the most remarkable of Constantine's successors. His magnificent portrait in San Vitale in Ravenna suggests a person of dominating personality (Plate 20). He may be described as the ideal type of Byzantine Sovereign, devoted to duty, possessed of abounding energy, a great builder of towns, fortresses, bridges and churches, and famous as codifier of the Canon Law. He had profound religious convictions, was sober, even ascetic. In his magnificent palaces, surrounded by elaborate ritual, he drank no wine, ate little, slept on a bed of wood. His main interest was theology, and nothing gave him more satisfaction than to spend time in his library, studying the writings of the Fathers

and discussing doctrinal issues with bishops and monks. He was greatly assisted in the exercise of his Imperial duties by his able wife, Theodora (*d.* 548) (Plate 21), a woman of humble origin (her father was a bear-tamer in a circus). She carried the burden of government with dignity and imagination and shared her husband's passion for theology and doctrinal discussion.

The gifted couple had great ambitions: they embarked on a grandiose plan of restoring the Empire to its former glory and bringing peace and concord to the Church. Their exceptional energy and dedication achieved spectacular results: the Barbarians were expelled from North Africa and Italy; the Western Empire was restored; the Council of Constantinople (the Fifth Ecumenical Synod of 553) was accepted by the majority of Christians; and that miracle of architectural perfection, the Cathedral of the Divine Wisdom (Plates 1 and 2), rose on the shore of the Golden Horn, to crown their long and arduous reign. But these victories were too forced to be permanent: the conquests in the West exhausted the Empire's military strength and were but a temporary check to the Barbarian advance; Church unity, cemented by a liberal use of intimidation, proved illusory. In fact, Justinian did irreparable harm, for his persistent efforts to achieve an enforced reconciliation between the Chalcedonians and the anti-Chalcedonians resulted in their final separation.

His ecclesiastical policy was based on two principles: that State security and prosperity depended on orthodoxy of faith confessed by the Sovereign and his people; and that the Emperor's supreme duty was to safeguard the integrity of the Church and the soundness of its teaching. In the preface to his *Sixth Novella* (535) he wrote:

'There are two main gifts bestowed by God upon men: the priesthood and the Imperial authority (*sacerdotium et imperium*). Of these, the former is concerned with things divine, the latter with human affairs. Proceeding from the same source, both adorn human life. Nothing is of greater importance to the Emperors than to support the dignity of the priesthood, so that the priests may in their turn pray to God for them. We, therefore, are highly concerned to maintain the true doctrines, inspired by God, and to honour the priests. The prosperity of the realm will be secured if the Holy Canons of the Apostles, preserved and explained by the Holy Fathers, are universally obeyed.'

Because of this belief Justinian intervened in the life of the Church and produced one scheme of reconciliation after another. He con-

66

sidered himself one of the leading theologians of his time and composed several doctrinal statements which he tried to press upon Church members. His conviction that the Emperor was responsible to God for the orthodoxy of his subjects, made Justinian a ruthless persecutor of Jews, Samaritans, heathens and heretics; he degraded exiled and imprisoned those bishops and priests who dared to disagree with his ecclesiastical proposals. His Imperial predecessors were content to support one or other episcopal party; but Justinian went further; he elaborated his own theological formulas and imposed them on the Christian community. His efforts were directed to finding ways of reconciling the main body of the anti-Chalcedonians, led by Severus the Patriarch of Antioch (d. 538), with the supporters of the Fourth Ecumenical Council.

Justinian and Theodora never classed Monophysites among heretics, and treated their dispute with the Chalcedonians as a split within the Catholic Church. Among many attempts to bridge the gulf, the most important one was known as *The Three Chapters*. Imperial censure was here directed against three eminent East Syrian Theologians of the Antiochian school; the latter were vindicated by the Chalcedonian Council, and sharply criticized by the Monophysites. They were Theodore of Mopsueste (d. 428), Nestorius's teacher, Theodore of Cyrus (d. 458) and Ibas of Edessa (d. 457). In 543, Justinian issued a dogmatic edict condemning the writings of these theologians who had all died at peace with the Catholic Church and who were highly venerated by the East Syrians both within the Byzantine Empire and outside its borders, in Persia, Central Asia and India. This Imperial Order was unpopular among the Chalcedonians and met with strong resistance in the West. But Justinian was determined that all the bishops should accept his condemnation. After a prolonged struggle with the opposition he convoked a synod in Constantinople in 553, which sanctioned his decree. Pope Vigilius (538–55), who was brought to Constantinople and was virtually Justinian's prisoner, at first resisted the Emperor, but eventually gave up the unequal contest and signed the acts of the synod. Many Christians were disturbed by the novelty of this censure directed against the dead, who had been revered during their lifetime for their piety and learning.

The Emperor's zeal, his use of intimidation and his harsh treatment of the Pope, did not produce the desired result. The Monophysites were not impressed: nothing less than the rejection of Chalcedon could bring them back into communion with Rome and Constantinople; but Justinian was not ready to make this final concession.

In the West, especially in North Africa, Northern Italy, and Illyricum, the decrees of the Council of Constantinople were received with hostility, and for some time a schism existed between Rome, where the Council of 553 was recognized, and other Western Churches which repudiated it.

Justinian's successors, Justin II (565–78), Tiberius II (578–82) and Maurice (582–92), alternated between repression and toleration of the anti-Chalcedon opposition, and all equally failed to reconcile the contesting parties. Meanwhile, a remarkable man called Jacob Baradai (*d.* 578), disguised as a beggar, was travelling all over the Asiatic provinces of the Empire, consecrating bishops and ordaining priests for the Monophysites. He was pursued by the police but always managed to escape, and he succeeded in making two Patriarchs, twenty-seven bishops and thousands of priests and deacons. Owing to his ingenuity and energy, a parallel body of clergy to that recognized by the Empire came into being in Syria and Palestine. The bishops ordained by Jacob bore the same titles as the Chalcedonian hierarchs, and became known as the Jacobites.

Another leading anti-Chalcedonian was an Egyptian monk called Peter. He was secretly ordained bishop in 575 by the opponents of the Imperial Church and took the title of Patriarch of Alexandria. He ordained at once more than seventy bishops and thus laid the foundations of an independent ecclesiastical organization in Egypt. Only the State officials and the Greek minority remained under the jurisdiction of the official hierarchy, which was nicknamed *Melkites* (King's men), by the indigenous population, who stood solidly on the side of St Cyril and his condemned successor, Dioscorus.

By the end of the sixth century the unity of Eastern Christians was irreparably lost. The Patriarchs of Constantinople and the majority of the Greeks had accepted the Chalcedonian formula; Egypt had rejected it. Syria, Palestine and the rest of the Asian provinces were split into Chalcedonian and anti-Chalcedonian factions, which were identified with the Greek and the Syriac-speaking communities. The Christians of Armenia ignored Chalcedon. The Christians of the Persian Empire refused to recognize the Council of Ephesus and were treated as Nestorians by the Orthodox. They supported the theology condemned by the Fifth Ecumenical Council. Only Constantinople remained in communion with the West. The rest of the Orient was hostile to Rome and the only bond of unity among all these non-Byzantine Christians was their withdrawal from any brotherly relations with Latin-speaking Christians.

The Chalcedonian definition and the separation of the Oriental Churches

The story of the Monophysite schism and the disintegrating consequences of the Chalcedonian Council raise a number of perplexing problems, the solution of which is vital to an understanding of the Christian religion. How, for example, was it possible for a Council, convoked to remedy injustice committed by its predecessor and attended by more than 500 bishops, a synod rightly claiming to be the most representative of the Ecumenical assemblies, to provoke such hatred among Christians that it led to civil wars? How could an ecclesiastical gathering, which at its concluding session had displayed such enthusiasm and unanimity, become a stumbling block to unity and concord? Why did persistent efforts at reconciliation, made by genuinely devout Emperors, supported by some of the best theologians, end in a fiasco? The most puzzling side of this bitter conflict is the moderation of the doctrinal formula evolved at Chalcedon, deliberately couched in negative terms to avoid the danger of inadequate definition of the mystery of the Incarnation.

At first sight there is something inexplicable in the passionate quality of debate and the innumerable acts of violence committed on both sides during the Christological controversy. Chalcedonians and anti-Chalcedonians professed the same religion, recited the same creed, often quoted the same Fathers of the Church, worshipped in a similar manner, and adhered to the Apostolic hierarchy; and yet they fought so fiercely against each other that many preferred exile and even death to communion with their co-religionists, and were so enraged that they burned the Churches and profaned the rival sacraments. This animosity was so widespread that when the Mohammedans invaded the Empire the Monophysites welcomed them as liberators and opened the gates of their cities to these enemies of Christianity. And yet, if any one examines the point of contention between the two parties, the one or the two natures of Christ, he is confronted with distinctions so subtle as to be imperceptible except to a trained theologian.

In studying the schism the first point to be stressed is the fact that the struggle was not between orthodoxy and heresy (as was the case during the Gnostic disputes in the second and third centuries, or during the Arian controversy in the fourth century), but between two recognized traditions which represented equally venerable and ancient schools of thought. The Chalcedonian conflict was a genuine tragedy, for its actors were all Orthodox, of sincere convictions, deeply devoted to the Church, and yet unable to recognize each other as members of the same body. One of the causes of such blindness was the aggressive intervention of the Empire. It was the State that forced the unwilling members of the Chalcedonian Council to produce their doctrinal definition of the two natures. It was the State that imposed the formula upon the restive Egyptian and Oriental Christians. It was the State that by banishing and imprisoning the leaders of the opposition made them so belligerent and bitter. It was the State again that, by pressing for its own candidates, provoked the clandestine ordinations of local men, and thus created parallel and conflicting hierarchies.

The dangers of State intervention were increased by the inner condition of the Church which was affected by two opposite tendencies: the longing for greater uniformity and the spread of virulent nationalism.

Christianity and Nationalism

At the time when the leaven of Christianity began to stir the Eastern world, Imperial administration had successfully imposed a cosmopolitan civilization upon the majority of the subject peoples. The city population was hellenized, the Greek language widely used, the other ancient languages of the East were reduced to the level of dialects spoken by rustics without culture. Only the Jews had resisted this process of assimilation and retained their own script and sacred writings, but even they increasingly used Greek in the synagogues of the Diaspora. People and races mixed freely within the framework of the universal State, forgetting their own exclusiveness. National barriers were crumbling, and the memories and legends of the past lingered mainly among the most backward communities.

In the early days Christianity represented a final state of this cosmopolitan development, for it admitted everybody and stressed the unity and equality of all, independent of race or social origin. When, however, it spread from town to country and beyond the fringes of the Empire, penetrating into the barbarian regions, it began to produce opposite effects. It stirred the national consciousness of peoples and created a sense of special vocation.

A mature and spiritually awakened person is not only a fully developed individual, but also an articulate representative of his race and culture. Christianity did not level down its converts, but brought out potentialities peculiar to each nation. This process of national self-realization however, clashed with the sense of ecclesiastical universality, and the tension created by these seemingly opposite principles caused conflict and strife within the Christian community.

The Church in the East grew too quickly in the course of the fourth and fifth centuries. Practically the entire multi-national population of the Empire became, at least nominally, Christian. The anti-pagan

70

legislation of Justinian brought into the fold of the Church a mass of ill-instructed and undisciplined people. They were stirred by the new religion; the awakening of nationalism was one of the consequences of their baptism, yet the sense of brotherhood with Christians of different language and temperament was still beyond many of these new converts. The Church having always been a supra-national community recognized the equality of all its national groups. As long as the local characteristics in worship and teaching were acknowledged as legitimate, unity remained; but with the increase of state pressure aiming at uniformity, and accompanied by the fear of divergency among Christians themselves, the variety of national traditions became an explosive which shook the whole fabric of the Catholic Church.

The idea of God as a stern ruler who required from his worshippers strict adherence to prescribed forms, and who approved only one doctrinal formula and was angered by those who used another verbal expression of the same faith, gained ascendancy among many Christians. It was especially popular among the monks who were trained to obey rules carefully drawn up by their superiors. The gap between them and the parochial clergy gradually grew wider. Even when other Christians were ready for reconciliation, the ascetics refused to make peace. Although they were men who were supposed to have left the world behind, they were the most active carriers of nationalism and their militant mood was an irresistible obstacle to peace. The ideal of uniformity, mixed with nationalism, led inevitably to sectarianism and schism. The Egyptians claimed that their confession of faith was the only one acceptable to God; the Romans insisted that it was their special prerogative to be the guardians of Orthodoxy; the Greeks were equally confident of their superiority. Yet all realized that unity was one of the indispensible marks of their religion and hence those desperate efforts to preserve it, which were frustrated by determination to make peace only on their own terms. The Christological conflict became a struggle between Egyptian and Syrian nationalisms and the centralized authority of the Empire. It became a mass movement which could no longer be appeased by theological arguments and agreements.

The rejection of the Chalcedonian formula was used as a standard under which the rebels against Constantinople united their ranks. The awakened nationalism in Egypt, in Syria and in other parts of the Empire had no normal channel of expression. Their old native dynasties had died out, the aspiration for political independence was dormant, the only form of self-determination that offered itself to people was in the sphere of ecclesiastical policy. The prestige of the presiding bishop, the theological victory of their native leaders were manifestations of a growing opposition to Imperial dictates. Neither politicians, nor generals, nor athletes, were the heroes of the subject nations, but bishops and theologians. Competitive theological formulae were used as weapons for fighting Christians whose language and outlook differed from their own.

The confusion and bitterness were greatly increased by the fact that none of the contesting parties realized the importance of the national element in their disputes. They were convinced that the only point that mattered was a correct definition of the Orthodox faith, and regarded their opponents not as nationalists searching for self expression but as dangerous heretics, wilfully distorting the gospel truth and exposing themselves to the sinister control of the powers of darkness. Such blindness to the real issues doomed all efforts towards reconciliation from the outset.

Nationalism, ignored officially by the Church, burst out in the ugly form of religious chauvinism. Christians in Egypt and Asia, which had given so many martyrs, saints and ascetics to Christendom, were its main victims. Hatred of foreigners led to doctrinal exaggerations and ultimately to such intolerance as resulted in a permanent schism. Only the revival of local autonomy could have preserved the unity of the Church. But neither the Empire nor the majority of Church leaders were ready for such concessions. They preferred an enforced uniformity with its inevitable consequence of rebellion. The Christians were being steadily forced into a position in which the price of unity was the disappearance of local initiative and tradition. Their choice lay between submission to the State dictatorship and schism, with the result that many favoured schism.

Christianity outside the Byzantine Empire

The new national awareness arising from belief in the Incarnation produced almost opposite results outside and inside the Empire. It disintegrated the Byzantine State but consolidated the independent nations of the East and gave them stability and vigour. The first nation to identify itself with the religion of the Incarnation was Armenia. In 301 King Tiridates III (261–314) proclaimed Christianity to be the faith of his people. By this act he erected a permanent barrier against the Persians, his powerful neighbours, who were ardent Zoroastrians.

The King was converted by St Gregor Loosavorich (St Gregory the Illuminator, *d.* 325) who also belonged to the royal family, but for a long time was persecuted by Tiridates and spent more than fifteen years in prison. In 302, St Gregor was ordained Bishop. In 303 he founded Etchmiadzin, which to this day is the seat of the Catholicos, the head of the Armenian Church. The mass conversion of the Armenians, who knew neither Greek nor Syriac, the two languages in which the Holy Scriptures circulated in Asia at that time, created the problem of translation. This task was successfully achieved by two heroes of Armenian history: Bishop St Sahak I (387–439) and St Mesrop Mashthotz (354–440) a former secretary to the King and a man of exceptional learning. They not only rendered the Holy Scriptures into Armenian but also invented a special alphabet for their people, consisting of thirty-six characters which were excellently suited to the sounds of their language. The Armenians as a nation came into being after their joining the Christian Church. Their literature and culture date from that time. Their allegiance to Jesus Christ became a sign distinguishing them from their non-Christian neighbours, and they retained it through all the trials of their stormy history.

A similar conversion took place almost simultaneously among the Georgians, who inhabited the south-western region of the Caucasus. The Apostle of Georgia was a slave girl, Nina (d. 335). Her unusual personality, her ardent faith and her gift of healing so impressed King Merian and Queen Nana that they were baptized, and in 330 adopted Christianity as the religion of their people. Later, the Georgian Church also acquired its own alphabet and translated the Bible and the Service books into its own tongue. The Georgians have always been the staunch allies of the Byzantine Empire, and so preserved their link with the Church of Constantinople. The Armenians followed the same policy, but sent no representatives to the Chalcedonian Council for they were, at the time, in the midst of a devastating war against the Persian invader. In 491, the Synod of Valarshapet repudiated the Chalcedonian definition and the Armenians subscribed to the formula of compromise between the Chalcedonian and anti-Chalcedonian Council, the *Henoticon* of the Emperor Zeno. Consequently their Church became branded as heretical and Monophysite by the Byzantine theologians. Various attempts at reconciliation between Constantinople and Etchmiadzin made in the course of the seventh and again in the tenth centuries, were never brought to successful completion, owing mainly to the political unrest of the time.

In the middle of the fourth century Christianity penetrated into Ethiopia. The first Bishop, St Frumentius, was ordained by St Athanasius in 350. In the sixth century the Bible was translated into Ghiez, which is still the liturgical language of the Church, although no longer understood by the people. The Ethiopians, like the Copts and the Syrians, repudiate the Chalcedonian Council and are Monophysites.

The most controversial problems are raised by the origins of Christianity in India and Ceylon. According to the firm belief of the Indian Christians their Church was planted by the Apostle Thomas, who met a martyr's death in their country; this was *circa* 72. In the absence of any reliable records this story cannot be substantiated, but a number of indirect proofs suggest it is based on fact. Nothing further is known about the early history of the Indian Church until 345, when a group of Persian Christians, led by the merchant, Thomas of Cana, and by a bishop, Joseph, fled to India from persecution in their own country and reinforced the local Christians. The members of this group today still form a separate community and do not inter-marry with the rest of the 'St Thomas' Christians. Cosmos Indicopleutes, 'The Indian Voyager', who in 522 visited the Malabar coast, found in south India and Ceylon long-established and flourishing communities.* At that time the Indian Church was in communion with the Churches of Mesopotamia, but was not in contact with the main centres of Christendom.

The Indians, in contrast with the other Oriental Christians, did not translate the scriptures and services into their own tongue but used the Syriac version until the nineteenth century. This failure, combined with the caste system, prevented the growth of Christianity in their land, and the Orthodox Church of Malabar has remained a restricted community, confined to the Malayalam-speaking people, who belong to the higher castes. The Orthodox Church in Ceylon died out, and Christianity was reintroduced there by Western missionaries.

The hardest trials befell the Church in the Persian Empire. Christianity had penetrated there in the first century, but it did not find favourable conditions among the Iranian people. Christians in Persia worked at great disadvantage: their scriptures and literature were written in Syriac, a language unfamiliar to the inhabitants; and the despotic Oriental monarchy made no such provision for the protection of its citizens as the Roman State. The Zoroastrian religion sponsored by the Persian kings was more intolerant of the new faith than the Hellenized paganism of Rome. In spite of all these obstacles, the Christian faith made a number of converts, many of whom were martyred.

The peace secured by Constantine between Church and State still further complicated the Christian position in the Persian Empire;

* He described his adventures in a book called *Universal Christian Topography*, written between 535 and 550.

Christians were identified by their rulers with Rome, the main enemy of their own country. For forty years they were fiercely persecuted, but in 383, Shapur III (383–88) reversed the policy of his predecessors, and established friendly relations with Constantinople. He allowed Christians to extend their missionary work, which carried the message of the Gospel to the furthest ends of the Persian Empire.

The period of peace did not last long, and to avoid the threat of being constantly accused of plotting with Byzantium against their own rulers, Christians in Persia decided to break with the Greeks. In 480, led by the Metropolitan Barsuma (457–84), they proclaimed their independence on the ground that the true faith, which they identified with the Antiochian School of Theology, was suppressed by their Byzantine neighbours. The Persian Christians were consequently styled Nestorians by the Greeks, and all contacts suspended. Nizibis became the centre of learning for the Persians, and there for several centuries they trained their theologians and scholars. The sixth century was a time of intense missionary activity in the Persian Church. Bishoprics were founded in Merv, Herat, Samarkand and still further East. Central Asia and Afghanistan were dotted with Christian communities. Some of these Persian missionaries went to the West, and one of them, Ivan, conducted his apostolic labours in St Ives, Cornwall.

Thus as far as the Eastern neighbours of the Roman Empire were concerned the Gospel preaching helped some of them to grow into articulate nations with a culture and literature of their own; to others Christianity brought trials and persecution, which prevented the Church from becoming the consolidating factor in the life of these people. Christianity acted as a stimulating and disturbing factor all over the East, making its converts mature persons, and distinguishing them from the rest of the population by their enterprise, better education and sense of responsibility. Thus in the course of the first six centuries of its history Christianity spread over a considerable part of Asia and penetrated into Ethiopia. It had no success however among the more primitive inhabitants of tropical Africa and it met with little response among Buddhists and Hindus.

Rome and the Christian East

A special problem for the Eastern Christians was their relations with Italy, North Africa and Gaul, all of which regarded the Pope of Rome as their presiding bishop. From the time of the reconciliation between the Church and the Empire the organization of the Christian community tended increasingly to follow the pattern of Imperial administration and the bishops of bigger cities received the title of Metropolitan, and authority over their episcopal neighbours. By the middle of the fifth century five Metropolitans were given yet further authority and called Patriarchs. The first among them was the Pope of Rome, whose jurisdiction extended over the entire Western half of the Empire and over a considerable part of the Balkans (Illiricum).

The second place belonged to the Ecumenical Patriarch of Constantinople, the Archbishop of the New Rome who supervised thirty-nine Metropolitan districts with some four hundred diocesan bishops. The Provinces of Thrace, Pontus and Asia were controlled by him. The Pope of Alexandria was the third hierarch and ruled over Egypt with its fourteen Metropolitans and one hundred and fourteen bishops. The fourth, the Patriarch of Antioch, had thirteen Metropolitans and one hundred and forty bishops in Syria and Arabia. The fifth, the Patriarch of Jerusalem, presided over Palestine with its five Metropolitans and fifty-nine bishops. In theory all the five Patriarchs were equal, and the destiny of the Church was entrusted to their fivefold leadership. In reality however, the importance of Patriarchates differed considerably and the rivalry among the principal sees became one of the main problems of Church life in the course of the fifth and sixth centuries. First there was strife between Constantinople and Alexandria which ended in the defeat of Egypt. Later a still more serious conflict arose between Rome and the Eastern Patriarchs. Its roots lay not only in the altered political position of the Roman bishops, who were increasingly regarded as temporal as well as spiritual leaders of their people, but also in the belief that the Popes were the successors of St Peter and as such endowed with special prerogatives.

Since the third century the Roman State had been ruled by two Emperors, one supervising the Eastern, the other the Western half of the Empire. In 476 the last Western Emperor, Romulus Augustus (475–76) was dethroned by Odovacar, a barbarian chieftain, and theoretically the Empire was reunited under the Eastern Emperors, but in reality Italy and Gaul were no longer controlled by Constantinople. The collapse of the Western Empire released the Popes from the Imperial control and St Leo the First (440–61) raised high the prestige of his see, by opening negotiations with the barbarians as the authorised spokesman and protector of the entire Christian population. His claims found support in the fictitious donation of Constantine, according to which Pope Sylvester (314–35) received from the great Emperor the sovereign rights over the lands around Rome. Amidst the chaos and uncertainty of life during the barbarian invasions, the Popes acquired an aura of stability and power that reflected the glory of the Eternal City. They were the sole guardians of a superior civilization, and as such the recognized leaders of the whole Western Church. Appeal to the papacy became the best defence for clergy against the arbitrary rule of barbarian chieftains. This significant evolution of the papacy did not affect the Byzantine East, where the Pope was still treated only as the first Metropolitan among equals. The Orthodox often appealed to Rome in asking its Patriarch to be an impartial arbiter in their numerous conflicts and the Popes as a rule efficiently performed this service, but the idea that the Roman prelate was the head of the Church remained foreign to the Orthodox mind, and the Oriental Christians outside the Empire were even less aware of the growth of papacy.

Until the Iconoclastic Movement of the seventh century no major dispute arose between the four Eastern Patriarchs and their Western brother although the communion between them was often interrupted; yet the seeds of the coming conflict were sown in the fifth century when the Popes secured greater political independence and at the same time began to be regarded in the West as St Peter's exclusive successors.

Eastern Monasticism

One of the most impressive characteristics of Eastern Christendom after its reconciliation with the Empire was the spectacular growth of monasticism which originated in Egypt. St Antony (251–356) was regarded as the pioneer of this movement. He withdrew into the desert of Nitria around 270. His lonely fight against the temptations of spirit and flesh fired the imagination of many admirers who flocked to his cell and a number of them started to imitate his austerities. No exact figures of the number of Egyptian monks are available, but the movement acquired such dimensions that towns and villages were abandoned and the desert was populated by ascetics, eager to undergo the most severe mortification for the sake of fuller communion with God. The popular enthusiasm for this type of Christian discipline became so powerful that many members of the Church considered that monks alone were the faithful following of Christ, who obeyed without compromise His Commandments.

The next stage in the evolution of the monastic movement was reached under the direction of Pachomius (*d.* 348). He had experienced the dangers of isolation and to counter them organized a communal life for the ascetics. His monastery had several houses each inhabited by thirty to forty monks, under the supervision of an experienced elder. Pachomius's scheme met with general approval and he himself became

77

the founder of nine monasteries and two nunneries.

From Egypt monasticism spread rapidly to Palestine, Syria, Asia Minor, Greece and Mesopotamia. In all those countries it acquired special characteristics, and yet retained its original purpose. In Palestine for instance, the monks congregated in the Lauras, which consisted of separate hermits' cells built around the Church and the central building used for the training of novices. The hermits gathered together for services on Saturdays and Sundays and recognized as their superior the elected abbot. Several of them, like St Euthymius, St Theodosius, and St Sabas, enjoyed a wide reputation for their holiness and wisdom. St Sabas was instrumental in building seven Lauras including the Great Laura.

It was in Syria that asceticism reached its most extravagant forms. St Simeon Stylites (d. 450) spent thirty years on the top of a pillar. He exercised great influence over the surrounding population and both Christians and heathens flocked in thousands to him in search of his spiritual help and advice. Other stylities like St Daniel (d. 489) and St Symeon the Younger (d. 593) imitated him. In Cappadocia monasticism took another direction. Under the leadership of St Basil the Great (d. 379) the coenobitic or communal life started by Pachomius was perfected. St Basil reduced the numbers of monks in each monastery, so that the abbot could know intimately each of them and be sure that the right balance between prayer and labour, study and rest was preserved. In his rules St Basil advocated a more moderate form of asceticism and he left a permanent mark on the development of Eastern monasticism. It would be, however, inaccurate to call the Orthodox monks 'Basilians' as some Western writers do, for the idea of religious orders has never appealed to the Orthodox mind.

The Christological disputes caused by the Chalcedonian Council split Eastern monasticism in two. The Mohammedan conquests in the seventh century arrested the development of its Oriental branch, but among the Byzantine Orthodox monasticism continued to flourish. From the tenth century, Mount Athos, with its numerous monasteries and hermit cells became the great centre of ascetic tradition. Constantinople, too, until its fall in 1453 contained many monasteries and convents and in later centuries the monastic movement found a favourable soil in Russia where it spread wide over the entire country, reaching the shores of the Pacific Ocean.

The motives that promoted the growth of Eastern monasticism were varied. The main impulse came from Christ's words addressed to the young man 'If thou wilt be perfect go and sell that thou hast and give to the poor'.[19] Many recruits joined the monastic communities in search of this perfection and they were encouraged by the unusual prophetic and healing gifts displayed by ascetics, which were regarded as a proof of divine approbation for this type of life.

Undoubtedly there were others who wanted to exchange the transient joys of life in the world and its manifold troubles and sorrows for the shelter of a well organized community. But although personal concern for security and safety often played an important part, it would be a onesided approach to the mentality of the Eastern monk if his longing for communion with God were understood only in terms of the individual's search for his own salvation.

Monasticism was essentially a corporate movement aiming at realization of the new Christian order in its integrity. Monks and nuns not only discarded their family ties and obligations, but they contracted at the same time fresh and tighter bonds, sharing their labour and property with like-minded brothers and sisters. They exchanged one type of allegiance for another which was more exacting and required a complete obedience to freely chosen leaders. The ascetics were compared to the angels, and they were conceived as forming well-ordered angelic legions animated by the spirit of love and obedience to their Creator. The change of name which accompanied the joining of a religious community indicated the readiness of the monk to die in the old world in order to be reborn into a new society. The monks did not despise those who stayed behind; they wanted to help and uplift the rest of the Church. Hospitality to the poor, help to the sick, readiness to assist and advise those in need of wise council were from the start characteristics of the monastic communities; yet charity, manual labour, bodily mortification and even psalmody were treated not as ends in themselves, but only as the means for achieving the main object of ascetic withdrawal from the ordinary life, that is worship and adoration of the Triune Creator. The desert Fathers thought that there was no other activity as noble, as all absorbing as this, and no one could perform it better than in close fellowship with other like-minded ascetics. Throughout the vicissitudes of its long and troubled history Eastern monasticism has never given up this ideal and Orthodox monks have always been dedicated to the praise of God which is the chief purpose of their communal existence.

The life of the Christian community has been greatly enriched by the monastic movement. It helped to accentuate those Charismatic gifts of the Holy Spirit, prophecy, healing, the knowledge of man's inner state, which the Church offers to its members but which are often unexplored by Christians. The ascetics and mystics penetrated deeply into the mystery of communion between God and man and have made the path of its further discovery easier for others. They also greatly enriched worship and the services of the Orthodox Church received their eventual shape in monastic communities. But the monastic movement had its negative as well as its positive features and its main defect was a desire to hasten the coming of the kingdom of God by cutting short the process of gradual transformation of human society.

The determination to subdue the flesh to the dictates of the spirit acquired a disproportionate importance. The fight against sexual temptations and the fear of heretical deviations dominated the mind of many ascetics and this created a spirit of intolerance which made the monks a menace to the Church in the troubled years of Christological disputes. Their fanatical bands were ready to assault their doctrinal opponents, and those who claimed to be the promoters of an integral Christian order introduced hate and enmity into the ranks of the believers. The monks failed to realize that the use of force could be disastrous; that zeal for correct doctrine did not justify violence; and that asceticism did not exempt them from charity towards doctrinal opponents.

The Eastern monks were largely responsible for the disruption of Church unity; their uncompromising stand contributed to the passionate atmosphere that surrounded theological debates. They were heroic followers of their Lord, but deficient in self-restraint. The religious outlook of many Eastern monks, indeed, became so unbalanced that it facilitated the victory of Islam. The ascetics were audacious pioneers, creating a new society based on faith in the Incarnation. They tried to storm the heavenly Jerusalem, but in so doing became victims of their own impatience and, against their own original intentions, the standard bearers of an aggressive nationalism.

THE ARCHITECTURE OF THE
CHRISTIAN EAST

1
In 548 AD the Emperor Justinian founded his magnificent
cathedral of Santa Sophia in Constantinople, still the
most important building in Eastern Christendom

2
The dome of Santa Sophia reflects the Orthodox vision
of the unity and harmony of the cosmos

Byzantine Interiors

3 and 4

The traditional splendour of the Eastern court extended to its religious buildings. The Empress Galla Placidia's fifth century mausoleum at Ravenna (*above*) shows the Byzantine rulers' love of decoration. Later, the Byzantine influence spread as far as the twelfth century Capella Palatina at Palermo (*below*)

Domes and Cupolas of the East

5 and 6

One of the earliest churches still preserved, St Ripsima at Etchmiadzin, Armenia (*above*), built in the seventh century, has a large centralized pointed dome, a local development from the Byzantine tradition. A Russian interpretation of the Byzantine dome is in the eleventh century church of Santa Sophia at Novgorod (*below*)

7 and 8
The Kings and Princes of Serbia built and endowed
many churches: the thirteenth century King's Church at
Studenitca (*above*). A gem of Serbian architecture, the
monastery church of Gracanitca, built *c*. 1320, has
elaborately carved vivid red brickwork (*below*)

Pre-Tatar Restraint

9
The twelfth century church of the Intercession on the river Nerl reflects the harmony and restraint of Russian architecture before the coming of the Tatars

10

Restraint in form was sometimes set off by elaborate
decoration. St Dimitry of Vladimir, a grander edition
of the church at Nerl, has striking stone carvings

Post-Tatar Exuberance

11 and 12

The originality of the sixteenth century St Basil's Church in Red Square at Moscow (*left*) derives from the attempt to reproduce the early wooden churches of Russia in stone. These predominated in the north where stone was hard to come by. The early eighteenth century church of the Transfiguration at Kizhi (*above*) is an extravagant example of the style

Decorative Profusion

13
The tomb of St Athanasius (*d. 1004*) in the Convent Church which he founded at Lavra, Mount Athos, is adorned with impressive frescoes and hanging lamps under a marble baldacchino

14
Continually reminding the worshipper of his fellowship with the Saints, the *ikonastasis* (rood screen) and pillars of the Cathedral of the Assumption, Moscow, of the late fifteenth century, are entirely covered with frescoes of the holy figures of Christendom

15
Built in the twentieth century as a burial place of the kings of Serbia, the modern church at Topola is in the traditional Orthodox style. Its whole interior is covered with mosaic reproductions of ancient frescoes from all the Serbian monasteries

IKONS AND MOSAICS
Twenty Centuries of the Ikon Style

16, 17 and 18
Byzantine ikon painting is indebted to the vivid, naturalistic Egyptian portraits of the first and second centuries AD (*left*). In the beautiful fourteenth century ikon of St Paraskeva, Novgorod (*above*), the features have become stylized and spiritualized. In the twentieth century the tradition of ikon painting continues to live but the style has become insipid (*right*)

The Glory of the Empire

19

(*above*) Sobriety and discipline: characteristics of the Emperor's court which are reflected in this imperial procession of martyrs holding crowns of glory, at Sant' Apollinare in Ravenna

20 and 21

The great Justinian (*above right*), empire-builder and theologian, was equally interested in the reconquest of the western lands lost to the barbarians and in the preservation of Orthodoxy among his subjects. He is surrounded by courtiers and bishops. His wife, the Empress Theodora (*below right*), was born a circus girl but developed the qualities of a great statesman. She shared her husband's passion for theology and doctrinal discussion

MAXIMIANVS

Saviour of the World

22, 23 and 24
The beardless Christ in Galla Placidia's fifth century mausoleum (*above*) was an attempt to show the Saviour as a mighty hero, triumphantly holding his Cross. But a more Oriental approach, at Cefalu in Sicily, emphasizes His role of Ruler of the Universe and Sage (*above right*). This mosaic was made by artists of the Constantinople school in 1147. The twelfth century Pantocrator at Daphni, near Athens (*below right*), is stern and forbidding. The Saviour is seen above all as Judge

25
The ascending Christ, in the ninth century dome of
Santa Sophia at Salonika, is surrounded by Apostles and
angels. The style is also monumental but movement has
been introduced into the composition

26
The twelfth century *Deisis* in Santa Sophia is a climax of
Byzantine art. It introduces profound human feelings of
sorrow and compassion into the traditional setting, in
which Christ is no longer the stern Judge but the
Redeemer

Christ and the Emperor

27 and 28

A close relationship was felt to exist between the Byzantine rulers and the Heavenly Ruler: the Emperor Leo (*above*) prostrates himself before Christ; Constantine IX Monomachius is on Christ's right and his wife, the Empress Zoe, on His left (*below*). Mosaics in Santa Sophia

29
A striking example of a highly stylized yet realistic
treatment: St Demetrius of Salonica stands between two
donors whose square haloes indicate that the mosaic
was executed during their lifetime

30
The influence of Byzantium on mid-sixth century
Roman art was considerable: mosaic of St Peter and St
Damian in the church of Cosmas and Damian, Rome

31
St Gregory, St Basil and St John Chrysostom are the three great ecumenical teachers of the Eastern Church. They are shown together in this mosaic from the Capella Palatina, Palermo

From Byzantium to Russia

32
The last flowering of Byzantine art gave rise to complex and elaborate compositions: the fourteenth century mosaic of the Census in the church of Kahrieh Djami, Constantinople

33
Painted in twelfth century Constantinople and later
brought to Russia, the ikon of Our Lady of Vladimir is a
supreme example of the blending of deep emotion with
the traditional stylization

34
Characterized by large staring eyes and simplicity of
gesture, the Ustug ikon of the Annunciation belongs to
the earliest period of Russian ikon painting

35
A sixteenth century head of
St John the Baptist shows the
expressionist treatment adopted
by later ikon painters

36
A very elaborate, almost miniature type of decoration with
great attention given to detail.
A typical seventeenth century
ikon: portrait of the fourteenth
century Metropolitan of Moscow, St Alexis (*d.* 1378)

37 and 38
The highly stylized setting of the
fifteenth century ikon of the
Annunciation (*above*) shows the
Orthodox love of symbols: the
hanging curtain in the background, a conventional representation to indicate that the
scene takes place indoors, was
copied by Duccio in his *Washing
of the Feet* (*below*) without any
understanding of the real purpose of the device

39
The ikon of the Nativity represents in detail the words of
the traditional Christmas hymns sung in the Orthodox
Church

40 and 41

Meeting of the First and Sec
Adam: the painter of the Des
from the Cross (*above*) draws
eye of the beholder down f
Christ's body to Adam's sku
the foot of the Cross. Prob:
by the same early sixte
century artist, the Entombr
(*left*) is another traditional
ject among Russian ikon p
ters. The movement of
woman's hands reflected in
shapes of the hills changes
sorrow into cosmic grief

42
The *Anastasis* (Descent into Hell) is a scene often chosen
by Byzantine artists to represent the Resurrection.
Christ breaks down the Gates of Hell, at his feet, and
liberates Adam and Eve

Doctrine and Speculation

43
Painted in the golden age of the Russian ikon, Rublev's
famous Holy Trinity (*c.* 1411) uses the scene of the three
angels' visit to Abraham to state the Christian belief in
the Holy Trinity

44
A sixteenth century ikon illustrating the Eucharist
Hymn: the Only Begotten Son the Word of God

45
The Arian controversy which split the unity of the
Church is symbolically represented by the torn robe of
the angel in the early seventeenth century ikon of the
mystical Vision of St Peter of Alexandria

46

One of the special feasts of the Church interpreted in
seventeenth century ikon: the Procession of the Venerable
and Life-Giving Cross recalls an ancient festival held in
Byzance to celebrate the consecration of a pool of healing
with a piece of the True Cross

CEREMONIES AND LIFE
OF THE CHURCH

Monks and Ascetics of Mount Athos

47–51
Monasteries still play a very important part in the life of
the Eastern Church. Athos, Holy Mount of the East, is
one of the most famous. Since the tenth century it has
remained an entirely male community. Traditions such

as the uncut hair and beard of Eastern monks and the
enthusiasm for ikon painting still thrive. The head of one
of the monastic communities is the Archimandrite
(*above right*)

Rock Monasteries

52 and 53
The rocky peninsular of Mount Athos has twenty separate monastic communities whose buildings often overhang the precipices (*above*). Equally isolated and almost inaccessible are the *meteora*, the 'monasteries of the air', in western Thessaly, to which the only means of access till recently was to be hauled up in a basket (*right*)

54
On January 21, 1956, Patriarch Timotheus of Jerusalem
was buried. Clothed in all his vestments his body is on
view to Orthodox Arab and Greek mourners

55 and 56

The Orthodox Easter Service, always held at night, is the most important festival and is celebrated with great joy and splendour. With candles in his hand the priest, assisted by the deacon, announces the Resurrection to the congregation (*above*). At the end of the Easter service a row of priests, holding the books of the Gospel, crosses and ikons, receive the salutations of the rest of the clergy and the congregation (*below*)

57 and 58

There are no chairs or benches, the congregation crowds around the clergy (*above*). Eastern worship lacks the precision and restraint of the West but conveys a powerful impression of the reality of the Divine Presence and has a strong corporate sense. Frequently a service is presided over by many priests and deacons together (*below*)

59
Separating the sanctuary (the Heavenly Jerusalem) from the main body of
the church (the Earthly Jerusalem): the *ikonastasis* has three doors of which
the central 'Royal' door opens onto the 'Throne' or altar. The profusion of
ikons, candles and frescoes creates an impression of the Saints and
congregation, gathered together in one body

60
Processions and services in the open air form an integral part of the life of the
Church. The relics of St Spyridon are carried annually through the streets of
Corfu

Religious Dance in Ethiopia

61
The Ethiopian Church forms an isolated and most
original outpost of Eastern Christendom, preserving
many Old Testament customs such as these religious
dances performed by the priests

PERSONALITIES OF THE CHURCH
Bishops and Prophets

62
An example of holiness at a time of scepticism: St Tikhon (1724–1783), Bishop of Voronezh (*right*), retired to sixteen years of seclusion at Zadonsk in protest against the spread of Western rationalism among the educated Russians. He is 'Bishop Tikhon' in one version of Dostoevsky's *The Possessed*

63
Cautious adviser to the Tsar, a wise statesman and brilliant theologian: Philaret, Metropolitan of Moscow (1782–1867), was a leading mind in the nineteenth century Church and author of the Imperial Decree in 1861 announcing the emancipation of the peasants

64
An ardent Slavophil in argument with Philaret: Alexey Stepanovich Khomiakov (1804–1860) was a lay theologian and philosopher of history

65
Prophet of the Revolution who warned the Russians of the results of the atheistic materialism advocated by the Intelligentsia: Feodor Mikhailovich Dostoevsky (1821–1881), greatest of the Russian novelists, was a convert to Orthodoxy after four years of Siberian prison

66
Vladimir Sergeievich Soloviev (1853–1900) provided a philosophical basis for Dostoevsky's prophecies. He foresaw the ascendancy of China and the coming of totalitarianism

67
Preparing the Russian Church for its approaching trials by his preaching on purity and dedication: Father John of Kronstadt (1829–1908) also had a nationwide reputation for healing

68

Bishop Nikolay Velimorovich of Ohrid (1880–1956), an outstanding preacher and national leader in the revival of the Church in Serbia

69

Convert from Marxism to Christianity: Father Sergey Bulgakov (1871–1944) was an ex-professor of economics and an outstanding theologian of the Russian Church

Church Leaders Today

70
The senior hierarch of the Orthodox Church is the Ecumenical Patriarch Athenagoras of Constantinople, one of the four original patriarchates of Byzantium

71
Head of the largest Orthodox community, consisting of about 100 million members, Alexey, Patriarch of Moscow and All Russia, holds a key position in the Church today

THE CHRISTIAN EAST BETWEEN ISLAM AND THE CRUSADES

(VIII–XIII CENTURIES)

Islam—The Sixth Ecumenical Council (680–681)—The revival of the Western Empire—The Filioque controversy—The conversion of the Slavs—The Photian schism—Byzantine short-comings and achievements—The significance of Humbert's excommunication—The coming of the Crusaders—The sack of Constantinople on Good Friday, 1204—The Slavonic speaking Churches—Russia's conversion to Christianity—The first fruits of Russian Christianity

AT THE BEGINNING of the seventh century the two rival Empires of the East, Byzantium and Persia, entered upon the fiercest of all their contests, with fatal consequences for both. At first the Persians led by Chosroes II (590–628) were victorious. In 612 they entered Syria; in 614 Jerusalem was taken, and the true Cross, discovered by Constantine's mother, Helen, was carried away by the triumphant enemy to their capital. The next year the Persians appeared on the Asiatic side before Constantinople, whilst the Avars approached the capital from the north-west. The Empire was saved by Heraclius (610–41). Undismayed by these defeats he consolidated the government and launched a counter-attack in 622. His five campaigns against the Persians were enthusiastically supported by the Christian population. Sergius, Patriarch of Constantinople (610–38) placed at the Emperor's disposal the treasures of the Church. Heraclius not only recovered all the lost territories, but penetrated into the heart of the enemy's domain, and in 628 he took Seleucia-Ctesiphon, and there found the Holy Cross which he brought back to Jerusalem. He was an outstanding military leader and a wise statesman. He recognized the vital importance of religious unity in this time of extreme danger to his Christian state, and spared no efforts to reconcile the Chalcedonian and the anti-Chalcedonian parties. The scheme he and his grandson Constans II (642–68) sponsored is known as Monotheletism. According to it, Jesus Christ, although he had two natures, had only one will. The advocates of this proposition hoped to bridge thus the gulf between the Monophysites and Duophysites. They argued that the acceptance of two wills in Christ logically led to the possibility of inner conflict within his person.

A number of the supporters of the Chalcedonian Council, including Pope Honorius I (625–38), approved this theological speculation, but two staunch Orthodox, Maximus the Confessor (580–662) and Sophronius, Patriarch of Jerusalem (634–68), resolutely opposed it, for they taught that will was a function of nature and not of person. If Christ had two natures, divine and human, then according to them he must also have two wills. The West followed the lead of Maximus and rejected Monotheletism. Constans II tried to force the Popes into submission. He arrested and deported Pope Martin I (649–55) who died in the Crimea a confessor to the Catholic faith. The only result of the Emperor's efforts was the appearance of a third Monothelete party among the Eastern Christians.*

Islam

At a time when the Byzantine Emperors made their last desperate attempts to reunite Christendom a new enemy suddenly appeared on the Eastern horizon: Islam. There is no greater puzzle in the religious history of mankind than the spectacular spread of Mohammedanism and the hold it has had ever since on the minds of Oriental peoples. Nothing had indicated, even remotely, the possibility of the rise of a new world religion among the poor and ignorant tribes of Arabia who spent their energy in interminable skirmishes with their neighbours.

The early life of Mohammed (570–632) did not suggest his later significance. He was distinguished neither by learning nor asceticism. He was employed as a trade agent by a wealthy widow, Khadija, whom at the age of twenty-five he married and so improved his social standing. In 619 Mohammed heard the call to be the prophet of the Almighty and embarked on the career of religious reformer. This date is one of the great turning points in the history of mankind. When he died, in 632, he was the master of Arabia and the inspired leader of his people.

The early spread of Islam was irresistible. Damascus and Edessa were taken in 636, Jerusalem in 638, Caesarea in 640, Mesopotamia was conquered in 641, Egypt surrendered in 642, North Africa was overrun in 647, Spain invaded in 711–15. Persia was also attacked, the Sassanian dynasty (226–651) destroyed, together with Zoroastrianism, which for more than a millennium had been the sole religion of its people. Iran was incorporated in Islam and gave up its ancient faith and tradition. These astonishing victories, the fascination the *Koran* exercised over its followers, and the number of converts it made among the subjugated nations create several perplexing questions. What was Islam's main source of strength? Why did it overrun the Christian lands

* They survived only in Lebanon and are known today as the Maronites.

with such ease? How did it extinguish belief in the Incarnation, among those who had so firmly accepted it? Why has there not been any significant return to the Christian faith among the people conquered by the followers of Mohammed? There is no doubt that one of the major factors in the Mohammedans' initial success was the fratricidal struggle between the Chalcedonians and anti-Chalcedonians in the Byzantine Empire.

For the Monophysites the Mohammedans came as supporters and liberators. The invaders advanced under the green banners deliberately chosen as the colour traditionally associated with the anti-Chalcedonian party. At a time when every aspect of social life had acquired theological significance, even the Blues and Greens, the two factions in the Hippodromes that contested for popularity in the Byzantine cities, were split on the Chalcedonian issue. The Syrians and the Copts thought the invaders would offer them better terms than the exacting imperial administration, which tried to impose upon them Chalcedonian definition. Many Byzantine strongholds gladly opened their gates to the armies of the Prophet, welcoming them as their co-religionists.

It is usually insufficiently realized how close Islam was in its early years to the Oriental version of Christianity. The *Koran* taught not only the virgin birth and Christ's freedom from sin, but also regarded Him as the God appointed Judge of mankind at the Last Judgment. As late as the eighth century St John of Damascus (*d.* 749), the outstanding theologian of his time, still looked upon the Mohammedans as a Christian sect. He wrote: 'At that time a false prophet named Mohammed arose, who having read the Old and New Testaments, in all likelihood through association with an Arian monk, organized his own sect.'*[1]

It was only much later that the real opposition between Christianity and Mohammedanism became apparent, both to the conquerors and to the conquered. This confusion as to the nature of Islam explains in part its initial lightning advance, but other causes contributed to the permanence of its hold. Islam not only defeated the Empire; it also superseded Christianity. At first sight this seems inexplicable, for it drastically lowered the cultural, social and artistic life of the Eastern nations whose passionate intellectual curiosity and all-absorbing preoccupation with theological speculations were arrested by the acceptance of final truth as proclaimed in the *Koran*. Women, hitherto allowed

* Recent research has conclusively proved that Mohammed was much influenced by Nestorianism. At the time of the rapid expansion of Islam its supporters and its opponents treated each other as professing together a religion based on the Biblical revelation.

equality with men, and an active part in the affairs of the Christian community, were forbidden public life, veiled and confined to their homes. Magnificent frescoes and mosaics of Christian art were defaced or whitewashed, so as not to offend the sight of 'true believers'. Self-government was suppressed everywhere, the arbitrary rule of sultans, sheiks and other Islamic chiefs replaced the elected representatives of the people. Scholarship was confined to the study of the sacred Islamic texts; most of the crafts were relegated, as inferior occupations, to the defeated Christians.

After three centuries of absorbing intellectual and artistic activity, drastic social experiments and tense conflicts, Egypt, Syria and Meso-potamia slowly but irresistibly sank into a state of mental resignation, political stagnation and fatalistic acceptance of Oriental despotism. God, who had been revealed to the Mediterranean people through the Incarnation of His Son, who had been seen by them face to face, became once more a remote and inaccessible Being raised high above the miseries and vicissitudes of earthly life, inscrutable in his dealings with men.

The chief attraction of Islam was that it was practical: it did not demand seemingly superhuman efforts. Keeping the fast of *Ramadan*, almsgiving, the daily repetition of five short prayers, a pilgrimage to Mecca, the Holy War and belief in One God and in His Prophet, was all that was required for salvation. The Christian East on the eve of the Islamic conquest had forgotten the limitations of human nature. Many members of the Church desired to imitate the angels: hence the mass movements towards the sexless life of monks and nuns; hence the exodus from towns and villages into the desert; hence extraordinary feats of self-mortification which showed to what an extent men could subdue their bodies at the dictates of the spirit. Some of these Eastern ascetics slept only in a standing position, others immured themselves in dark cells or lived on pillars, or ate only herbs, and even those not more than once a week.

Islam stopped all these excesses. It swept away the exaggerated fear of sex, discarded asceticism as unnecessary, banished the fear of hell for those who failed to reach perfection, quenched theological inquiry and ended the argument between Monophysites and Duophysites. Islam was like the sand of the desert, burying rich and varied vegetation. But at the same time it extinguished the flames of hate. It created a sense of solidarity and brotherhood which had been lost among the contending Christians.

The Eastern Christians had displayed heroic virtue, but had been

84

wilful and uncharitable towards their theological opponents, and this was their undoing. They were not ready for the Christian order and were reduced to the status of a despised and enslaved minority.

The Sixth Ecumenical Council (680–81)

The Emperor Constans II was murdered in Sicily in 668. His son Constantine IV (668–85) was an able leader who after a five years siege of Constantinople (673–78) by the Saracens, defeated them by land and sea and saved his realm from extinction. But the revived Empire was no longer so multi-national as before; it was mainly confined to the Greek speaking population. Egypt, Syria and Palestine had been given up; Greek was made the official language of the state and officials were renamed accordingly. The status of the Patriarch of Constantinople was also changed. He became sole spokesman of the Byzantine Church, for the other three Eastern Patriarchs were not only enslaved by the Mohammedans, but also lost the major part of their flocks who went over to their anti-Chalcedonian rivals.

These changes deprived the Monophysite dispute of its previous significance. The new task was to strengthen the link between Rome and Constantinople. This was achieved in 680 when the Sixth Ecumenical Council met in the capital. It held eighteen sessions, from 7th November 680 to 16th September 681. Its proceedings were tedious, mere reading and discussion of various doctrinal documents, but the Council's work was free from violence or state interference. The Chalcedonian party obtained complete satisfaction. No one advocated any concessions to the opponents of the Fourth Ecumenical Council. All who in the past had been inclined to compromise were anathematized, including the Pope Honorius, listed by the synod among the heretics. The Sixth Ecumenical Council closed the controversy raised by Nestorius at the beginning of the fifth century and marked the end of a period in the history of Eastern Christendom.

Iconoclasm and the Seventh Ecumenical Council (787)

The victory of Constantine IV over the Arabs in 668, though it rescued the Empire from subjugation to Islam, did not remove the menace of this formidable opponent. The entire Eastern and Southern frontiers were henceforth permanently exposed to attack. The Empire needed a strong and efficient government, which it found in the Isaurian Dynasty (717–867).

Leo III (717–41), the founder of the house, and his son, Constantine V (741–75), were vigorous rulers who consolidated the Empire, and considerably enlarged its territory. They were both social reformers and legislators. In 740 Leo III promulgated a new legal code which marked an important advance on Justinian's *Novellae* and showed a further increase in Christian influence. Marriage was no longer to be considered as a dissoluble contract, but as a lifelong union. Equality between men and women was confirmed by giving the mother the same rights as the father; the death sentence for crimes was drastically limited; women found guilty of adultery were exempted from flogging. This tendency towards more humane treatment of criminals and greater respect for women were accompanied by an attempt to reform Church life, which caused a new split in its ranks.

Disputes within the Christian community had usually been provoked by bishops and theologians, accusing each other of heresies. But Iconoclasm, the new conflict, had a different origin. The initiative was taken by the Basileus, supported, however, by a number of prominent bishops. Its object was to check the excessive veneration of sacred pictures representing Jesus Christ, His mother and the saints and to oppose monasticism, pilgrimages and special devotion to various shrines.

Iconoclasm may be described as the last Oriental protest within Christianity against Hellenism, which was interwoven with the tradition of the Byzantine Church. It was part of that movement towards Monotheism and simplified theology, the most powerful expression of which was Islam itself. Although the Emperor and the army valiantly resisted the formidable pressure of Islam, they nonetheless fell under its influence and tried to alter the life and worship of the Church on points which were particularly criticized by the Mohammedans, viz. the veneration of holy pictures, the cult of the saints and celibacy.

It is not likely that the Iconoclastic Emperors thought of bridging the gulf between Islam and Christianity, and so reconciling the two religions. It is more probable that they, being themselves non-Greek in origin, shared the view that God cannot be depicted by any human form. The army supported its leaders in their campaign against images, most soldiers of that period being recruited amongst Armenians, Mardaites, Isaurians and other Asiatic peoples.

The first edict, ordering the removal of the ikons from the churches, was issued in 725. It met with strong opposition in Greece and Italy, but was accepted in Asia. Germanus, the Patriarch of Constantinople (715–30), Pope Gregory II (715–31) and the best theologian of the Eastern Church of that period, John of Damascus (676–749), all protested. Germanus was expelled from Constantinople, but John of

Damascus was out of reach; he lived in territory occupied by the Mohammedans. The Pope, still a nominal subject of the Empire, was too far away to be dethroned. But Leo III punished him by confiscating the estates of the Roman see in Sicily and Southern Italy, and transferring the dioceses in Illyricum from Rome to Constantinople. These measures had fatal consequences for Christendom. They created antagonism between the Old and the New Rome, and forced the Popes to look for new friends and protectors; these they found in the Franks. The revival of the Western Empire as a rival to Byzantium was prepared by the Iconoclastic Emperors who tried and failed to enforce their policy in the West.

Constantine V, Copronymus (741–75), was more of a theologian than his father, Leo III, and his campaign against the ikons was still more vigorously pursued. He convoked a council in Constantinople in 753 which gathered some three hundred and forty bishops. They declared that the only lawful representation of the Saviour was the Eucharist, and that figures and pictures which could depict only his human side were therefore heretical. Neither Rome, nor Antioch, nor Alexandria sent delegates to this council. Constantine's son and successor, Leo IV, the Khazar (775–80), relaxed his father's oppressive measures against the Ikonodules. On his death the regency fell upon Irene, an accomplished Athenian, an ardent devotee of the ikons. She managed to elevate to the Patriarchal see of Constantinople a learned Secretary of State, Tarasius (784–806), and under his presidency the Seventh Ecumenical Council was convoked at Nicaea in 787. About three hundred bishops attended it. The Pope sent two legates. The decisions of the Council of 753 were repudiated and veneration of the ikons was approved. The Council drew a distinction between adoration, which could be addressed to God alone, and the honour paid to holy pictures, which were venerated for the sake of their prototypes. The Seventh Council reaffirmed the true humanity of the Saviour, by proclaiming that Jesus Christ could, like any other human being, be represented in portraiture. The Council stressed the independence of Church from State in the third of its twenty-one canons.

As far as the East was concerned the work of dogmatic definition was completed by the Seventh Ecumenical Council and the Orthodox Church does not recognize the authority of later councils convoked in the West. The Catholic faith had triumphed, but in the course of these long and often confused struggles, the Eastern part of Christendom was split, and as a result the Oriental wing of the Church became separated from Rome and Constantinople and, under Islam, stagnated.

The revival of the Western Empire

During the period of troubles caused by the Iconoclastic Emperors, relations between Rome and Constantinople were often strained. Meanwhile political conditions in the West underwent important alterations. The barbarians who had destroyed the Western half of the Empire had begun to settle down and form more permanent political units. The Popes, increasingly cut off from the Byzantine Sovereigns, sought the friendship and protection of the barbarian rulers, who were flattered by association with prelates reflecting the ancient glory of the Imperial city—mistress of the world for so many generations.

The Iconoclastic controversy exacerbated the new situation, for Rome supported the Orthodox and suspended communion with the East whenever the Iconoclasts were in control of the Patriarchal see of Constantinople. During this time of tension an event occurred which had momentous consequences for the future of Christian Europe. In 800, Pope Leo III (795–816) crowned Charlemagne (771–814) as Emperor, in the old Basilica of St Peter in Rome. This elevation of a Western barbarian upset relations between Eastern and Western Christians. Since Justinian's time it had been generally believed that divine Providence had established two institutions for the salvation of men: the Church and the Empire. The first was responsible for the spiritual welfare of people, and guided them to the eternal kingdom, while the second was responsible for the peace and order of temporal life, affording protection to the Church so that it might serve men undisturbed. The Empire, like the Church, was one and indivisible, guided and protected by God, but as the unity of the Church did not exclude the co-existence of many bishops, so the Empire could and often did have several co-Emperors.

In theory the reappearance of an Emperor in the West should have been welcomed, but the crowning of Charlemagne was not a friendly action or a proper extension of Imperial authority over the Western lands occupied by barbarians. It was a revolutionary blow, a challenge to the Basileus. A Western barbarian had been elevated to the throne without the knowledge and consent of the legitimate Monarch.

The crowning of Charlemagne set up a rival universal state, and because only one Empire was conceivable, a disquieting choice was thereby offered to Christians. This was clearly understood by both parties, yet an open clash was at first averted. The Eastern Emperor was in trouble in 800, and closed his eyes to the offence; he even sent a message of welcome to his 'illegitimate' brother. Charlemagne, similarly, was not ready to attack the Eastern Emperor. He started a search for heresy, however, hoping to establish his claim as the only rightful successor to Constantine. At a time when uniformity of ritual, and even of custom, was increasingly regarded as an indispensable sign of doctrinal orthodoxy it was not difficult to label any Christian community 'heretic'. Eastern and Western Christians had always followed their own traditions, and by the ninth century these had diverged considerably, so the Western bishops who supported Charlemagne easily provided him with the required evidence, the most weighty accusation being the alleged corruption of the Creed by the omission of the phrase *Filioque*. Such was the beginning of the so-called *Filioque* controversy which till today has remained a stumbling block in the way of Eastern and Western co-operation.

The Filioque controversy
Before Nicaea a neophyte was expected to confess his faith in the words of a creed which proclaimed belief in the Triune God and in the Incarnation. Local churches had their creeds which differed verbally, but were identical in essence.

After the recognition of the Church by the Empire in the fourth century the wording of all these baptismal creeds was standardized and the text which was finally adopted at the Second Ecumenical Council of Constantinople in 381 became the Creed of the Catholic Church. The later Councils, the Third and Fourth (Ephesus 431 and Chalcedon 451), prohibited all alterations and additions, and decreed that communion among local churches would depend on acceptance of the Nicean-Constantinopolitan confession of faith. This decision was approved by all Churches, and when, therefore, the Western prelates accused the Byzantine bishops of altering the creed, they raised a major issue which profoundly shook the Orthodox. The point of the controversy centred on two Latin words *Filio que* 'and from the Son'. This contested phrase refers to the relation of the Holy Spirit to the other persons of the Holy Trinity. The Western bishops insisted that the creed should state 'I believe in the Holy Spirit . . . who proceeds from the Father and from the Son'. The Eastern Christians said 'I believe in the Holy Spirit who proceeds from the Father'. Who was right, and who wrong in this dispute? Historically speaking, the Orthodox were correct. The creed, as sanctioned at Constantinople, and as finally approved by the Eastern and Western Bishops at the later Councils, adhered to the text of St John's Gospel, chapter XV, verse 26, which describes the Holy Spirit as proceeding from the Father. The Frankish prelates of the ninth century who knew little history, were genuinely convinced that their version of the creed was the right one, and had no idea how, when, or where the fatal addition was made.

Pope Leo III (795–816) was a better informed person. He was annoyed by the opening of a controversy which did not contribute to the prestige of Western learning. He tried to stop it by ordering the text of the original creed to be engraved on silver plates which he prominently displayed in his Cathedral. His efforts produced no permanent results. The Western Emperors supported the addition and in 1014 Pope Benedict VIII (1012–24) sanctioned the recitation of the altered creed in Rome at the Coronation of the Emperor Henry II (1002–24). After that the creed with the *Filioque* clause became the accepted confession of faith for all Western Christians.*

The place, the time, and the reason for this change in the text of the creed is one of the most obscure points in Church history and a detailed account of it lies outside the scope of this book. It suffices here to state that a number of Western divines like St Augustine (*d.* 430), the Popes, St Leo I (440–61) and St Gregory the Great (590–604), spoke about the Holy Spirit as proceeding from the Father and the Son, and similar expressions were current also among some Eastern theologians. But these expressions did not affect the text of the creed which was treated both by East and West as finally settled. The alteration of the creed occurred some time in the sixth or seventh century in Spain, probably by mistake, for the Spanish Church had few men of learning in those centuries, and it is most likely that those who first introduced the *Filioque* clause thought that they were using the original version. It is improbable that the men who were responsible for this addition had any intention of challenging the authority of the Ecumenical Councils. They were motivated by the desire to stress the equality of the Father and the Son, which was denied by their opponents, the local Arians, and the statement that the Holy Spirit proceeded from the Father and the Son seemed to serve this purpose. The altered creed gradually penetrated into Gaul and Britain, but remained a local peculiarity of the barbarian Churches and therefore caused no offence to the East. The dispute arose only when the Carolingian Bishops accused the Orthodox of suppressing what had never been there. The question, once raised, became the cause of endless theological debate. Each side tried to prove that the other professed a heretical doctrine of the Holy Spirit. No satisfactory solution of this controversy has yet been found. There are theologians on both sides who ascribe the utmost doctrinal significance to this different wording, and there are others who think

* The Sorbonne resisted the innovation however till the 13th century.

that both versions, if rightly interpreted, can express the same catholic faith.

The conversion of the Slavs

The end of Iconoclasm brought about a powerful revival of Byzantine Christianity. A remarkable artistic inspiration swept across the Empire; Churches were redecorated, and mosaics, frescoes and ikons, superior to those of the earlier period, appeared everywhere. Learning was encouraged and the University of Constantinople attracted a number of outstanding scholars. This was also a time of intense missionary work, which reached its greatest success in the conversion of the Slavic peoples, who entered the Orthodox Church equipped with the Bible and Liturgical books translated into their own language. Yet this great missionary enterprise helped to increase hostility between East and West, although at first it was jointly sponsored by Rome and Constantinople.

The Apostles of the Slavs were two brothers, Cyril (d. 869) and Methodius (d. 885). They were natives of Salonica, a Greek city surrounded, in the ninth century by Slavonic-speaking rural populations, and they were probably fluent in this tongue. Cyril and Methodius belonged to the cultural élite of their time. Educated in Constantinople they retired to a monastic life but were soon recalled to the Capital and entrusted with missionary work. The evangelization of the barbarians was considered by the Byzantine Empire as an expression of its Christian vocation, and also as an important part of its consistent policy of maintaining good relations with its neighbours, whose conversion was expected to make them less aggressive. In 863, the two brothers, equipped with a Slavonic translation of the Holy Scriptures made by them, were dispatched from Constantinople to remote Moravia, in response to the request of Prince Rastislav.

This unexpected demand, and the eager response of the Empire, were part of the complex political situation in Central Europe in the middle of the ninth century. The Moravians, inhabiting Central Europe, wanted to be associated with the superior civilization of Christendom, but their Germanic neighbours, led by the Archbishop of Salzburg, were more intent on imposing their political rule over them than on acquainting them with the message of the Gospel. In order to join the Church and yet retain their identity and independence, Prince Rastislav and his chieftains decided to ask Byzantium to come to their aid. This request coincided with the appearance on the Empire's Western frontiers of a new enemy, the Bulgarians—the Asiatic nomads who invaded the Balkans, conquered the Slavs, adopted their language, and formed a strong militant state situated between the Empire and Moravia. Thus, if the Greeks could help the Moravians against the Germans the Moravians could help the Greeks against the Bulgarians, and an alliance between Rastislav and the Empire was beneficial for both sides. The missionary brothers, who were able to preach the Gospel in the language of the Moravians and Bohemians had a resounding success. Princes, nobles and common people were baptized, churches were erected. The Frankish clergy were alarmed and accused Cyril and Methodius of heresy alleging that only three languages, Hebrew, Greek and Latin, used for the inscription on the Cross, could be lawfully employed in Christian worship. In order to vindicate their cause the two brothers had to go to Rome where they were favourably received, for both Hadrian II (867–72) and his successor, John VII (872–82), were disturbed by the growing independence of the Germanic bishops, and welcomed the unexpected help of the Greek missionaries in checking their ambitions.

Cyril died in Rome in 869 but his brother was consecrated by the Pope Archbishop of Sirmium, with an independent jurisdiction over Moravia and Pannonia, also inhabited at that time by Slavs. On his way to his diocese Methodius fell into the hands of the Archbishop of Salzburg and spent a long time in prison, but eventually he managed to reach Moravia and complete his work there. He died in 885.

The Slavonic-speaking Church did not survive in Central Europe. In 906 another wave of Asiatic nomads, the Hungarians, destroyed the Moravian Empire. The Germanic clergy exploited this disaster and suppressed the use of Slavonic. The last stronghold of the Slavonic liturgy, the Sazava Monastery in Bohemia was latinized in 1096. But the Slavonic speaking Christians, defeated in Moravia and Bohemia, found a refuge in Bulgaria, where Tsar Boris (852–89) offered them every encouragement and protection. The alphabet invented by the brothers, the so-called 'glagolitic', in its modified form 'Cyrillic', became the script used by all Slavs in the Orthodox Church, and the translations by Cyril and Methodius facilitated the birth of Slavonic literature in Bulgaria, and later in Serbia. The missionary work of the two brothers deeply affected the history of Europe. The Bulgarians became strong supporters of Byzantine Orthodoxy. Their neighbours the Serbs, after a period of hesitation between Rome and Constantinople, also joined the Eastern half of Christendom. In the next century, Vladimir, Prince of Kiev (d. 1015), followed the same path, and thus the majority of the Slavs found their spiritual home in the Orthodox Church, which spoke to them in their own language.

The other Slavs, however, embraced the Latin tradition. The Croats, the Slovenes, the Czechs, Slovaks and Poles became incorporated in the society of Western Christian nations and looked to Rome for spiritual leadership.

The Photian schism

The foundation of the native-speaking Church in Bulgaria, so important for the future growth of Slavonic culture, brought about an alarming deterioration of relations between the Eastern and Western parts of Christendom. Tsar Boris is remembered in Church history not only as the first Christian ruler of his nation, but also as the man who provoked the acute conflict between Rome and Constantinople, known as the Photian Schism.

Photius (820–91) was a distinguished civil servant, one of the most learned men in Constantinople. Although a layman he was recognized as a theologian of repute. In 857 Ignatius, Patriarch of Constantinople (846–57 and 867–78), was deposed by the Emperor, Michael III, the Drunkard (842–67). In the ensuing crisis Photius was hastily ordained and installed as Patriarch (858–67). The Pope, Nicholas I (858–67), whose relations with Constantinople were already strained, refused to recognize Photius as a lawful bishop. He sent two legates to Constantinople with a letter in which he asserted his right to supervise the affairs of all Churches, including that of Constantinople. The legates were commissioned to investigate the election and report on it to the Pope. Nicholas, however, mentioned in his epistle the possibility of Photius's recognition if ecclesiastical provinces in South Italy, Sicily and Illyricum, cut off from Rome during the Iconoclastic controversy, were returned to his jurisdiction.

In 861, a council was held in Constantinople at which the legates presided. After prolonged deliberation, they declared, in the name of the Roman Pontiff, that Photius was legitimate holder of the office. This victory of the newly-elected Patriarch was bought at a high price. Not only had Papal legates acted as supreme judges in the case of the two rival claimants to the Ecumenical throne, but their right to do so had been acknowledged by the Empire and the Church.

Nicholas was much embarrassed by the complex situation. He was pleased that his authority had been recognized but disturbed because return of the desired provinces was withheld, and this was especially important for the ancient province of Illyricum partially coincided with a powerful Bulgaria, whose ruler Boris was contemplating his own and his people's conversion to Christianity. The question whether he would join Eastern or Western Christendom was of the utmost importance for the far-seeing Pope, who realized all the consequences of such a momentous decision. In the ensuing acrimonious correspondence between Rome and Constantinople the question of Bulgaria acquired central importance. The devious policy pursued by Tsar Boris led the antagonists to accuse each other of departing from the Apostolic tradition. Thus the competition between Rome and Constantinople, till then concerned with their spheres of influence and jurisdiction, suddenly assumed a sinister tone. Each side charged the other with heretical innovations, and thus transferred their controversy to new and dangerous ground.

Boris shrewdly tried to make best use of this rivalry. At first he corresponded with Rome, but in 864–65 he accepted baptism from the Greeks, asking the Emperor, Michael III, to be his sponsor. He was so impressed with the splendour of the Patriarchal service that he requested a Patriarch of his own in his capital; he was politely refused. In anger he turned once more to the Pope and in 866 two Latin bishops came to Bulgaria carrying with them a long epistle composed by Nicholas in response to the questions raised by Boris. Most of them were of a practical nature and typical of Boris's mentality; for instance he asked whether women could wear trousers without endangering their salvation. The Pope's replies were wise and helpful, but at the end of his long epistle he made some bitter attacks on the Greeks, warning the Bulgarians against their Patriarchs' departure from sound tradition.

The Latin intrusion excited Greek indignation. In 867 Photius convoked a synod in Constantinople, at which Pope Nicholas's action was condemned, and the Latin missionaries in Bulgaria were accused of many errors and innovations. The most serious was the heretical teaching about the procession of the Holy Ghost from the Father and the Son. Thus the *Filioque* controversy, first raised by Charlemagne at the beginning of the century, and successfully dealt with by the Pope, was reintroduced.

In the same year Pope Nicholas died and Photius was expelled from his throne by the new Emperor, Basil (867–88), who had murdered his benefactor, Michael III. Ignatius was restored but did not show much gratitude for the defence of his cause by Rome and maintained the anti-Latin policy of his predecessor. In 878, after Ignatius's death, Photius once again became Patriarch. This time he resumed communion with Rome and the schism was brought to an end.[2] He himself died in 891, in exile, having been for the second time deprived of his Patriarchate in 886 by the Emperor Leo VI (886–912).

Meanwhile Tsar Boris once more changed his mind; in 869 he expelled the Latin Bishop and brought back the Greeks. This incorporated his realm finally into the orbit of Byzantine Orthodoxy.

The sad story of the Photian schism was an indication of creeping disease in the Church. There was nothing surprising in a barbarian's concern with minute questions of daily custom in food and dress, but it was distressing that the occupants of the two principal sees of Christendom were ready to accuse each other of heresies on account of similar trivialities: the Greeks objected to the Latin rule allowing cheese to be eaten in Lent, and the Latins fulminated against the alleged Greek disapproval of taking baths on Wednesdays and Fridays. Such a mentality made concord impossible in a community of diverse nations. The Church meanwhile suffered for its leaders' lost vision of its true Ecumenical nature. Having publically denounced each other as heretics, nothing could prevent East and West from drifting further apart.

Byzantine shortcomings and achievements

The Byzantine Empire attained one of the summits of its long and glorious history under the able rule of the Macedonian Dynasty (867–1056). For two centuries Constantinople, unsurpassed in wealth, culture and artistic achievement, dominated the Mediterranean world. Its magnificent churches, adorned with marble and mosaics, and numerous palaces, libraries, hippodromes, monasteries and hospitals, made it an object of wonder to all. The efficiency of its civil administration, the discipline of its armed forces, the skill of its artisans and the experience of its bankers and merchants made Byzantium the most prosperous and stable country of Christendom. Its gold *besant* was for centuries the only universally recognized currency, commanding the same confidence from China to Ireland, from Africa to the steppes of South Russia. The idea maintaining this vigour and stability was the belief that Jesus Christ was ruler of this extraordinary realm. The Empire was His and the sovereignity of the Incarnate Lord was realistically interpreted. The Imperial Palace contained an empty throne on which the book of the Four Gospels was placed and this seat of honour was reserved for the invisible presence of the Heavenly Master. The laws were promulgated in the name of Jesus Christ and His head crowned with the Imperial diadem was stamped on the gold besant. The army marched shouting rhythmically, 'Christ is Conqueror', and carried His image on their banners. The Emperor was only His vice-regent and his dress and behaviour emphasized his role as a visible ikon of the invisible King (Plate 28).

Acceptance of the Incarnate Logos as Sovereign of the State meant that its constitution was based on the Gospels. The Byzantines took their religion seriously, they tried to build up their political, social and intellectual life on the basis of Christ's teaching. The first consequence was a profound sense of equality. Any inhabitant of the Empire, whatever his race or social class, might rise to the highest positions in the state, including the Imperial throne. Women were as eligible for sovereignty as men, and enjoyed esteem and freedom unknown elsewhere. The centralized power of the monarch was not arbitrary, but controlled by Christ's commandments so that, paradoxically, the democratic spirit permeated this highly centralized and minutely regulated society.

The foreign policy of Byzantium was directed towards conversion of the heathen and establishment of good relations with neighbouring peoples. The army was called 'Christ-loving', for its task was to protect the Christians from barbarian aggression. Care of the poor, the sick and the helpless was a function of the state. Many charitable institutions were endowed and maintained at the Emperor's expense. Some of these hospitals housed several thousand inmates who were looked after by doctors and priests. The builders of the Byzantine Empire had a great and inspiring vision; they saw themselves as chosen servants of the Creator of the Universe. Constantinople was a divinely protected city; its golden domes reflected the celestial glory resting on this earthly capital of the Eternal King.

This noble belief was the source of many remarkable achievements but like all things human it had its negative sides. The main weakness was a too close identification of the divine prototype with the imperfect human counterpart. The Byzantines were tempted to take the symbolic for the achieved. They considered a ritualistic action sufficient in itself and neglected its moral implications. They were burdened and immobilized by the pretence that in their realm Christ's kingdom was realized and they closed their eyes to many flagrant violations of New Testament teaching on the pretext that their social and political order was approved and sanctioned by their divine Master. They became self-satisfied, and this prevented them from further scientific and technical exploration, the two spheres in which they showed little interest or acumen. This over-emphasis on symbolism led them to such a curious abuse as the appointment of eunuchs to a number of important offices in the Palace. They were supposed to represent angels, and as Christ was surrounded by the celestial host, so the Emperor was attended by sexless human beings. The Basileus himself occupied a paradoxical position. He was a sacred figure and any action directed against him was not only a political crime, but sacrilege and was cruelly punished; yet if a plot against him was successful his defeat was taken as a sign of divine displeasure and the new Emperor who had probably murdered his predecessor was acclaimed as God—chosen ruler of his people. Byzantine political life was full of intrigues; the centralized administration mistrusted local self-government and suppressed economic initiative; equality was not confirmed by freedom; the static conception of life hindered progress. These shortcomings of the Byzantine social order were the more serious because they also affected the structure of the Church, and in parts were even caused by a distorted vision of its mission among both leaders and the rank and file.

The Byzantine Christians handed too many of their responsibilities and functions over to the Empire. They endowed the state with religious significance, which made the Empire as indispensable for the salvation of mankind as the Church itself, and raised the Emperor to the status of a member of the ecclesiastical hierarchy. The Empire and the Church became so closely allied that at times they could hardly be distinguished and this fusion made the Church increasingly vulnerable and dependable on State support.

The Byzantine break with Rome

Having united Empire and Church in an indissoluble union, the Orthodox exposed themselves to the political rivalries between Byzantium and Western Europe. At the beginning of the second millennium the papacy enjoyed a remarkable revival, after its almost total eclipse during the Dark Ages. A number of energetic Popes were elected in succession. This change occurred at the time when the Ecumenical Patriarchs also reached the height of their power, sharing in the authority and prestige of their victorious Empire.

The new clash between Rome and Constantinople was caused principally by the cultural competition between the Greeks and Latins, both sides being firmly convinced of the superiority of their own tradition.

Two parallel movements of reform were started within the Western Church in the eleventh century, one, directed by the Cluniac monks, aimed at the improvement of monastic life; the other, associated with Lorraine, was determined to tighten ecclesiastical discipline, suppress simony, and prevent the appointment of unsuitable men to episcopal office. Both these movements hoped to succeed by strengthening the authority of the Popes and by enforcing celibacy upon the clergy. They drew their inspiration from the same source—the renewed appreciation of Latin learning and culture. The Germanic and Slav converts to Christianity were so fascinated by the majesty of the vanished Roman State that they considered their own languages unworthy of use in divine worship and did not feel properly incorporated in the Church until they had mastered not only the Latin language but also the outlook that went with it.

The Germanic Emperors backed the reform movement, for they needed a better educated and disciplined clergy for their civil and ecclesiastical administration. In order to strengthen the papacy the Emperors raised their own kinsmen to the papal throne and this policy affected radically the relations between the Popes and the Patriarchs. Until the eleventh century the occupants of the two principal sees belonged to the Mediterranean world, and though they argued with each other they had much in common. The situation changed when men of different temperament and background became heads of the Latin Church.* Born and bred in France and Germany, they were strangers to the Greeks and Italians. They assumed that their customs represented the authentic Apostolic tradition, and they pressed two of their innovations, the *Filioque* addition to the creed and compulsory celibacy of the clergy, upon the unwilling southerners.† When they had achieved their victory in Italy the reformers decided to impose the same novelties upon the Greeks, and this naturally provoked the greatest indignation in Byzantium.

The Christian West was inspired by a vision of the centralized authority of the papacy, not only independent but superior to all other powers. The celibate clergy, obedient to the head of the Church and exempt from the control of secular rulers, provided the basis for the monarchy of St Peter. This majestic edifice of medieval Catholicism, boldly conceived by strangers to the climate of earlier Christianity, found its visual expression in the grandeur of romanesque and later gothic church architecture.

The consolidation of papal autocracy in the thirteenth century
It is significant that the transformation of the papacy from one of the Patriarchates of the Roman Empire into a sacred monarchy coincided with the appearance of the Normans in Italy. They were invited there

---

* The first German pope was Gregory V (996–999). Silvester II (999–1003) was French. Between 1009 and 1058 came five Germans, and there were two more Frenchmen before 1100.

† The decrees against married clergy were passed by the reforming Synods of Augsburg 952, Poitiers 1000, Goslar 1019, Pavia 1022, Selingstad 1023, Bourges 1031, Rome 1047. Finally Pope Gregory VII excommunicated all married priests in 1074.

by Pope Benedict VIII (1012–24) in 1016 to help him in his struggle against the Arabs and Byzantines. The Normans soon took control of Sicily, penetrated into Southern Italy and became a major political force. They played a decisive part in the drama of the schism between Rome and Constantinople, and without their active participation it would not have occurred in the middle of the eleventh century.

It started in 1049 when a Frenchman, Bruno of Toul, became Pope Leo IX (d. 1054). At that time Constantine Monomachus (1042–55) occupied the Imperial throne of Constantinople (Plate 28). The Normans coveted the Byzantine provinces in South Italy and were an equal menace to the papal possessions. It was natural for the Emperor and the Pope to consider closer co-operation, and after an exchange of letters Leo IX sent three legates to Constantinople to secure an alliance with the Empire. His legates were Humbert of Mourmontiers, the Cardinal Bishop of Silva Candida (1010–63), Frederick of Lorraine, Chancellor of the Roman see, later Pope Stephen IX (1057–58), and Peter, Archbishop of Amalfi, a city which contained a large Greek population and was a vassal state of Byzantium.

The legates reached Constantinople in April 1054 and at once entered into acrimonious dispute with Michael Cerularius, Patriarch of Constantinople (1043–58), a person of distinction, once thought a suitable candidate for the throne of the Empire, a stern disciplinarian, narrow minded and much aware of the exalted position of his see. He was a stronger person than the easy-going Constantine Monomachus, and the Patriarch enjoyed greater popularity in the city than the Emperor. This encouraged him to take an opposite line of conduct, and instead of welcoming the envoys from Rome he resolutely opposed them. This hostility was due to a previous encounter between Michael and Humbert which arose in the course of the Patriarch's attempts to enforce Greek practices on the Armenians recently brought under the political control of the Empire. In his campaign for uniformity Michael had declared the use of unleavened bread at the Eucharist a heretical innovation, but the Armenians who practised it had pointed out that Rome, together with the entire West, was on their side. The Patriarch, irritated by this resistance, had in 1052 ordered the Latin clergy in Constantinople to follow Greek usage, and when they refused he closed their churches. This move was accompanied by publication of a belligerent epistle written at the Patriarch's command by Leo, Archbishop of Ohrida, and addressed to John, the Greek bishop of Trani in Apulia. Leo of Ohrida criticized Western liturgical customs and condemned not only the use of unleavened bread but fasting on Saturdays in Lent and the manner of singing *Alleluia*. All these deviations from the ritual approved at Constantinople were treated as serious offences against Orthodoxy, and Bishop John was asked to send the letter to the Pope and the rest of the Frankish clergy.

A reply to this attack had been written by Humbert who had shifted the controversy to ground particularly attractive to supporters of the Lorraine movement. He discussed at length the prerogatives of the Roman see basing his arguments on the forged Isidorian decretals dating from the middle of the ninth century, which in the eleventh century were regarded in the West as the most important vindication of papal supremacy, but were still unknown in Constantinople.

Such having been the first contact between Michael and Humbert, the Patriarch treated the legates from the West when they reached Constantinople as men ignorant of the Apostolic tradition, while Humbert explained to Constantine that before any alliance between the Empire and the papacy could be concluded, Michael must submit to Leo IX. The Emperor tried in vain to come to terms with the papal envoys, but the Patriarch obstructed his negotiations.

News soon reached Constantinople that Leo had died on 19th April a prisoner of the Normans. Michael at once suspended all contacts with Humbert and his companions declaring that they had now lost their credentials. Humbert took advantage of the Pope's death to act independently and on Saturday, 16th July 1054, he marched into the Cathedral of St Sophia just at a time when the celebration was to begin, and laid on the altar a bull of excommunication. He then left the church, solemnly shaking the dust off his feet and shouting at the dumbfounded congregation, *Videat Deus et judicat*. The bull was at once taken to the Patriarch, and when it was translated into Greek it proved to be one of the most curious documents in the history of Christian disputes. The excommunication was directed, not against all Orthodox Christians, but only against Michael Cerularius, Leo of Ohrida, Michael Constantine, the Patriarchal Chancellor, and those who followed their lead.

The justification of their expulsion from membership of the Catholic Church was a unique collection of facts and fiction. The facts were trivial, the fiction grotesque. Cardinal Humbert accused the Patriarch of erroneous teaching that the Eucharistic bread had a soul, that women in labour could not be baptized, that men who shaved their beards were not worthy of receiving the Sacrament; other incriminations were simony, the approval of castration and re-baptizing Latin Christians. The greatest of all his crimes was the wilful corruption of the Nicene creed from which, it was alleged, the Patriarch had deleted the words *Filioque*.

This extraordinary document revealed not only the bigotry of its author but a surprising ignorance of history. Humbert was respected as a learned man, but he was so ill-informed that he had no idea that the original creed did not include the *Filioque* clause, and that compulsory celibacy of the clergy was not an Apostolic tradition. Michael lost no time in convoking a local council of bishops and excommunicating Humbert and the other legates, calling them impostors. The Emperor, refusing to be dragged into this unedifying exchange of ecclesiastical hostilities, sent back Humbert loaded with presents hoping that the new Pope would repudiate the action of the hot-tempered Cardinal. This expectation was not gratified, for the Normans were determined to prevent an alliance between the Pope and the Emperor and they made the resumption of further negotiations impossible.

It is remarkable that the breach of communion between Rome and Constantinople happened when the papal see was vacant and that the act of excommunication was never confirmed, nor indeed, repudiated by any Roman Pontiff.

The significance of Humbert's excommunication

The year 1054, once accepted as the date of the schism between East and West, has recently been challenged. Some historians minimize the importance of 1054: they point out the continuance of friendly inter-course between Latin and Greek Christians after the 'excommunication' and the absence of any reference to it in the Byzantine chronicles of that period. Other historians say the rupture between Rome and Con-stantinople took place earlier under the Patriarch Sergius II (995–1019). In 1009 Pope Sergius IV (1009–12), on the occasion of his election, sent the customary profession of his faith to Constantinople. It contained, for the first time, the *Filioque* clause. As the result of this the Patriarch refused to include the Pope's name in the list of lawful bishops and thus official communion between the two leading sees was suspended.

It is arguable, however, that this omission of the Pope's name from the diptychs at Constantinople did not suggest to contemporaries that the unity of the Church was broken. Even Cardinal Humbert described Constantinople as *civitas Christianissima et Orthodoxa* and he treated the Emperor with due respect as a Catholic sovereign. The rest of the Eastern Churches did not consider that their relations with Rome had under-gone any drastic alteration either in 1009 or in 1054, and they continued to regard the Latins as members of the Catholic church. Yet, in spite of all this evidence Humbert's excommunication was a tragic landmark in the history of the Church. Both sides firmly believed in the unity of Christendom, but their vision of what the Catholic Church ought to be was no longer the same. Not only were their worship, discipline, customs and outlook different, but there was a serious divergence in regard to the structure of the Christian community. The West saw the Church as a sacred monarchy, and the Pope as the source of all authority in teaching and administration. The Greeks had no place for that type of papacy in their system. They were ready to treat the Bishop of Rome as the senior hierarch, but the idea that the Pope was an ecclesiastical monarch to be obeyed by the rest of Christendom was alien to the Byzantine tradition and neither side was prepared to make any concessions.

Division

This refusal to recognize as legitimate the divergence in the structure of the Church encouraged an endless controversy between Greeks and Latins, which included not only constitutional problems, but also minute details of ritual and custom, each side producing catalogues of heresies, such as the wearing of rings by Western bishops, the use of organ music or genuflection. It was obvious that for such minds the unity of the Church could only be expressed through complete uniformity, and that required the powerful assistance of the secular arm if it was to be enforced. This wrong idea of unity led to compulsion which was the fatal breeding ground of hatred and disruption. From the ninth century onwards the Eastern and Western branches of the Church, each allied to its own Empire, harassed each other whenever political circumstances were favourable.

Nevertheless the secular arm was not strong enough by itself to disrupt the Eucharistic communion between the Eastern and Western Christians and so bring to an end their sacramental unity. This last act of schism could only be authorized by a hierarch having the right to speak and act in the name of the whole body.

The concentration of power and authority in the hands of a single bishop, the Pope in the West and the Ecumenical Patriarch in Byzantium, made the disaster of the schism possible. Cardinal Humbert thought that he was entitled to sever the Patriarch and his associates from the Church. The Greeks were equally convinced that the Latins could be deprived of their membership in the Catholic Church by the act of a synod presided over by the Patriarch. In an atmosphere of disputes and quarrels, embittered by acts of violence and oppressions, the weapon of excommunication in the hands of individual prelates acquired a truly menacing character. Its destructive power was amply demonstrated by the sad story of the eleventh century schism.

And yet, despite all these internal deformations and widespread misconceptions, the Church still possessed its power of unity, as the time taken to consummate the schism proves. There were also a certain number of Christians on both sides who were not entirely committed to a static conception of the Church, and who objected to the prevalent tendency towards uniformity; but these ecumenically-minded Christians were constantly defeated, not so much by argument as by their opponents' liberal use of coercion, which frustrated all efforts towards reconciliation.

The story of the schism between East and West is not, however, so discreditable to the Christian religion as might at first appear. The Christians were deprived of their Eucharistic fellowship only because they conceived it on a basis which clashed with their own teaching and because they applied methods which the New Testament explicitly condemned. No wonder, therefore, that their purposes were defeated. The really astonishing fact was that it took another four hundred years to destroy their unity finally.

The coming of the Crusaders

While the Byzantines were fighting the Normans in South Italy and the Eastern and Western Christians were evolving their own systems of ecclesiastical order, new enemies of Christendom appeared in the East and began a steady advance upon Constantinople. These were the Seljuk Turks, originally nomads from Central Asia. At an early stage they had embraced Islam. This conversion, on the one hand, arrested their cultural development, for they became imitators of the Arabs, adopting their outlook and script, ill-suited to their own mentality and language; on the other hand, it helped their rise to leadership among Islamic nations. The Turks were invariably victorious, for they were a unified group, bent on conquest, whereas their enemies were divided, irresolute and foolish enough to solicit Turkish help against their neighbours. In 1055 the Seljuks invaded Mesopotamia and took Baghdad. In 1071, owing to the dissensions among the Christians, they inflicted a disastrous defeat upon the Byzantine army at Manzikert, from which the Eastern Empire never fully recovered. It was a black year for Constantinople, for the Greeks also yielded at the same time their last foothold in Italy to the Normans.

The end of the eleventh century may be regarded as the beginning of the Empire's downfall. Islam in the East and the Latin Christians in the West were equally determined to annihilate the Christian East. For four hundred years the Empire struggled on two fronts, but its fate was sealed; it might have defeated one adversary, but the combined power of both was too great for successful resistance.

One of the most able Byzantine Emperors of that period was Alexius Comnenus I (1081–1118), and it was during his reign that the Latin Christians launched their crusade against Islam.

To many Christians in the West, the heroic and romantic aspects of the Crusades have obscured their negative results, for the Crusaders antagonized the Orient and introduced the spirit of brutality and persecution into their own Church. In the end they destroyed the last traces of fellowship between Eastern and Western Christians. Their greatest crime was the barbarous sack of Constantinople, an act that opened the way for the Turkish invaders into the heart of Europe.

The beginning of the crusades was spectacular: on 27th November 1095 the Pope, Urban II (1088–99), preached his epoch-making sermon at the Council of Clermont, in which he summoned the Christian West to rescue the Holy Places from the tyranny of infidels, and make the road safe for pilgrims to Christ's birthplace and to the city of His death and resurrection. The response was enthusiastic and several armies of Crusaders soon started on their march to the East. In 1096–97 they entered the well cultivated lands of Byzantium. The first contact between these undisciplined and rapacious Western warriors and the local population was not encouraging to either side. The Crusaders were bewildered by the prosperity and refinement of the Empire's inhabitants, and inhibited by the unfamiliarity of Eastern customs. The Orthodox Churches, with domes and ikons, were unlike their own buildings; the services were equally different. The simple soldiers felt that they were encountering a religion alien to their own. The Knights were dazzled by the achievements of Byzantium and envied its wealth and civilization. The Emperor Alexius urgently needed men for his campaign against the Turks and would have welcomed recruits to his own army, but the sight of an independent force marching across his territory, conducting the war on its own terms with the purpose of creating independent Western principalities in the former domains of the Empire, greatly alarmed him. He was, however, a clever diplomat and able administrator. He concluded an agreement with Western leaders, stipulating that any reconquered province should be restored to the Emperor. Some of the Crusaders, exemplified by Godfrey of Bouillon, were men of honour and high ideals and kept faithfully to their agreements. Others insisted that everyone should retain his own conquests.

Alexis efficiently protected his own people against the pillage and rapine of the Crusaders by creating a special body of police which accompanied the passage of Western armies across his state. In spite of all these precautions, Baldwin's soldiers sacked a suburb of Constantinople; another detachment of Crusaders ruined Castoria, a prosperous city in Macedonia. The Eastern Christians looked with surprise and indignation at the coarse and violent Latin warriors. The idea of a Holy War of aggression was abhorrent to them. They were especially shocked when they saw bishops, abbots and monks fully armed and behaving like ordinary soldiers. The Orthodox were also puzzled to find so great a difference between the Latin approach to the Church and their own and many of them were reluctant to recognize Western Christians as professing the same religion.

The Crusaders were at first victorious and in 1099 took Jerusalem. The expansion and consolidation of their territory did not, however, improve their relations with Eastern Christians. When a new city was taken by assault the entire population suffered at the hands of the invaders, the Crusaders showing no respect for the lives and property of Christians. Conditions became even worse when their rule was firmly established, for they tried to replace the local clergy by their own men, and in 1100 John, a Greek Patriarch of Antioch, was forced to quit his city; he was replaced by a Latin prelate. This date marked a further step in the alienation of East and West and created a new reason for antagonism between their clergy. The most unprincipled crusaders were the Normans who made no secret of carving out private kingdoms for themselves. Bohemund of Taranto, son of Robert Guiscard, had fought in Italy against the Emperor before the crusades began. When he took Antioch, he refused to hand it over to Alexius. And so the gap between Greeks and Latins quickly widened and they soon mistrusted each other as much as the Mohammedans. The same Bohemund conceived the idea of a crusade against the Orthodox Christians. In 1103, after his release from captivity by the Turks, he toured Europe recruiting a new army, this time not against the infidels but against the Empire, accusing Alexius of double dealing and collusion with the enemies of the Cross. He failed, but the idea of a Holy War against schismatics was born, and it cast its sinister shadow on relations between the Crusaders and Byzantium.

The sack of Constantinople on Good Friday, 1204
The twelfth century saw the rapid decline of the Eastern Empire and the moral and political degeneration of the Crusaders who, although unable to dislodge the Mohammedans and establish a permanent political

settlement, secured several strongholds in Syria and Palestine, and became a third partner in a contest in which, before their arrival, only Eastern Christians and Mohammedans were involved. The Italian merchant republics, Venice, Genoa and Pisa, following in the Crusaders' wake, established trading posts wherever possible, and their conflicting interests still further complicated the confusion created by the Latin arrival in the Near East.

Meanwhile the Empire suffered several military setbacks. In addition the throne was contested by rival candidates who did not scruple to invoke the aid of foreigners. The Crusaders behaved increasingly like mercenaries, ready to serve any master and treated Eastern Christians and Mohammedans alike, as their enemies. This gradual sinking of the original ideal to the level of a war for conquest reached its nadir at the beginning of the thirteenth century, in the so-called Fourth Crusade. The great Roman Pontiff Innocent III (1198–1216), inspired by the same vision as Urban II, wanted to see Christian nations marching as a united force against the followers of the false prophet. But if the Pope was faithful to the old ideal the men who responded to his call were unlike the first Crusaders. They were led by Marquis Boniface of Montferrat, who accepted the Venetian offer to transport his army by sea to Egypt if he would capture the city of Zara and hand it over to that Republic. So the first military exploit of the Knights of the Cross was to take and sack a Christian city which belonged to the King of Hungary, a good Catholic and faithful servant of the Pope (1202).

Innocent indignantly excommunicated the Crusaders, but soon forgave them, hoping that they would turn their attention to the war against the Saracens. But this was not to be, for whilst the army was still celebrating its victory over Zara, a Byzantine Prince, Alexius, son of the deposed Emperor Isaac Angelus (1185–96), arrived at their camp and asked Boniface to help him to recover his father's throne. The Crusaders agreed to assist the Pretender and the Venetians gladly offered their fleet. In April 1203 the Crusaders sailed from Zara and reached Constantinople in June. The Emperor Alexius III (1195–1203) made no preparations in defence of the city, but although he was unpopular, he found loyal support among the inhabitants and the citizens refused to admit the Pretender. The Crusaders were baffled, for they had expected an easy triumph; instead, they had to fight hard against the defenders of the capital. Alexius III, however, was not a man of courage; he fled from Constantinople and the officials hastily reinstated the blind Isaac Angelus. The Crusaders agreed to a truce, on condition that their candidate, Alexius IV, was proclaimed Co-Emperor with his father.

Alexius on his side confirmed his readiness to stand by all the obligations he had contracted at Zara, including submission to the papacy and trade concessions to Venice.

The rash promises made by the young prince proved hard to fulfil. The treasury was empty, the Patriarch and people refused to acknowledge the Pope as head of the Church, the Venetians were hated and no one had any respect for the puppet Emperor. In February 1204, the excited population dethroned Alexius IV. Both he and his father perished, and another nobleman called Alexius Murzuphulus was proclaimed Emperor.

The Crusaders decided to strike, and, after a short but fierce struggle broke into the city on Good Friday, 1204, and for three days savagely sacked the great capital of the Christian East, which had never before been conquered. The looting of Constantinople is one of the major disasters of Christian history. The city contained innumerable and irreplaceable treasures of classical antiquity and of Christian art and learning. All the best that the Mediterranean world possessed was gathered there. For three days, a wild crowd of drunken and blood-thirsty soldiers killed and raped; palaces, churches, libraries and art collections were wantonly destroyed; monasteries and convents were profaned, hospitals and orphanages sacked. A drunken prostitute was placed on the Patriarch's throne in the Cathedral of St Sophia and sang indecent songs to the applause of the Crusaders, whilst the Knights were busy hacking the high altar to pieces; it was made of gold and adorned with precious stones.

In those three days mankind lost some of its greatest masterpieces of art. The Church lost its unity, the Empire the strength to resist the Asiatic invaders. The sense of fellowship between Eastern and Western Christians, which had survived so many setbacks and trials, and resisted so many attempts at disruption, at last finally collapsed. One could no longer speak of the Latins and the Greeks as being members of the same Church. The polluted altars, the sacred vessels stained with blood, the ravaged religious houses too eloquently declared the end of Christian unity.

Pope Innocent was at first horrified at the results of his efforts, but later he became reconciled to the act of destruction, for the Crusaders hastily elected their own Emperor and Patriarch, both of whom recognized the supremacy of the Pope in the name of the ruined city. The Latin Empire of Constantinople led a shadowy existence for half a century (1204–1261). It was an artificial construction, which lasted as long as it did only because of the weakness and divisions among the

Greeks. At last Michael VIII Palaeologus (1260–82) expelled the Crusaders and returned to Constantinople from Nicaea, where the Greek government had found a temporary abode. Byzantium survived for another two hundred years, but it was no longer a normal life, but death agony. The Crusaders had undermined its effective resistance against the Turks. It was only a question of time till the city fell into their hands. The Turks, when they came, came to stay. The Crusaders failed to rescue the Holy Land from the Mohammedan yoke; instead they delivered the Christian East into the hands of its Oriental oppressors.

The Slavonic-speaking Churches

After the rise of Islam, the Byzantine Church and culture lost their hold on the bulk of the inhabitants of Asia Minor, Syria and Egypt, but found a new domain among the Slavonic-speaking peoples.

The Byzantine version of Eastern Christianity became the religion of the Serbians, Bulgarians, Macedonians and Russians. After their conversion to Christianity in the ninth century the Bulgars twice created an impressive Empire and tried each time to subdue the Greeks and make Constantinople their capital. Simeon (893–927) was the first Bulgarian ruler to assume the title of Tsar. In 913 he brought his army up to the walls of Constantinople, but failed to take the city. In 923 he had a private conference with the Basileus and secured an annual subsidy from the intimidated Greeks, together with recognition of the Bulgarian Church as an independent body under an Archbishop resident in the capital, Great Preslav. The Empire founded by Simeon lasted, however, only till 972. His successor, Tsar Peter (927–69), was unable to control his unruly nobles and the might of his State was undermined. During the reign of his son, Boris II (969–76), Bulgaria was invaded by Sviatoslav of Kiev (945–73), who devastated Great Preslav and captured the Tsar. The Emperor, John I Tzimisces (969–76), marched into Bulgaria in 972 and divided the defeated Empire into two independent realms. One of them, Western Bulgaria, under the rule of Tsar Samuel (976–1014), with its capital in Ohrid on the shore of a beautiful mountain lake, became a centre of Slavic art and learning. Samuel resumed the wars against Byzantium but Basil II (976–1025), surnamed Bulgaractonus, for his resounding victory, completely routed the Bulgarian Army (25th July 1014). Samuel died the same year and his State was dissolved.

The Second Bulgarian Empire flourished from 1186–1241. It reached its zenith under the rule of John Asan II (1218–41) who called himself the Tsar of the Bulgars and the Greeks. This time, the capital was fixed in Tirnovo. Profiting by the rivalry between the Greek and Latin Empires, the Bulgarians were able to maintain ascendancy over their neighbours. In 1236, John Asan attempted to take Constantinople, then occupied by the Crusaders, but he was repulsed. After his death, anarchy sapped the Bulgarian realm, and the continuous strife among Balkan Christians facilitated the advance of the Turks. In 1382 they took Sofia; in 1393 Tirnovo; in 1398, Vidin, the last Bulgarian stronghold. For five hundred years, till 1878, the Bulgarians were reduced to slavery under the Islamic invaders.

The story of their neighbours, the Serbians, was similar in its main outlines. These gifted and spirited people, who had settled in the Balkans some time in the sixth century, had periods of greatness when led by able rulers; but tribal rivalry and lack of co-operation invariably ruined their attempts to establish a stable political order. The founder of the dynasty which made the Serbians a nation was Stefan Nemanja (1151–95), who extended his rule over the neighbouring tribes and enlarged his territory at the expense of the Byzantine Empire. The fruits of his labours were in danger of being squandered by his sons, but disaster was avoided by the youngest, called Rastko, who became the Patron Saint of Serbia and the true builder of national unity. This remarkable man became a monk when still a youth, and received the name of Sava. In 1207 he returned to his country from Mount Athos and succeeded in restoring peace among his brothers. In 1217, he went to Nicaea, the temporary capital of the Byzantine Empire (for Constantinople was occupied by the Latins) and was consecrated there by the Ecumenical Patriarch as Archbishop of all the Serbian lands. In 1222, he crowned his brother Stefan in the monastery of Žiča as the first King of the Serbs. He died in 1236 in Tirnovo but his relics were solemnly transferred to Mileševo Monastery two years later. They were burnt in 1595 by the Turks in an attempt to stamp out the longing of the Serbians for freedom. St Sava's part in the history of the Serbs has no parallel in the life of other nations. He was more than an able organizer of the Church or a patron Saint. He remains their beloved teacher, a living example of a truly Christian man, the symbol of Serbian unity and of their indestructible link with Byzantine Orthodoxy. There is no Serbian who does not venerate St Sava. His feast is a national holiday.

The climax of Serbian political might was reached during the reign of King Dushan (1331–55). He proclaimed his realm an Empire in 1345 and called himself the Emperor of the Serbs, Bulgars and Greeks. The Serbian Archbishop became a Patriarch in 1351 with his seat at

Peč. Dushan was not only a military leader but also a legislator and patron of the arts. He was regarded as a dangerous enemy by the Greeks and the Ecumenical Patriarch refused to recognize the title of Patriarch assumed by the head of the Serbian Church. Only in 1375 when the Byzantines and the Serbians were equally menaced by the Turks did they come to an agreement, but it was too late. In 1389, at the battle of Kosovo, the Turks destroyed the independence of Serbia. The flower of the Serbian nation perished on the battlefield with their Tsar, Lazar (1371–89). Long centuries of slavery lay ahead of the defeated people. Though Kosovo was a national disaster, it was a heroic fight remembered with pride as well as mourning. Lazar's widow, Militsa, founded a convent for widows of the slain and became their abbess. She is counted among the saints of the Church. She displayed fortitude and faith in the ultimate victory of Christianity, in the darkest hour of her nation's defeat and humiliation.

The story of the Orthodox southern Slavs reveals the overwhelming attraction for them of Constantinople, and of its brilliant civilization. Serbian and Bulgarian ecclesiastical architecture and painting dating from the centuries of their rivalry with Byzantium are a remarkable achievement. Most of these artistic treasures can be found in the monasteries built and endowed by Serbian and Bulgarian rulers in the twelfth, thirteenth and fourteenth centuries, such as Studenica, Peč, Dečani, Gračanica. Ohrida, the one-time capital of Bulgaria, contains remarkable churches adorned with magnificent frescoes dating from the eleventh and twelfth centuries.[3] But the proximity of Constantinople, which they called *Tsargrad* and 'Queen of Cities', was the cause of their undoing.

Instead of concentrating their strength on building up their own national states they wasted it on grandiose schemes of Empire building which involved them in constant struggles with their neighbours. The Slavic Tsars tried to imitate the Basileus, hoping to make their archbishops equal to the Ecumenical Patriarch. These exaggerated ambitions contributed to the instability of the Christian states in the Balkans and aided Turkish victory, for when in 1353 the nomads crossed the Straits and landed in Europe, they found the disunited Balkan nations, who were unable to stop their advance. The fall of Constantinople dragged the rest of the Orthodox Christians, settled on the former territory of the Empire, into the same abyss.

Russia's conversion to Christianity
The Russians also felt the fascination of Constantinople, but their

geographical remoteness and their particular national problems led to their different historical development from that of the Southern Slavs.

Russia's conversion to Christianity took place in the midst of growing tensions between East and West, but at first it promised an improvement in their relations. The prime mover was the Grand Prince Vladimir of Kiev (979–1015), one of the most remarkable rulers in Russian history. Kiev in the tenth and eleventh centuries was an important centre of international trade, for the Mediterranean Sea, the main thoroughfare between East and West, was blocked at that time by Islamic pirates. It was therefore safer to carry goods along the protected shores of the Black Sea and up the Russian rivers to where these approach but do not meet other rivers flowing down to the Baltic. There, Eastern merchandise was distributed among Western countries. Kiev stood at the centre of this river traffic and the city's wealthy population included Slavs, Greeks, Germans and Scandinavians. The Princes of Kiev were themselves of Viking origin.

In the tenth century, native paganism was losing its hold on many Russians and the number of Christians was rapidly increasing. At the beginning of his rule Vladimir was opposed to the new religion, but he changed his mind and decided to be baptized and to convert also his people to Christianity. Such a step had important political consequences, for the entry into the community of Christian nations implied recognition of the sovereignty of the Christian Emperor, who was deemed to be the sole supreme master of all Christian princes and people. Vladimir, like other heathen rulers of Europe, had been confronted with a choice between the Eastern and Western Empires, and on his decision depended the incorporation of his vast domains in one of these big political and cultural units which were just then beginning to compete with each other.

Prince Vladimir was a great monarch. He can be compared with Charlemagne in the breadth of his political schemes and in his skill in carrying them out. His Empire covered the majority of European Russia, the Baltic States and part of Poland. His leadership was also recognized by the Princes of Hungary and Moravia. The realm of Kiev therefore included Eastern and Western areas of Europe, and Vladimir might have joined either. He refused to commit himself, and by an adroit use of diplomacy and military force managed to obtain from Constantinople an ecclesiastical settlement which corresponded with his desire to found a Church independent of outside authorities. His Church had a Western organization, as the Cathedral of Tithes he built reveals, for Tithe was a Western method of securing ecclesiastical income not an Eastern one; but the ritual he adopted was Eastern and the language of the services was Slavonic. In the tenth century, Vladimir made use of the earlier translations by Cyril and Methodius and their disciples. The Russian chronicle describes in dramatic form the Prince's search for the best religion. It tells how Vladimir sent out his envoys to all neighbouring countries. They studied Islamic practices among the Arabs, Judaism as professed by the Khazars whose Kingdom was situated in the lower region of the Volga, and the Latin Church in action in the West. None of these religions impressed them favourably. They were carried away however by the splendour of Byzantine liturgy when they visited St Sophia in Constantinople. The narrator of the Russian chronicle records that the envoys declared to Vladimir that they did not know whether they were still on earth or in heaven, when they assisted at divine service. It was the beauty and glory of the Byzantine ritual at the height of its artistic perfection which brought the Russians into the Orthodox fold. The actual story of the sending of the envoys to neighbouring countries may be a legend, but it accurately states the importance of aesthetic appeal in Byzantine worship. The love of beauty has been one of the chief characteristics of Russian Christians. The word 'Orthodoxy' was translated into Slavonic as '*Pravoslavie*', which means true glory, or right worship, and this aspect of religion has always been prominent in the Russian mind.

In 989 Vladimir organized the mass baptism of his people after a successful campaign against Kherson, the Byzantine stronghold in the Crimea. His military victory allowed him to dictate his own conditions to the defeated Empire; he not only obtained bishops of his own choice, but also a wife, Anna, the Emperor's sister. Vladimir entered the circle of civilized nations not as a suppliant but as a powerful Christian sovereign.

His attempt to hold the balance between East and West was not followed by his successors. The Russian converts were influenced by the anti-Latin feelings which animated their Greek teachers. Vladimir's son, Yaroslav the Wise (1019–54), accepted the Patriarch of Constantinople as supreme overseer of the Russian Church, and as a sign of this new ecclesiastical orientation a second cathedral was consecrated in Kiev in 1039, this time dedicated to the Divine Wisdom (Santa Sophia), in imitation of the mother church of Constantinople. After this ecclesiastical revolution the Russians became the most faithful adherents of Byzantine Orthodoxy, and its most ardent supporters.

The first fruits of Russian Christianity
The Russian Christians from the beginning of their history displayed a

number of characteristics which put them apart from the rest of Christendom.

Prince Vladimir astonished his Byzantine advisors by proposing to abolish capital punishment as incompatible with the Christian religion. He also impressed his teachers by charity so great that all the poor of his capital were fed and cared for at his expense. His two youngest sons, Boris and Gleb, were canonized for a deed without precedent in Christian history.

The news of their father's death reached Boris when he was returning home at the head of his troops after a successful expedition against the marauding nomads. He heard simultaneously that his eldest brother, Sviatopolk, intended to attack him and thus secure Boris's domain. The young prince, to the surprise of everybody, refused to lead his men into battle against his brother. He told them it was their duty to fight for the protection of their country, but not to be involved in the rivalry between him and his brother. He preferred to be slain rather than cause the death of others when this could be avoided. His murder in 1015, and that of his brother, Gleb, who shared his views, so deeply stirred the nation that Sviatopolk had to flee from the country and perished in exile.

A similar emphasis on the social implications of the Christian faith was manifested in the remarkable life of St Theodosius (*d.* 1074), the founder of the famous monastery of the Caves near Kiev. He was the son of well-to-do parents and as a youth he voluntarily shared the manual work of the serfs and wore the same poor dress, desiring in this identification with the humble and oppressed to follow Christ, who, being God, lived among the poor as one of them.

Even when Theodosius became Abbot of his monastery he continued to work as one of the servants. The same spirit of charity and forgiveness is seen in the testament of Prince Vladimir Monomakh (1113–25), one of the most successful rulers of pre-Tatar Russia. This remarkable document is inspired by a consistently Christian outlook. During his long and brilliant political career Vladimir practised the principles and virtues he preached.

He was a peacemaker in dealing with other Russian princes, but a bold and successful warrior when defending his country against the nomads. Christianity for him was the rule of life and he advised his sons to practice daily self-examination, and always to pray before going to sleep and to give alms. He wrote:

'Above all, do not forget the poor; feed and protect them as well as orphans and widows. Do not allow the powerful to oppress others. Do not kill anyone, and do not allow the death sentence to be pronounced, even on the worst criminals, for they too have Christian souls. Fight against pride in your minds and hearts. Remember we are all mortal: today we are alive; tomorrow we shall be in our graves. All that we possess is not ours, but God's. Never bury your treasures in the ground; this is a great sin. Respect the old as if they were your father, and treat the young as your brothers.'

The deeply Christian spirit of his testament and the popularity it enjoyed witness to the strong hold of the new religion on the Russian people.

Russia, during the Kiev period (980–1240), reached a high level of civilization. Its capital was the second largest city in Europe, next to Constantinople. The cathedrals of St Sophia, erected by Yaroslav in Kiev and in Novgorod, were the finest buildings outside Byzantium.* (Plate 6.)

The use of the Slavonic language in worship, and translation of the Bible and other Christian literature into that tongue, facilitated the growth of Russian culture. In the West, access to higher education was made difficult by the necessity of learning Latin. However, this disciplined the minds of barbarian converts, and helped to create a body of people bearing a tradition superior to and distinct from their own. Such division between clergy and laity did not take place in Russia. Russian Christianity was grafted on to an undeveloped paganism, and the new faith quickly secured the people's allegiance. This process, however, left various national defects unchanged, such as lack of self-control and a tendency to anarchy, weaknesses characteristic of Slavonic history.

The Russia of the Kiev period was culturally advanced, but politically unstable owing to the rivalry of its numerous princes, and the independence of its commercial cities. This deficiency in statesmanship proved fatal when Russia was suddenly invaded by the Mongols in the middle of the thirteenth century.

* Both Cathedrals are still standing in spite of all the vicissitudes of Russia's stormy history.

CHAPTER FOUR

THE MONGOL INVASION AND
THE FALL OF BYZANTIUM

(XIII–XV CENTURIES)

Russia under the Mongol yoke (1240–1480)—Sergius of Radonezh (1314–1392)—The missionary work of the Nestorian Church—The Mongols and Christendom—The Mongols and the conversion of Asia to Islam—The last years of the Empire

THE SACK of Constantinople in 1204 was followed by another major calamity for Eastern Christians: the sudden irruption of the Mongols. The nomads of Mongolia were split into many rival tribes, and despised by their more civilized neighbours; no one expected any serious danger from those wild desert horsemen. Their spectacular rise to power in the thirteenth century was as unforeseen as the Mohammedan conquest of the Near East and North Africa in the seventh century. The builder of the Pan-Asian Empire was Temuchin (1167–1227), the son of a small chieftain. He begun his military exploits by attacking and defeating the Tatars, a neighbouring tribe which had treacherously poisoned his father. It is ironical that his hordes became known in Europe by the name of that annihilated clan, changed however to Tartars, the men of horror bursting out from 'Tartarus'.* After many adventures Temuchin, having united all the Mongols, was proclaimed supreme Khan or Emperor in 1206 and took the name of Genghis Khan. In the next four years (1211–15) he subdued the powerful and populous Chinese Empire, and after this victory turned West and devastated Transoxania, Bokhara, Azerbaijan, Georgia and Persia. He captured all the principal cities of Central Asia and of Afghanistan: Samarkand, Merv, Nishapur and Herat.

The sweeping raids of his horsemen were irresistible, owing to their iron discipline and to their mobility, which upset all the calculations of contemporary military experts. The Mongols, using two horses alternately, could travel day and night, for they were able to doze in the saddle and eat rough meat, which made long camp halts unnecessary.

But such energy was not sufficient to build an empire, and here Genghis Khan skilfully employed experienced Chinese bureaucrats, led by Eliu Chu Tsai. The speed and efficiency of the Mongol postal system

---

* The chronicler Matthew Paris (thirteenth century) wrote: 'The detestable race of Satan the Tartars . . . rushed forth like demons loosed from Tartarus.' (Matthew Paris, I, 312.)

and the excellence of their methods of taxation brought stability to their conquests. The Pax Mongolica made travelling safe in Asia and opened regions in the heart of that vast continent which before and after its time were closed to the outside world.

The military skill of the nomads and the experience of the Chinese bureaucrats do not, however, explain the secret of Genghis Khan's drive, which ultimately lay in a sense of mission dominating all his plans. He believed that the supreme God of the Eternal Blue Sky had commissioned him to establish universal peace, and would grant him victory over all his opponents as long as he obeyed the divine decrees. Although Genghis Khan and most of his followers were Shamanists he made no attempt to impose his creed upon the conquered. On the contrary he displayed a genuine respect for every type of religion and, believing that the supreme deity accepted diverse cults, he punished every sacrilege or disrespect shown to any priest, monk or soothsayer.

Genghis Khan died in 1227 in the middle of his victorious campaigns. Under his elected successors in the course of the next two centuries, Russia, Mesopotamia, Syria and Palestine, and later India, were added to the domains ruled by the Mongols.

The Mongol conquest had far reaching repercussions in the history of Eastern Christians. On the one hand it temporarily relaxed the Turkish pressure on the remaining Byzantine possessions, for on two occasions the Tatars inflicted heavy blows upon the Mohammedans in Mesopotamia and Asia Minor, first in 1256–58, and again in the fifteenth century. Their last victory at Ankara in 1402 prolonged the life of the tottering Empire for another half century. On the other hand the Tatar rule for two hundred years cut off the Russian Church from the rest of Christendom and retarded and partially distorted the growth of Russian culture.

Another disastrous result of Mongol imperialism was the destruction of the Nestorian Church by Tamerlane (1369–1405), the fiercest of the Asian despots.

Russia under the Mongol yoke (1240–1480)
The Russians, like the rest of Europe, had heard little of the Mongols until their sudden invasion of the country. After three devastating campaigns (1237–41) Russia ceased to exist as an independent nation. The small and unco-ordinated Russian forces were crushed by successive waves of advancing nomads. Kiev and all other principal cities were burnt to the ground, the people were massacred or carried away as slaves. The greatest calamity struck the richer southern provinces; the

Franciscan papal envoy to Mongolia, John of Plano Carpini, crossing Russia in 1245, recorded in a description of his voyage that he found no inhabitants in the once thickly populated region. Only two cities sheltered by the marshy lands of the north escaped destruction: Novgorod and Pskov.

The Mongols intended to subjugate the rest of Europe, and when they reached the Adriatic Sea in 1242 no military power could have stopped them; but the West was saved by the death of their Supreme Khan, Ugedey, in 1241. As soon as the messenger from Mongolia reached the Tatar army quartered in Hungary, its commander, Khan Batu, ordered his men to move back to South Russia. He wanted to be nearer the scene of the election of the Supreme Khan. He had intended to resume his conquest of the West, but intrigues and disagreements at the Court forced him first to postpone and later to abandon his campaign. So Europe escaped the Mongol yoke, while Russia became solidly incorporated in the pan-Asian Empire.

As soon as the news of the disaster that had befallen the Russian people reached their Western neighbours a crusade was organized, not against the heathen nomads, but against the small Russian territory near the Baltic Sea, which had by chance been left undestroyed. In this desperate hour of Russian history a remarkable prince, Alexander Nevsky (d. 1263), saved Novgorod and Pskov from the Crusaders. At the head of a handful of men he defeated first the Swedes (1240), and later the Teutonic knights (1242). This double victory made possible the survival of Orthodoxy in Russia, for the Mongols took the Russian Church under their protection.

The Russian recovery was slow and painful. Most of the survivors were scattered either in the forest lands of the north-east or in Galicia and the Carpathian mountains. They were allowed to resume their labour, and the administration was left to the Russian princes closely supervised by the Mongolian overlords. The Tatars took possession of the Steppes and continued their nomadic existence, despising the Russians engaged in agriculture.

At first the latter periodically rebelled against their enslavers, but their uprisings were invariably suppressed and their hopes of liberation gradually faded. Throughout these years of trial the only light left to them was their Church. The Mongols showed marked respect for the Metropolitans of Kiev whom they exempted from taxation, with freedom to travel over the whole country. Several prelates showed courage and zeal worthy of their calling. They had no permanent seat for their cities were in ruins, but moved from place to place, bringing people consolation and acting as living symbols of their unity.

Russians and Greeks were usually appointed in turn to these responsible posts. One of them, Theognost (1325–52), decided to fix his residence in Moscow, which was an important event in the history of Russia. At the time of the Tatar invasion Moscow was an insignificant township. It had a number of able princes, however, who instead of plotting against their neighbours concentrated on improving the administration of their small domain. One of these, Ivan Kalita (John the Purser) (1328–41), so named for his charity and financial skill, made his principality an oasis of peace and order in the midst of rivalry and anarchy. The transfer of the Metropolitan's see to Moscow greatly enhanced its prestige, and from the middle of the fourteenth century it became the unchallenged centre of religious and national revival.

In 1380 Prince Dmitry of Moscow (1359–89) presiding over an all-Russian coalition inflicted the first defeat on the Tatars at the battle of Kulikovo Pole. This victory did not mark the end of the Tatar yoke. The Mongols were still stronger than the Russians and re-established their control, but Kulikovo Pole is nevertheless an important landmark in Russian history, for it delivered the Russians from their fear of the nomads by destroying the belief in their invincibility. This liberation from fear was prepared by the labours of one of the greatest saints of the Russian Church, St Sergius of Radonezh.

Sergius of Radonezh (1314–92)

As a young man St Sergius withdrew into the green wilderness of the virgin forests some fifty miles north of Moscow. After several years of seclusion he was joined by other men who desired a life of prayer and contemplation. Gradually a community was formed and St Sergius became its Abbot. He was not a man who sought promotion; his only wish was to dedicate himself to the worship of his Creator, but his humility, single-heartedness, and freedom from anxiety and fear made him the teacher of his people. Rich and poor, prince and peasant sought him out to ask his advice. Prince Dmitry of Moscow, on the eve of the Kulikovo Pole, also went to the elder and obtained St Sergius's blessing.

The encouragement given by the Abbot to military resistance to the Tatars appears at first sight to contradict his characteristic work of peacemaking. The first church he built was dedicated to the Holy Trinity in order that his disciples, inspired by the vision of the perfect unity of the Three, might learn to live at peace among themselves. Several times he undertook long and exhausting journeys to restore concord among the quarrelling princes. As a rule he was successful, for all recognized his impartiality and holiness. In the case of the Tatars, however, he acted differently, for refusal to fight meant the massacre and deportation of the helpless. The almost total depopulation of central Asia wrought by the hordes of Tamerlane early in the next century explains the action of the Russian saint. War was evil, in his view, but the abandoning of victims to their fate was still more evil, and on this ground St Sergius encouraged Prince Dmitry to advance into the Steppes and there meet the formidable enemy. The Russian victory was the result of this bold action. The peace-loving saint contributed more than anyone else to the liberation of his nation from fear and from the Mongols.

St Sergius had many disciples, and the fifteenth century was a period of Russia's spiritual renewal. Religious houses were founded all over the country, learning was revived and ikon-painting reached its golden period; the greatest of the artists, Rublev (1370–1430), dedicated in 1411 his masterpiece, the ikon of the Holy Trinity (Plate 43), to the memory of St Sergius, his teacher.

By the end of the century Russia had acquired considerable military power. In 1480 another Muscovite Prince, Ivan III (1462–1505), at last repudiated the Tatar sovereignty. By that time Ivan had the title of Grand Prince of Russia, for he controlled most of the north-eastern provinces. But south-west Russia, with Kiev, was not under his rule. It had been incorporated into the Polish-Lithuanian State, and its recovery became the main political concern of post-Tatar Russia.

The liberation of Moscow from the Mongols coincided with the fall of Constantinople in 1453. In 1472 Ivan III married Sophia, niece of the last Byzantine Emperor, and assumed his prerogatives as his successor. Moscow, now the only free capital among the Eastern Christians, became their recognized centre and their only hope of ultimate liberation from Islam.

The missionary work of the Nestorian Church

The Tatar conquest altered the course of Russian history and left a lasting imprint upon its Christianity. The Mongols had an even more decisive impact on the destiny of the Nestorian churches which had spread all over Asia in the early middle ages.

The destruction of the Sassanian Empire by the Arabs (638–50) had brought temporary relief to the native Christians. The Mohammedans annihilated Zoroastrianism, but showed tolerance to the Christians. Caliph Omar (634–44) granted them the status of a *milet*, an autonomous community within the Islamic state. The Christians were allowed to maintain their schools, to convoke councils and to be judged by their trusted men. They were forbidden to proselytize among the Moslems, but were free to convert heathen to their faith. They were treated as socially inferior, but were valued for their skill and learning.

The Persian Christians were enterprising travellers and ardent missionaries. Their lively communities could be found far beyond the frontiers of the Abbasid Caliphate. They reached China, India, Ceylon, and even penetrated into Mongolia and Tibet, bringing light and a wider vision of life to these isolated and inaccessible regions. Their chief centre of learning was Nisibis, the seat of the famous theological school, where not only theology but also Greek Philosophy was taught, first in Syriac and later in Arabic. Thence the knowledge of Plato and Aristotle was transmitted by the Arab and Jewish scholars to Spain, and from there it reached the rest of Europe in the later middle ages. Another important school of theirs was in Seleucia where medicine was studied. The Nestorians were renowned doctors. Some of them exercised considerable political influence, being confidants and advisers of such Caliphs as Harun al Rashid (785–809) and his successors.

The third centre of Christian scholarship was Merv, where many translations were made from Greek and Syriac into the languages spoken in Samarkand and Bokhara.

The Nestorian Church reached its widest expansion during the time of the Patriarch Timothy the Great (778–820). He was resident in Baghdad and commanded the allegiance of twenty-five Metropolitans and more than a hundred bishops. Many of his flock lived outside the Abbasid Caliphate, and bishops from such remote places as Sumatra, Malabar, Mongolia and Eastern Siberia recognized his authority. He sent out missionaries to Tibet and to various nomadic tribes and consecrated bishops for them who moved with their flocks over the vast open spaces of central Asia.

Timothy's successors continued the policy of expansion. One of these missionary bishops Subhaliso, for instance, supervised the Christians scattered in Dailam and Gilon on the south side of the Caspian Sea. In 1009 the Metropolitan of Merv converted twenty thousand heathen Turks to Christianity. Simultaneously a Mongol tribe, the Keraits, who lived south of Lake Baikal also joined the Nestorian Church.

In the same period during the T'ang Dynasty (618–907) a considerable number of Chinese were converted. In 781 an important monument was erected in Sianfu the capital of China of that period which gives a description of the history of the Chinese Church, and shows the importance it had in the life of the nation. The later history of the

Chinese Church is less known, though the periods of persecution were relieved with toleration.

The thirteenth century saw another revival of the Church in China. In 1275 the Archbishopric of Peking was created, and churches were built in Chen-Kiang, Yang Chou and Hang Chou. A special department of the administration was established to look after the affairs of the Christians. This expansion of the Nestorian Church was brought to an end by the Mongols. At first their victories seemed to offer new possibilities for the spread of Christianity in Asia, but these hopes were not justified. The close of the fourteenth century saw the catastrophic collapse of the Asian Churches brought about by Tamerlane's hordes.

The Mongols and Christendom

The coming of the Mongols and their conquest of China, Central Asia and Persia placed the Nestorian Christians in the forefront of an entirely new situation. The new masters of Asia were in search of a more consistent religion than their primitive Shamanisms. It was obvious that Jesus Christ, Mohammed, or Buddha would eventually become their supreme teacher.

At first, Christianity had a considerable advantage over its rivals, for the Uighur Turks who were the first to be incorporated in the Mongol Empire, and who represented a higher civilization than Ghenghis Khan's own tribe, were mostly Christians. The Keraits, the Naimans and the Ongut Turks, who were all closely allied to the Mongols, were also predominantly Nestorians. The Kara Khitai were Buddhists and Taoists, and only the Western Turks were Moslems. Christianity exercised greater influence in the headquarters of the Mongol Empire than other religions, for many of the wives and mothers of the Khans were Christians, being members of the Kerait Royal family. Several of these masterful women played decisive roles in politics: for instance Baigi, the mother of Kublai Khan (1260–1294), and Duluz Khatum, the wife of Hulagu (1256–1265). Many high officials were also Christians, such as Chinkai and Bolgai, both chancellors, and Kitbaka, the chief lieutenant of Hulagu.

Pope Innocent IV (1241–54), with the foresight of a great statesman, grasped the extreme urgency and importance of the religious problem raised by the Mongol victories and despatched several missions. The first papal envoys were John of Plano Carpini and Lawrence of Portugal, both Franciscans. They spent two years on their long journey to Karacorum, the tent capital of the new empire (1245–47). They carried with them two papal bulls addressed to the Emperor of the Tatars.[1] I the first, Innocent IV stated his claim to be St Peter's successor and urged the Khan to accept his authority; in the second he reprimanded the Mongols for devastating the Catholic kingdoms of Hungary and Poland.

The Tatars, then contemplating the conquest of Europe, replied in a document revealing their religious interpretation of their amazing military successes. Khan Kuyuk (1240–48), author of this epistle, expressed the typical Mongol reaction to the Papal demands. He wrote:

'By the power of Eternal Heaven we are the ruler of all nations and this is our command: if it reaches thee, thou who art the great Pope together with all the Princes shalt come in person to pay us homage and to serve us. Thou hast also said that it would be well for us to be baptized. This request we cannot understand. Thou likewise sayest that we should become a trembling Christian like the Nestorians and worship God and be an ascetic. How dost thou know whom God absolves, and to whom He shows mercy? How dost thou know that thy words have God's sanction? From the rising of the sun to its setting all lands have been made subject to us. Who could do this contrary to the will of God? Now thou shouldst say with a sincere heart "I will submit and serve you", and we shall recognize thy submission. If thou dost not observe God's command we shall know thee as our enemy.'

This letter, sealed in November 1246, spoke a language unfamiliar to European diplomacy, the language of a world where the claims of the papacy to control Emperors and Kings were met with surprise. The Pope was disappointed but he persevered, and several other missions were despatched by him and his successors. The most important were those of Brother William of Rubruck, another Franciscan (1253–55) who has left a vivid description of his stay among the Tatars, and that of John of Monte Corvino, who spent twelve years at the Court of Timur (1294–1307).

These later envoys met with a much more friendly reception, for the Mongols had by that time embarked on a great military campaign aiming at the annihilation of Islam, and were eager for Christian co-operation. A unique chance of mass conversion was suddenly offered to the Church and probably only one man at that time realized its supreme importance. He was St Louis, King of France (1226–70), but he was misled by his ambitious brother, Charles of Anjou, King of Naples and Sicily (1268–85), and died during the disastrous expedition against Tunis. After his death no one in Europe was equal to the task of meeting the Mongols' request for friendship and collaboration.

This little-known episode in the long contest between Asia and Europe contained potentialities of major significance for the history of the world and the fatal mistakes committed by the Christians had tragic consequences. The Mongols led by Hulagu started their campaign against Islam in 1255; their intention was to restore Palestine to the Christians and to end Mohammedan control over the Near East. Mesopotamia was conquered in 1257, Baghdad in 1258 and the Abbasid Khalifate abolished with the execution of Mustasim, the last Kalif. The next year Hulagu advanced into Syria and took Edessa; his General, Kitbaka, a Nestorian Christian, captured Aleppo and Damascus in 1260. The only remaining Mohammedan realm was Egypt where the majority of the population was Christian. Hulagu, sure of his victory, sent envoys to the Mamluk Sultans to demand submission. They were put to death and the Mongols began their march towards the Nile Valley. At this crucial moment a civil war in the Caucasus forced Hulagu to withdraw his main force from Palestine. The news of the retreat reached Egypt and encouraged the Mamluks to start a counterattack. They were uncertain of their chances and appealed for help to the Crusaders, who controlled the shortest and safest route for the Egyptian advance. The Barons of Outremer met in Acra and decided to assist the Moslems. They were antagonized by the favours which the Mongols showed to the Eastern Christians and thought that the defeat of the Mamluks would not bring any advantage to the Latin Christians. The Egyptian Army safely crossed the Crusaders' territory and in a decisive engagement at Ain-Jalut the greatly reduced detachment of the Mongols was defeated (1260). It was a decisive victory. The Mongols never repeated their drive towards Egypt.

In 1268 the Mamluks rewarded their Christian allies by annihilating them. Sultan Baibar (d. 1277), a Kipchak Turk who had assumed supreme power over Egypt, expelled the Crusaders from Antioch, their most important possession. Its fall was followed by the quick surrender of other strongholds until the last, the island fortress of Ruad, was captured in 1303. The entire coast of Syria and Palestine was devastated by the victorious Moslems; this time they did not spare Christian populations and turned fertile regions into a desert. The barons had miscalculated the temper of their Islamic rivals and paid in full for the mistake, which their hostility to Oriental Christians had caused them to make.

The defeat in Ain-Jalut did not, however, end negotiations between the Christians and the Mongols. Khan Abaka (1265–82), Hulagu's son, sent an embassy to the Council of Lyons in 1274, offering his alliance. Edward I, King of England (1272–1307), wrote an enthusiastic letter to the Mongol Khan hoping to meet him soon in Palestine liberated by their joint efforts from the enemies of the Holy Cross. In response, six Mongol envoys visited England in 1277, but they failed to stir the King and his barons and the expected crusade was indefinitely postponed. In 1286 Abaka's son, Argun (1284–91) sent the last and the most impressive mission to Europe. In order to create a favourable atmosphere a prominent Christian, Rubban Sauma, was appointed as the head of the delegation. He was a Chinese Christian and confidant and schoolmate of the Nestorian Patriarch, Mar Jahballaha III (1281–1317) who was an Ongut Mongol born and bred in Peking. The Mongol mission visited Rome, Paris and London in 1287. It was received everywhere with honour; the learned and devout Chinaman was much admired. He acquainted Western Christians with a Church, the existence of which was not suspected in Europe. His efforts to conclude a military alliance between the Mongols and Christian rulers, however, came to nothing, although Khan Argun announced that he would be baptized in Jerusalem as soon as he recovered the city from the Moslems. In anticipation of this event he baptized one of his sons and gave him the name Nicholas in honour of the reigning Pope. Christian Europe remained deaf to these appeals from the East. Its rulers were absorbed in their quarrels and problems. Khan Argun died in 1291. The same year Acra was taken by the Mamluks and Palestine was finally lost to the Crusaders. Khan Ghazan (1295–1304) drastically altered the policy of his father. He embraced Islam and this led to the conversion of the rest of the Mongols. The whole of central Asia with the exception of Tibet became, like the Near East, solidly incorporated into the Islamic community.

The Mongols and the conversion of Asia to Islam
The Mongol Empire which spread from the China Sea to the Black Sea and temporarily provided stability and ease of communication all over this vast territory offered a unique opportunity for Christians to convert Asia to their religion. The Mongols showed increasing friendliness towards Christians and their hostility to Islam made them eager for closer links. Their ultimate conversion to Islam therefore requires some explanation.

The Tatars encountered Christianity under three distinct forms. The most congenial to them was the Oriental Christianity professed by several tribes akin to them. The court of the Great Khan was full of Nestorians mostly employed as craftsmen, scribes and doctors;

they were valued as experts, but despised as a subject race. Khan Kuyuk described them as 'trembling Nestorians' in his epistle to the Pope, and for the conquerors of Asia it would have been humiliating to accept the faith of these subservient and at times underhand men.

The Russian Orthodox Church impressed the Mongols more favourably, and some of the Russian princes and bishops, such as St Alexander Nevsky (d. 1263) and the Metropolitans Cyril (1242–81) and Alexis (1353–78) were highly esteemed by the Khans. Yet conversion to the Russian Church would have meant giving up their national customs. Later such acceptance of Christianity became frequent, and led to the incorporation of Mongols in the Russian community; but at this decisive moment, at the end of the thirteenth century, when the Tatars ceased to be ferocious invaders and began to co-operate and inter-marry, the Russians missed their opportunity, for they conceived Christian life in too narrow a manner. The Russians were intensely ritualistic; they observed the Old Testament distinction between clean and unclean food, and the Mongol habit of eating any kind of meat and drinking the fermented milk of mares (*kumis*) revolted them. They treated the Tatars as impure and several princes and envoys preferred death to the pollution entailed by conformity with Mongol customs. Most notable among these martyrs was Prince St Michael of Chernigov and his boyar Fedor, killed by the Mongols in 1246 for their refusal to follow the prescribed ritual of the Khan's court.

The Latin missionaries represented another extreme tendency. The Franciscan Friars who came to Mongolia from Rome astounded the Tatars by their courage, simplicity and complete disregard of earthly advantages and riches; but the Mongols were baffled by their declaration that all kings should owe allegiance to the Vicar of Christ. The Khan and his courtiers inquired as to the number of horsemen and camelmen serving in the Pope's army, and when they realized that their own military strength was far superior, they declined to submit to the Pope's authority if that was the price of baptism. To men bred in the wild deserts of Asia, controlling territories the size of which surpassed the imagination of medieval Europe, such submission was incomprehensible. Even the Nestorian Christians were unable to grasp the implications of the papal doctrine. When Rabban Sauma reached Rome in 1289 no one there had ever heard of his Patriarch Mar Jahballaha III. The cardinals wished however to learn whether that unknown prelate recognized the Pope as the Head of the Church. Sauma answered, 'Never has any man from the Pope come to us Eastern Christians. The Holy Apostles taught our fathers the true faith and so we hold it intact to this day.'[2] If the papacy meant nothing to a learned Chinese Christian how could its significance be understood by a Shamanist Nomad?

Islam was more accommodating. Its simple rules of faith and conduct, its unity and its strength of conviction impressed the Mongols, who were able to enter into its orbit without abandoning their national customs and habits of thought. The acceptance of Mohammed as their master by the Mongols closed Asia to Christianity for many centuries to come. This conversion also meant the almost complete annihilation of Oriental Christians. Tamerlane (1363–1405), the last great military leader of the Mongols, was a fanatical Moslem, and in his devastating march across Asia he virtually exterminated Christianity. Pyramids of skulls, cities levelled to the ground, fertile plains turned into desert, marked the triumphant progress of this scourge of Asia.

The Nestorian Christians did not apostatize. They were physically exterminated, and with their destruction the cultural and intellectual life of Central Asia rapidly declined. Their tragic history was a curious mixture of glory and failure. They were learned and zealous Christians, most of them doctors, merchants and clerks in state offices. They were excluded by their Islamic masters from any leading posts in the government and had no right to serve in the army. They belonged to a tolerated community which was nevertheless looked down upon and despised by the master race. They therefore acquired many features common to such minorities. They were affected by enforced recourse to cunning and intrigue. They lived in constant danger of being suddenly attacked by the Mohammedan mob and put to death by an ill-tempered and suspicious Sultan. They lived under a political order which did not restrict the arbitrary will of the irresponsible rulers who were equally free to lavish favours or to inflict punishment indiscriminatingly on all their enslaved subjects.

The Nestorian Church perished, for the wind of the desert blew it away before it had time to establish firm roots in the shifting sands of Central Asia.

The Florentine Council (1439)

During the years of the Empire's agony the Basileus had continued to make desperate efforts to secure military help from the West. This was to be purchased only by submission to the Pope, and negotiations for such a surrender went on all the time. Once they seemed to have succeeded at the Council of Lyons in 1274. Michael VIII (1260–82) was an able diplomat who by accepting Roman protection acquired temporary immunity from another attack from the West. His main adversary was Charles of Anjou, King of Naples and Sicily. This aggressive brother of St Louis IX of France (1226–76) invaded Southern Italy in 1266, on the invitation of Pope Urban IV (1261–64). Having defeated King Manfred of Sicily (1255–66) and executed the fifteen-year-old Conradin, the last offspring of the Hohenstaufens (1268), Charles embarked on building up an Empire of his own at the expense of Byzantium. The reconciliation of Michael VIII with the Pope postponed Charles's campaign. The Sicilian Vespers (1282), the successful revolt of the local population against Charles and his French troops, removed the danger of Western aggression, and the Byzantines recovered their ecclesiastical freedom by repudiating the union with Rome concluded at Lyons.

The last attempt at reconciliation with the papacy was made on the eve of the fall of the Empire. The Emperor, John VIII (1425–48), was determined to obtain reinforcements from the West, the last hope of saving his realm, which was now confined to Constantinople and a narrow strip of land on the Asiatic coast of the Sea of Marmora. On 24th November 1437, the Basileus, accompanied by his brother Demetrius, the Patriarch Joseph II (1416–39), and twenty-two bishops, set sail for Italy. They reached Venice on 8th February 1438, and at once opened negotiations with the Pope, Eugenius IV (1431–47), who convoked a Council for the purpose of restoring unity with the Greeks. The first sessions of this synod took place at Ferrara, but on 10th January 1439, the assembly was transferred to Florence where the act of reunion was signed by both sides in July of the same year.

The Council of Florence was a representative gathering; the Patriarchs of Alexandria, Antioch and Jerusalem sent envoys, and Isidore, Metropolitan of Moscow (d. 1463), acted in the name of the Russian Church. The Orthodox Bishops were divided. One section led by Bissarion, Archbishop of Nicaea (1395–1472), and Isidore of Moscow, who was a Greek, desired reunion with the Latin West, not only for political but also for religious reasons. The other section, led by Mark, the Archbishop of Ephesus (d. 1443), thought that surrender to Rome meant betraying the Apostolic tradition preserved by the Christian East. The Latins were led by Cardinal Julian Caesarini (1398–1444). The trivial points which had loomed so large in the polemic between Greeks and Latins in the preceding centuries were brushed aside. The whole problem of the schism was considered from a purely doctrinal point of view. It was believed that if theological understanding could be achieved the unity of Christendom would be immediately restored and the Islamic menace eliminated.

Five main items were selected for deliberation, the *Filioque* clause, purgatory, papal primacy, Eucharistic bread, and the words of consecration of the elements for Holy Communion. Consideration of the *Filioque* clause took the longest time. Mark of Ephesus attacked the Western addition, both on the ground of its theological implications and also as a violation of the agreement reached at the earlier Ecumenical Councils not to alter the creed sanctioned by the synods. This doctrinal debate was opened on 2nd March and lasted until June. It ended with a Western victory. The scholastic theologians had by that time elaborated an intellectual scheme defending the double procession of the Holy Spirit; they were well equipped for the dispute and drove Mark of Ephesus and his supporters into a merely defensive position. The Orthodox tried by quotations from the Fathers to prove that the original formula alone represented the Apostolic tradition which excluded the doctrine of double procession, but the Latins showed that a number of ancient and revered ecclesiastical writers had described the Holy Spirit as proceeding from the Father through the Son. On the strength of these expressions, Bissarion of Nicaea and other Greeks, being urged by the Emperor to make concessions to the Latins, accepted the theology of the double procession and agreed to restore their unity with Rome. The minority, led by Mark, protested in vain.

The other points of divergency, the bread of the Eucharist, Purgatory, and the words of Consecration, were amicably solved, both sides accepting the Eastern and Western practice and teaching in these matters as traditional, and therefore lawful.

The most interesting side of the Florentine Council was the solution of the papal problem. This crucial point of divergence escaped the attention of the debating parties for some time. The Greeks were genuinely surprised when the Latins raised it towards the end of the discussions. The Byzantine theologians having solved the *Filioque* problem, deemed that no further doctrinal obstacle stood in the way to reconciliation. The Greeks were unaware of the centrality of the papacy for the West. This fact was proved by the quick agreement reached by both sides. The Orthodox accepted a formula proposed by the Latins with the proviso that the privileges and rights of the Eastern Patriarchs should remain unaltered.

Having secured their independence, they declared: 'We recognize the Pope as Sovereign Pontiff, Vice-Regent and Vicar of Christ, Shepherd of all Christians, and Ruler of the Churches of God.' These impressive titles conveyed a different meaning to East and West. The East was not concerned with the extent of the papal power within the Latin Church. Its sole desire was to remain free from it in its own domain.

The Florentine Council was concluded by a solemn proclamation of the unity achieved. Mark of Ephesus refused to sign the declaration of reunion however, and his defiance indicated the strength of Byzantine resistance to the surrender to Rome made by the hard-pressed Emperor and his prelates.

The reconciliation proved to be an illusion. The returning Greek delegates were met with undisguised hostility. People openly said they would rather be ruled by the Turks than by the Pope. The Moslems, at least, would not interfere with their ecclesiastical affairs. Even more uncompromising was the reception of the news in Moscow; the Metropolitan Isidore had to flee from Russia. Both Prince and people unanimously repudiated the terms of capitulation; only Bissarion and his supporters stood firm in defence of the Florentine union. They eventually joined the Roman Church, and Bissarion ended his life as a prominent Cardinal.

The capture of Constantinople by the Turks was interpreted by many Eastern Christians as a deserved punishment for the betrayal of Orthodoxy by Emperor and Patriarch. No negotiations for reunion have been conducted between Rome and Constantinople since 1439.

The history of the schism between the East and the West reveals two important facts: (a) that it did not occur suddenly, but took some five hundred years to develop; (b) that the main cause in the separation, the growth of papal authority in the West, was at no time recognized by the contesting parties as the root problem.

Eastern and Western Christians argued all the time on side issues like the use of leavened or unleavened bread, or the lawfulness of the addition of the *Filioque* clause to the creed, or the rival claims to jurisdictions. Such blindness in itself contributed to their ultimate defeat. They had lost understanding of one another, and were talking at cross purposes. It is only in the present century that some of the underlying reasons for their divergency of outlook have been discovered. They will be discussed in the chapters on Eastern Orthodox doctrine and worship.

The last years of the Empire

During the last two hundred years of its history Byzantium, though moribund as a state, remained spiritually and artistically alive. It was a time of artistic inspiration when mosaics and frescoes of exquisite harmony and beauty were created. Although only few of them have survived, some can still be seen in the recently restored Church of St Saviour in Constantinople (Kahrieh Djami) (Plate 32), and in the ruined churches of Mistras, capital of the Peloponnese, the last stronghold of Greek resistance to the Turks. Its numerous churches, precariously perched on the slope of a precipitous mountain overlooking the plain of Sparta, speak eloquently of the profoundly humane and genuinely Christian outlook of these doomed defenders of orthodox freedom.

The revival of art was accompanied by a remarkable mystical movement known as Hesychasm. It originated in Mount Athos which, after 963, had become the exclusive preserve of monks. Gregory Palamas (1296–1359) who ended his life as Archbishop of Salonika was one of the most outstanding of the Hesychasts. His writings reveal deep penetration into the mystery of man's communion with the divine. He taught that God is inaccessible in His inner self but that the entire creation is permeated with the divine energy which illuminates the universe and establishes the most intimate personal relations between man and the Creator. He maintained that the light in which Christ was seen by the Apostles on the Mount of Transfiguration was that uncreated energy and that it has been observed since by other men with purified hearts and minds.

A contemporary of Palamas was Nicholas Cabasilas (*d.* 1380). He was one of the most powerful Byzantine writers and two of his works, *The Life of Christ* and *The Explanation of the Divine Liturgy*, are classics of Orthodox literature. Cabasilas was a layman, but his exceptional erudition and rare religious insight made him an authority on Eucharistic worship and a recognized teacher of spiritual life. Philosophy also flourished in the works of Planudes, Plethon and Bissarion. Several distinguished historians among whom were John Cantacuzene, Niciphorus, Gregoras, Ducas and Chalcocondylas left well-documented records of their time.

The Ottoman Turks and the fall of Constantinople

The Byzantines were living an intense and highly articulate life, but they had no physical strength to resist the incursions of the Turks. These nomads, without culture, but obedient to the will of their sultans, gained ascendency over the rest of the Moslems and steadily advanced towards the West. Defeated by the Mongols in 1243, they recovered under a new dynasty whose founder was Othman (1290–1326) and he gave them the name by which they are known as the conquerors of Constantinople.

From the fourteenth century onwards it became clear that these Asiatics were the unquestioned masters of the Near East. Their progress was at first slow, but once a city was taken no recovery of the lost territory could be attempted. In 1326 the Turks took Brusa, in 1331 Nicaea, in 1337 Nicomedia. Their advance was not only facilitated but even actually encouraged by the dissensions and rivalry among their Christian opponents. So the Emperor, John VI Cantacuzene (1347–54), foolishly invited the Turks to come to his rescue. On his instigation they landed on the European shore and defeated the Serbians in 1353. In the next year they established themselves at Gallipoli, and having acquired this foothold rapidly began to expand their rule over Thrace.

In 1365 the Sultan Murad (1353–89) transferred his capital to Adrianopolis and so sealed the fate of the Byzantine Empire. It was now solidly encircled by the Turks and its only contact with the rest of the world was henceforth by sea.

The founding of an Islamic State on European soil alarmed the Christian West. But the attempts to unite the European powers against it failed. Amadeus of Savoy hastily organized a crusade, but his force was inadequate and he was repulsed by the Turks in 1366. In 1402, however, the scene suddenly changed; once again on account of the Mongols. In the battle of Angora, Tamerlane annihilated the Turkish army with its Christian auxiliaries supplied by the conquered Balkan nations. The Christians were offered a chance of liberation, but the unique opportunity was missed and the Turks resumed their conquest of Europe. In 1430 they took Salonica, the city next in importance to Constantinople. In 1472 they invaded Hungary and thus reached the heart of Europe. The last attempt at their expulsion was made by King Vladislav VI (1434–44) of Poland and Hungary. Betrayed by the Venetians and unsupported by the Balkan Christians, his army of Hungarians, Poles and Bohemians was crushed at Varna in 1444 by the Turks. The King was killed and with him any hope of saving Constantinople was lost.

Mohammed II (1451–81) laid siege to the great capital in February 1453 when the city had been largely depopulated by civil war and the ravages of plague. The Emperor Constantine XI (1449–53) had only 10,000 men to defend his capital, yet its prestige was so great and its high walls so formidable that Mohammed almost gave up the attempt although he had brought 150,000 men with him. He was persuaded, however, to continue the siege by a Hungarian renegade, Urban, who constructed heavy artillery for the Turks. After several days of bombardment a breach in the wall was made on 29th May

1453. On that day the last Eucharist was celebrated in S Stophia; the Emperor and the remnants of his army, Greeks and Latins, all made their communion. That same morning the Islamic hordes poured into the city massacring the population, burning and ravaging everything on their way. The Emperor, who bore the name of the Founder of the City, died fighting in its streets. The Patriarch was slain. When Mohammed rode on horseback into the cathedral he found it filled with the dead bodies of those who had vainly sought refuge in the temple. According to a legend, the onslaught started before the celebration of the Holy Communion was completed, and the priest in his sacred vestment vanished miraculously behind one of the marble columns, carrying the Chalice with him. The Eastern Christians still believe that Hagia Sophia will one day be restored to Christian worship and the divine service interrupted by the Turks will again be sung in this Cathedral of the Holy Wisdom.

Mohammed wanted to repopulate Constantinople with his own people, but the Turks felt strangers in a city built by men of another race, culture and religion; so the Sultan allowed the scattered Christians to return to their homes and resume life as artisans and traders, being treated as a subject race by their proud Asiatic conquerors. This was the end of the great realm, but the Orthodox Church survived the disaster and continued to minister to its enslaved members.

The defects and limitations of Byzantine political and social order facilitated the decline of the Empire; its bureaucracy was over-organized, private enterprise was too narrowly supervised, and constant wars sapped the strength and wealth of the people. Yet the Empire perished not from internal disease but from external attacks. Without the stab in the back inflicted by the Crusaders in 1204, Byzantium would perhaps have been able to resist the Turks and so preserve for posterity its unique treasures of classical and Christian art and learning.

CHAPTER FIVE

THE CENTURIES OF ISOLATION
AND OPPRESSION

(XV–XVIII CENTURIES)

The Ottoman Empire—The Orthodox Church under the Turkish yoke—The Orthodox East between Rome and the Reformation, Cyril Lukaris (1572–1638)—The Orthodox Church and the Moscow Tsardom—Two tendencies in Russian Orthodoxy—The schism in the Russian Church— The Orthodox in Poland and the Ukraine—The incorporation of the Ukraine into Moscow Tsardom and the Council of 1666–67—Archpriest Avvacum (1620–82)—The Russian Church on the eve of the reforms of Peter the Great (1668–98)—Peter the Great (1682–1725) and the abolition of the Moscow Patriarchate—The Nonjurors and the Orthodox Church—The St Petersburg Empire and the Russian Church in the eighteenth century—St Tikhon of Zadonsk and Paisy Velichkovsky—Western ascendancy over the Christian East—The Church of St Thomas in South India—The Church of Ethiopia—The Nestorian Church of the East—The Church of the Armenians—The Coptic Church—The Jacobites—Balkan Christians in the seventeenth and eighteenth centuries—The Eastern Orthodox under Hapsburg rule—The Christian East at the time of its decline

The Ottoman Empire

THE CAPTURE of Constantinople by the Turks in 1453 removed the last obstacle to their advance. For the next two centuries Islam pressed hard on Southern and Central Europe. Mohammed II (1451–81) extended his power over the greater part of the Balkans; the Aegean islands were conquered in 1457–62, the Ionian Islands in 1479, and the Crimea in 1476. Egypt was incorporated by Selim I (1512–20) in 1517 and this victory delivered Palestine and Arabia to the Turks. The possession of Mecca and Jerusalem entitled the Sultan to proclaim himself Caliph, or supreme ruler of Mohammedans all over the world. The Ottoman Empire reached its greatest expansion under Suleiman the Magnificent (1520–66). He expelled the Knights Hospitallers from Rhodes in 1522 and in 1526 the larger part of Hungary was brought under his control. In 1538 the entire coast of the Red Sea fell under the Turkish sway and this enabled them to raid India. In September 1529 120,000 Mohammedans appeared before the walls of Vienna but failed to take the city. Three times (1526, 1529, 1532) the Turks invaded Austria. These attacks on the Hapsburgs had important repercussions in the religious history of the West, for they enabled the Protestant Princes of Germany to consolidate their political power whilst their Roman Catholic opponents were engaged in a struggle against the Turks. In 1541 the Turks captured Budapest and in 1547 forced the

Emperor to become their tributary. Nevertheless they were unable to advance further West or to establish their hegemony in Europe. In 1571 they suffered their first serious setback in the naval battle of Lepanto. This, however, did not much affect their formidable military strength and they were able to go on fighting simultaneously in Tunis, Persia, the Caucasus, Hungary and Austria.

During this period of Turkish expansion, civil administration and even military command were to a large extent in the hands of foreigners, recent converts from Christianity. For example, Ibrahim Pasha (1523–36), the famous Vizier of Suleiman the Magnificent, was a Greek; so too was the skilful naval commander, Khaireddin Pasha; Mohammed Sokolich, Grand Vizier (1560–79) under Selim II (1566–74) and Murad III (1574–95) was a Serbian; the dynasty of Kiuprili Viziers (1656–91) was Albanian.

The Turks showed little interest in routine administration, delegating it to men recruited from the conquered nations. This indolence demoralized the Sultans and led to the political decline of the Ottoman State. In 1606 the Turks signed a peace treaty with the Hapsburgs at Zsitva-Torok by which they recognized the Austrian Empire as a power equal to their own and the Emperor ceased to pay tribute to the Sultan. After a second unsuccessful attempt to capture Vienna in 1683, the Turks concluded a disadvantageous peace with a European coalition in 1699, at Karlowitz, by which they ceded Hungary, Transylvania, Croatia and Slavonia to Austria, Podolia to Poland, and the Morea and Dalmatia to Venice. For the first time Russia was a partner in a joint European action and received the fortress of Azov. This peace treaty was the turning point in relations between Turks and Christians. After Karlowitz the Ottoman Empire began its long and tortuous retreat from the West.

The Orthodox Church under the Turkish yoke

As long as the Turks were at the height of their power the subjugated Eastern Christians had no means of open resistance and were obliged to adapt their religious and cultural life to adverse conditions. The Mohammedans forced the heathens they conquered to choose between conversion to Islam and extermination; subjugated Christians and Jews were recognized as 'people of the Book' and were allowed to practise their religion, although exluded from citizenship. Christians, therefore, enjoyed a certain autonomy but suffered from many limitations; the Turks divided Christians not according to nationality but confession. So all the Byzantine Orthodox, whether Greeks, Arabs, Serbians or Albanians, were grouped together; the non-Chalcedonian Copts were treated as a separate body; so were the Armenians and the Nestorians. Each of these communities was governed by a Hierarch approved by the Sultan. The Patriarch of Constantinople was the only officially recognized spokesman of all the Byzantine Orthodox. He was their Supreme Judge with direct access to the Sultan. Other Patriarchs and bishops lost their independence and were reduced to the rank of his subordinates and spent much of their time in Constantinople in order to be near the source of intrigue and power.

The Patriarch's position was exalted and precarious at the same time. Of one hundred and fifty-nine Patriarchs during five hundred years of Turkish rule, only twenty-one died a natural death in office. Six were murdered, twenty-seven abdicated, one hundred and five were arbitrarily removed. The Sultans could at any moment dismiss the Patriarch or any other bishop who incurred their displeasure. Few were able to exercise their pastoral duties in peace. Some were expelled and restored as many as four or five times, and yet in spite of all these dangers the post, although obtained and kept through bribery, and exposed to the rivalry and machinations of the envoys of Western powers, was eagerly sought after.

In these circumstances the Christians suffered acutely. No new churches were built. No church might call attention to its existence either by ringing bells or by putting a cross on the building. Systematic training of the clergy was abandoned, higher education made impossible, the schooling of children reduced to a few rudiments. Bribery and corruption, as the basis of Turkish administration, had a specially adverse effect on the authority of the clergy. Every office had to be purchased and the bishops and priests were obliged to recoup the money from their flock. The greatest calamity, however, was the obligation to provide the Sultans with slaves.

At five-yearly intervals Christian boys between eight and fifteen were inspected by the Turks; the strongest and most intelligent were selected, converted to Islam and made the slaves of the Sultans. The majority were drafted into a special army corps, called Janissaries. These ex-Christians were the main instrument of oppression, for they were often turned into fanatical Moslems. Later they acquired considerable political power which was used to end the rule of many Sultans. The rest of the Christian recruits were assigned to other kinds of service in the Sultan's household and some reached important positions in the State.

This constant loss of the most vigorous males was one of the reasons for stagnation in the Christian East. This iniquitous tribute of boys

135

lasted for more than two centuries (1430–1685) and when it was at last abolished the position of Christians soon improved. But even under these degrading conditions Eastern Christians did not lose their enterprise and natural abilities. Some went to Italy for their studies, others received instruction from a few learned monks who heroically maintained the tradition of scholarship amidst the greatest obstacles and hazards. Trade, crafts and diplomatic service were in most cases in Christian hands.

The Orthodox East between Rome and the Reformation

While the Byzantine Church was making its last vain attempts to reach a working agreement with the papacy, the Western Christians were in the grip of the Conciliar Movement, which aimed to suppress abuses and generally to improve Church life. The Conciliar movement was supported by many high-minded clerics, but its leaders lacked unity and practical wisdom. The papacy was resolutely opposed to these attempts at curtailing its authority, and by the end of the fifteenth century these plans for peaceful reformation had failed. The religious revolution of the sixteenth century took place when the Christian East was absorbed in the struggle for mere survival. The Russians were engaged in fierce fighting against the Tatars on their Eastern and Southern frontiers. The Greeks were too harassed by political troubles, too isolated psychologically and politically from the West, to participate in the debates between Catholics and Protestants. The Reformation was thus an exclusively Western concern and this led to peculiar limitations in theological thinking and liturgical changes.

But if the Orthodox were unable to influence events in the West, both parties in the Reformation dispute were eager to find support in the East for their claims to represent authentic Christianity. The first attempt to secure allies among the Greeks had been made by the Hussites as early as the fifteenth century. These Czechs who revolted against Rome sent several emissaries to Constantinople and tried to link their movement with the Orthodox Church. The fall of the city ended these negotiations. Martin Luther and his collaborators were no less determined by letters and personal interviews to have their activities approved by Eastern opponents of the papacy. These contacts revealed the gulf between the Christian East and West in the sixteenth century.

The Orthodox were bewildered by the Reformation; some merely regarded Protestantism as a new error born of Rome, 'the mother of all heresies'. Others hoped to persuade Calvinists and Lutherans to return to the sound doctrines of an undivided Church and to discard all Latin innovations. Few of the Orthodox realized that Protestantism carried the Roman premises to their logical conclusion and for the time being, therefore, had no common language with the East. But this fact was not grasped, and various schemes of reunion based on doctrinal agreement and propounded either in Tübingen, the stronghold of Lutheranism, or in Geneva, the home of Calvinism, were favourably received by some of the Eastern Christians. The Roman Catholics, stimulated by the counter reformation, and having found a new militant force in the Jesuits, were alarmed and spared no efforts to break up these attempts at co-operation. Constantinople became the focal point of intense competition which reached a dramatic climax when Cyril Lukaris became Patriarch.

Cyril Lukaris (1572–1638)

Lukaris, a native of Crete, belonged to a well-to-do family. He studied in Padua where the more fortunate Greeks of the Islands sent their sons for higher education. As a youth he became known to Meletius Pigas (1592–1602), an enlightened Patriarch of Alexandria, who ordained him in 1593 at the age of twenty-one. Meletius was keenly aware of the importance of raising the standard of education among the clergy and of forming closer links with the non-papal West. He encouraged Cyril to accept an invitation to Lithuania where the Roman Catholics had begun an energetic campaign against both Protestants and Orthodox. Cyril spent some years teaching theology, first in Vilna and later in Lvov, the capital of Galicia. He was present with his friend, Nichiphorus Pataschos, at the Council of Brest-Litovsk in 1596, where the majority of the Orthodox bishops went over to Rome, but the parochial clergy and laity remained faithful to their tradition. The ensuing persecution of the Orthodox by the Poles cost the life of his companion, but Cyril escaped arrest and returned to Egypt. On the death of his benefactor he was elected Patriarch of Alexandria (1602–20). His experiences in Poland and Lithuania, and the Jesuit propaganda in Turkey had convinced him that the Orthodox needed the help of the Protestants in order to resist the increasing aggressiveness of the Latins. Accordingly he despatched one of his best priests to the West, Metrophanes Kritopulos, who spent five years in Oxford (1617–22), six years in Germany and Switzerland, and two years in Venice. After his thirteen years' sojourn among the Protestants and Romans Metrophanes returned to the East and ended his life as Patriarch of Alexandria (1636–39). His mission was successful; he had gained first-hand knowledge of religious conditions in England and on the Continent and could provide Cyril with the information he needed for an energetic campaign against Rome. This he began while still in Alexandria, but he soon realized that the battle had to be fought from Constantinople and he managed to be transferred there in 1620. This made him the central figure of a highly dramatic contest in which Rome, Geneva, France, Austria, Holland and England all took part.

The story of the Patriarch reveals the internal state of the Orthodox Church, the pressure it had to withstand from the divided Western Christians, and the peculiar mixture of religious, political and commercial interests at work in Constantinople in the seventeenth century. The main actors in this drama were the French, Austrian, Dutch and English ambassadors. Since 1535 France had been recognized by the Turks as the protector of Christians in their Empire, which privilege encouraged the Jesuits to campaign for the submission of the Orthodox to Rome. The election of Cyril, their opponent, was a challenge to French prestige, and her envoy, the Comte de Cézy, helped by his Austrian colleague, and using all the methods of Oriental diplomacy, denunciations and bribes, succeeded in removing Cyril from office. The Protestant diplomats defended Cyril and helped him regain his position. This game was repeated several times. Meanwhile Cyril conceived the plan of establishing a union between the Orthodox and the Protestants. It is impossible to ascertain whether he envisaged the possibility of doctrinal agreement or whether he aimed only at practical co-operation. His daring scheme caused the Jesuits to see him as a dangerous heretic, the Turks as a cunning political intriguer, for the French accused him of instigating raids by the Ukrainian Cossacks, which had become a serious menace to Turkish security on the Black Sea. Cyril tried to avoid publicity about his negotiations, but his Protestant friends desired tangible proof of his approval of reformed theology. A fatal role in this complicated plot was performed by Antoine Léger, a Calvinist from Geneva, Chaplain to the Dutch Legation. He was instrumental in publishing Cyril's *Confession of Faith* which appeared in Latin in 1629, in Geneva. This document contained several Calvinistic articles, which were at once refuted by other Orthodox prelates. Nevertheless, the majority of the clergy and the people remained loyal to their Patriarch and when the Jesuits replaced Cyril by a Romanizing bishop, Athanasios Patelarios, the intruder was expelled after twenty-two days. Cyril was reinstated for the fourth time, but his new victory made his enemies determined to get rid of him altogether. The first plot to murder him failed, but in 1638 he was once more defeated and thrown into prison. His Roman opponents bribed his jailers to strangle him while the Sultan was away. Cyril was murdered on 27th June. His body was thrown into the sea but was found by a fisherman and now rests in the Patriarchal Church in Phanar.

The story of Cyril Lukaris indicates the determination of both Romans and Protestants to drag the Orthodox into their controversy, and the political and theological dangers which this entailed for Eastern Christians under the Turkish yoke. The assassination of Cyril stopped for a time attempts at reunion between Protestants and Orthodox. Negotiations were resumed only at the beginning of the eighteenth century when a new factor had appeared—the rising power of Russia— and the offer of unity came from England, not from the Continent.

Cyril's active interest in Western theology was an exception, rather than a typical example of the Orthodox attitude of the rest of Christendom. The majority of the Greeks, embittered by the West's unbrotherly behaviour during the last years of the Byzantine agony, wanted nothing to do with any Westerners. Only a minority realized the futility of such a negative attitude and the need to remain in touch with Western thought, which was progressing unhampered by Islamic oppression. Those Orthodox who desired higher education could obtain it only in Western universities, and both Roman Catholics and Protestants were ready to accept a certain number of Eastern students, for both parties were anxious to increase the number of their supporters among the future leaders of the Church in Constantinople. This training in the West was purchased in most cases by temporary apostasy, though most Greeks were staunchly Orthodox and looked upon their studies abroad as a means of arming themselves against their teachers' propaganda. Once they returned home, therefore, they resumed membership in their own Church. Nevertheless, few altogether escaped the theological impact of their heterodox training: intellectually they lost touch with their own tradition; their opposition to Rome was based on Protestant principles, and that to the Reformers on Jesuit teaching. The Orthodox could no longer speak with their own voice and the rest of Christendom stopped listening to their message.

The Orthodox Church and the Moscow Tsardom

From the time of her liberation from the Tatars in 1480, Russia had been expanding and this growth of political power was accompanied by a sense of special vocation associated with the belief in Moscow as the third and last Rome. This idea was the outcome of the conviction shared by Eastern and Western Christians that the Empire was as indispensable as the Church to the divine plan of salvation. The fall of Byzantium was interpreted as a sign of the approaching end of the world. (This was generally expected to take place in 1492—seven thousand years from the creation, according to an accepted calculation.) As an alternative another theory was propounded, that of the transference of Imperial prerogatives from one nation to another. The foundation for this vision of succeeding Empires fulfilling their missions and being replaced when they proved unfaithful is found in the book of the Prophet Daniel.[1] His Four Empires were interpreted in the light of the commentary by St Hippolytus (d. 236) who identified them with Babylon, Persia, the Empire of Alexander the Great, and Rome. During the ascendancy of the last kingdom the greatest events of history were to take place including the Incarnation and the Last Judgment. Rome was to have no successors, but the capital of Christendom might change its locality, although retaining its sacred name. So the Orthodox called Constantinople the second Rome, after the schism with the West and when it was taken by the Turks Moscow became the third Rome. This belief shaped Russian thinking; the latter saw themselves as the guardians of unpolluted orthodoxy. Linking their history with the glories of antiquity they felt called to world-wide service, failure in which duty would entail divine rejection and punishment.

These thoughts, mingled with awe and exaltation, were expressed by a monk, Philothey, who wrote in an epistle to Basil III, Grand Prince of Moscow (1505–33):

'The Church of old Rome fell for its heresy; the gates of the second Rome, Constantinople, were hewn down by the axes of the infidel Turks; but the Church of Moscow, the new Rome, shines brighter than the sun over the whole universe. Thou art the ecumenical sovereign, thou shouldst hold the reins of government in awe of God; fear Him who has committed them to thee. Two Romes have fallen, but the third stands fast; a fourth there cannot be. Thy Christian Kingdom shall not be given to any other ruler.'

These words, written in Pskov in the fifteenth century, were prophetic. Philothey foresaw the greatness of his country at a time when the very existence of Moscow was scarcely acknowledged by Europe. In 1547, fifteen years after Philothey's epistle was composed, Ivan IV (1533–84) assumed the title of Tsar, which the Russians interpreted as equivalent to Basileus; and in 1596 the Metropolitan of Moscow was made a Patriarch. The document announcing this event reproduced the words of the learned elder almost verbatim, and they were confirmed by the signatures of the four Eastern Patriarchs.

The Russians accepted the challenge of responsibility predicted by Philothey, but their interpretation of the essence of Orthodoxy differed considerably from that of Byzantium. The first Rome bequeathed to Christendom law, order and discipline, and proclaimed the universality of the Church. The old Rome represented the paternal authority of the Father. The second Rome—Constantinople—offered intellectual leadership. It had done much to formulate creeds and combat heresies. Its function was appropriate to the Logos, the second person of the Holy Trinity. The third Rome, Moscow, expressed the conviction that the entire corporate life of a nation should be inspired by the Holy Spirit.

The Russia of the Muscovite Tsardom which rose out of the ruins of the Tatar occupation was different from the Russia of Kiev. So was the Church, which transferred the seat of its chief bishop from the old to the new capital. The Russia of Kiev was a young and enthusiastic disciple of Byzantium; the Russia of Moscow was a Christian outpost of the Asiatic world. It was behind Europe in science, in military and technical skill, but there was one domain where the Russians were masters, and this was the sphere of worship understood as covering all aspects of personal, social and national life. In that art of Christian conduct described by the Russians as *bitovoe blagochestie* (the piety of daily life) the Muscovites were unrivalled. Orthodoxy, etymologically understood as 'True Glory' (*Pravoslavie*), permeated their whole culture. The Russians achieved a remarkable spiritual unity. Tsar and boyars, merchants and peasants, all were members of the same Orthodox community, speaking the same language, sharing the same ideal, observing the same pattern of behaviour and completely understanding each other. Their inspiration came from their belief in the Incarnation, confirmed by the drama of the Eucharist, performed on each feast day by the entire nation. The parish church was the Russians' university, their concert hall, their art gallery, and above all the holy place, which reminded them that this world, in spite of its imperfections, was the temple of the Holy Spirit, and that man's vocation was to work for its transfiguration. The bright cupolas of the Russian church adorned with golden crosses, the innumerable ikons depicting the triumphant saints, the joy of the Easter celebrations, all these typical manifestations of Russian Christianity eloquently declared the determination of the Russian people to sanctify their national life and uplift it to holiness and brotherly love.

A Russian of that period was a dedicated person expressing his joys and sorrows in a manner attuned to his religion, regulating his diet in commemoration of the events described in the New Testament, facing death as a person ready to meet his judge and Saviour, and from his first to his last breath playing a part in the cosmic drama of redemption.

The Byzantines saw in Jesus Christ the Emperor; the Russians regarded their community as protected by the saints, the chosen vessels of the Holy Spirit, the greatest among whom was the Mother of God, the Virgin Mary.

Neither Constantinople nor Moscow lived up to their ideal; but their failure does not rob them of significance, for they beheld a great vision, ennobling and uplifting mankind.

Two Tendencies in Russian Orthodoxy

The growth of Russian Orthodoxy was accompanied by the appearance of two distinct tendencies, both traceable to St Sergius of Radonezh. The spokesman of one of them was St Nil of Sorsk (1433–1508). His school of thought, known as Nonpossessors, stressed freedom of spiritual life, was opposed to any use of coercion in religious matters, disapproved of too close a relation between Church and State, and welcomed fellowship with the rest of the Orthodox. St Nil himself was a good scholar, he had spent some time on the Holy Mount of Athos and his spirituality was in tune with the Hesychast movement. The name of Nonpossessors was applied to St Nil and his followers for their refusal to acquire lands and control the peasants labouring on them. They considered preoccupation with the management of property incompatible with the monastic profession, and thought that an ascetic had to endure poverty and privation as part of his religious training. St Iosif of Volotsk (1439–1515) represented the opposite viewpoint. He was an able administrator, a lover of Russian piety, a patron of art and a keen promoter of good works. He stood for the right of the monastic communities to possess lands and serfs, and on this basis to maintain educational and philanthropic institutions. His friend and ally Gennady, Archbishop of Novgorod (d. 1505), advocated severe punishment of heretics and other disturbers of religious peace, considering it a duty of the State to protect Orthodoxy and suppress errors, but to the Nonpossessors such persecution was forbidden by the gospels.

As long as these two schools of thought co-existed in Russia the balance and freshness of its religious and cultural life were preserved. Unfortunately, however, matrimonial troubles in the family of the Grand Prince of Moscow, Basil III (1505–33), brought about the defeat of the Nonpossessors. Their adherent, the Metropolitan Varlaam of Moscow (1511–22) who disapproved of the Prince's second marriage, was removed and Daniil (1522–39), a determined enemy of the Non-possessors, took his seat. He used every means to suppress their movement and consequently their influence began to decline from the middle of the sixteenth century. Russia's cultural development became one-sided, ritualism was over-emphasized, learning neglected, dependence on the State increased, and the appreciation of freedom lost.

The victory of the Possessors played a part in the tragic fate of one of the most interesting personalities of that epoch, St Maxim the Greek (1470–1556); his coming to Moscow in 1516 offered the Russian Orthodox a unique opportunity of enlarging their mental and spiritual horizon by linking their cultural life with the Renaissance in Italy. For a long time mystery surrounded his origins, but his identity has recently been established.[2] He was a native of Greece, who had gone to Italy in 1492 and there plunged into the intellectual and artistic controversies of the Renaissance. An admirer of Girolamo Savonarola (1452–98), he joined the Dominican Order (1502–04), but feeling dissatisfied with its spirit he returned to Greece and spent eleven years on Mount Athos (1505–16). In 1516 he went to Russia on the invitation of the Grand Prince of Moscow, who desired to improve Russian scholarship. Maxim stood for the best in Christian learning. He was a man of great integrity, dedicated to Orthodoxy, fearless and uncompromising in his attitude to sloth, ignorance and abuses. He had something of the flame which burned in his teacher, Savonarola. He was received with open arms by the Nonpossessors and roused the enmity of the Iosifians, who, having consolidated their position, attacked Maxim as a dangerous innovator and critic of Russian customs.

His arrest and long imprisonment (1531–51) ended, for centuries to come, the possibility of any profitable exchange of ideas between Moscow and the rest of Christendom. The Possessors drove the Russian Church into isolation and provincialism. Their victory was confirmed by the Council of the Hundred Chapters, convoked in Moscow in 1551, at which the bishops in their replies to Tsar Ivan IV (1533–84) asserted the supremacy of Russian Orthodoxy over the Greek version.

Ivan IV, the first Russian tyrant, was a militant representative of the idea of sacred autocracy as conceived by Iosif of Volotsk. When St Philip, Metropolitan of Moscow (1566–69), rebuked Ivan for his cruelty and oppression, the Tsar found sufficient subservient clergy to condemn and degrade him. Philip was murdered and so the Russian Church began to pay for too close an alliance with Moscow Tsardom.

During Ivan's reign the Russian drive towards the East began. In 1552, the Russians took Kazan and thus broke through the Tatar barrier which had prevented them from extending their domains eastwards. In 1556, Astrakhan surrendered to Moscow and the whole course of the Volga River became open to Russian navigation. Siberia was entered in 1555, and in less than a century the Muscovites had reached the Pacific Ocean (1640). These conquests were commemorated by the erection of one of the most original of Russian churches, St Basil, on the Red Square in Moscow (Plate 11). The architects, Barma and Postnik, by providing each of the seven cupolas with its own design and colour, expressed the vision of Asia converted to Christianity by the Russian Church. Persian, Turkish, and Indian architectural motifs are interwoven with the pattern of Russian wooden structures. St Basil's reveals the fusion of Oriental and Byzantine elements in post-Tatar Russian art and culture.

The schism in the Russian Church

Russia's remarkable achievements, and no less obvious limitations, were fully revealed in the tragic story of the schism which occurred in the middle of the seventeenth century. Early in the century Russia passed through a major political crisis known as the Time of Troubles (1598–1613), when the end of the dynasty of Rurik, on the death of Tsar Feodor (1584–98), caused civil war and anarchy, aggravated by the invasion of Poles and Swedes. The enemies penetrated into the heart of Russia and even Moscow was captured by the Poles. The Russians recovered their unity under the leadership of Patriarch Germogen (1606–12) and the monks of St Sergius monastery. The national revival was inspired by the faith and love for the Orthodox Church.

In 1613 Michael Romanov, a boy of sixteen, was elected Tsar of Moscow by the National Assembly and order was gradually restored. The shattering events of the interregnum, when foreigners and bandits ravaged the country, and when sanctuaries were polluted and Christian customs discarded, provoked a movement of reformation among the younger clergy who desired to see their people morally purged. Most of these zealots came from humble homes but the popular character of the Russian Church did not bar them from reaching leading positions. One of them, Nikon (1605–81), the son of a blacksmith, became Patriarch of Moscow in 1652; others, like Avvacum (1620–82), Ivan Neronov (1591–1670), Longuin and Lazar, received the charge of leading parishes in Moscow and neighbouring cities. These men of integrity and faith started a vigorous campaign for the spiritual renewal of the people and they were particularly concerned with the responsibility of the upper classes to set an example of genuinely

Christian conduct. The second Tsar of the Romanov family, Alexey (1645–76), was a devout Christian and gave wholehearted support to this movement. He was particularly attached to Nikon, who had gained popularity by his stand for justice and Christian probity. When Nikon was elected Patriarch a wave of expectancy passed through the country, but instead of a speedy advance to further triumphs of Orthodoxy the Russian Church suffered an unexpected disaster, due to a split within the reforming party. Its immediate cause was a decree issued by the Patriarch in 1653 ordering Russians to follow the Greek ritual in all cases when this differed from their own. These differences of ceremonial affected among others such customs as the manner of making the sign of the Cross and the number of Alleluias sung at church services.

The reforming priests led by Avvacum refused to obey the Patriarch. Nikon, instead of explaining the reason for his order, banished the protesting clergy. This only inflamed their zeal. A large number of laity also repudiated the amended ritual and thus the Russian Church lost its unity. Nikon's opponents formed their own community and to this day remain a separate body known as Old Believers, or Old Ritualists.

It was common in the past among Russian historians to see in this schism a proof of the intellectual backwardness of the Muscovites before their Westernization in the eighteenth century. The cause of the schism was said to be an obscure dispute about details of ritual, and the Patriarch's opponents were stigmatized as narrow-minded fanatics who preferred to split the Church rather than consent to minor alterations. In reality there were serious political considerations which promoted the Patriarch to start his campaign for the unification of the Muscovite and Greek and Ukrainian rituals and no less weighty reasons for the repudiation of his reforms.

In the middle of the seventeenth century Russians were the only independent nation among the Orthodox and they received urgent appeals for help both from Christians suffering under the Turks and from their kinsfolk oppressed by the Poles in the Ukraine. Moscow became an important centre for Eastern Christians who came to Russia for alms and protection. These contacts with Greeks, Arabs, Balkan Slavs and Ukrainians revealed the existence of a number of differences in ritual between the Muscovites and other Orthodox. At that time, when the static conception of the Church prevailed, any disagreement on such matters was explained as a departure from the Apostolic tradition and caused bitter arguments. The Russian government, now planning a campaign for the liberation of Eastern Christians beginning with the Ukraine and extending to the Balkans, required unity and concord among all the Orthodox. Tsar Alexey and his friend the Patriarch were moved by a vision of the Eucharist being celebrated once more in Hagia Sophia, in Constantinople, when the Russian Tsar, surrounded by all five Patriarchs, would announce the end of the Turkish yoke and the deliverance of the Orthodox from their subjection to Islam. For the sake of this mission they were both ready to sacrifice the beloved customs of Moscow Orthodoxy, arguing that the Greeks, teachers in Christ of the Russians, must know the original patterns better.

The Patriarchs' policy implied that the Russians were wrong when they claimed that the centre of Orthodoxy was transferred from Constantinople to Moscow, and this was precisely the belief which Nikon's opponents were not ready to give up. They were convinced that the Greeks and the Ukrainians, deprived of political freedom and obliged to train their clergy in Roman Catholic and Protestant seminaries, no longer preserved the authentic tradition. Recent research has confirmed the Old Believers' assertion. The ritual of the Russian Church at the time of schism faithfully reproduced the Byzantine liturgical customs of the eleventh century, for the Russians had altered nothing in the order of services, whereas the rest of the Orthodox under the impact of the West modified some of their customs and teaching. These changes were particularly noticeable in the neighbouring Ukraine which at the very time of the schism appealed to Moscow for help and protection.

The Orthodox in Poland and the Ukraine

The Ukraine, the original home of the Russian people, fell into the hands of the Lithuanians in the fourteenth century. At first the invaders readily accepted the cultural leadership of the Russians and many of them joined the Orthodox Church. In 1386 the Grand Duke of Lithuania, Jagiello (1377–1434), married Jadwiga, the Queen of Poland (1384–99), and the two countries became dynastically united. One of the conditions of this union was Jagiello's conversion to Rome; he also promised to make Latin Christianity the religion of his people. He himself was duly re-baptized, for he was already a member of the Orthodox Church, but his attempt to bring others into the Roman fold met with opposition. He wisely refrained from using force and Lithuania secured autonomy and religious toleration under the rule of his cousin Vitovt (d. 1430). Until the second part of the sixteenth century Lithuania and Poland co-existed peacefully. The Russians in Lithuania and in the

Ukraine followed their Orthodox tradition and were not pressed to change their religion. The situation was altered, however, in 1569, when Poland and Lithuania, menaced by the growing power of Moscow, concluded a much closer union at Liublin: Kiev, with a part of the Ukraine, was handed over to Poland, which had always been a militant Roman Catholic state. This transfer coincided with the rapid spread of Protestantism in Lithuania and Poland, where the considerable German colony turned Lutheran; and many Lithuanians became Calvanists. In order to stop this desertion the Jesuits were invited to Poland and their arrival greatly changed the position of the parties. The Jesuits opened excellent schools for the sons of the gentry, and quickly stamped out Calvinism among the leading families of Lithuania.

Having obtained this victory they cast their eyes on the Orthodox, who had just been brought under the political control of the Poles. Poland was an aristocratic State; only the nobles had political rights, and only those of them who belonged to the Roman Church were entitled to the privileges of the gentry. Many of the leading Russian Orthodox families, therefore, deserted their Church and nation, and went over to Rome. This apostasy strengthened the resolve of the rest of the Orthodox in the Ukraine and in Lithuania to stand firm for their faith and language. Numerous lay brotherhoods were organized which opened schools and printed books in defence of their religion.

This resolute resistance showed the Jesuits that they could not expect an easy victory. They conceived a new plan of conversion; the Russians were to keep their Eastern tradition intact, the only change being recognition of the Pope as Supreme head of all Christians. This scheme met with the approval of several Orthodox bishops who were promised, in case of success, equality with the Roman episcopate which enjoyed many privileges (including seats in the Senate) denied to the Orthodox hierarchs. King Sigismund (Vasa) III (1587–1632), an ardent Roman Catholic, gave his full support. The negotiations between Rome and the Russian bishops were conducted in great secrecy for the influential lay brotherhoods were expected to resist.

When all the details were agreed upon a Council of the Orthodox Church was convoked in Brest Litovsk (1596). It was divided from the first. The majority of the bishops and a minority of the priests and laity were for union with Rome; the rest were against it.

In spite of this division, the pro-Romans proclaimed their recognition of the Pope, and the King at once declared them the only lawful representatives of the Russian Church in his dominions. Those who refused to surrender were outlawed, bishops and priests were expelled, churches closed, persecution began. Deprived of their bishops the opponents of union were harassed on all sides, and a number of them began to despair, a despondency aggravated by the events of the Time of Troubles, during which the Poles occupied even Moscow. The turning point, however, occurred in 1620 when Theophanes, the Patriarch of Jerusalem (1608–45), on his way to Moscow, secretly ordained seven Orthodox bishops in the Ukraine. The Polish government ordered their immediate arrest, but unexpectedly a new force came to the rescue— the Cossacks. These pirates of the steppes, outlaws from Poland and Russia, were mostly Orthodox, but originally they showed little respect for any religion. They recognized no authority and their camps in the no-man's land of the lower reaches of the Dnieper and the Don were a menace to Tatars, Turks and Poles alike. Yet when the Orthodox fell victim to organized persecution, the Cossacks protected them and forced the Poles to make important concessions. Under this unexpected patronage the Orthodox reopened their schools and restored their Church life.

The Theological Academy of Kiev became the centre of resistance to Rome. It was no longer sufficient to train men for the priesthood; they had to be equipped to contend with the Uniates, who had behind them the support of the Roman Church with its scholastic achievements, financial resources and political influence. The Orthodox in the Ukraine felt isolated. Moscow had no understanding of their position, the Greeks were fighting for survival and the Kievan theologians could not expect help from anywhere. At this critical moment a man of outstanding personality and learning became their leader—Peter Mogila (1596–1647). He was the son of a Moldavian Prince educated in Paris; a Sorbonne graduate, he enjoyed every refinement of European culture, but unlike many other Orthodox nobles he had remained faithful to his Church and offered it his services. In 1633 he was elected Metropolitan of Kiev, and during the fourteen years of his episcopate he revised the whole policy of his Church in regard to the West.

Mogila realized that it was impossible to fight against Rome with those remnants of learning which the Ukrainian Orthodox had preserved from better days. Men who knew only their own Slavonic language and some Greek had no access to contemporary literature, most of which was in Latin; he therefore made Latin the language of instruction in his Academy and forced the reluctant Orthodox to study in the original the writings of their opponents.

The Councils held in Kiev in 1640 and in Jassi in 1642 supported his reforms and approved the service books and catechisms he compiled which contained several adaptations from Latin sources. Mogila trained a number of men skilled in dialectics and capable of arguing against the Uniates. Those Eastern Christians who had submitted to Rome now found themselves at a disadvantage. They were thought of as inferior Catholics. Their bishops were not, in spite of promises given, of equal standing with the Roman prelates and were not admitted to the Senate. The Orthodox despised them as traitors, and whenever Eastern Christians gained freedom of action, the Uniates were the first to suffer.

Peter Mogila bought his success, however, at a price. The training in the Latin language, the study of the manuals of Roman and Protestant theology, inevitably affected the thinking of his pupils. Their theology avoided Western extremes, but lost sight of genuinely Orthodox teaching. The Ukrainian Orthodox were Latinized and when the Muscovites met them they could feel at once their deviation from the familiar tradition, without always being able precisely to formulate the points of departure in question.

The incorporation of the Ukraine into Moscow Tsardom and the Council of 1666–67

In 1648 the entire Ukraine rose against Polish rule. Bogdan Khmelnitsky (d. 1669), leader of the rebellion, liberated his people; he expelled all Jesuits, Uniates and Jews from the Orthodox lands. Later, defeated and hard pressed by the victorious Poles, he appealed for help to Tsar Alexey. The National Assembly in Moscow, after long hesitation, agreed to declare war on Poland. On 8th January 1654 the Rada, the assembly of the Cossacks, recognized the Moscow Tsar as Sovereign.

The war between Russia and Poland lasted till 1667, neither side being able to secure a decisive victory. This exhausting conflict was aggravated by the intervention of the Swedes, the Crimean Tatars and the Turks. A peace of compromise was at last concluded; the Ukraine was divided, Kiev and its theological Academy handed over to Russia. In this way the ecclesiastical isolation of Moscow was brought to an end. A school equipped with Latin manuals, directed by scholars familiar with the intricacies of Western controversy, was incorporated in the Russian Church, which since the thirteenth century had lived without contact with Western thought.

During the war with Poland the Tsar was often away from Moscow; he left the government in the hands of the Patriarch who used his power for a vigorous campaign against the Old Believers. When in 1657 Alexey returned to Moscow his relations with the Patriarch were no longer the same. The Tsar lost his previous blind confidence in his friend and Nikon, realizing this, tried to restore his authority by a dramatic step. He suddenly left Moscow and declared that he would not return until the Tsar made peace with him. Alexey refused to open negotiations and for nine years the Russian Church had an absentee Patriarch who did not govern it. This new crisis was more than a mere disagreement between two former friends; it reflected another and even deeper cleavage among the leaders of Russia than the one provoked by the vexed question of the changes in ritual.

From the start of his rise to power Nikon had aimed at the establishment of the independence of the Church from the State. He used the same title of Great Lord (*Veliki Gosudar*) as the Tsar and never failed to emphasize the moral ascendency of the sacred ministry over the secular power. His determined opponents were the boyars who wanted to take control of vast ecclesiastical lands and to deprive the hierarchy of its legal independence.

The devout Tsar at first shared Nikon's aspirations, but later changed his mind and sided with the boyars. This was a decisive conflict in Russian history, which prepared the ground for the drastic secularization of the country in the eighteenth century. Nikon was defeated because his rash policy and ill-advised reforms offended and antagonized many of his supporters and with his defeat the cause of Church independence was lost.

The struggle between the Tsar and the great Patriarch was brought to an end by the Moscow Council of 1666–67. Its convocation was a major disaster in the history of the Russian Church. The Council was presided over by two Eastern Patriarchs, Paisius of Alexandria (1665–85) and Macarius of Antioch (1647–72), specially invited to Moscow for the purpose. But the main actor in this ecclesiastical gathering was an unscrupulous Greek adventurer, the ex-Uniate Bishop Paisius Ligaridis. He had been an admirer of Nikon when the Patriarch was in power, but had turned against his benefactor when Nikon fell.

The Council first excommunicated all who opposed the Patriarch's reforms and so cut off the Old Believers from the rest of the Russian Orthodox. Secondly, it condemned the Patriarch and deprived him of his orders. Thirdly, it declared that the Council of the Hundred Chapters of 1551, much venerated by the Russians as voicing their conviction of the superiority of their own Orthodoxy, had no authority on the ground that it was composed of ignorant men. The Russian bishops were reluctant to sign such a humiliating statement, but they were forced to do so by the Eastern Patriarchs and Paisius Ligaridis. Nikon died in 1681, having outlived the Tsar Alexey and most of his foes. During his years of exile he was treated as a simple monk, but he was buried as a Patriarch with all the honours belonging to this office, and as such is remembered by the Russian Church. He was a man of great gifts and equally great limitations, a born leader who unexpectedly failed, when he reached the summit of power, for want of wisdom and moderation.

Archpriest Avvacum (1620–82)
The chief opponent to Nikon's reforms was Archpriest Avvacum, a man of outstanding zeal and courage, a talented writer who personified Moscow culture. An acquaintance with him is essential to an understanding of Russian Orthodoxy. Avvacum, like Nikon, came from a humble home, that of a poor village priest. He was ordained at twenty-one, and was immediately involved in a struggle with men of authority. He was a fearless reformer who refused to keep silent in the face of abuses and injustices. Transferred to Moscow he became known to the Tsar and his household and won the admiration of many fervent Christians in high positions. His fierce denunciation of Nikon's surrender to the Greeks caused him to be sent into exile. He and his family spent ten years (1653–63) in Eastern Siberia with a small detachment of Cossacks sent to explore that wild region. In his autobiography, composed in 1673, Avvacum, with superb literary skill, described his adventures. This book marks an epoch in Russian literature. Written in prison, with the purpose of strengthening the partisans of his movement, this first autobiography in the Russian language not only reveals its author's strength of personality, but also presents a magnificent example of seventeenth-century spoken Russian. Avvacum discarded the conventional literary style of contemporary writers and created a masterpiece which stands far above the rest of the literature of Moscow Tsardom.

Avvacum did not spare his opponents; he used crude words, and expressions more suited to the market place than to ecclesiastical controversy, but his sincerity, his fervent faith and his readiness to expose his own faults and weaknesses, captivate the reader.

A central figure in the gallery of persons described by Avvacum was Pashkov, head of the Siberian expedition. He was a law unto himself, a brute used to being feared and obeyed by all his subordinates. Avvacum was his helpless prisoner, but undismayed by flogging and tortures he stood firm against his formidable opponent and finally won the battle. Avvacum was the stronger of the two personalities. The priest was respected by all members of the expedition, including the wife and son of the dreaded commander. Avvacum had an iron constitution; even when exposed naked to the frost of Siberia he refused to surrender. Left alone in charge of the sick and wounded, without arms or protection he brought his party safely back to Russia after six months travel across unmapped country inhabited by hostile tribes. In summarizing this dramatic part of his life he wrote: 'For ten years Pashkov tormented me, or maybe I tormented him. I know not which: God will decide on the day of Judgment.'

Avvacum's wife was a woman of the same courage and strength. Two scenes from his autobiography introduce her. Avvacum is describing their forced march in Eastern Siberia:

'The country was barbarous, the natives hostile, so we feared being separated from each other, and yet we could not keep pace with the horses—for we were a hungry and weary pair; and my poor old woman tramped along and at last she fell. And I came up to help her, and she, poor soul, began to complain to me saying "How long, Archpriest, are these sufferings to last?" And I said, "Till death," and she with a sigh answered, "So be it, let us be getting on our way." '

The second episode was the most decisive in Avvacum's life. He relates that when after ten years of suffering in the wilderness of Siberia, he at last reached the Russian settlements and learned that many men of his faction had either perished or yielded to pressure, his courage failed him, and he began to think about reconciliation with the Tsar and the Patriarch. He turned to his wife for advice and asked her, 'What must I do? Am I to speak or to hold my peace?' Honour, prosperity and freedom for him and his family depended on this decision; but this was not the road chosen by her for her beloved husband. Her reply was 'I and the children give our blessing to continuing the preaching of the word of God as heretofore'. 'And,' adds Avvacum, 'I bowed to the ground before her, and shook myself free from blindness.' The crown of martyrdom awaited him at the end of his long and stormy life, and he was sent to win it by his faithful wife. In 1682 Avvacum was burnt alive with three of his closest companions. They suffered this punishment, as the official act runs, because of 'the great blasphemies they uttered in regard to the Tsar and his household'.

Avvacum's death by fire deeply stirred his followers and many men and women among the Old Believers chose to die in their burning homes to which they themselves set fire rather than be contaminated by conformity with the Nikonites, the name they gave to the rest of the Russian Orthodox.

Avvacum was a passionate man, extreme in his views and actions, but he was a dedicated priest for whom the overwhelming reality of the divine presence made the sufferings and privations of earthly existence of no account. He was the true spokesman of Moscow Orthodoxy, a firm believer that his beloved city was the third Rome. When, at the Council of 1666, the Eastern Patriarchs tried to extract his submission and pointed out the duty of conformity Avvacum replied,

'O you teachers of Christendom, don't you know that Rome fell away a long time ago and lies prostrate, and that Poles and Germans fell in the same manner, being the enemies of Christendom to the end. Even among you, Orthodoxy has become particoloured, and no wonder, if by the violence of the Turkish Mohammed you are impotent today. It is you who henceforth should come to us to be taught. By the gift of God there existed among us a sacred autocracy, till the time of Nikon the apostate. In our Russia, under our pious princes and Tsars, the Orthodox faith was pure and undefiled and the Church knew no seditions.'

Such was Avvacum's creed and he was ready to die in witness to the special Christian calling which he believed was assigned to Holy Russia. Nikon and Avvacum were typical representatives of Russian culture, a culture rich in devotions and artistic achievements but deficient in intellectual discipline and self restraint. The Muscovite outlook was integral, inspired by faith in its unpolitical Orthodoxy; its convinced upholders had an overwhelming sense of their mission but their interpretation of Orthodoxy was so restricted, and their attachment to their own customs so blind, that, in spite of knowing their gifts should be shared with the rest of Christendom, they chose to split their own community for the sake of uniformity on such matters as the correct way to make the sign of the Cross, or the proper direction of Church processions. This tragedy of isolation and of the lost sense of proportion occurred when Russia was once more entering the society of Christian nations. Avvacum's contest with Nikon was the end of Moscow's self-sufficiency; Russia could no longer remain cut off from the rest of Christendom.

The Russian Church on the eve of the reforms of Peter the Great (1668–98)
The withdrawal of Nikon's opponents, the Old Believers, from participation in the life of the Church increased the speed and one-sided-

ness of the Westernization of Russia. The merchants, the free peasants of the East and North and the Cossacks, the hard core of the Old Believers' community, were the most independent and enterprising classes, and their loss was calamitous for the main body of the Church at a time when the country was exposed to the impact of Western civilization. One of the most urgent needs of the Church was the improvement of theological knowledge. Tsar Alexey was aware of this. Among several scholars he invited to Moscow from Kiev, the most notable was a learned elder, Epiphany Slovenetsky (d. 1676), of the old Kiev school of theology.

Versed in the Greek Fathers, but not in the Latin scholasticism introduced by Peter Mogila, Epiphany was a genuine scholar, conservative but not reactionary. He wanted to raise the educational standard of the Muscovite clergy, but was opposed to slavish imitation of the West. He was retiring but courageous, and spoke in defence of the Patriarch Nikon after his fall, although he had not been one of his friends when Nikon was in power.

Epiphany wished for gradual progress, not drastic change, and was warmly supported by Boyar Feodor Mikhailovich Rtishchev (1625-73), one of the most attractive characters of seventeenth-century Moscow. He and his sister Anna were Christian humanists, patrons of learning, founders of charitable institutions, imbued with Christian humility and a genuine sense of brotherhood. They granted freedom to all their serfs and their charity was boundless. They were both deeply attached to the Church and observed all the ritual of daily life evolved by Muscovite Orthodoxy; but they were open to new ideas and welcomed Epiphany and other Greek and Ukrainian scholars who brought with them the intellectual discipline lacking in Russian culture.

Enlightened conservatism aiming at gradual reform was, however, soon superseded by another tendency, introduced by the pupils of Peter Mogila, and in particular by another Ukrainian monk, Simeon Polotsky (d. 1680). Simeon knew no Greek but was at home with Latin, and his eloquence and polished manners were a novelty in Moscow. His urbanity made him indispensable at court functions. Tsar Alexey entrusted the education of his children to this persuasive cleric who taught them Latin and Polish and acquainted them with the manners of the West. Simeon looked down on the Muscovite clergy as uncouth and boorish. He was himself a man of superficial mind but he had acquired a large amount of miscellaneous information and at first greatly impressed his unsophisticated hearers; but his Latinized theology and his haughty behaviour eventually provoked the suspicion and animosity of the higher clergy of Moscow. His chief opponent was the Patriarch, Joakim (1674–90), who was supported by two learned Greeks, Ioanikius and Sophronius Lichudis, sent to Moscow by Dositheus, the Patriarch of Jerusalem (1663–1707), a staunch defender of Orthodoxy who was alarmed by the spread of Westernized theology in Russia.

The Greek brothers were well trained in anti-Latin polemics, for they had been educated in Venice and Padua. As soon as they arrived in Moscow, in 1880, they attacked Sylvester Medvedev (d. 1691), who had succeeded Simeon Polotsky as the leader of the pro-Latin Ukrainian party.

The chief point of contention was the moment of consecration of the Eucharistic elements. The Latin tradition identified this moment with the words 'Take, eat, this is my body', pronounced by the celebrant. Sylvester Medvedev followed this teaching, but his opponents considered that the invocation of the Holy Spirit which follows the words of institution was the moment of consecration. The Council of 1690 brought victory to the anti-Latins. Medvedev was condemned and several manuals of theology, printed in Kiev, were declared heretical and withdrawn from circulation.

The Muscovite clergy had only a short time to enjoy their victory. The new Tsar, Peter, was not interested in gradual change but was determined to make a European nation of Russia, at a single stroke.

Peter the Great (1682–1725) and the abolition of the Moscow Patriarchate
Peter was the thirteenth child of Tsar Alexey, and at his birth in 1672 no one could have foreseen that he would ascend the throne and alter the course of Russian history.

His father was married twice. The feuds of the Miloslavskys and the Narishkins, the families of the two wives, interfered with Peter's education and distorted his character. He was four years old at his father's death; ten when his eldest half-brother, Tsar Feodor II (1676–82), died childless after a short and promising reign. His other half-brother, Ivan, was a passive, sickly youth, and Peter, a vigorous and healthy child, was hastily proclaimed Tsar by the partisans of the Narishkin family.

Sophia, Peter's masterful half-sister, organized a counter plot. Her armed supporters invaded the Kremlin and proclaimed Ivan and Peter as co-rulers. In this palace revolution several of Peter's uncles and other relatives were savagely butchered before his eyes and this scene of horror was never erased from his mind. From that fatal day Peter became the enemy of Moscow and an irreconcilable opponent of its way of life.

For the next seven years the country's government remained in Sophia's firm hands. This ambitious princess kept Peter, the nominal Tsar, away from the capital and deliberately neglected his education. Alexey saw that his eldest children were carefully brought up. Feodor spoke Latin fluently and was refined in his manners, but Peter grew up self-willed and undisciplined, unable even to spell, but with a strong bent for mechanical and practical things, usually overlooked in Muscovite Russia. One of his passions was for sailing, a sport previously unknown in Russia, which he learned from foreign craftsmen settled in Moscow. In 1689 Peter had a decisive clash with his sister. He forced Sophia to retire to a convent. His main ambition was to secure for his country an outlet to the sea, and after twenty-one years of hard fighting against Sweden (1700–21), he gained control of the Baltic, and made Russia a first-class military power.

During these strenuous years under the constant menace of foreign invasion, Peter undertook far-reaching internal reforms. He substituted for the paternal rule of the Moscow Tsars a centralized and absolutist monarchy on the Western model. The administration was handed over to a bureaucracy, copied from Sweden. The army was properly trained and armed, industry and commerce encouraged and education improved. These changes, accompanied by heavy taxation and other oppressive measures arising from firmer state control, provoked strong discontent. Conservatives, who resented the privileges granted to foreigners and disliked Western customs, expected the Church to voice their grievances. Peter decided to deprive the Church of its freedom and so prevent its being the mouthpiece of the Russian people. It was a difficult task, for although the Church was greatly weakened by the Old Believers' schism, it remained the strongest bond the Russian deople knew, and was more real to them than state or nation.

It took Peter twenty-one years of careful manoeuvring and planning to defeat the Church. In 1700, after the death of the Patriarch Adrian, one of Peter's favourites, Stefan Yavorsky (1658–1722), was appointed guardian of the vacant Patriarchal throne. During the next twenty years Peter filled the episcopal seats with men of his own choice, mostly Ukrainians, who were unpopular in the Muscovite dioceses and dependent therefore on the Tsar's favour. The most subservient and the most learned was Bishop Feofan Prokopovich (1681–1738). He was well versed in Western Theology and had Protestant leanings. He favoured secular control of Church administration as it existed in Lutheran

countries. Peter wanted to introduce this into Russia. Under his supervision Feofan composed the *Ecclesiastical Regulations* published in 1721,
giving a new and subordinate position to the Church. In this document
the old forms of ecclesiastical government were ridiculed and attacked,
the Muscovite customs were criticized and the advantages of the new
system highly praised. The central point of this legislation was the
abolition of the Patriarchate and its replacement by a permanent council
of clergy called the Holy Governing Synod.

Various reasons for this drastic change were presented. One was the
alleged greater impartiality and efficiency of a collegiate organ as compared with the rule of a single man; another was the dangerous idea of the
great importance of the Patriarch entertained by 'ignorant people' who
thought him equal to the Tsar. The final argument was that the
Emperor, having absolute power, could not tolerate rivals who, like the
Bishop of Rome, or some of the Byzantine Patriarchs, might have the
audacity to claim authority over the secular ruler. In order to eradicate
such misconceptions a collegiate body was instituted composed of
persons chosen by the Tsar and obedient to him. The Synod consisted
of a president, two vice-presidents and eight other members who were
either bishops, monks or married priests. Each member, including the
president, had one vote and all resolutions had to be approved by a
majority.

The Synod had no precedent in the history of the Orthodox Church,
being not a representative body, as every member was nominated by the
Tsar and could be dismissed by him. Every one of them had to take a
special oath and declare 'I acknowledge the Monarch of all Russia to
be the final judge of this college'. The total dependence on the Emperor
was still further emphasized by the appointment of a secular official
called the Procurator of the Synod. 'This watchful eye' of the Monarch
was not a member of the Synod and he had no vote, but he occupied a
key position for he alone was responsible for the agenda of the sessions
and he submitted decisions to the Emperor for his signature. Only
resolutions thus approved were acted on. If one adds to the functions of
the Procurator his right to suggest to the Sovereign suitable candidates
for the Synod one realizes the supreme importance of these
officials.

The first members of the Synod were all Ukrainians. The Muscovite
bishops, though excluded, were required individually to sign a document approving the Synod, on pain of expulsion from their dioceses.
The more stubborn, like Ignaty, Bishop of Tambov, and Isaiah,
Metropolitan of Nizhni-Novgorod, were by then already removed. The

rest gave their unwilling approbation. In 1723 the Eastern Patriarchs, depending on Peter's favour, also recognized the strange college as 'their beloved brother in Christ'.

There were several reasons for the failure of the Russian hierarchs to avoid having this grotesque caricature of ecclesiastical government imposed on them. The main one was, of course, the withdrawal of the Old Believers. The other was that the Orthodox would have stood firm in defence of their faith and resisted any attempt to alter their sacramental tradition, but Peter did not touch these sides of Church life. He attacked the weakest feature of the Russian Church—its constitution. Orthodox Canon law prescribes a carefully designed system of ecclesiastical administration. Bishops and clergy are to be elected. Bishops must convoke diocesan councils and be consulted regularly by the senior hierarch. These regulations safeguarding the freedom and authority of the Church had never been observed in Russia. The bishops were few (up to the eighteenth century only sixteen), distances were enormous and councils held only in exceptional circumstances. These defects were mitigated by the family spirit prevalent in pre-Petrine Russia. Although the rights of the bishops and the Patriarch were never clearly defined and the Tsar had a good deal to say in their election, their spiritual authority was universally recognized and the Tsars were always the first to set an example of filial obedience to the Patriarchs. The latter had the customary right to remind the sovereigns of their Christian duties of mercy and forgiveness whenever measures undertaken by the government seemed too harsh or unjust to Christian people.* One symbol of the Tsar's acceptance of authority of the Church was the Palm Sunday procession: on that day the Patriarch, representing Christ, rode through the streets of the capital on an ass whilst the Tsar humbly led the animal.

Peter ended this moral ascendancy of the Church. He silenced the bishops, abolished the Patriarchate, suppressed parochial freedom and paralysed the Church. The Moscow Tsars had always been such faithful and devout members of the Church that no provision had been made to protect it from their unlawful interference. The majority of Russians hoped and prayed that the next monarch would deliver the Church from bondage. No call to organized opposition was sounded and as a result, for more than two hundred years, the Russian Church lost the right to speak freely on any major moral or religious issue.

Peter himself was the first to suffer the evil consequences of his policy. In 1718 he clashed with his son and heir, Alexey, who fled abroad. The

* This right of intervention was called *Pechalovanie.*

young man was persuaded to return home by his father's word that no punishment would be inflicted upon him. Peter failed to keep his promise and his son perished under torture during interrogation. The Tsar was obviously tormented by his conscience and before the fatal act was committed he asked the leading bishops to advise him. In the old days the Patriarch would have voiced the Christian mind of the nation. Now the bishops, nominees of the Tsar, were afraid to interfere, although they did mention the virtue of forgiveness in their non-committal reply. Peter's action upset the lawful succession to the throne and plunged the country into the turmoil of palace revolutions which convulsed Russia for the whole century.

But neither Peter nor his agents, the Procurators of the Synod, were able to alienate Russians from the Church who remained faithful to their forefathers' tradition. The Orthodox never accepted the idea that the Emperors, or anybody else, had the right to control the Church of God. The Church was much older than the Empire, it might be temporarily subdued, but not substantially altered or destroyed. The Empire collapsed in 1917, but the Church survived the catastrophe made inevitable by Peter's suppression of the voice of free Christian opinion.

The Nonjurors and the Orthodox Church

During Peter's reign a curious episode in the relations between Eastern and Western Christians occurred, an attempt at corporate reunion between them made by the Nonjurors. These learned and conscientious divines of the Anglican Church, who refused to break their oath of allegiance to the Stuarts, encouraged by Peter, sent three letters to the Patriarch of Constantinople stating the conditions of reunion acceptable to them and received two replies. The correspondence lasted from 1716 to 1725. Nothing came of this first attempt at reunion between the Anglicans and the Orthodox, for the Nonjurors wanted the Eastern Christian to alter several liturgical customs, notably the direct invocation of the saints, the veneration of ikons and the adoration of the Eucharistic elements. Above all, they objected to the special devotion shown to the Mother of God. The Eastern bishops advised the Nonjurors to give up their Calvinistic-Lutheran heresy and this suggestion offended the English divines who were highly critical of the continental Protestants. In the eighteenth century neither side was willing to listen to criticisms and suggestions yet this exchange of letters began discussions which became more fruitful in the course of the next two centuries.

The St Petersburg Empire and the Russian Church in the eighteenth century
St Petersburg, the new capital of Russia, was a strange city, neither
Russian nor European, a city of beauty and grandeur but with a feeling
of doom and unreality hanging over it. Equally bizarre was the Empire
which replaced the old Moscow Tsardom. Socially it was sharply
divided from the beginning until its tragic end. The ruling class was
Westernized, wore European dress, preferred to speak foreign languages
and treated Paris as their metropolis. They sought wisdom and instruction at German universities and read French books and newspapers to
keep in touch with the latest political thought. They imitated Europe
with ardour in the conviction that Western philosophy and social
science offered a panacea for all defects and failures, including those
affecting their national life.

Peter rebuilt Russia in accordance with Western plans. Two centuries
after him Vladimir Ulianov-Lenin (1870–1924), another admirer of
European wisdom, blew up the Empire when attempting to complete
the work started by the revolutionary Tsar. Both of them represented
the minority of the Russians. The rest of the nation, especially the
peasants, considered the West an enemy and an oppressor, for the
Empire had extended the burden of serfdom which became especially
degrading in the second half of the eighteenth century, and was
abolished only in 1861.

After Peter's death in 1725 the Empire seemed very insecure. Neither
Russian nor foreign observers believed it would survive. Several attempts
were made to reverse the process of Westernization and to restore
Moscow to its previous place of honour. But these efforts produced no
permanent results. The contact with Europe, secured at a high price,
was too valuable to be given up and it was not only kept but deepened.

The eighteenth century was a turbulent period in Russian history.
The nation was stirred by its attempts to adjust itself to new conditions.
The government was mostly in the hands of incompetent and ignorant
adventurers, many of foreign origin, whilst the throne was occupied by
women and children who had neither moral nor legal right to this
exalted position. Peter, in his desire to assert his absolutist claims, had
decreed that the reigning sovereign was alone responsible for the choice
of a successor. He himself failed to make use of this doubtful privilege,
but by this law he destroyed all semblance of legality or stability in the
Russian succession.

The state of the Russian Church was deplorable. The Synod was
exposed to all the intrigues and vicissitudes of court revolutions. The
bishops were promoted or degraded on grounds which had nothing to

do with religion. The parish clergy were utterly dependent on the arbitrary decisions of bishops recruited among the monks, mostly newcomers from the Ukraine. New theological schools for the training of the clergy slavishly followed Western patterns. The textbooks were in Latin and so was the teaching.

This state of oppression reached its climax during the long reign of Catherine II (1762–96). This gifted and ambitious German woman who usurped the Russian throne regarded herself as the enlightened and benevolent ruler of a barbaric people. She was responsible for the spread of the most inhuman forms of serfdom. She professed the sceptical rationalism of Voltaire. The Orthodox Church was for her contaminated by ignorance and superstition. Among the Procurators of the Synod she appointed were free thinkers and men openly hostile to Christianity. One of her actions was to sequestrate lands belonging to the Church and drastically to reduce a number of religious houses. These measures met with resolute protest from a few of the more independent bishops. Their leader was Arseny Matsievich, Metropolitan of Rostov, starved to death in 1772 by order of the Empress for his criticisms of her policy. Other bishops were imprisoned or unfrocked.

During Catherine's reign St Petersburg blossomed in all its extravagant beauty; the Empress and her entourage followed the latest Paris fashions and copied the great capitals of Europe; but this refinement and luxury were purchased by the slave labour of Russian peasants, who made unsuccessful but formidable attempts to get rid of foreign rule under the Cossack, Pugachev. For a short while the rebels controlled most of the Eastern provinces (1773–75).

Catherine was fortunate in securing the services of several men of exceptional ability. Among her generals the greatest was Alexander Suvorov (d. 1800). In the course of two wars against the Turks, the Russians for the first time penetrated deep into the Balkans, in 1768–74 and again in 1787–92. The peace treaty concluded at Kuchuk Kainarjie in 1774 established Russian control over the Black Sea and granted Russian monarchs the right to protect the Orthodox population in the Ottoman Empire. This was a turning point in the history of the enslaved Eastern Christians whose hopes of liberation ceased to be an unrealizable dream.

The three partitions of Poland in which Catherine unwillingly took part (1772, 1793 and 1795) brought into the Empire another large section of the Orthodox Ukrainians and White Russians, but it also added a territory inhabited by Roman Catholic Poles and by a considerable number of Jews. The Russian Empire was greatly enlarged,

L 161

but as it grew its political, social and religious conditions also became more complex.

In the second half of the eighteenth century the upper classes of Russia began to desert their Church in search of other ways of life, some of them emancipated from Christian faith and morals altogether. Some regarded themselves as Voltaire's disciples; others joined the Freemasons. These deserters were few at first, but they all belonged to the aristocracy and their outlook gradually penetrated to the lower classes.

The inrush of new ideas, closer contact with the West, the subjugation of the Church to bureaucratic control, had not only negative, but also positive results for Russian Christianity. The closing of many monasteries relieved the Church of the burden of men and women without genuine religious vocation; acquaintance with Christian literature of the West introduced Russians to some of the great works of Christian piety; mixing with Balkan Orthodox, unrestricted by the St Petersburg bureaucracy, stimulated the revival of Russian monasticism.

St Tikhon of Zadonsk and Paisy Velichkovsky

Two Church leaders of that period deserve special mention: St Tikhon of Zadonsk (1724–83) and Paisy Velichkovsky (1722–94). St Tikhon was born in the family of a poverty-stricken Church cantor. He was sent to one of the newly-opened seminaries in which the sons of the Russian clergy were drilled in Latin scholasticism. Endowed with a lively mind and a vivid imagination, he progressed rapidly in his studies. He was ordained, took monastic vows, and was appointed teacher of theology (Plate 63).

In 1763, at the early age of thirty-nine, he became Bishop of Voronezh. The city was a frontier town at that period, facing the open steppes inhabited by the Cossacks. The unruly people, the undisciplined clergy, the general atmosphere of unrest and violence which he encountered there taxed his health. In 1767 he gave up ecclesiastical administration for which he was ill-suited and withdrew to a small monastery in Zadonsk. For the next sixteen years he lived there in seclusion and poverty as a simple monk. This flight from the world and its conflicts did not mean severing himself from suffering mankind. On the contrary, St Tikhon dedicated himself to the service of all in need of help and advice. He maintained a large correspondence and wrote several books of devotion in which he freely incorporated the elements of Western Christianity which he found congenial to Russian Orthodoxy. His love, humility and patience won him the deep attachment of many disciples and admirers. Even during his lifetime he was venerated as a holy man, and he was canonized by the Russian Church in 1861.

Father Zosima of *The Brothers Karamazov*, and still more Bishop Tikhon in *The Possessed*,* give us Dostoevsky's portrait of this Russian saint and prove the impact St Tikhon had upon the greatest of Russian novelists.

Paisy Velichkovsky was born in the Ukraine in 1722. He entered the theological Academy of Kiev, but he disliked its scholasticism and longed for the Orthodox patristic tradition. He left Kiev and became a monk on Mount Athos, the home of unpolluted Orthodoxy.

There he started his great work of translating into Russian the Greek classics on asceticism and contemplation. He collected a number of ancient manuscripts and took them to Moldavia where, in 1779, he was elected Abbot of Niamez Monastery. There, until the end of his life, he worked day and night on translations, surrounded by an increasing number of faithful disciples. He made the experience of the great Eastern mystics available to the Russian Church. Many of these writings had never been translated before, others could only be found in rare ancient manuscripts. One of his books called *Dobrotolubie*, containing extracts from the writings of the Eastern Fathers on prayer, acquired especially wide popularity.† It became a manual of instruction in the art of Christian living and helped many Russians to lead a better Christian life.

Paisy himself was an experienced spiritual director, and revived the true monastic tradition of the Orthodox Church which had fallen into decay in many parts of the Eastern world in the eighteenth century. He recalled the Orthodox to the sources of their tradition. He taught patristic Greek to his pupils and advised them to read the Fathers of Eastern Orthodoxy instead of studying the writings of the Roman Catholic and Protestant controversialists.

The eighteenth century ended in Russia with the short and tragic reign of Paul I (1796–1801). He was a maniac and visionary, obsessed by the desire to revive the sacred kingship profaned by the rationalist monarchs of his time, including his own mother, Catherine II.

In his deranged mind the ideal of an Orthodox Empire was combined with Prussian militarism and medieval knighthood. He invited the Knights of Malta to settle in Russia and he accepted the title of their Grand Master. He made a statute describing himself as head of the Church. It was a meaningless claim, for it contradicted Orthodox

* The chapter describing Bishop Tikhon is however usually omitted from the text of the novel.

† An English abbreviated translation was published in 1951. See *Writings from Philokalia* translated by E. Kadlonbovsky and G. Palmer (London, Faber & Faber, 1951).

teaching and, besides, the Russian Church was only one member of the community of Eastern Christians. Nevertheless this assertion gave rise to the misconception that the Russians professed Caesaro-papism.

In reality Paul I's declaration was the arbitrary act of an irresponsible ruler and was repudiated by the Russian Church as soon as it was able to express its true opinion at the freely elected Council in 1917.

Western ascendancy over the Christian East

The sixteenth, seventeenth and eighteenth centuries were the dark period in the history of the Christian East. Political oppression, poverty and ignorance undermined the strength of this community. It was also the time of Western ascendancy when both the Roman Catholics and the Protestants took for granted their superiority over the Byzantine and Oriental Churches.

The unequal contest between the Christian East and the West went on both in Europe and Asia; one of its battlegrounds was the remote outpost of Eastern Christendom, the Orthodox Church of the Malabar coast in South India.

The Church of St Thomas in South India

The Portuguese discovered the existence of St Thomas Christians after Vasco da Gama landed near Calicut on 14th May 1498. The Christian community in India consisted of some 30,000 families at that time and was governed by the Metropolitan, Mar Yahballaha, assisted by three suffragan bishops, Mar Denha, Mar Jacob and Mar Johanes, all natives of Mesopotamia and representing the Nestorian version of Oriental Christianity.

The arrival of the Portuguese coincided with Moslem incursions into South India. In 1502 the Indian Christians asked Vasco da Gama to take them under his protection. This was a political move and the Orthodox did not expect that their alliance with the Portuguese would affect their church life and at first it did not. The newcomers made no attempt to interfere with the affairs of the Malabar Christians; St Francis Xavier, the great missionary of that epoch (1506–52), who spent three years in South India, and baptized several thousand pagans, did not proselytize among the Orthodox and maintained friendly relations with them. He even recommended to Portuguese King John III (the Pious, 1521–57), one of the bishops, Mar Jacob, 'as a virtuous and saintly old man, who has well served God and Your Majesty for forty-five years'.

These amicable relations began to deterioriate in the second part of the sixteenth century. As early as 1455 Pope Callistus III (1455–68) had granted to the Portuguese jurisdiction over the whole of Africa and Southern Asia. For some time this privilege was nominal, but with the rapid growth of their overseas possessions, the Portuguese started to make practical use of it. As far as the Indian Church was concerned this implied that the King of Portugal had the right to nominate its bishops and supervise its administration. The Indian Orthodox were totally ignorant of the Papal claims to universal jurisdiction. However, being used to acknowledging the authority of the Nestorian Patriarch of Babylon, they had no difficulty in transferring their allegiance to the even more remote figure of the Pope. But things began to look different when the Portuguese started to Latinize their worship and alter their ancient traditions. These were strikingly different from the Western ways, for they incorporated many Hindu customs; the priesthood, for instance, was a privilege open only to the sons of certain families; much teaching was oral; the services were celebrated in Syriac, like the Sanskrit of the Hindus, a sacred but incomprehensible language. All the bishops were foreigners who came from Mesopotamia and they lived like Hindu saints, in isolation, never mixing with their flock. Portuguese attempts to bring these unusual Christians into line with their own ecclesiastical policy provoked many conflicts, which came to a head at the end of the sixteenth century.

In 1595 Alexis de Menez, as Portuguese Archbishop of Goa, was entrusted by Pope Clement VIII (1592–1605) with the task of disentangling the confused situation. He spent several months visiting the scattered communities of the Malabar Christians, travelling down crocodile infested rivers and crossing hills in tropical jungle. He impressed the Orthodox with his zeal and courage and he managed to persuade clergy and laity to merge their Church with that of Rome. On 21st June 1599 a synod was held at Diamper. Eight hundred and thirteen delegates representing this ancient Church made a solemn confession of faith as prescribed by the Council of Trent (1565): they acknowledged Papal supremacy, accepted the compulsory celibacy of their clergy and agreed to alter the ritual of their worship.

This complete victory was partly the result of a display of Portuguese military power, for the Viceroy sent a detachment of troops to Diamper to watch over the council's proceedings. This seeming triumph of the Latins was accompanied by the wholesale burning of Orthodox service books and other ecclesiastical documents. This destruction was so thorough that hardly any reliable information is available today about the life and teaching of the Indian Church prior to the sixteenth century.

The next events were typical of Eastern people who visibly yield under strong external pressure, but are capable of long and stubborn inward resistance. The Latinization of their Church was strongly resented by the St Thomas Christians, but it took them more than half a century to reassert their independence. Rebellion flared up in 1653. Its immediate cause was the arrest and murder by the Portuguese of Bishop Ahatalla, who had come secretly to India from Babylon at the invitation of Rome's adversaries. When the news of his assassination reached the Orthodox their leaders met at Mattancherry and held a synod in the vicinity of the much revered ancient bent (*coonen*) cross. All the delegates solemnly pledged themselves to return to their old tradition and to repudiate their submission to Rome. As a visible token of their unanimous determination they all took hold of the ropes tied to the cross and repeated together their oath to defend their religious freedom.

A confused struggle between the Portuguese and the Indians followed this act of defiance; the rebels had no bishop and were obliged to resort to irregular ordinations by presbyters, in order to supply their parishes with clergy. This action gave the Jesuits the chance to persuade many of the Indians to resume obedience to Rome; while others continued their resistance.

In 1663 the Dutch expelled the Portuguese from Malabar, which allowed the Orthodox to regain their lost contacts with other Eastern Christians. Mar Gregorious, a Syrian bishop, arrived in 1665 and restored the Apostolic ministry among the Indians by reordaining their clergy. He represented, however, not the Nestorian, but the Jacobite tradition of Oriental Christianity, and since his time the St Thomas Christians have acknowledged the Syrian Patriarchs of Homs as their ecclesiastic superior.

Those Indians who returned to Rome have formed a separate community, known today as Syro-Romans. Their worship and teaching are Latinized, but they have retained certain features which keep them apart from the ordinary Latins of their country.

Thus the Orthodox Christians of South India, who had preserved their faith and unity in the midst of Hinduism for sixteen hundred years, became divided through meeting the Christian West. Their community was split into two halves, and the gulf between them is as unbridgeable today as it was in the seventeenth century.

The Church of Ethiopia

The story of the contact between Rome and the Ethiopian Christians is in some ways similar. The Negus David (1505–40) maintained a correspondence with King John III of Portugal, and with several Popes. At first the Latins seemed natural allies against the Moslems. In 1603 a Jesuit, Pedro Paez, converted the Negus Za Donghel to Rome. The King was murdered the next year, but his successor, Susneyos, in 1623, declared Roman Catholicism the religion of Ethiopia. In 1626 Alfonso Mendez arrived from Rome with the title of Patriarch of Ethiopia, and began drastic reforms. A regular persecution of those who opposed these Western innovations was pursued with great vigour. This policy made the Roman Church so unpopular in Ethiopia that the next Negus, Fasilidas, expelled the Jesuits and repudiated the union with Rome. This time no schism resulted for the Ethiopians unanimously returned to their traditional forms of Church life. Up to the Italian invasion in 1936 their mountain realm remained closed to all outside influences. Some of its customs, such as circumcision and the use of sacred dances in worship (Plate 62), link the Ethiopian Church to Old Testament religion more closely than any other branch of Christianity.

The Nestorian Church of the East

No other Christian community had such ups and downs in its history as the Nestorian Church of the Persian Empire. In the fourteenth century its outposts in Central Asia, Turkestan and Persia were annihilated in the massacres which accompanied Tamerlane's campaigns. Only a small remnant survived in Mesopotamia and in the wild mountains of Kurdistan. Five dioceses were left out of more than two hundred which had existed in the previous centuries. The Patriarchs moved to Mosul. Ecclesiastical administration degenerated into a system of hereditary appointments; the Patriarch selected one of his relations, usually a nephew, as guardian of the throne, *Natar Curaga*, who succeeded him in the religious and secular control over all Nestorians.

In 1552 this order was upset by a conflict between the Abbot Sulaka and Shiman Dinkha, the *Natar Curaga* of the late Patriarch, Shimanbar Mama. The Nestorians of the plain—the communities of Mosul and Nisibis—supported Abbot Sulaka as their candidate for the Patriarchate —the Nestorians of Kurdistan, Shiman Dinkha. The latter happened to be the only bishop among the Nestorians at that time, so he assumed the title of Patriarch and seized control of Church property. His opponents appealed to Rome to consecrate Abbot Sulaka. The Pope, Julius III (1550–55), welcomed this unexpected request; Sulaka was consecrated and received the title of Patriarch of the Chaldeans, as the Nestorians reconciled to Rome are still called.

Sulaka consecrated five other bishops when he returned to Mosul and since then the Nestorian community has been divided between the Church of the Plain and the Church of the Mountains.

Both communities adhered at first to the *Natar Curaga* system and for some time there was little difference between them; switches in allegiance from one to the other were common during the sixteenth and seventeenth centuries. Some Nestorian bishops submitted to Rome; some of the Chaldeans returned to their Mother Church. At last the Roman authorities began training their clergy in the Western tradition and this stabilized the Chaldean Church as a body with Latinized ritual and outlook. In 1778 the Christians of the Plain made their final submission to Rome, and the Nestorian Church of the East was irreparably split. The Chaldeans still have their centre in Baghdad, but the Nestorians who used to have their stronghold in the mountains of Kurdistan were massacred by the Mohammedans at the end of World War I, and their remnants dispersed over Lebanon and Palestine.

The Church of the Armenians

The strongest resistance to the Islamic invaders was made by the Armenians. This valiant nation has fought, undismayed, against its many invaders and found in its Church the mainstay of its national independence.

The Armenians were overrun by the Saracens in the ninth century. Etchmiadzin, their ecclesiastical capital, was destroyed, and for five hundred and forty years the Catholicos had no fixed residence (901–1441).

During that troubled time many Armenians migrated to the West and in the eleventh century they founded the Kingdom of Little Armenia in Cilicia (1080–1395). It was the period of the Crusades and the Armenians were valuable allies to the Western knights. King Lavan II (1185–1219) opened negotiations with the Crusaders convinced that nothing short of close co-operation among all Christians in the Near East could save the latter from defeat. In 1199 he recognized the Pope as his Sovereign and was crowned by the papal legate. The majority of the Armenians were unwilling to become Latins and the King was therefore anointed by his own bishop too in conformity with the Orthodox ritual. He persuaded the papal legate, however, to accept the submission of twelve bishops as a token of the nation's incorporation in Western Christendom. This first act of union had little practical effect. At the end of the thirteenth century the need for greater military assistance from the West induced King Hetoom II (1289–1305) to adopt a more accommodating policy towards the Latins. In 1307 a synod at Sis sanctioned various changes in worship and teaching in compliance with papal requests. These concessions proved to be of no real value, for the Crusaders' days were numbered, and the Armenians, abandoned by the West, lost their political independence in 1375 but regained their religious freedom. Their link with the Latins has left however a permanent mark on their ritual. For example, Armenian bishops wear Western mitres and carry pastoral staffs after the Latin model.

The fifteenth and sixteenth centuries were a dark period in Armenian history. Moslem oppression, aggravated by internal disorders, decreased their opportunities but not their desire for learning. This tenacious people never gave up hope of regaining independence and were determined to preserve their cultural inheritance. The Catholicos, Michael of Sebastia (1545–76), started a printing press in the Armenian language. He sent one of his agents, Abgar of Tokat, to Italy and, in 1565, the first Armenian book was published in Venice. Other printing houses later appeared in Rome, Constantinople, Amsterdam and Etchmiadzin. This longing for education was the source of acute conflict in Constantinople, where an influential and prosperous colony of Armenians had settled. Roman emissaries used both force and persuasion to win these Armenians over to their side by promising them educational facilities and political protection. The French Ambassador, Marquis Feriol, abducted the Armenian Patriarch of Constantinople, Avedic Tokat, to France, where he was tried and condemned by the Inquisition in 1711.

In spite of these acts of violence, the Armenians, either scattered all over Europe and Asia or persecuted in their own country, were forced to look to the West to maintain their learning and cultural tradition. One of these scholars, Mikhitar, after many wanderings, found refuge on the little island of San Lazaro, near Venice, and there in 1717 he started a community of learned monks which has remained an important cultural centre for Armenians.

One condition which was imposed upon Mikhitar was submission to Rome. But he held aloof from the campaign of conversion and a tradition of impartial scholarship has been retained by the religious community he founded.

The Armenians, like other Oriental Christians, lost their unity as the result of Roman and Protestant propaganda. Three million remained Orthodox, and one hundred thousand are divided between the Roman and Protestant confessions.

The Coptic Church

The National Church of Egypt, strongest opponent of the Chalcedonian Council, broke away from the Byzantine Orthodox in the sixth
century. At first it was favoured by the Moslems, but conditions
gradually deteriorated and it was reduced to a minority group called
The Copts by their Islamic masters.

In 1594 the Jesuits made a determined attempt to persuade the Copts
to submit to Rome: this failed. In 1630 a French priest, Father Agathen-
gelo of Vendôme, worked among the Copts, but his zeal and eloquence
could make no converts. The Uniate Copts date only from the nineteenth century and number forty thousand, as against two and a half
million of the Orthodox Copts.

The Jacobites

Roman propaganda had far greater success with another group of
anti-Chalcedonians, the Jacobites of Syria and Palestine. The scattered
Jacobites, harassed by the Mohammedans, needed financial help and protection. This was willingly offered to them by Western Powers, especially
by France, on condition of their submission to the papacy. In 1701
Andrew Akhidian, a supporter of union with Rome, became bishop of
Aleppo. His designs became known to his flock and his attempts to
effect reconciliation led to riots. His supporters among the clergy were
thrown into prison by the Turkish authorities and for seventy-seven
years no one dared reopen negotiations with Rome.

In 1783 the Jacobite Patriarch of Antioch nominated as his successor
Mar Michael Yarweh, Archbishop of Aleppo, who submitted to Rome.
The Orthodox expelled him with the help of the Turks and Yarweh
fled to Lebanon. He started the line of Syrian Patriarchs reconciled to
the papacy. Thus the Jacobites were split, in the eighteenth century,
into two groups of almost equal numbers (about 80,000 at present).

Such is the story of the impact of the Christian West upon the Oriental
Christians. Many of them hoped to find friendship and much-needed
assistance in the West. They recognized the West as better equipped
and more enlightened, and some were ready to accept the Roman
leadership in exchange for improved education and greater order and
efficiency in their own Church life. The price of such submission was
invariably the Latinization of their rites, the abandonment of their
ancient traditions and acceptance of Latin clergy as supervisors. As a
result, only a minority became Uniates; the majority remained faithful
to their own community, although it had morally and intellectually
deteriorated under Mohammedan oppression, Bribery, intrigue and

spiritual isolation sapped the vitality of the Oriental Christians; but conversion to the West was not an antidote against these evils, for both Rome and Protestantism looked on the Christian East as inferior and degraded, to be redeemed only by absorption. Western recognition of the value of the Christian East came only in the twentieth century.

Balkan Christians in the seventeenth and eighteenth centuries

The state of the Eastern churches was more hopeful in the Balkans than in the rest of the Ottoman Empire, for Balkan Christians had the advantage of being a majority in their own lands, whilst the Oriental Christians were minorities scattered among Mohammedans. The Balkan Christians lived nearer to the free Christian countries and an occasional breath of fresh air reached them, which was denied to the peoples of Asia.

The end of the seventeenth century displayed unmistakable signs of Turkish decline. In 1688 the Hapsburgs captured Belgrade and Vidin, and were enthusiastically welcomed as liberators by the Serbs. This success was short-lived, however. In 1690 the Turks drove the Austrians out of Serbia and Bulgaria. This defeat meant a national catastrophe to the Serbs, who, led by their Patriarch, Arsenie III, left their homeland in large numbers and fled to Banat with the retreating Austrians (1691). The lands abandoned by the Serbs were partially occupied by the Arnauts of Albania, which upset national equilibrium in the heart of the Balkan peninsula. The Turks, alarmed by this mass exodus, abolished the last remnants of ecclesiastical autonomy in the Serbian Church, and handed over its administration to the Phanariot Greeks, who were the best-organized body within the Ottoman Empire and who hoped in due time to replace their Asiatic masters.*

The eighteenth century was thus a time of intensified competition among the Balkan Christians. The Phanariots, being engaged in trade, amassed considerable fortunes and were able to purchase from the Turks all the remunerative ecclesiastical and civil appointments open to Christians. This system of organized bribery enabled the Greeks to control most of the bishoprics and they began systematically the work of Hellenizing the non-Greek Orthodox, who were in the majority. Greek was made the language of worship, the few parochial schools also taught their pupils in Greek. The Phanariots hoped to restore the Byzantine Empire, but for the time being they were most obedient and pliable Christian subjects, and the Turks trusted them more than the rest. The

---

* The name *Phanariot* is derived from the part of Constantinople which was reserved for the Greeks and where all the best families had their residence.

Phanariots also obtained secular control of the rich provinces of Moldavia and Wallachia. From 1712 until 1821 the posts of Gospodars of these provinces were sold by the Turks to the rich Greek families of Constantinople. A Gospodar enjoyed his privileges for only three years during which he extracted all he spent, and more. Such rapacity naturally increased mutual distrust among Balkan Christians.

The Phanariots had miscalculated: they failed to Hellenize the Slavs and the Rumanians, and instead of becoming the leaders of liberation they incurred the hostility of other Orthodox. The secular nationalism of the West was still unknown at that time in the Balkans where Christians regarded themselves as members of the same Orthodox family, the only difference being linguistic. The Phanariot policy created however a spirit of rivalry among them and in consequence the Balkan Christians were unable to act together in their struggle against the Turks.

These inner divisions provided opportunities for the Western powers, in particular England and Austria, to interfere and this led to the fatal policy of dividing the Balkans, which eventually dragged Europe into the disastrous wars of the twentieth century.

The Eastern Orthodox under Hapsburg rule

In 1699, by the peace of Karlowitz, the Austrian Empire acquired considerable territory ceded by the Turks. This victory greatly increased the number of Orthodox within the Hapsburg domain and the government multiplied its efforts to induce the Eastern Christians to submit to Rome. As early as 1652 an isolated branch of the Russian Orthodox Church in the Carpathian mountains had been forced into union. In the eighteenth century the same policy was vigorously pursued in Transylvania. The majority of the Christians there were Orthodox Rumanians, but they were treated as outcasts. Only four Western confessions, Roman, Lutheran, Calvinist and Unitarian were recognized. The Orthodox clergy were degraded to the level of serfs and had to carry the burden of heavy taxation and manual labour, from which other Christian ministers were exempt. The Orthodox laity was systematically oppressed. Union with Rome was offered to the Rumanians as an immediate remedy for these evils. The clergy were promised the same treatment as those of Western confessions; the laity was assured improved status. In 1701 the majority of the Rumanians of Transylvania accepted union with Rome, though a substantial number remained Orthodox. This remnant, deprived of its own bishops, was temporarily put under the supervision of the Serbian clergy, for the

Serbs stubbornly resisted the policy of Latinization and all efforts to turn them into Uniates had failed. They were newcomers in Austria and they retained that spirit of independence which they had kept alive for centuries under the Turks. They were also a valuable military force occupying the frontier zone between the Ottomans and the Hapsburgs and therefore they enjoyed certain privileges denied to other Orthodox. Their resistance gave such courage to the rest of the Eastern Christians that the Austrians were unable to enforce union with Rome upon all their orthodox subjects.

The Christian East at the time of its decline (fifteenth–eighteenth centuries)
The fall of the Byzantine Empire in the middle of the fifteenth century was a great landmark in the evolution of Eastern Christianity. The State which was believed to be indestructible collapsed, the Queen city elected by God was sacked by the infidels. Since the time of the Emperor Constantine the Orthodox regarded the Empire as their shield and protector and handed over to it many functions previously exercised by the Christian community itself. The blow suffered by the Church was shattering but not fatal. It survived the disaster but life was greatly impoverished and deprived of several essential activities. The main change was that its further growth became difficult. Under Islam, Christians had a comparative security of tenure, but were forbidden to expand and this crucial limitation profoundly affected their psychology. Instead of looking forward, they remembered with longing their glorious past. The Eastern Christians became intensely conservative, Orthodoxy was identified in their minds with immobility, rigorous adherence to forms shaped in better days became the only policy available to them. Such arrested development damaged many sides of Church life. Its theology lost originality and vigour, worship became stereotyped, philanthropic and educational work was reduced to a minimum, missionary activities ceased altogether.

This decline coincided with renewed pressure from the West. The Eastern Christians, fighting in self defence on ground chosen by Western controversialists had produced a number of defective formulae. From this time dates the idea that the first seven Ecumenical Councils form the final and unalterable authority for the Orthodox Church, that there are only seven Sacraments and that there exists a precise moment when consecration of the Eucharistic elements takes place. Pressed on two sides by Islam and the West, the Eastern Christians so closely associated Church with nationality that they confined Orthodoxy to their own people and became indifferent to the religious condition of the rest of the world. And yet, in spite of all these failures, Christianity did not die out among them.

The Eucharist spiritually fed the faithful, the Gospel illuminated their minds, and their undying love for freedom gave them strength to continue their struggle for their liberation from the Islamic yoke. The Christian East was chained to the walls of its prison, but it refused to surrender, trusting that God in his mercy would one day deliver his servants from captivity.

The only exception to this state of slavery were the Russians; their Church was expanding with the growth of the Moscow Tsardom but it also suffered from excessive conservatism, and was even more suspicious of the West than the Greeks and Orientals. The confusion between essential and secondary elements in religion was so widespread in Russia that its leading Christians split their community just at a time when unity was required for their campaign to liberate their oppressed co-religionists.

This gloomy picture has, however, one redeeming feature. The static conception of the Church universally accepted by all Christians during those centuries seriously distorted their thought and actions. Most of the Western controversies of the sixteenth and seventeenth centuries were therefore lamentably one-sided and many decisions taken at that time upset the balanced presentation of Christianity. The Eastern Christians, deprived of their freedom, escaped the dangers of doctrinal sectarianism and of liturgical inadequate improvisation. Their conservatism saved them from many mistakes committed by the West. The Orthodox were behind the West in scholarship and organization, but they were sustained by their firm conviction that they kept the Apostolic teaching intact and that in their worship they faithfully preserved the Patristic tradition.

At the end of the eighteenth century the Christian East sank to its nadir. Islam was shattered but still undefeated, and its grip over the Orthodox remained as oppressive as ever. The Russian Church was paralysed and humiliated, the West was aggressive and confident of its superiority over the East. In that hour of darkness a faint light appeared on the far horizon. It came, most unexpectedly, from France, the old enemy of the Orthodox: the explosive ideas of liberty, equality and fraternity proclaimed by the French Revolution politically and intellectually stimulated the Christian East, and contributed to the recovery of its freedom.

CHAPTER SIX

THE PERIOD OF INTELLECTUAL STIRRING AND NATIONAL LIBERATION

(XIX CENTURY)

The Russian Church at the beginning of the nineteenth century—St Serafim of Sarov (1759–1832)—Optina Pustin—The Metropolitan Philaret of Moscow (1782–1867)—The revival of missionary work—The Slavophils—Alexey Khomiakov (1804–60)—The emergence of national autocephalous Churches in the Balkans—The Serbian Church—The Prince-bishops of Montenegro—The Church of Greece—The Church of Rumania—The Church of Bulgaria—Success and failure of the Balkan Churches—The Orthodox in Austria-Hungary—The Russian Intelligentsia and the Orthodox Church—Feodor Mikhailovich Dostoevsky (1821–81)—Vladimir Sergeevich Soloniev (1853–1900)

The Russian Church at the beginning of the nineteenth century

THE TRANSITION from the eighteenth to the nineteenth centuries was a highly dramatic period, charged with tensions and revolutionary turmoil throughout Europe. In Russia the unbalanced and unpredictable Emperor Paul I was assassinated in 1801, to be succeeded by his son, Alexander I (1801–25), an enlightened and liberal ruler who at first commanded an enthusiastic admiration from his subjects. Napoleon's invasion of Russia in 1812, and his defeat, raised Alexander to leadership among the Great Powers, and brought the Russian army into the heart of Europe. In 1815 the Cossacks lit their camp fires in La Place de l'Opéra, in Paris.

Alexander's reign was remarkable for the appearance among Russians of a body of a genuinely Westernized people. Since Peter the Great's reforms, the upper class had borrowed their dress, speech and manners from the French, but even these Russians had remained cultural strangers to the Western world. By the end of the eighteenth century a change had begun. Nikolay Karamzin (1766–1826), author of some sentimental novels and one of the first Russian historians, visited Western Europe in 1789–90. In 1791–92 he published *Letters of a Russian Traveller* in which he expressed a novel sense of belonging to the Western World. Homer and Virgil, Molière and Racine, Voltaire and Kant were no longer mere names to this educated Russian. He was moved by classical ruins, shed tears reading sentimental stories and was uplifted by the desire to see his fellow men liberated from the bondage of political oppression.

This close association with European culture had important repercussions in religious ideas. Suspicion of the Christian West was replaced by the desire to discover a common language with Roman Catholics and Protestants. The Emperor himself took the lead; for the momentous historical events in which he had played such a prominent part changed his previous rationalist outlook. He became a mystic and searched for signs and symbols revealing divine providence. Alexander professed a religion of the heart and rejected both doctrines and sacraments as mere formalized manifestations of Christianity, unnecessary to true initiates. He was convinced that not only all Christians but all believers in God could join in a common endeavour to promote goodwill among men. In his friend, Prince Alexander Golitsin (1773–1844), he found an enthusiastic supporter of his creed. Golitsin was appointed head of a dual ministry of education and religion, with the task of building up the entire educational system of the Empire on religious foundations acceptable to all confessions. This plan was supplemented by encouragement of the Bible Society, founded in 1812, modelled after the British Bible Society, started in 1804. At first it had a resounding success but when Alexander's brother, Nicholas I (1825–55), ascended the throne, circulation of the Holy Scriptures in spoken language was forbidden as politically dangerous, and the Society's work was restricted to circulating the Bible in languages other than Russian.*

The emphasis on the emotional, pietistic elements of Christianity, so marked among the higher circles of St Petersburg society, was accompanied by similar tendencies in the lower classes. This may be seen in the success of various sects, some of which promised their followers liberation from sin and carnal desires by orgiastic experience. The most active was the Khlisti sect. Its adherents claimed to be possessed by the Holy Spirit and, this stage once reached, they could do no wrong; they indulged in ritual dances which often ended in sexual promiscuity. In contrast to this clandestine sect was another, the Skoptsi, founded by Kondraty Selivanov (d. 1832), advocating voluntary castration as the surest road to bliss and salvation. Other sects drew their inspiration from German pietism, calling themselves Spiritual Christians because they repudiated the Sacraments and the hierarchy and preached anarchism in social matters. In this irrational atmosphere of confusion, emotional tensions and official disapproval of confessionalism, the position of the Orthodox Church was far from easy.

During the eighteenth century the clergy of the Russian Church had been increasingly isolated from the common people. Candidates for the

---

* The *New Testament* in Russian was allowed to be printed again in 1863. The *Old Testament* in Russian was published in 1875.

priesthood and episcopate were restricted to the graduates of the *seminaria* where sons of the clergy were trained. Latin was used in these schools and their textbooks were copies of either Roman Catholic or Protestant manuals. This unsatisfactory education in an alien spirit cut off the parochial clergy from the lower classes, who adhered to traditional Orthodoxy. The upbringing in Seminaries did not, however, raise bishops and priests to the level of the Westernized upper classes with their preference for the French language, literature and manners. This cultural isolation of the Russian clergy was further aggravated by their legal status. The Imperial legislators had suppressed Church self-government but had not provided the clergy with an adequate state subsidy. Parishioners no longer had any say in appointing their pastors whom the bishops selected at their will. But the upkeep of a parish priest and his assistants remained as in the old days a parish responsibility and often this led to friction and discontent. The bishops too were nominated without consulting the members of the Church and were controlled by the Synod, which could move them from one diocese to another, promote or demote them. Yet the Church was not dead: it remained the most vital force in the life of the Russian people; it gave them their sense of brotherhood and dedication to the service of God and man. The Church was the only meeting place for Russians of all classes and conditions; it was the bond uniting them to their past and reminding them that they were all primarily Orthodox Christians and only in the second place masters and serfs, peasants and nobles.

St Serafim of Sarov (1759–1832)
The significance of the Church to the nation can be seen in such men as St Serafim of Sarov, one of the most beloved saints of the Russian people. Born in Kursk, in central Russia, he belonged to the artisan class little touched by Western influence. His father and mother were in the building trade and deeply devoted to the Church. At the age of eighteen Prokhor Moshin (his secular name) joined the monastic community of Sarov, lost in the immense forests of the Eastern province of Tambov. There he passed through all the stages of Orthodox asceticism, gradually increasing the severity of his exercises until he attained to such contemplation of the divine love that he could abstain for days and nights from food and sleep. He spent a thousand consecutive nights kneeling in prayer on a stone near his lonely forest hut. All these tests of endurance and obedience to the divine will found their consummation in service to suffering mankind. In 1825, after seventeen years of seclusion, St Serafim opened the doors of his cell to all who wanted to consult him.

Physically he was drastically changed; the bent old man bore little resemblance to the strong healthy youth who had come to Sarov, but the elder's shining blue eyes, his radiant love and his knowledge of men showed that his sufferings and trials had not been wasted. For the remaining seven years of his life he was visited by an endless stream of people; as many as four or five thousand a day came to see him, to touch him, to be comforted. He remained humble, retiring; often he gave enigmatic counsel, but boundless compassion was poured out on all. St Serafim was both a healer and a seer. One of his disciples, Nicholas Motovilov, cured by St Serafim of an apparently incurable disease, has left a remarkable document describing his conversation with the elder.

At the end of a discourse about the ultimate purpose of life consisting of perfect union with the Holy Spirit, which transforms and illuminates human nature, Motovilov saw the light of transfiguration about which St Serafim had been telling him. Motovilov wrote:

'After these words, I looked at his face and there came over me an even greater awe. Imagine in the centre of the sun, in the dazzling brilliance of its midday rays, the face of a man who talks with you. You see the movement of his lips and the changing expression of his eyes, you hear his voice. You feel someone grasp your shoulders yet you do not see the hands, but only a blinding light spreading several yards around and throwing a sparkling radiance across the snow blanket on the glade and on to the snowflakes which besprinkled the elder and me.'[1]

St Serafim did not stand alone. A genuine revival of monasticism and spirituality took place in Russia in the nineteenth century. Rare gifts of holiness and prophecy were revealed by men and women of all classes and orders.

Optina Pustin

The ascetic tradition, revived by Paisy Velichkovsky in the eighteenth century in Moldavia (see p. 163), was brought to Russia by his numerous disciples. One of them, Leonid (1768–1841), settled in Optina Pustin, a monastery near Tula, and became well-known as a spiritual adviser. He was succeeded by another man of holiness and wisdom, Makary (1788–1860), and later by the most famous of the Optina elders, Amvrosy (1812–91), whose disciples, Anatoly (d. 1922) and Nektary (d. 1928), met the storm of the Communist Revolution, were ejected from their monastery and died as confessors. Optina was not only an important centre of monastic life: it was also a meeting place for the bearers of the authentic patristic tradition of Eastern Orthodoxy and for Westernized intellectuals in search of Christian teaching unpolluted by bureaucratic interventions or Western controversies. Gogol (1809–52), Dostoevsky (1821–81), Tolstoy (1828–1910), Vladimir Soloviev (1853–1900) and Rozanov (1856–1919) were among the visitors to Optina. Ivan Kireevsky (1805–56) and Constantin Leontiev (1831–1891), two remarkable Russian thinkers, made Optina their permanent home. Yet Optina, like all Russian monasteries, was not reserved for intellectuals and the spiritual élite; it was open to all; the elders were ready to discuss intricate problems of mystical theology or homely peasant problems—selling a cow or arranging a marriage. The whole of life, with its daily labour, financial concerns, personal relations, was brought before them and then seen in the light of man's ultimate destiny, that of a creature whose earthly task was to learn to love God and his neighbours in joyful freedom.

The Metropolitan Philaret of Moscow (1782–1867)

St Serafim, the elders of Optina and other representatives of genuine Russian Orthodoxy, held aloof from ecclesiastical administration by the Procurators of the Synod. They did not argue with official circles, where their spiritual freedom created suspicion, but neither were they ready to support the anti-canonical system introduced by Peter the Great. Among the bishops of that period were not only time-servers and bureaucrats but also scholars and ascetics; few, however, were statesmen. The exception was Philaret (Drozdov), Metropolitan of Moscow from 1821–67 (Plate 64). Son of a poor Church cantor, he was educated in a seminary where he learnt good Latin but little theology. He took monastic vows and in 1809 at the age of twenty-one was ordained and sent to St Petersburg as one of the best young preachers. There he imbibed that spirit of open-mindedness and religious tolerance which emanated from the Throne. For the rest of his life Philaret remained a liberal but the main part of his ecclesiastical career coincided with the reactionary reign of Nicholas I (1825–55) which prevented him from making his full contribution to the Church.

Philaret was a frail man of retiring disposition but with such a brilliant mind that he dominated the entire Russian scene and no major decision on any ecclesiastical problem was ever settled without him. He was ordained Bishop in 1817 and four years later transferred to Moscow. This appointment secured him a permanent seat in the Synod, though during the tenure of the Procurator's office by General Protasov

(1836–55), Philaret was not invited to attend the Synod sessions. But even during that time he was asked for his opinion which often crucially influenced the Synod's decisions.

Under Protasov's rule the Russian Church had to keep silence. That dashing cavalry officer was appointed by the disciplinarian Emperor to look after ecclesiastical affairs and keep the bishops in due subordination. Protasov's ideal was uniformity and obedience. He tried to copy Roman discipline and one of his projects was to declare the Slavonic text of the Bible authentic, in imitation of the Roman attitude to the Vulgate. Philaret was too cautious to oppose the all-powerful Procurator openly, but his carefully formulated comments on this and other similar proposals were so cutting that the General had to give up some of his most cherished plans. Philaret was a born theologian; his vast reading made him the leading divine in the Russian Church but he refrained from writing books, and only his printed sermons acquaint us with the vigour of his original thought. He also left several volumes of letters, many of which contain his judgments on problems of Church administration. His wisdom raises his opinions to the level of authoritative pronouncements expressing the true mind of the Russian Church.

He was opposed to the confessional chauvinism then prevalent in official circles. He never missed an opportunity of stating that Protasov's attempts to treat Western Christians as heretics were not binding, and that declarations made in this spirit by bishops and theologians were only their private opinions. He even went further, declaring that so long as the Russian Church was deprived of canonical organs of administration any doctrinal decision made in its name had no validity.

Philaret survived both Protasov and Nicholas I. He lived long enough to see the liberal reforms inaugurated by Alexander II (1855–81) and had the honour and satisfaction of being author of the 1861 manifesto in which the Tsar released the Russian peasants from serfdom. The Russian Church owes a great debt to Philaret for he prevented ignorant and self-confident men from making pronouncements in its name which contradicted its genuine tradition.

The revival of missionary work

The Russian Church never lacked men who regarded missionary work as their vocation but the seventeenth century schism and the oppressive state control of the St Petersburg Empire were unfavourable to such work and for a time it declined. Nevertheless, the urge to spread the message of salvation was so strong that a remarkable expansion of missionary activities took place in Russia in the middle of the nineteenth century. It was due to several outstanding men. The pioneer was Makary Glukharev (1792–1847), an enthusiast, always ready for adventure, yet a devoted admirer of cautious Philaret, who never failed to support his unconventional disciple. Influenced by Philaret, Makary took monastic vows and spent some time at the Monastery of Glinsk whose abbot was another Philaret (d. 1841), a well-known saintly elder. Makary, widely read in Eastern and Western mysticism and an excellent linguist, translated the works of St Augustine (d. 430), St Teresa of Avila (d. 1582) and Pascal (1623–62) into Russian. He was so ecumenically minded that he hoped for a Church where Orthodox, Roman Catholic and Protestant altars might stand under the same roof. When in 1819 he met two Quakers, Stephen Grillet (1773–1855) a former atheist and French Royalist and William Allen (1770–1843) a distinguished Professor of Chemistry, both touring in Russia, he felt a deep spiritual affinity with these two devout men. He prayed with them and discussed the question of religious education. In 1830 Makary went to the Altay mountains of Central Siberia and was confronted by the task of evangelizing a people whose language, outlook and culture had never before been studied. He soon mastered the Telengut dialect, the most widely used among these nomadic tribes. He translated the Bible and extracts from the Liturgical books and conducted services in the vernacular. Makary lived in the same primitive conditions as his flock, using the limited means at his disposal for building schools and helping the converts to start a new life based on Christian teaching. He was reluctant to baptize people unless convinced they had really accepted the message of the Gospel. During the fourteen years he spent in the wild Altay mountains he made only six hundred and seventy-five converts. But he laid a sound foundation for further work, and under his devoted disciples, the Archpriest Landishev and the Archimandrite Vladimir, twenty-five thousand of the forty-five thousand inhabitants of the Altai region, became Christians. The mission founded by Makary remains one of the best organized and most successful of the Russian Church.

Makary was too active a spirit to forget the condition of his Mother Church. He was grieved at its lack of freedom and particularly indignant at the suppression of the Russian text of the Bible. He himself had worked hard on it and could not understand how the privilege of worshipping God in the spoken language could be granted to the Altay people and denied to Russians by the same authorities. He wrote to the Synod but his unsolicited advice was interpreted as a sign of insubordination. Makary was ordered to do penance by celebrating the Eucharist daily for six weeks. The zealous priest was surprised to learn that members of the Synod regarded frequent communion as a punishment. So wide was the gap between these officials and the true spirit of Orthodoxy. Makary died prematurely in 1847, while planning to travel to Palestine through Germany where he hoped to publish his Biblical translations, forbidden in his own country.

Another equally indefatigable missionary of this period was Father John Veniaminov (1797–1879). During his first sixteen years of missionary work, he was a priest (1824–40), and for twenty-eight years an itinerant bishop (1840–68) under the name of Innokenty. He was a self-educated man, equally gifted in languages and mechanics. He became a parish priest in Irkutsk, capital of Eastern Siberia, but soon asked to be sent to Alaska, part of the Russian Empire until 1864. He settled down in Unalaska, the administrative centre of the Aleutian Archipelago, one of the most inhospitable parts of the world, where frost, fogs and storms made life hard and perilous. He mastered the Aleutian language, a task which no foreigner had attempted before him because of its many guttural sounds. He composed an alphabet and grammar and in this tongue wrote a remarkable book *The Way to the Kingdom of Heaven* which later was translated into Russian, gaining wide popularity for its simple and direct appeal.

Veniaminov taught the Aleutians not only religion but various useful crafts and he himself learned the art of navigating a seal-skin canoe and travelled fearlessly from one island to another undismayed by raging storms or polar darkness. Ten years spent among the Aleutians resulted in the mass conversion of these people. Transferred to Sitka, he learned the language of the Kolosh Indians and became their tutor in Christ. Raised to Episcopal dignity in 1840, he received as his charge the Aleutian and Kurile Islands, the peninsulas of Kamchatka and Alaska and the entire province of Yakutsk. He was constantly on the move, using canoes, sailing boats, reindeer and dog-sledges and snow-shoes as means of transport. His knowledge of local languages and dialects was prodigious and he was universally trusted and loved by the natives. When in 1868 he succeeded Philaret as Metropolitan of Moscow he left four separate and well-organized dioceses: Alaska and the Aleutian Islands; Vladivostok and Kamchatka; Amur and Blagovekchensk and Yakutsk and Viluisk. As Metropolitan of Moscow he maintained a keen interest in missionary work and inaugurated the Orthodox Missionary Society which continued its activities up to the time of the Communist Revolution. During the second part of the nineteenth century more than twenty-five thousand people, mostly natives of Siberia, were converted by missionaries from this Association.

The story of Russian missions would be incomplete without mentioning two other men who also laboured at that time. One was a layman, Nikolay Ivanovich Ilminsky (1822–1891), the other was Nikolay (Kasatkin), first Orthodox Bishop of Japan (1836–1912). Ilminsky, like his two illustrious predecessors, was also an exceptional linguist. His special interest was missionary work among the Mohammedans, and he completely reorganized it.

He graduated in 1848 from the Theological Academy of Kazan and was appointed Professor of Oriental languages. Besides Hebrew, Greek and Latin, he could speak Arabic, Persian, Tatar, Cherimis, Chuvash, Mordvin, Kirgiz, Yakut and several other Siberian languages. He was perplexed by the failure of Christian missions among tribes in the Volga and Ural regions and by the spread of Islam there. After much research, he spent two years in Cairo, at the Moslem university, without being recognized as a stranger, he concluded that the literary language of the Tatars and Kirgiz was so infused with the Mohammedan theology and so closely associated with the Koran, that no Christian message could be delivered through that medium. Ilminsky therefore decided to use the spoken language of these people, a vocabulary without Islamic associations. He abandoned the complex Arabic script, known only to men trained in Islamic schools, and produced a phonetic script easy for the common people to learn. This change produced remarkable results; the Christians in the Eastern provinces of Russia increased, for services conducted in their spoken tongue made the Christian message intelligible to them. An immediate consequence of this change was ordination of pupils of schools opened under Ilminsky's direction. During his lifetime forty-four Tatars, ten Chuvash, nine Cheremis and two Votiaks were ordained. Christianity became rooted in the life of these people and spread so rapidly that Meshera and Mordva were entirely converted, the majority of the Chuvash and Cheremis entered the Church, and only among the Tatars did Christians remain a minority.

The greatest success of Russian missions was achieved, however, not within the Empire but in Japan. The Apostle of the Japanese was Ivan Kasatkin (1836–1912). In 1853 the Russians, with other European Powers, were allowed to establish diplomatic missions in Japan. Kasatkin, who took monastic vows and changed his name to Nikolay, was sent as Chaplain to the Russian Embassy in Tokio in 1861. He was interested in Japanese religion and culture, learned the language and began to celebrate in Japanese in the Embassy Chapel. An increasing number of Japanese attended this novel service. The first convert to the Orthodox Church was Paul Savabe, a Buddhist priest, baptized in 1868. By 1874 there were four hundred Orthodox Japanese; in 1875 Paul Savabe and John Sakai were ordained Priests. In 1880 Kasatkin was made bishop and the Church began to grow rapidly. The Russo-Japanese War (1904–05) was a testing time for the growing community. Bishop Nikolay stayed with his flock and identified himself with them. He died in 1912 leaving a Church about thirty thousand strong, divided into thirty parishes, having some forty priests and deacons and one hundred and forty-six catechists. The Orthodox Church in Japan, isolated after the Communist Revolution, survived and has continued its steady progress till today.

Such are the main outlines of the missionary work of the Eastern Orthodox in the nineteenth century. None was possible except in the Russian Church, for the rest of the Orthodox were either still under the Mohammedans or only just emerging from their long captivity. For some time an impression has existed in the West that Eastern Christians have no missionary spirit. This is due to ignorance of the facts. In a volume dedicated to Ilminsky's memory in 1891, the following incident was reported. The curator of the Biblical Museum in Mulhausen wrote to the authorities of the Russian Church inquiring whether any translations of the Bible had been made by its members. He was staggered when in response he received a crate of books containing translations into more than sixty languages. The Russian Church in 1899 had twenty missions inside the Empire and five foreign missions in Alaska, Korea, China, Japan and Persia.

The Slavophils

The Russian Church under Nicholas I was a strange body ruled by a cavalry officer and bishops who, though socially inferior, were ranked with military and state officials and were awarded similar decorations. In spite of being in the bureaucratic grip the Church pulsated with its own independent life, and men and women with exceptional prophetic and healing gifts, saints, missionaries and mystics were not lacking among its members. Its chief defect was the growing alienation of the Westernized minority. For example, Alexander Pushkin (1799–1836), the greatest Russian poet of the nineteenth century and a man who deeply loved and understood his people, was a contemporary of the greatest Russian saint of that period, St Serafim of Sarov (1759–1833) but it is unlikely that either ever heard of the other. They lived in separate worlds.

A group of gifted Russian intellectuals, known under the misleading name of Slavophils, were the first who tried to end this harmful state of affairs. They belonged to the landed gentry and had deep roots in the Russian soil. The best known among them were the brothers Ivan (1806–56) and Piotr (1808–56) Kireevsky, the brothers Constantine (1818–60) and Ivan (1823–86) Aksakov, Nikolay Yazikov (1803–46), Alexander Koshelev (1806–83), Yury Samarin (1819–76) and Alexey Khomiakov (1804–60). They had been brought up like the rest of their class in an atmosphere of Western culture, were fluent in European languages and had travelled in Germany, France and Italy. But they differed from other Westernized Russians in retaining their link with their Church whose traditions they loved and understood. The Slavophils were painfully aware that most of their class were strangers in their own country. They were convinced that Russia had as much to offer Europe as to receive, if only the originality and value of Orthodox culture were recognized. The Slavophils were suspected by the Government and prohibited from disseminating their ideas through the Press. They met in drawing rooms of the old capital and spent hours in heated debates with their opponents, the Westernizers, men like Alexander Herzen (1812–70) and Nikolay Ogarev (1813–77).

One of the Slavophils, Yury Samarin, enumerated in a letter the topics of conversation in his circle:

'We used to argue about the relation between Orthodoxy, Latinism and Protestantism. Is Orthodoxy the undifferentiated and primitive form of Christianity from which other higher expressions of religion have arisen? Or is Orthodoxy the unchangeable fullness of religious truth? What is the difference between Russian and European culture? Does it depend on their respective stages of development or is it something fundamental? Must Russian culture be increasingly swamped by the West or should the Russians penetrate deeper into Orthodoxy and discover the foundations of a new universal culture?'[2]

These animated discussions were centred on subjects which the Russians had debated in the sixteenth and seventeenth centuries when belief in Moscow, as the third Rome, had brought about the schism within their Church. Again two parties appeared. The Westernizers denied the originality of Russian culture. They were convinced that their country was backward and needed to learn both wisdom and technical knowledge from the West. They did not believe that the Orthodox Church had any message. The Slavophils on the other hand were practising Christians who were firmly convinced that the Orthodox Church had preserved the original fullness of the Christian revelation. Rome, with its over-emphasis on authority, and Protestantism with its excessive stress on individualism, typified for the Slavophils the defects of nineteenth-century European civilization with its egoism, aggressiveness and self righteousness. The Slavophils thought that the recognition of the importance of a sense of community was essential for a more balanced social and political order. They were ostracized by the majority of their contemporaries, and ridiculed as eccentrics; but their work had a permanent value and led to the spiritual and cultural renaissance which took place in Russia on the eve of the Communist Revolution. The leading figure and the most original mind among the Slavophils was Alexey Stepanovich Khomiakov.

Alexey Khomiakov (1804–60)

Khomiakov (Plate 64) received his first instruction from a French tutor, an emigrant Roman priest who taught him French and Latin. He later added Greek, English, German and Sanskrit to these languages. Khomiakov's mother, strong in character and deeply devoted to the Orthodox Church, helped him to revere the faith of his forefathers. He never deserted Orthodoxy, his spiritual home. Khomiakov was a man of many gifts, a poet of distinction, a painter and the inventor of an engine that won a medal at a London exhibition. He was also a historian of original insight and he compiled the first Russian-Sanskrit dictionary. He was a competent landlord, an amateur doctor and above all, a theologian who opened new vistas to the Russian Church and delivered its thought from entanglement with Western controversies and slavish imitation of foreign patterns. Outwardly his career was uneventful. As a cavalry officer in the Imperial Guard he took part in the Russo-Turkish War of 1829, but soon retired to spend the rest of his life as a well-to-do landlord, dividing his time between Moscow and his estates. He was happily married and had eight children. He died prematurely from cholera whilst treating his peasants for this deadly disease. A man of his intellect, knowledge and dynamic personality would have occupied a leading position in the political or educational life of any country but Russia of his time. Nicholas I distrusted men of initiative and imagination and, above all, he feared that freedom which for Khomiakov was indispensable. Khomiakov was a great Russian patriot, but he was above all a genuine Christian and therefore suspected by the police of being a revolutionary and a free-thinker. None of his books was allowed publication in Russia during his lifetime. History, philosophy, politics, all

186

attracted his attention, but his main contribution was to theology. He was familiar with philosophy, and able to clothe traditional beliefs of Eastern Orthodoxy in the language of contemporary thought.

His approach was so unusual, and the true image of Orthodoxy had been distorted for so long by ecclesiastical bureaucrats that Khomiakov was accused of modernism and only recognized after his death as the authentic spokesman of his Church. His most striking assertion was that both Rome and Protestantism represented the same individualistic approach to religion, whilst the Christian East had preserved the original corporate interpretation of Christianity. (He taught that Western Churches, by fixing Church authority in the Pope or in the Bible, had equally departed from the earlier tradition, according to which the entire community was inspired and guided by the Holy Spirit.)

Before Khomiakov's time Orthodox theologians had been hard pressed by Western controversialists and had tried to defend themselves with Western arguments. Khomiakov broke away from these tactics by placing the Orthodox Church not between Rome and Geneva, but above them. For Khomiakov the Church was not an institution, but a living organism. He dismissed as wrong the search for an external source of infallibility in which the Christian West had been engaged since its separation from the Orthodox Church. He wrote: 'Infallibility resides solely in the ecumenical fellowship of the Church united by mutual love; the guardianship of dogmas and the purity of rites is entrusted, not to the hierarchy alone but to all members of the Church who are the body of Christ.'[3]

For Khomiakov the communion of love was indispensable for the understanding of truth, to the balanced sacramental life and to constructive social action; but love presupposed freedom. Whenever freedom was suppressed, man's creativity was curtailed and intellectual and moral life stagnated. This emphasis on freedom and personal responsibility was linked with an equally strong stress on the importance of community. 'Man's loneliness,' wrote Khomiakov, 'is the cause of his impotence; whoever separates himself from others creates a desert round himself. A self-centred individual is powerless; he is the victim of irreconcilable inner discord.'[4]

Such ideas were unacceptable to the Westernized Russian liberals who demanded unrestricted liberty for the individual, and to the Imperial Government which insisted on obedience and subordination as indispensable to stable political order.

Seven years after Khomiakov's death the liberal reforms made possible the appearance of his theological works in Russia, and in the preface to the first edition Yury Samarin boldly described his teacher as a Doctor of the Church. He was right. The title of Doctor of the Church belongs to Khomiakov as a landmark in the history of Russian Christianity, as a man who revived the patristic tradition within the framework of nineteenth century thought and made Orthodoxy intelligible to educated Russians.

The emergence of national autocephalous Churches in the Balkans

In the nineteenth century the Mohammedan occupation of the Balkans was five hundred years old; yet the Turks remained aliens in creed, race and political outlook, neither absorbed by the conquered nor able to make them part of Islam. The spark of freedom that had been kept alive in the subjugated people by the Orthodox Church at last flared up in a consuming flame. One cause was Russia's steady advance against the Turks; another was the penetration of French revolutionary ideas into the Oriental world. Napoleon's conquest of Egypt and his acquisition of the Ionian Islands in 1797 stirred the Christian East and gave it new courage to break away from slavery.

The Serbian Church

The Serbs were the first to rebel. In 1804 they rose under Karageorge. Defeated, they rebelled again in 1815 under the banners of Obrenovich and after long and bitter strife secured their autonomy.

In 1830 the Turks recognized Milosh Obrenovich as hereditary prince of Serbia. The Serbians obtained the right to build churches and schools, and to organize their own administration, though still obliged to pay tribute to the Sultan. As a guarantee of their obedience Turkish garrisons remained in strategic positions. In 1831 the Patriarch of Constantinople granted autonomy to the Serbian Church within the newly-created principality and so freed it from Phanariot control. Milentije Pavlovich was consecrated the first Archbishop of Belgrade and Metropolitan of Serbia.

In 1879 the Serbian Church became autocephalous, which means not only self-governing, but equal of the other Churches in the Orthodox-Byzantine tradition. The first decades of freedom were full of trials for the Serbian Church. It had few experienced and educated clergy, while hampered by political instability, personal rivalry and intrigues. Nevertheless, constructive work started. Petar Jovanovich, Metropolitan of Serbia (1833–58), founded a theological seminary on the Russian pattern and started to send the more promising young men to complete their training in Russia. One of these, Mihajlo Jovanovich, became the best known of the great Serbian Archbishops of the nine-teenth century (1859–81 and 1889–98). Under him the Serbian Church, once having acquired autocephalous status, came into conflict with the State. He was exiled for eight years. The cause of this conflict was the anticlerical bias of the political leaders of liberated Serbia. They had mostly been educated in France and Germany and uncritically imi-tated the West. They aimed at founding a secular state and disregarded the Serbians' deep attachment to the Orthodox Church which had saved them from spiritual and moral collapse under the Turks.

This anticlericalism and positivism remained fashionable to the end of the Serbian monarchy, among the Westernized minority. Intellectual confusion, moral instability and superficiality characterized this class, which showed little understanding and still less appreciation of the nation's cultural and religious tradition.

The Prince-bishops of Montenegro

A unique ecclesiastical situation developed among the Orthodox Montenegrins. They were racially akin to the Serbians, but their mountain stronghold had never been completely subjugated by the Turks and they were the first to secure their political independence. Their resistance had acquired a religious character so that the bishops had become their national leaders. Danilo Petrovich (1697–1735) was the first bishop to establish contact with Russia and to acquire a position akin to that of a secular ruler. The morale of the Montenegrins was greatly strengthened by this alliance. Danilo's successor was his nephew, Sava Petrovich (1735–82), who collaborated with his cousin, another bishop, Vasilje Petrovich. The latter visited Russia three times and managed to publish *The History of Montenegro* in Moscow in 1754, which stimulated widespread sympathy for his tiny country and secured considerable help.

This dynasty of bishop-rulers reached its most glorious stage in Petar I Petrovich Negosh (1782–1830) and his successor, Petar II Petrovich Negosh (1830–51). In 1799 the Sultan Selim III (1783–1807) recognized the independence of Montenegro and simultaneously its Church gained autonomous status. Petar I was canonized by his Church for incessant and self-sacrificing labours for his people. His nephew, Petar II, was a philosopher and poet of originality and power, a man of wide outlook and a capable administrator.

His successor, Danilo Petrovich (1851–60), brought the rule of the Prince-bishops to an end. He married and became his country's first secular prince.

The Church of Greece

The Serbian revolt did not attract Western attention but the Greek uprising in 1821 stirred Europe profoundly.

It began in several places at once: on 6th March Prince Alexander Hypsilantis, one of the Phanariots, unfurled the flag of Greek freedom in Moldavia; on 25th March Germanos, the Metropolitan of Patras, called on his people to rise against their Mohammedan oppressors, and the inhabitants of several Greek islands simultaneously proclaimed their independence.

This rebellion had been prepared by secret societies, the most important of which was *Philiki Hetaireia* (Association of Friends). It numbered some 200,000 members who disseminated an education directed towards patriotism and a desire for political liberation.

News of the Greek uprisings reached the political leaders of the West at the time of the Conference of Laibach. In this reactionary period, Alexander I of Russia was in an awkward position. Traditionally, the Russians regarded themselves as supporters of the oppressed Balkan Christians, but the Holy Alliance, initiated by Alexander, included the Turkish Sultan whom he was thus obliged to support against the Christian revolutionaries.

Prince Hypsilanti was easily defeated for he had entirely miscalculated the attitude of the Moldavians. They had no sympathy with the Phanariots and were therefore unwilling to aid his small army. The uprising in Morea, however, was enthusiastically supported by the entire population, and in spite of Turkish military superiority it ended in a Greek victory. A wave of phil-Hellenic sentiment induced the governments of Russia, England and France to intervene on the Greek behalf.

At the battle of Navarino in 1827 the Turko-Egyptian fleet was destroyed, and after a defeat suffered during the war with Russia (1828–29), the Sultan agreed to grant Greece independence. The first King chosen by the great powers was Otto of Bavaria (1833–62) under whom the government of the country fell entirely into the hands of Germans who neither understood nor respected the people they had to rule. They pursued a policy of strict control over the Church and instituted a Synod on the Russian pattern. An early problem was the regularization of relations with the Patriarch of Constantinople. In 1821, as soon as the news of the rebellion reached the capital, the Patriarch Gregory V (1797–98; 1806–08; 1818–21) was murdered by the Turks, together with some 30,000 Greeks. Under such conditions it was difficult to maintain relations with Constantinople and in 1833 the thirty-three bishops of liberated Greece proclaimed the autocephalous status of their Church. The Patriarch Constantius (1830–34), however, refused to sanction this action. A deadlock ensued which adversely affected the status of the Greek church. Meanwhile, the German bureaucracy had grown suspicious of a Church that voiced the anti-foreign feelings of the bulk of the people. The number of bishops was reduced to ten and soon to four, all old and decrepit. Protests led to the arrest of the more vigorous clerics and laymen.

Conditions improved, however, in the second part of the nineteenth century. Reconciliation between Constantinople and the Synod of the Greek Church was achieved in 1852 when the latter's autocephalous status was sanctioned by the Ecumenical Patriarch Anthimus IV (1840–41 and 1848–52). The number of dioceses was increased to twenty-four, and a movement for raising the standard of Christian knowledge and education was started by the people themselves, who remained devoted to the Orthodox Church, in spite of the apostasy of a Westernized minority.

The difficulties encountered by the zealots of Orthodoxy are well illustrated by the story of the Archimandrite Eusebius Matthopoulos (1849–1929), founder of the Zoë brotherhood. He was a remarkable monk who joined a religious community at the age of fourteen and was ordained deacon when he was seventeen. As a youth he came under the influence of several staunch defenders of Orthodoxy like Ignatius Lampropoulos (d. 1869) and Apostolas Makrakis (d. 1905) who boldly opposed the abuses and corruption in their Church. The old evil of simony introduced by the Turks was renewed after the liberation by some Greek politicians and in 1875 a public scandal arose when three bishops were found guilty of obtaining their sees by bribing Cabinet ministers. Makrakis, Eusebius and their friends led the protest against this violation of public morality and ecclesiastical canons, but the Synod of the Greek Church, composed of similarly compromised men, brought the defenders of Orthodoxy to trial and condemned them in 1879 on a false charge of heresy. The new Synod revised this sentence, however, and the three bishops were degraded and the exiled zealots released from confinement in remote monasteries. Eusebius resumed his evangelistic campaign of preaching and teaching all over the country and gained wide popularity. But Apostolos Makrakis, embittered by the episode, refused to recognize the Synod's authority and formed his own sect. This drifted into an unhealthy state of credulous belief in his political predictions based on his interpretation of the Book of the Revelation. Makrakis was endowed with a vigorous and original mind and had an exceptional knowledge of theology, but the self-confidence which led him to assume the role of prophet separated him from the Orthodox Church. After his death in 1905 his sect came to an end, but his writings enjoy considerable popularity and he has many admirers, especially among the Greeks in the United States.

Father Eusebius was as learned and uncomprising as Makrakis, but he was free from self-assertion. He realized that Greek religious progress depended on the co-ordinated efforts of many devout Christians, and with this idea he founded a community of evangelists. The Greek Church owes a debt of gratitude to him for a remarkable institution, the Zoë brotherhood, inaugurated in 1909. It had a noteworthy success, though its full impact was felt only after the First World War.

The Church of Rumania

Russia's victory over the Turks in 1828–29 secured recognition of autonomy to Wallachia and Moldavia, two provinces mainly inhabited by Rumanians. For five years (1829–34) they were under the enlightened government of Count Kiselev, who organized a militia, improved finance and brought order into the administration. The economic prosperity consequent on his reforms encouraged a liberal movement among intellectuals. France, its politics, literature and culture, attracted young Rumanians, and in 1848 a successful revolution secured a liberal constitution for Wallachia, ruled at that time by Prince Guika.

Nicholas I, who acted as self-appointed guardian of reactionaries all over Europe, stepped in and used Russian troops to suppress the liberals. His intervention provoked a conflict with the Turks, who claimed sovereignty over the two Danubian Principalities, and the tension thus created between Russia and the Ottoman Empire was ɔne of the contributory factors to the Crimean War (1853–55). As long as hostilities lasted, the Austrians occupied the Principalities. At the Congress of Paris (February–March 1856), England insisted that Turkish rule of Rumania be restored, but the combined French and Russian opposition prevailed. In 1858, at another Conference of Paris, the Great Powers agreed to allow the Principalities to establish similar constitutions on condition that they remained separate. This artificial arrangement collapsed when Wallachia and Moldavia elected the same man, as their ruler, Prince Alexander Cusa (1859–66). Their fusion in one realm called Rumania was accepted by the Turks in 1862 and England had no choice but to concur.

In 1866 Alexander Cusa was forced to abdicate and was replaced by

Prince Charles of Hohenzollern-Sigmaringan (1866–1914), who in 1881 was proclaimed King. In 1864 the Church of Rumania declared its independence of Constantinople. A land reform in the same year deprived it of many of its possessions, mostly the property of Greek monasteries endowed by the Phanariots, who controlled Church and State in the Principalities up to 1821. In 1885 the Ecumenical Patriarch recognized the autocephality of the Rumanian Church and its canonical position was regularized.

The condition of the Church in Rumania in the nineteenth century was far from satisfactory. An anti-clerical government treated it as a department of the State, the bishops were appointed by politicians and the parochial clergy, recruited from peasants, were looked down upon by the Westernized upper classes. Only towards the end of the century did the Rumanian Church begin to adjust itself. In 1890 a theological faculty was added to the University of Bucharest (founded 1869). The training of priests was improved and the output of Christian literature increased. Like the Greeks, most Rumanians remained deeply attached to the Church and the monasteries continued their beneficent influence though the ruling class had neglected religion.

The Church of Bulgaria
The Bulgarians were the last of the Balkan Orthodox nations to gain independence. Geographically nearest to Constantinople they suffered more than others from the dual oppression by Turks and Phanariots.

The first sign of Bulgarian revival appeared in 1762, when the Monk Paisy published his *History of the Bulgarian People*. By the middle of the nineteenth century schools had been founded which taught the Bulgarian language and propagated the idea of liberation. The other Balkan states had freed themselves from the Turks before rejecting Phanariot control in ecclesiastical administration. In Bulgaria the order was reversed so that when in 1870 the Sultan permitted the Bulgarians to have an independent Church organization the Patriarch, Anthimus VI (1845–48; 1853–55; 1871–73), excommunicated them (September 1872). This act was not approved of by the other Eastern Churches, and the schism between Constantinople and Bulgaria did not cut off the Bulgarian Church from the rest of the Orthodox. Anthimus, Bishop of Vidin, became their first Exarch (1872–88).

This ecclesiastical victory encouraged the Bulgarians to claim political freedom. In 1875–76 an uprising was put down by Turkish irregulars, with much cruelty and bloodshed. Russia came to the rescue and defeated the Turks. The creation of a strong and united Bulgaria was opposed by Britain. The Berlin Congress of 1878 split Bulgaria into three sections: the largest was handed over to the Sultan; Prince Alexander of Battenberg (1879–86) was elected ruler of the central part of Bulgaria; the remainder became a separate State called Eastern Rumelia, which in 1885 after a referendum rejoined the main body. The encouragement given to it caused Alexander's downfall, and Prince Ferdinand of Saxe-Coburg (1887–1918) was elected in his place. The political leader during that confused time was Stefan Stambulov (1887–94), an ambitious and unscrupulous man with radical views on religion and openly hostile to the Church. He met a strong opponent in Clement, Metropolitan of Tirnovo (d. 1901), who firmly defended the freedom and dignity of the Bulgarian Church. Under Ferdinand the country was brought into the sphere of German influence and most Bulgarian theologians went for their studies to Germany and not as before to Russia.

Success and Failure of the Balkan Churches

In every Balkan country the national survival under the Turks was made possible by the Church. The Orthodox Church brought these nations to the threshold of independence but its clergy were unable to maintain their authority in the next period of their evolution. The chief cause of failure was their lack of intellectual preparedness for their new role. Deliverance from suffocating Turkish control opened to the Balkan nations the exciting world of Western civilization, with its conflicting ideas, radical, social and political theories and unrestricted facility for learning and discussion. The young men sent to train in the West eagerly and uncritically absorbed the rudiments of a superior civilization and came back to their own countries with a firm belief in Western ability to provide ready-made solutions to all their problems. They were determined to reshape their own countries in accordance with the most up-to-date Western doctrines. The leaders of the Orthodox Church could not meet this challenge. Some were patriotic and devout men, but hardly any of them had had Western training and their outlook and manners seemed obsolete to politicians educated in Paris or Germany. Even those theologians who had studied abroad and had university degrees (at first rare exceptions) were of little use, for they regarded their own Church as backward and in need of reform.

Russia, which had experienced the same turmoil a century earlier, could not be of much help, for those who understood the situation, like the Slavophils, were made ineffectual by official censorship and the antagonism of the Westernized classes, whilst most Russian intellectuals still copied Europe and the Balkan Christians naturally decided to go to the original source themselves. This wholesale imitation of the West was encouraged by the German Protestant rulers of the Balkans. These potentates had no knowledge of their subjects' history and were alien to the Orthodox Church and its genius.

This division between the Orthodox background and the new imported ideas damaged the growth of Balkan culture. In the nineteenth century it lacked originality and cohesion, for past achievements were forgotten and ignored.* Only after the First World War did the Balkan intellectuals realize that they possessed a tradition of their own with many remarkable achievements.

The Orthodox in Austria-Hungary

The tragic lack of understanding between the Church and the Westernized leaders of the Balkan nations was due to their long isolation from the rest of Christendom. It might have been expected that those Orthodox who were incorporated earlier in the Austrian-Hungarian Empire would have been able to help their co-religionists both culturally and theologically in emerging from the Turkish yoke. They were the Carpatho-Russians, the Ukrainians of Galicia and Bukovina, the Rumanians of Transylvania, the Serbians of Bonat and Voivodina, the Dalmatians and Bosnians. These scattered Orthodox were unable, however, to accomplish this task, being themselves oppressed in their own lands. The Viennese government looked with deep suspicion upon the Balkan national revival, and patronized the Uniates to counterbalance the danger of reunion of its own Orthodox subjects with their fellow Christians outside the borders of a dual monarchy. When it met with strong resistance the government tried to inflame national frictions among the Orthodox. Accordingly, Eastern Christians in Austria-Hungary were divided into several separate ecclesiastical provinces which received different treatment from the State. These were the Serbian Church under the Metropolitan of Karlovci; the Rumanian Church in Transylvania under the Metropolitan of Hermannstadt (or Sibiu); the Church of Bukovina and Dalmatia, which included Rumanians, Ukrainians and Serbians, people of different national and linguistic background; and the Church of Bosnia and Herzogovinia, two provinces annexed by Austria in 1875.

Altogether two and a half million Orthodox were under the Haps-

---

* Serbian medieval architecture is among the finest in the Orthodox world, but the Serbian cathedrals and churches built in the nineteenth century after liberation were second rate copies of a decadent Austrian style.

burgs in the second half of the nineteenth century. Disunited, treated as an undesirable minority, hindered in their cultural and religious activities, these Orthodox were in need themselves of help and encouragement from the Balkan Christians who were culturally less advanced but spiritually more alive than their fellow Christians under the Austro-Hungarian domination.

The most oppressed Church in the Empire was that of Transylvania. Its priests were regarded as serfs; an Orthodox could not be appointed to any government post, and the only escape from the status of a pariah was to join the Uniates. Yet many Rumanians resisted all attempts to induce them to submit to the Pope. In 1810 they succeeded in obtaining their own bishop, Vasilie Moga (1810–46). The conditions attached to his appointment were curiously similar to those governing the lives of the Christians under the Turks. He was forbidden to persuade ex-Orthodox Uniates to rejoin his Church or to prevent any of his flock from going over to Rome. Even if an entire Uniate parish deserted to Orthodoxy, their Church and school would remain the property of the Uniate priest, who retained his stipend. The bishop was particularly reminded that he represented a religion which was not 'received' in Transylvania, although it was the creed of its original inhabitants, and that he could not claim the same rights as the Roman Catholic and Uniate clergy. In spite of everything Bishop Moga rebuilt his diocese on a sound basis and gave his people fresh courage. His successor, Andrey Shaguna (1848–73), was a still greater man. He had received a good education, spoke fluent Hungarian and German and his love of and dedication to his Church and people were such that a number of Uniates returned to Orthodoxy in spite of all its disadvantages, and after one and half centuries of obedience to Rome.

Orthodox status in other provinces of the Austrian Empire was more favourable. They gradually gained the right to erect churches with such visible signs of buildings dedicated to worship as bells, towers and crosses, and with an entrance on the street and not in a backyard.* In 1875 the seminary for the training of priests in Chernovci was reformed and made into a faculty of theology. Until 1848 all instruction was in Latin but later both the Rumanian and Ukrainian languages were introduced.

The most vigorous of all Orthodox communities was the Serbian which came to Austria at the end of the seventeenth century as allies in the war against the Turks, and which, therefore, had retained facilities for worship and instruction denied to other members of the Orthodox

* The Turks imposed the same prohibition upon the Orthodox.

Church. They had their own Seminary in Karlovci and this small city, not far from the Serbian borders, was made the centre of their religious and cultural life.

Towards the end of the century the Orthodox in Hungary and Austria acquired a veneer of Western civilization, but were further removed from their original tradition than their less educated compatriots of the Balkans, who fought for and obtained political freedom to shape their own destiny.

The Russian Intelligentsia and the Orthodox Church

The defeat suffered by the Russian Empire during the Crimean War (1853–55) discredited the militaristic and bureaucratic order which Nicholas I (1825–55) had imposed on the Russian nation for thirty years. Its artificial rigidity was at last ended and his son and successor, Alexander II (1855–81), inaugurated liberal reforms, the most important being the emancipation of the serfs in 1861. This belated change in the social structure of the Empire coincided with the appearance of the intelligentsia, a phenomenon without parallel in the life of other nations. The Russian intelligentsia was neither a social class, nor an intellectual élite, nor a political party. It contained people drawn from all classes, of different standards of education, of opposing political ideas but with certain fundamental convictions, which may be summarized under three headings: that the injustice from which the peasants suffered was a national sin and that the privileged minority was morally responsible for it; that autocracy was an evil which caused economic backwardness and social inequality and ought therefore to be ended; and that the radical political and philosophical theories of the West if applied to Russia were bound to produce immediate improvements in all spheres of life. These principles were accepted with religious fervour which came from the Christian background of the majority of the intelligentsia, although atheism and materialism were regarded as marks of a progressive outlook. These Russian enthusiasts of European radicalism and socialism identified Europe with irreligion.

It was typical that the most popular leaders of the intelligentsia, such as Nikolay Chernishevsky (1828–89) and Nikolay Dobrolubov (1836–61), were sons of priests, and retained a sense of service to a sacred cause when they embraced positivism and nihilism and dismissed Orthodox Christianity as obsolete. The Church's main crime in their eyes was its negative attitude to violence and its unwillingness to fight autocracy with revolutionary weapons. The intelligentsia passionately wanted to uplift the Russian peasants but despised the people's faith and therefore remained misunderstood and mistrusted by the bulk of the population. The left-wing leaders of the intelligentsia believed in automatic progress; they predicted that an ideal social order would suddenly arise out of the bloodshed and destruction of revolution. They therefore concentrated on undermining the political structure of the country without giving thought to the practical consequences of its collapse. Among those few who foresaw the sufferings which would result from the victory of atheistic materialism in Russia was one of the greatest of Russian thinkers and writers, Feodor Dostoevsky.

Feodor Mikhailovich Dostoevsky (1821–81)

Dostoevsky (Plate 66) was a doctor's son, born in Moscow. As a youth he fell under the influence of French Socialism. He was arrested and condemned to death in 1849 for participating in a clandestine society where radical political ideas were discussed. The sentence was commuted and instead Dostoevsky spent four years in a Siberian prison. These terrible experiences altered his outlook and he returned to St Petersburg in 1859 a convinced Christian.

He had met sin in men in its most appalling and revolting forms; he had lived in enforced intimacy with hardened criminals and observed the mentality of torturers and executioners. He was absorbed in the study of evil but was even more fascinated by his experience of the reality of human freedom in the choice between hatred and love. He predicted with the authority of a prophet that mankind was preparing a rebellion against God, on an unprecedented scale, in the name of progress and emancipation. He realized that the muddle-headed and naïve Russian intelligentsia was heading straight for the disaster of despotic totalitarianism. He wrote: 'The preachers of materialism and atheism who proclaim man's self-sufficiency are preparing indescribable darkness and horror for mankind under the guise of renovation and resurrection.'[5]

Amidst the suffering of his Siberian exile Dostoevsky 'met Christ, whom', as he said, 'I learned to know as a child but whom I had deserted when I became a liberal European.'[6] He foresaw that those who rejected Christianity and the Church did so to prove to themselves and to others that men were masters of their own destiny and that no moral power higher than man's existed in the Universe. These 'benefactors' were building a gigantic prison of compulsory uniformity and would show no mercy to those who refused to be slaves in the future totalitarian realm. Men were afraid of freedom, according to Dostoevsky, and eager to exchange it for security and material prosperity. But men could never be truly happy without freedom and therefore having once lost it they would struggle for its recovery, even at the cost of suffering and death.

In his greatest work, *The Legend of the Grand Inquisitor**, Dostoevsky confronts a defender of totalitarianism with Christ. The Inquisitor accuses Jesus Christ of disregarding the frailty of human nature, for men cannot fulfil the self-denying requirements of unadulterated Christianity. The Inquisitor represents himself as the true lover of men who would satisfy their material needs, take the burden of freedom away from them and make them prosperous and happy.

During this passionate diatribe against the teaching of the Gospel Christ keeps a silence so eloquent that *The Legend* is one of the few pieces of world literature, outside the New Testament, that gives a living picture of Jesus Christ.

Dostoevsky was not a theologian in the technical sense of the word. He never used the word 'redemption' but all his writings are based on a profound experience of Christ as the Saviour of mankind. Christ was not, for Dostoevsky, a teacher of wisdom, not an example of high moral conduct; He was truth, beauty and goodness incarnate in perfect humanity. By loving Christ, by clinging to Him, sinful and divided men could recover harmony and integrity. In Christ evil was conquered for in the light of His divine countenance the ugliness of self-centred existence was exposed in its ultimate wickedness.

Dostoevsky found his conception of Christianity embodied in the Orthodox Church. He believed that Russian Christians had a message for the rest of the world and that their community would play a central role in the inevitable conflict between Christian and anti-Christian forces. He predicted that this clash would occur at the end of the century. Dostoevsky's warnings were dismissed by the Russian intelligentsia. He was admired as a gifted novelist but the profound religious intuitions underlying all his fiction were overlooked. Dimitry Merezhkovsky (1865–1941) was the first to introduce Russian readers to this theology. Since that time Dostoevsky has been recognized as the foremost Christian thinker of Russia.

Vladimir Sergeevich Soloviev (1853–1900)

Among the intellectuals of the nineteenth century was one who fully shared Dostoevsky's convictions and who provided them with a solid philosophical basis. He was the most outstanding of Russian philosophers—Vladimir Soloviev (Plate 66).

Soloviev, like Dostoevsky, gave up his Christian faith for positivism

* Included in his novel *The Brothers Karamazov*.

and materialism but soon abandoned these. He studied first science and then philosophy. In his thesis, written in 1874 and entitled *The Crisis of Western Philosophy*, he asserted the need of a synthesis of faith and reason for further progress in creative thinking. Although his approach to philosophy was out of harmony with the outlook shared by his examiners, his ability was such that he was offered an academic appointment and sent abroad to complete his studies. Soloviev was, however, not only a gifted scholar; he was also a visionary and a prophet. During his stay in London, a mystical experience in the Reading Room of the British Museum compelled him to go to Egypt and there in the desert he had the crucial revelation of his life, a meeting with *Hagia Sophia*, the Divine Wisdom. On his return to Russia he gave up his academic career and for the rest of his life he remained a freelance philosopher and an itinerant teacher of wisdom. Soloviev was a poet, a social reformer, an original theologian, a forerunner of the Ecumenical movement but, like Dostoevsky, he was above all a prophet who foresaw the approaching cataclysm in the history of Russia and Europe.

Soloviev was a disciple of the Slavophils and a personal friend of Dostoevsky, but he went beyond them. He was not only critical of the Christian West, as were his predecessors; he realized the vital importance of reconciling East and West, for he was also acutely aware of the defects of Orthodox Christianity. Before his time the Russians either accepted the West as their teacher or stubbornly adhered to their own tradition. Few contemplated the possibility of restoring communion between Rome and the East and if they did thought in terms of surrender by one side to the dictates of the other. Soloviev saw the Church as consisting of three distinct and equally necessary elements personified by the Apostles, John, Peter and Paul. He identified the Gospel according to St John with the contemplative spirit of the Christian East. Rome represented the Petrine tradition of action and leadership. The intellectual and scholarly interests of the Protestants he linked with St Paul and with Pauline interpretation of the Gospel message. Soloviev was an optimist, believing in the possibility of Christian reintegration. He preached the responsibility of members of the Church for the social and economic conditions of mankind and prayed and worked for the victory of charity in relations between Jews and Christians. Though Orthodox he was ready to receive Holy Communion in the Roman Church. He was a lonely figure misunderstood on all sides: but his dedication to the Christian cause, the stimulus of his brilliant writings and his mystical intuitions were such that he was esteemed even by those who disagreed with his ideas.

In 1900 he published a book which seemed to repudiate his previous optimistic conclusions.[7] In the story of Antichrist he prophesied Church reunion, but not as a result of properly conducted deliberations. He foresaw the coming of a world dictator who, under the mask of benevolence and protection, would impose his iron rule on all religions. Only a minority of Christians drawn from diverse confessions would refuse to recognize the dictator as the Great Benefactor of mankind, and persecution would be launched against them till under the pressure of extreme danger the faithful remnant of the followers of the Messiah would relinquish their age-long prejudice and disagreement and restore their unity. This final act of Church history would coincide with the end of the world. Such is the theme of Soloviev's strange book. A spirit of tension permeates its pages. A vision of approaching catastrophe seems to have imposed itself upon the seer and constrained him to contradict his earlier opinions. The picture of Antichrist, the Universal Ruler, is so powerfully drawn that it seems like a realistic portrait and not mere fiction. Soloviev was made the vessel of this revelation but he could no longer endure its burden.

In the preface to his last book, composed at Easter 1900, Soloviev wrote:

'Even in this amended form I still feel there are numerous defects in this work, but the not far distant image of pale death quietly advises me not to put off its publication.'

Soloviev proved to be a good prophet even in his own case. His life ended suddenly on 31st July at the early age of forty-seven. The doctors failed to diagnose his case; his vitality seemed to be exhausted and his organism refused to serve any more. He was homeless all his life, and he died in the house of friends with whom he had found a temporary refuge. His extraordinary personality left an indelible mark upon Russian culture. His enigmatic figure concludes the story of the Eastern Church in the nineteenth century.

CHAPTER SEVEN

THE TIME OF TESTING AND TRIAL

(XX CENTURY)

The Russian Religious Renaissance—Four converts from Marxism to Christianity—Attempts at reform of the Russian Church (1905–14)—Father John of Kronstadt (1829–1908)—The All-Russian Council (18 August–9 November 1917 and 20 January–7 April 1918)—Reorganization of the Eastern Churches after the First World War (1914–18)—The revival of Christianity in the Balkans—The main characteristics of Eastern Christendom in the nineteenth and twentieth centuries—The Communists' godless campaign—The reaction of the Orthodox—The Russian Church in exile and its meeting with the Christian West—The Russian emigrants and the Ecumenical Movement—The present state of the Eastern Church

---

The Russian Religious Renaissance

THE TWENTIETH century brought a marked change in the European cultural and religious atmosphere which was particularly felt in Russia. The excessive utilitarianism and drab materialism of her intelligentsia, their exclusive preoccupation with social and economic problems, their cult of the peasants, faded away, and poetry, art, and religion regained the place of honour denied them in the last decades of the nineteenth century. This artistic and religious renaissance began among the intellectual élite in the two capitals of St Petersburg and Moscow, but it spread rapidly and on the eve of the First World War the younger generation of the Russian intelligentsia had moved away from the belief that Darwinism solved the mystery of creation and that materialism was the last word in enlightenment. Positivism was no longer accepted as dogmatic truth and was replaced by an intense search for other philosophic viewpoints. A desire to understand the symbolic language of Christianity became fashionable and brought some leaders of the intelligentsia into the Orthodox Church; others embraced Occultism and Theosophy or were satisfied with their own mystical intuitions. Poets like Alexander Blok (1880–1921), Andrey Biely (1880–1935), Viacheslav Ivanov (1886–1949), writers like Dimitry Merezhkovsky (1865–1941), Vasily Rozanov (1856–1919), composers like Alexander Scriabin (1871–1915), painters like Mikhail Vrubel (1856–1910), V. Vasnetsov (1848–1942), Michail Nesterov (1862–1942), Nikolay Reirih (1874–1947) and Vasily Kandinsky (*d.* 1944)[1] were all pre-occupied with religious problems and their approach to art was in sharp contrast with the moralistic and didactic tendencies of the older generation. The renewed interest in Christianity facilitated personal encounters between the intelligentsia and leaders of the Orthodox Church, the two sections of Russian society which had lost contact with each other.

In 1901, on the initiative of Merezhkovsky, his wife Zinaida Hippius (1869–1945), and of V. M. Skvortsov (1859–1932), a lay theologian and a keen missionary, regular and successful religious meetings were started in St Petersburg. The clergy and professors of the Theological Academy discussed with writers and noted intellectuals such questions as the mission of the Church, and its dogmas and ethics. It was an entirely new experience for both sides, for the intelligentsia had previously treated such problems as outside the realm of its concerns. Similar societies were organized in Moscow and in Kiev. The spiritual and cultural revival owed much to Vladimir Soloviev who thus achieved posthumous popularity. The poets regarded him as their master, the philosophers studied his works, the theologians became aware of the importance of his ideas.

Among his disciples the most notable were four ex-Marxists who at the beginning of the century abandoned materialism and atheism and joined the Orthodox Church.

Four converts from Marxism to Christianity

They were Piotr Struve (1870–1944), Sergey Bulgakov (1871–1944) (Plate 69), Nikolay Berdiaev (1874–1948) and Simeon Frank (1877–1950). Their conversion was an event of the first importance, a turning point in the evolution of the intelligentsia. In the nineteenth century there had been severe critics of the intelligentsia but most of them were political conservatives and their criticisms were therefore brushed aside.

This time the campaign against materialism was opened by recognized and respected members of the intelligentsia, by four philosophers and economists, who had acquired the reputation of being able exponents of Marxism, the latest doctrine borrowed from the West and accepted as a panacea for all social and economic evils. The desertion of these prominent men profoundly affected the temper of the intelligentsia. The old guard of radicalism was alarmed but younger people welcomed the stimulating ideas in the writings of these philosophers who in 1909, with several friends, published a symposium *Vehki* (*Signposts*) which provoked heated controversy. In five months six editions of the book appeared. Readers were impressed by its underlying unity though the authors did not see each other's articles before they were printed. Their main theme was the logical contradiction between social utopianism, which confidently expected economic justice, peace and prosperity to be achieved all over the world, and the belief that the universe was the outcome of blind physical forces and biologically dependent on a struggle for the survival of the fittest. The contributors to *Vehki* insisted that the hope of a moral organization of society rested on the belief that the cosmos had an author, and a purpose intelligible to men. Christianity was the most progressive force in the evolution of mankind for it gave the assurance that moral effort and aspiration were in harmony with the will of the Creator, who had revealed his design for the Universe through the life, death and resurrection of Jesus Christ. The symposium called the intelligentsia to return to religion, to give up terrorism as a legitimate political weapon and to recognize that disregard of the Christian code could only lead to revival of that enslavement to the despotic state from which men had been liberated by Christ. *Vehki* reiterated Dostoevsky's prediction that atheistic egalitarianism would bring about tyranny on an unprecedented scale. The weight of these warnings was augmented by their authors' intimate knowledge of Lenin and other exponents of Marxism, who had been their associates, and by their familiarity with the philosophical and economic theories according to which the communist social order was to be planned. The ex-Marxists had arrived at their conclusion after hard and long inner struggles in the course of which they had rejected atheism as a false interpretation of reality and embraced Christianity as the only satisfactory solution of life's mystery.

These former revolutionaries did not however surrender their intellectual freedom. On the contrary, they joined the Church intending to resume their campaign for a better social order and in the hope of seeing the Christian community released from bureaucratic control. Their expectations were justified. The Russian Church started to move away from the fixity which marked its life in the nineteenth century.

Attempts at reform of the Russian Church (1905–14)
Russia's defeat in the war against Japan (1904–05) led to open expression of popular discontent with bureaucratic inefficiency. Nicholas II (1894–1917) made concessions to public demands for greater freedom. One of the laws promulgated in 1905 guaranteed religious equality to all citizens of the Empire and offered the right of self-government to religious associations. The Russian Church alone had no share in the benefits. Count Witte (1849–1915), the initiator of these liberal reforms, recognized this anomaly and entered into negotiations with the Metropolitan of St Petersburg, Anthony (Vadkovsky) (1899–1912), with a view to securing greater liberty for the Orthodox. The Metropolitan

responded warmly to the offer and sent a memorandum to the Government suggesting improvements in ecclesiastical administration. This document when published broke the long silence imposed upon the Orthodox by State control. The revival of Church autonomy was demanded in all parts of the country. Even the bishops, carefully selected from the more obedient clergy, openly manifested a desire for far-reaching reforms. On 23rd March 1905, the members of the Synod sent a petition to the Emperor for a convocation of Church Council and the restoration of the Patriarchate. Nicholas II expressed his approval and, as a preliminary step, a commission was set up to prepare the council's programme. A careful questionnaire was sent out to all the bishops asking their opinion on the best ways of improving Church life. Their replies and minutes of the preconciliar committee were published in 1906 and are valuable material in illustrating the state of the Church on the eve of dissolution of the Empire. A remarkable feature of these documents is the unanimity with which the leaders of the Russian Church repudiate the order which had governed their lives for two hundred years. Only two diocesan bishops out of sixty-two did not advocate its abolition. The preconciliar committee included no defenders of the Synod. The question was, what organization should replace it? The Conservatives favoured restoration of the Patriarchate, the Liberals wanted something more democratic.

The news of the forthcoming liberation of the Church was enthusiastically received all over the country and newspapers and magazines devoted much space to discussions of the prospective reforms. These bright expectations were not fulfilled, however. The Empire founded by Peter the Great refused to release the Church. The urgently needed improvements were indefinitely postponed under various pretexts, and in the last years of the Empire's agony the ecclesiastical administration was further degraded, for it fell under the influence of Grigory Rasputin* (1872–1916), a peasant from the Urals who had gained a reputation for holiness in Court circles. It was a time when many false teachers and prophets attracted admirers and moral laxity was widespread; but the same period saw a strong revival of genuine Christianity, manifested in the appearance of a number of outstanding theologians like Fr Pavel Florensky (1882–1949), M. M. Kareev (1866–1934), V. Nesmelov (1863–1920), Metropolitan Antony (Khrapovitsky) (1863–1936), and of Christian philosophers like Prince Sergey Trubetskoy (1862–1905) Prince Evgeny Trubotskoy (1863–

---

* Rasputin is often mistakenly described as a monk. He was a married man and had two children.

1920), V. Ern (1879–1919) and N. Novgorodtsev (1863–1927). As the Russian Church neared the time when it would be put to its severest test, the grace of the Holy Spirit became abundant. Among charismatic Christians a special place belongs to Father John of Kronstadt.

Father John of Kronstadt (1829–1908)

Fr John Sergiev (Plate 67) was for many years Dean of the cathedral in the Russian naval base guarding the approaches to St Petersburg. He acquired a nationwide reputation for his exceptional healing gifts and his power to change the hearts of men. He could cure the sick even at a distance when requests for help reached him by letter or telegram. His crowded services were attended by people from all parts of the country. Fr John revived frequent communion among his followers and used public confession of sins as a means of conversion. He was also an excellent organizer and created a number of philanthropic institutions, which housed and provided employment for several thousand people in need of assistance (about 8,000 in 1902). His diary, entitled *My Life in Christ*, has become one of the most popular devotional books and is translated into many languages. Another priest of rare spiritual insight was Alexey Mechev (*d.* 1923). He had an exceptional gift of helping people to know themselves. In the years of the First World War and at the beginning of the Communist revolution his prophetic insight attracted crowds to his services. Nikolay Berdiaev visited him before his expulsion from Russia by the Communists in 1922 and was greatly comforted by Fr Alexey's assurance that his exile was providential and would offer him an opportunity of spreading widely his Christian message. Fr Alexey had never been outside Russia but he accurately diagnosed both the spiritual condition of Europe between the two world wars, and the response which Berdiaev's message would evoke among Western Christians.

The All-Russian Church Council (18th August–9th November 1917 and 20th January–7th April 1918)

In February 1917 the Empire collapsed in the middle of the world war. The liberal provisional government failed to maintain its authority and growing anarchy soon paralysed military operations and civil administration. In those months of chaos and privation the only constructive force was the Church. It was reorganized on a proper canonical basis and the most valuable reforms were achieved by the All-Russian Council. The speedy convocation of this Council was the work of the last Procurator of the Synod, Professor Anton Kartashev (1875–1960). He was appointed in July 1917 and at once gave up the title associated with subjugation of the Church. As Minister of religion he offered every possible assistance to the Church in bringing the bishops and other representatives together. The Council met in Moscow on 15th August 1917. It included all that was best in the Russian Church among clergy and laity. In spite of the anarchy preceding the Communist uprising in October 1917, which established Lenin's dictatorship, hostile to the Church, the Council accomplished a number of far-reaching reforms; the Patriarchate was restored and Tikhon (Beliavin) (1866–1925) was chosen (31st May 1917). Self-government was revived and central and diocesan organs of administration were established. The success of the Council was remarkable, for its members showed wisdom and maturity in their judgment when the rest of the nation, especially its political leaders, had lost all sense of proportion. The vitality and strength of the Russian Orthodox was proved by their ability to devise the proper constitution of the Church under the most unfavourable conditions of the civil war and after two centuries of subjugation to bureaucratic control by the Empire.

The Council was also the triumph of those leaders of the intelligentsia who returned to the Church before the outbreak of the Revolution, trusting in its constructive force. The outstanding man of this group, Professor Bulgakov, was elected to the supreme Church Soviet, instituted as a permanent organ of administration by the Council. Thus the necessary reconstruction of Church government was completed precisely at the moment when the Communists began their campaign against all religions.

Reorganization of the Eastern Churches after the First World War (1914–18)

The First World War caused the collapse of four empires, the Russian, German, Austrian and Ottoman. Their disappearance led to drastic changes in the life and destiny of all Eastern Christians.

To deal first with the Orthodox of the Byzantine rite: the Patriarchate of Constantinople, which included some eight million Christians before 1914, was reduced to some 80,000 Greeks resident in Constantinople; the Greeks remaining in Asia Minor were expelled from their ancient homes after the Turkish victory over the Greeks in 1922. The leaders of the Turkish Republic consented only under foreign pressure to allow the Ecumenical Patriarch to retain his residence in the Phanar and imposed many irksome restrictions on his movements. The Greeks of Rhodes and some other neighbouring islands and the Greeks of the

Diaspora, especially numerous in America, continued to recognize him as their spiritual head. These Greeks outside Turkey added some 500,000 to his flock. The Patriarch of Alexandria became a subject of independent Egypt; his jurisdiction extended over all Greeks in Africa and comprised some 120,000.

The Patriarchate of Antioch had its territory divided between the two republics of Syria and Lebanon. Some 280,000 Orthodox Arabs were left under his supervision, of whom 100,000 were scattered all over the world, the dioceses of North and South America containing the majority. The Patriarchate of Jerusalem suffered from the disturbing conflict between the Arabs and Israel. Most of its 50,000 people were Arabs, but the Patriarch himself and the leading clergy were all Greeks and this created friction and discontent.

The autocephalous Church of Cyprus (360,000) retained its status as did the smallest of the Orthodox Churches, that of Mount Sinai (300). The largest, that of Russia, restored its Patriarchate in 1917 and disappeared soon after from the scene of international relations, cut off from the rest of the world by the Communists.

The collapse of the Russian Monarchy revived the autocephalous status of the ancient Church of Georgia (2,500,000) which had been absorbed in the Russian Church at the beginning of the nineteenth century after the incorporation of Georgia to the St Petersburg Empire.

Five new autonomous Churches came into existence as a result of the Communist Revolution: the Orthodox Churches of Poland (4,500,000), of Finland (70,000), of Lithuania (55,000), of Latvia (160,000), of Estonia (250,000). Some of them accepted Constantinople as their Ecclesiastical Supervisor, others remained nominally linked to the Russian Church. Uncertain of their allegiance were the Church of Japan (40,000) and the Russian Orthodox Church in North America (1,500,000).

The Church of Greece greatly increased its numbers by the influx of refugees from Asia Minor. In 1910 it had two million, after the First World War six million. A vast extension in territory and numbers also took place in the Churches of Serbia and Rumania. The Serbian Church became a Patriarchate (in 1920) and absorbed the Church of Montenegro and the Serbian dioceses in Austria and Hungary. Its members mounted from 2,300,000 (1910) to 7,000,000 (1925). The Rumanian Patriarchate included the Orthodox of Wallachia, Moldavia, Bessarabia, Bukovina and Transylvania. In 1910 the Rumanian Church counted 4,550,000; after the War 15,000,000.

The Church of Bulgaria also grew but less than the others for the Bulgarians were twice defeated, in the Balkan War of 1912 and in the First World War. In 1910 their Church was 1,500,000 strong; its membership in 1924 had risen to 5,000,000.

The Albanian Church acquired autocephalous status in 1922 and numbered some 215,000 members.

Another Church came into being—that of Carpatho-Russia in Czechoslovakia. This isolated branch of the Russian Church had accepted Union with Rome in 1652. Several attempts by some of these Uniates to return to the Orthodox Church were treated by the Austro-Hungarian Government as political treason. When their land became incorporated in the Czech Republic, some 200,000 of the Uniates became Orthodox while some 500,000 remained under Rome.

No less important changes took place among the Oriental Orthodox. The worst fate befell the Armenians. During the war they were completely exterminated by the Turks in their own land and only those who happened to live in Constantinople survived. The Church in Soviet Armenia was at the same time exposed to Communist oppression. Nevertheless, that vigorous race continued to cling to its national Church, which numbered some 3,000,000 members in 1930.

The Copts of Egypt (900,000) and the Monophysites of Ethiopia (8,000,000) continued as before in their isolation, stubbornly opposing any deviation from the forms of Church life unchanged since the Middle Ages. The Syrian Orthodox Church of Travancore, on the contrary, showed signs of revival. The educational standard of its clergy was much improved, missionary work started and its representatives took an active part in ecumenical work and entered into contact with the Orthodox of the Byzantine tradition, with whom they had never been in touch before. These improvements, however, caused a split in 1908 in its ranks. The more conservative section remained under the control of the Syrian Jacobite Patriarch resident in Homs but the more progressive party, led by the Catholicos Gevarguese, rejected this tutelage and asserted its right to self-government. Each branch had at that time some 500,000 members. In 1959 both sides were at last reconciled. The Jacobites of Syria continued to decline in strength and numbers. From 400,000 they were reduced to 80,000 after the war. The Nestorian or Assyrian Church suffered even more grievously. After proclamation of Iraq's independence in 1920, the Mohammedans massacred their Christian compatriots. Out of 200,000 in 1910, only some 70,000 survived as fugitives from their own country. Their spiritual head, Mar

Shimun, was expelled and found a temporary refuge in England, later moving to the USA.

In general terms one may say that those Eastern Christians who remained under the control of Islam continued to decline, whereas those who secured freedom displayed considerable vitality in spite of manifold obstacles and trials.

The revival of Christianity in the Balkans

The main problem confronting the greatly enlarged Balkan Churches was to amalgamate Christians who for centuries had lived under diverse political and economic systems and developed their own characteristics. Some of these Christians had only recently emerged from Turkish oppression; others had a century's experience of independence; others had been for longer or shorter periods incorporated in Austro-Hungary. Rivalry, suspicion, misunderstandings were inevitable; the Orthodox from Austria looked down on others as less cultured; the clergy drawn from independent states claimed priority in Church Government for they had won their freedom by a hard struggle, whilst the rest had been liberated without the sacrifices and dangers of rebellion.

These clashes in ecclesiastical circles were aggravated by political conflicts in the newly-formed states which brought some of them to civil war, as in the case of Jugoslavia under German occupation (1940–44). But in spite of everything, these Christian communities were able to start work in earnest for the moral and religious education and improvement of their nations. Their efforts towards spiritual renewal took various forms, but all aimed at securing a wider and more responsible participation of the laity in the life of the Church, at reviving its missionary spirit and raising the standard of pastoral work among the clergy.

In Greece the renewal was associated with several missionary movements including the Zoë brotherhood of theologians and preachers. In 1938 the society had some eighty members, the majority lay theologians (only twelve were in Holy Orders) devoting all their time to preaching and teaching. Most had theological degrees, all were celibates and held all possessions in common. If they desired to marry, they might still work but were no longer treated as full members. The brotherhood organized Sunday schools (298 schools with 30,500 pupils), published popular religious literature, a magazine Zoë (circulation 76,000) and was responsible for catechitical instruction. All work was voluntary. No subsidies were accepted from outsiders. The new methods introduced by Zoë at first aroused suspicion and its activities were several times examined by the Synod. It finally received full approbation in 1923. Its success was such that other, similar societies have been formed under direct control of the Synod.

The Zoë brotherhood is a typical example of an unofficial Orthodox movement. Lay members of the Eastern Church have a strong sense of responsibility for the life and work of their community.

A similar movement started by ordinary peasants greatly improved the life of the Serbian Church. It began after the end of the First World War among soldiers returned from captivity. In the prisoner-of-war camps they had learned to read the Holy Scriptures together and to discuss religious questions. They continued to do so in their villages, bringing others into their study circles. This movement was spontaneous and at first had no recognized leader (the clergy kept aloof from it) but was Orthodox in teaching and spirit. It acquired a nation-wide significance when it attracted the attention of the most remarkable Bishop of the Serbian Church, Nikolay Velimirovich of Ohrid (1880–1956) (Plate 68), who consented to lead the movement. A powerful preacher and an original thinker, he was able to speak both to the learned and to the simple. Under his inspiring guidance, the Bogomolci, as they were called, stirred and renewed the life of the Serbian Church. One of their important contributions was the annual convention usually held near a famous monastery which attracted large numbers of pilgrims. In consequence, the religious vocation among women was revived. This had died out in the Balkans under the Turks but in the post-war years a number of convents were founded in Serbia. They were directed at first by Russian nuns who came as refugees to Yugoslavia, but the Serbians later assumed responsibility for them; several have even survived under the Communists.

A more complex movement known as the Iron Guard was started in Rumania between the two wars. It acquired a strong political colouring. Its main supporters were young men and women including university students. These Rumanians reacted sharply against that secularism of the West which had been so fashionable among older educated Rumanians, who despised their own culture and religion, and treated emancipation from the Orthodox Church as a mark of inclusion in the circle of civilized people. The Iron Guard regarded Church membership as the sign of true love and understanding of Rumania. The political bias of the Iron Guard towards Fascism compromised the religious value of the movement and diverted it from its original purpose of strengthening and purifying the life of the Rumanian Church.

The rise of National Socialism in Germany brought about a crisis in the political life of the Balkan people. Their sympathies were with the Western democracies but they found themselves caught between Communists and Fascists. The Second World War left all Balkan countries except Greece behind the Iron Curtain. The Communists after gaining power avoided direct attack on the Church and followed the example of Stalin's post-war policy, allowing the Church to maintain its organization on condition it complied with the law prohibiting religious propaganda.

The main characteristics of Eastern Christendom in the nineteenth and twentieth centuries
During the two last centuries the Russian Church was a dominant factor in the life of the Eastern Christians. It was not only a much larger body greatly exceeding in numbers all other Orthodox put together but it was also the recognized partner of a mighty Empire whilst the rest lived either under an oppressive rule of non-Orthodox, or were divided between small states.

The main problem for Eastern Christians during that period was the disintegrating impact of Western civilization which captured the imagination of the younger generation. Their desire to copy Europe led them to a critical and even hostile attitude towards the Orthodox Church, dismissed as part of the old, obsolete order. The defenders of Orthodoxy among the Westernized section at first were few. They increased markedly however towards the end of the period. Here again Russia occupied the key position, the most fanatical atheists and the most convinced defenders of Christianity could be found among her people. The battle between godlessness and religion which took place in Russia after the collapse of the Empire was an event surpassing the limits of Eastern Christendom. The Communist dictatorship pressed the Eastern Christians into the front line of a world-wide conflict and thereby ended that isolation of the Orthodox which had affected their life and thought during the past millennium. The Christian East and West once more became partners in the great adventure of building up a universal Christian order. The story of the contest between the Communists and Russian Christians provides one of the central themes in religious history of the twentieth century.

The Communists' Godless Campaign
The Communist attack on Christians, liberals and fellow-socialists in 1917 came as a shock to the majority of the Russian intelligentsia. Yet Vladimir Ulianov-Lenin (1870–1924), the indisputable head of the

Party, acted in exact conformity with the predictions of the authors of *Vehki*. He was not only convinced that he possessed the secret of human happiness; he was equally sure that he alone was able to bring felicity and prosperity to mankind and that, therefore, it was his revolutionary duty first to silence and later to eliminate altogether all those who had other ideas about the ultimate purpose of human life. Lenin realized that his most radical opponents were the Christians who saw the world and humanity in an entirely different light from dialectical materialism. He felt a deep personal aversion to God and never missed an opportunity of deriding the believers. In his eyes it was he, Lenin, not Jesus Christ who was the Saviour of mankind.

Lenin's passionate belief in the absolute truth of his doctrine has been unreservedly accepted by the Communists. The uncompromising opposition of the Party to Christianity reflects faithfully its founder's convictions. This determined enmity has been further exacerbated by a number of ideas which Christians and Communists share, but which they interpret in different ways. The notion of evil, for instance, is accepted by the Communists, but is identified with economic exploitation. Sin is understood as the support of the Capitalist order; providence as the law of progress defined by dialectical materialism. The Saviour of mankind is the Party which under the direction of its inspired leaders alone can secure to men the bliss and security of a classless society. The belief in these dogmatic statements excludes the possibility of a peaceful co-existence between Christianity and Communism and the history of the Church under Soviet rule reveals the persistent attempts of the Government to suppress all Christian influence. The tactics of the Communists can vary considerably and their frontal attacks have often been followed by intervals of temporary appeasement, but the Party leaders have never given up their final object of making dialectical materialism the only acceptable outlook for people under their control. As far as Russia is concerned, the Communist campaign against the Church three times reached the highest degree of intensity—this happened in the years 1918–23, 1929–32 and 1937–39. On all three occasions the Communists hoped to annihilate Christianity altogether, but each time they failed in their object and were obliged to retreat.

The first attack was planned and executed by Lenin himself. In his original optimism he expected to destroy the Church by one stroke and he issued in quick succession a number of drastic decrees against the Christians. On 4th December 1917, all Church property was confiscated; on 11th December all theological schools were closed; on 18th

December civil marriage was made obligatory. On 23rd January 1918 all these hastily promulgated revolutionary orders were incorporated in an anti-religious law aiming at undermining the material foundations of religious associations and at depriving them of any power to maintain order and discipline.

As a materialist, Lenin believed that people belonged to the Church either because they obtained some material benefit from it (the clergy) or because they were ignorant and obsessed with superstitions and fears (the laity). He was confident that the self-evident truth of his own teaching would without any difficulty defeat Christ and His Gospel and Lenin allowed therefore both religious and anti-religious teaching and propaganda. It came as a shock to the Communists to realize that the destruction of the Church was a much more difficult task than they had anticipated. There were some Christians, including priests, who publicly renounced their religion and, encouraged by the Government, the mob profaned some churches and murdered several bishops and priests. But in general Communist decrees produced results the very opposite of those Lenin expected. They consolidated the Church by relieving it of unstable members and thus increasing its vitality and power. The early years of Communist rule indeed witnessed a religious revival.

This unexpected resistance forced the Communists to use more brutal methods. The Patriarch Tikhon was imprisoned in 1922, whilst the Metropolitan Veniamin of Petrograd (1917–22), who was especially popular among the industrial workers, was executed together with some of his clergy. These measures were accompanied by an attempt to divide the Church by the Communist-sponsored so-called 'Living Church Movement' (1922–26), which attracted several ambitious bishops and priests who hoped to secure control of the Church with the help of the Party. This weapon of schism failed however; the vast majority of clergy and people remained faithful to the Patriarch and 'The Living Church' dwindled to nothing in spite of State protection.

The Patriarch died on 25th March 1925. His popularity was enormous; a hundred thousand mourners took part in his funeral, which was conducted by sixty bishops and hundreds of clergy. It was the striking manifestation of the people's devotion to the Church. The Government, alarmed by the undiminishing vitality of the Church, refused permission for the election of Tikhon's successor and started the systematic arrest and deportation to concentration camps of trusted priests and bishops. But Lenin's death in 1924, and the struggle for the control over the Party that followed, brought a temporary relaxation in the pressure of the anti-religious campaign, and for the next two years both people and Church enjoyed comparative freedom.

The second frontal attack was launched in 1929. This time it was conducted by the new dictator, Iosif Vissarionovich Djugashvili-Stalin (1879–1953). The Communists no longer misconceived the strength of Christian convictions. They realized that intellectual arguments were not adequate to combat belief in God and that therefore the best chance of eliminating religion was by complete prohibition of Christian teaching. The law published in April 1929 made it a criminal offence to preach the Gospel, to argue against materialism and atheism, or to make any attempt to bring any one into the Church. The only activity still allowed to believers was gathering together for worship. Each group of worshippers was treated as an isolated unit, which could continue its existence on condition that twenty people signed a document expressing their desire to pray in public. Those who did so exposed themselves to the secret police and were usually gradually arrested.

The Law of 1929 marked a Christian victory. The omnipotent Communist State, in complete control of all means of propaganda, education and instruction, was obliged to impose compulsory silence upon Christians, who were already deprived of press, schools and literature and yet remained undefeated in debates and discussions. The years 1929–32, the years of enforced collectivization and mass deportation of the peasants, witnessed the wholesale closing of churches and the exile and imprisonment of the parochial clergy. But the famine and general dislocation of economic life caused by collectivization obliged the Communists to make a halt in their anti-religious campaign. Stalin's constitution of 1936 even granted the right of citizenship to ministers of religion, a right that had previously been denied them.

The last and fiercest attack on the Church was made in 1937–39. These were the grimmest years in the history of the Communist State; thousands of people were uprooted and banished to the extreme north and Siberia; the army, the party, and the remnants of the intelligentsia were exposed to constant purges; spying and denunciation reached unheard of proportions. Fear and despondency brought almost all manifestations of organized Church life to a standstill. On the eve of the Second World War many careful foreign observers were under the impression that the Communists had succeeded in intimidating and demoralizing Church members to the extent that religion had been effectively destroyed, especially among the young, brought up in schools giving compulsory anti-religious instruction. The war dispelled this illusion. In 1941–42 the major part of European Russia was overrun by the Germans and as soon as the Communist pressure against religion was removed, the people spontaneously reopened their Churches. This took place all over the country and it happened in spite of twenty years of relentless efforts to exterminate Gospel teaching. Everywhere people disregarded the privations of the German occupation, repaired the buildings, unearthed the sacred vessels, recovered concealed service books, formed choirs and induced the clergy to resume their office. The figures for the important diocese of Kiev speak eloquently of the determination of the Orthodox to revive their Church life at the first opportunity:[2]

	1917 (Before the Communists)	*1939* (Under Stalin)	*1942* (A year after the temporary suspension of Communist rule)
Churches	1,710	2 (?)	616
Monasteries	23	–	8
Monks and Nuns	5,193	–	387
Priests	1,435	3	889
Deacons	277	1	21
Cantors	1,400	2	387

Christian faith proved so strong that Stalin was obliged to retreat from his uncompromising position and in 1943 he allowed the election of a Patriarch. The Metropolitan Sergy (Stragorodsky, 1861–1944) was chosen by the surviving bishops. On his death, Alexey (Simansky) became his successor (plate 71). Further concessions were soon made. The training of the clergy was resumed and eight seminaries and two theological academies were opened. Such theological books as had escaped destruction were returned to those schools and religious communities were recognized (before the War they existed probably in secret). A number of Churches were restored for religious use and a monthly Church periodical appeared in Moscow. The law of 1929 was not abrogated, however, and Christian propaganda remained still a criminal offence; but the right to worship, which, though legally guaranteed, had been practically denied to Christians between 1937–39, was no longer challenged. The victory which the Russian Church thus achieved was won neither by the strength of its organization nor by inspired leadership but by the faithfulness of countless men, women and even children who persisted in their love of Jesus Christ.

The reaction of the Orthodox

The Communists miscalculated the strength of the Church and have been obliged to stop their direct assaults against the believers. Now their hope of ultimate victory rests on the systematic re-education of the masses so as to persuade them of the falsehood of Christian teaching. The Christians have also been forced to learn by their mistakes and to revise their policy. At first many of their leaders regarded the Communists as criminal adventurers who had by accident established a temporary hold over the nation. The Patriarch Tikhon had issued on 19th January 1918 an edict of excommunication directed against those who profaned churches, blasphemed and murdered the faithful. This excommunication had held no terrors for those who had discarded all belief in God. Only gradually did both sides come to realize that the struggle would be hard and lasting.

In the course of the various stages of the anti-religious campaign four distinct attitudes towards the Soviet Government emerged among the members of the Church. First, uncompromising repudiation of the Communists as the enemies of Christ and his Church and a consequent refusal to have any dealings with the government. Secondly, recognition that there was substantial agreement between the Communist and the Christian ideas of social order and therefore an offer of collaboration with the Party. Thirdly, insistence on a clear cut separation between the Church and the State based on non-interference in the internal affairs of each other. Fourthly, acceptance of Communist rule as the legitimate form of government and submission to its political control on condition of being allowed to keep intact the Orthodoxy of doctrine and worship.

The first and the second points of view were held only by minorities. The uncompromising Christians usually ended their lives in concentration camps whilst the collaborators were unable to secure the Communists' support and were therefore rejected alike by both sides.

The majority of the Orthodox took one of the last two views. They had in common the conviction that the Church had to face the fact of the Communist order and to refrain from any political opposition to the Government. This was not a policy of opportunism, but the outcome of the belief that every State exists with the sanction of God, who is the ultimate ruler of the universe. The disagreement between the two parties in the Church centred on the amount and character of State control which could be legitimately accepted in return for the legal recognition of the Church.

Metropolitan Sergy Stragorodsky was one of the leading exponents of the fourth point of view and when the Communists came to the conclusion that the existence of the Church had to be recognized, he was elected Patriarch. His policy of acceptance of the Communist control over the Church except in the spheres of teaching and worship was followed by his collaborators after his death.

The Soviet Government created a special State department to deal with religious affairs. All matters related to the opening of churches, to their repair, to taxation of clergy, and to the general supervision of Christian activities are its responsibility. The Communists do not interfere in an open way with the inner life of the Church, but the Religious Regulations published in 1945 make it obligatory for every holder of an ecclesiastical office from the Patriarch to a parish priest to be registered with the Communist authorities before he can exercise his function. (§§ 16.26.48.) The government has a right to refuse a registration or to cancel it after it has been granted.

This means that neither the Patriarch nor a diocesan bishop can make any appointment without ascertaining beforehand that the suggested candidate is acceptable to the Communists. This is a compromise on both sides; the hierarchs are restricted in their choice, but the Communists are also obliged to register a certain number of clergy in order to make possible the continuation of organized Church life.

The status of religious associations in other Communist-controlled countries is based on the same principles, although it is usually more liberal than in the USSR; and in some countries, like Poland for example, even the Christian instruction of children is permitted, although only by persons duly registered and approved by the Communist authorities.

The struggle between Christianity and Lenin's doctrine of dialectical materialism is not yet over. The Communists have the advantage of a monopoly of education and they are able to exclude the Christians from all leading positions, but they rely upon obsolete scientific theories in support of their claims that science has proved the eternity of matter and the non-existence of God. They fear and mistrust freedom and refuse to the Christians the right to defend by argument their religion, and this is their main weakness.

The Christian cause suffers from the artificial restrictions imposed upon the activities of the Church, from the lack of intellectual freedom and from the exclusion from its leadership of men considered too independent by the Communists. Its strength lies, however, in the truth of its teaching and as far as the Russian Church is concerned, in the Eucharistic experience of its members, which assures them of divine love and of the reality of their fellowship with the risen and ascended Christ.

218

The Russian Church in Exile and its meeting with the Christian West
The years 1918–22 were a time of civil war in Russia. After the military defeat of the anti-Communist forces, a great exodus took place; more than a million people were driven into exile. These fugitives were of diverse nationalities, creeds and political opinions, but the majority of them belonged to the Russian intelligentsia. The hardship of life outside their own country and the bitterness of defeat altered their outlook. Many of them recognized the truth of the warnings in *Vehki*, which had predicted that godless Communism, for the victory of which Westernized Russians had laboured, would bring not equality and freedom but ruthless dictatorship. Political disillusionment helped many to find their way back to the Church, which became the centre for the colonies of Russian exiles, particularly numerous at first in the Balkans, France and Germany.

The younger generation of the intelligentsia had begun this return to Christianity even before the Revolution, but the process was hastened by the emigration. Members of the Russian Church in Exile were confronted with many difficult tasks: they were able to organize Church life without political interference, but they were handicapped by uncertainty, poverty and social degradation; they wanted also to help their harassed co-religionists in Russia; and they were obliged to define their attitude to Western Christians among whom they had to live and work. Different solutions of these problems divided the Russian emigrants. The most conservative, led at first by the Metropolitan Antony (Khrapovitsky, 1863–1936) and after his death by the Metropolitan Anastasy (*b.* 1873), seeing the Church as the natural ally of the Monarchy, thought they ought to struggle for the revival of the Empire. Convinced that their views prevailed also among Christians in Russia, they assumed the right to speak in the name of the whole Russian Church. They were suspicious of and even hostile to Western Christians, whom they blamed for failing to organize a crusade against the godless Communists.

The majority of the Russians were opposed to these extremists. Their leader for a long time was the wise Metropolitan Evlogy (Georgievsky, 1864–1946) appointed by the Patriarch Tikhon in 1921 to preside over the Russian Church in Western Europe. This central section considered that membership of the Church did not commit a Christian to any particular political views and they deprecated the claims of any group to speak in the name of Christians in Russia. In order to protect itself from Soviet interference, this party accepted in 1931 the Ecumenical Patriarch as its ecclesiastical superior who reappointed the Metropolitan

Evlogy as his Exarch. These Russians wished to establish more cordial relations with Western Christians and took an active part in the Ecumenical movement.

The third group remained faithful to the Church in Russia and, as soon as the Patriarchate of Moscow was restored in 1943 recognized him as their superior. Their attitude to the West was therefore partially conditioned by that of the Head of the Russian Church.

The clashes and tensions among these three groups disturbed the life of the Church in Exile but also bore witness to its vitality. One evidence of this was the distinguished work of a number of theologians and writers who have become famous for their original and vigorous thought. Foremost among them were the above-mentioned ex-Marxists, who after many adventures met again in Western Europe. Three of them, Bulgakov, Frank and Berdiaev, were expelled from Russia in 1922; Struve escaped to the West with the remnants of the White Army. To these names other Christian leaders must be added: Lev Karsavim (1882–1952), Anton Kartashev (1875–1960), V. Zenkovsky (*b.* 1885), G. Florovsky (*b.* 1893), G. Fedotov (1886–1951), Konstantin Mochulsky (1892–1948), B. Visheslavtsev (1877–1954), Vladimir Lossky (1903–1958), L. Zandes (*b.* 1893), and others who contributed to the spiritual and intellectual life of the exiled community. They were gifted men equally familiar with both Russian and Western European culture and able to interpret them to others.

The endeavours of the Russians in exile to help their co-religionists under the Communists were defeated. The Iron Curtain completely cut them off from their own country and people and only on rare occasions could even an exchange of news be attempted.

The organization of independent Church life in Western Europe and in America was more successful, although political tensions hindered progress. The exiled Russians made their most valuable contribution to the Ecumenical Movement and to theology, including Christian interpretation of social and economic changes brought about by the Communists.

The Russian emigrants and the Ecumenical Movement

The arrival of Russians in the West coincided with the beginning of the Ecumenical Movement, the idea of which was conceived within the Anglican communion and was warmly supported by most Protestants. The Movement aimed at including all Christian confessions; its purpose was to re-examine doctrinal differences in the hope of removing some obstacles by impartial and scholarly investigation, and to promote practical co-operation between divided Christian bodies. At first two independent organizations were started: the Faith and Order Movement, dealing with the doctrinal side of reunion; and the Life and Work Movement, with its social and economic implications. Between them they held a number of conferences (Stockholm 1925, Lausanne 1927, Oxford 1937, Edinburgh 1937, Amsterdam 1939 and 1948). In 1948 they amalgamated to form the World Council of Churches.

The Russians in exile played an important part in this work. The need for their participation was all the greater for two limitations affecting the Movement. The first was the refusal of the Roman Church to join; the second the unreadiness of the Christian East to give full support. These two facts made the Ecumenical Movement one-sidedly Protestant, Anglo-Catholics and Old Catholics representing a minority. The Russians in exile, although unable to speak officially in the name of their Church, nevertheless voiced the tradition of the Christian East and by their active interest in the Movement partially restored the balance. Besides participation in the Faith and Order, and Life and Work conferences, and numerous commissions, they also established fruitful relations with the World Student Christian Federation and with the Young Men's Christian Association. The main agents for these unofficial contacts were the Russian Theological College in Paris, St Sergius's Academy founded in 1925; the Russian Student Christian Movement started in 1923 and the Fellowship of St Alban and St Sergius inaugurated in 1927. The Russians who supported these three organizations were convinced members of their Church who, however, saw the West neither as their enemy nor as their superior, but as a partner whose gifts were complementary, and on whose co-operation the fullness and richness of Christian life and thought depended.

This new spirit of mutual trust was inspiring. The Christian East, in the person of these Russians, for the first time since the fifteenth century was not on the defensive. It was meeting the West on equal terms and this in spite of the fact that their Church seemed to be crushed by the Communists. These Russian Orthodox were confident that the Christian faith would triumph again in their country and this gave them strength to bear the hardships of exile and to speak with authority and frankness to their Western friends. The Christian West soon recognized their significance and offered them generous assistance. The Theological College in Paris and the Student Christian Movement were helped by the World Student Federation, the YMCA and other similar organizations, Anglicans in particular being generous and faithful supporters of these Russian institutions. The outstanding spokesman of the American

YMCA, John R. Mott (1865–1955), was the first who realized the intellectual and spiritual value of the exiled Russian theologians and secured funds to publish their works. The YMCA Press enabled these Russian thinkers to appear in print. Their books were later translated into many European languages. This literature, created at a time when silence was imposed on Christians in Russia, will sooner or later reach their compatriots who have been deprived of freedom of thought and speech for several decades in their own country.

One of the least expected consequences of the Russian exile was the conversion to Ecumenical work of the famous Abbé Couturier (1881–1953), a Roman Catholic Priest from Lyons. He met the Russians in 1923 when forty-two years old, and this encounter reorientated his interest and made him one of the most remarkable leaders of work for Christian reconciliation.

The Russian emigrants lost their country but not their Church; the complete freedom of action they enjoyed made possible their constructive contribution to the rest of Christendom by increasing mutual understanding between its divided members.

The present state of the Eastern Church

It is too early to make any detailed comment on the new period in the history of Eastern Christians which began after the Second World War. Two features are, however, sufficiently clearly marked to be mentioned. Firstly, the close identification of Church and people which had been one of the main characteristics of Eastern Christianity has ended, and the Church is becoming aware of its separateness. Secondly, the fear of the West that has haunted the Christian East since the fall of Byzantium has gone. The Orthodox in recent years have been exposed to the extreme pressure of Western materialism and atheism as represented by Marxism and they have survived. This victory has given them a renewed confidence in the vitality of their faith.

The trust in freedom as the best ally of truth which was so ardently preached by the Slavophils is a new experience for most Eastern Christians and promises much closer and friendlier relations with the Christian West, for a fruitful co-operation among the divided Christians depends on their repudiation of any form of compulsion and intimidation and on confidence in the guidance of the Holy Spirit.

So in spite of the present hardships and severe trials the Eastern Christians look with sober confidence to their future, believing that the good news of reconciliation contained in the Gospel is alone capable of satisfying the deepest religious needs of mankind and that no other teaching can ever replace the Christian revelation about the true nature of God and man.

In conclusion it may be useful to outline briefly the present state of Eastern Christians. They belong to two federations of self-governing Churches. The majority follow the Byzantine tradition in faith and worship, but the minority still reject the Chalcedonian Council and form the Oriental Churches. The Byzantine Orthodox are sub-divided into some twenty Churches, some large and influential, others small and poor, but all enjoying equality of status and freedom in self-government. No decision can be made in the name of the Orthodox Church unless approval is unanimous. There is no effective organ which co-ordinates their actions, but their unity is real and they usually display unanimity on all major issues. Their inter-Church relations reflect that sense of freedom and mutual responsibility which is a marked characteristic of the Christian East.

Five of these Churches have retained the titles and the territory which was theirs under the Byzantine Empire. These are the Patriarchates of Constantinople, Alexandria, Antioch and Jerusalem and the Church of Cyprus. The Ecumenical Patriarch of Constantinople (Plate 70) occupies the place of honour among the heads of autocephalous Churches of the Byzantine Federation. Today his flock is confined to Constantinople alone, for the Turkish government does not allow Greeks to live anywhere outside that city. The Patriarch, however, also exercises his jurisdiction over the Greeks in Diaspora, and Greek bishops in Europe and America recognize his authority. He is supposed to look after the general interests of the Orthodox, and to take the initiative in any discussions of wider interest than those relevant to a national Church.

The Patriarch of Alexandria is next in seniority and his congregation is composed mainly of the Greeks resident either in Egypt or scattered over Africa. In recent years some 20,000 negroes of Uganda have joined the Orthodox Church under the Patriarchate of Alexandria.

The Patriarch of Antioch, now resident in Damascus, the Syrian capital, takes third place. His people are the Christian Arabs, originally domiciled in Syria and the Lebanon, but now also scattered over the world. They are particularly numerous in North and South America.

The Patriarch of Jerusalem has only 50,000 Christians. Most of them are Palestine Arabs, but he is elected from the small group of Greek monks who form the Brotherhood of Custodians of Holy Places. There has been a long-standing conflict between these Greek monks and the

Arab Christians, and every election is usually a contested affair creating much bad feeling and mutual incrimination.

In addition to these four Patriarchates, the Church of Cyprus, which was not included in any of them in Byzantine time, still retains its autocephalous state. There is also the monastic community of Sinai in the Arabian desert, which has at its head an Archbishop, and also claims independence.

All these Churches with their Byzantine past enjoy their prestige, but are now circumscribed by adverse conditions. Their membership has dropped, their learning has declined, and their vitality has been sapped by long submission to Islam. They represent the former glory of Byzantine Christianity, but the real strength of the Eastern Church exists today in five leading national Churches, four of which are presided over by the Patriarchs. These are the Churches of Russia, Rumania, Greece, Jugoslavia and Bulgaria.

There are four more Orthodox Churches which enjoy complete independence, but are smaller than the great national Churches. These are the Church of Georgia, the Church of Albania, the Orthodox Church in Poland and in Czechoslovakia. Thus there are fourteen autocephalous Churches in the Federation of the Byzantine Orthodox. Most of them call their senior hierarch 'Patriarch'; others prefer such names as 'Catholicos', 'Metropolitan' or 'Archbishop'. The prerogatives of these presiding bishops vary in different Churches, but in most cases they act as constitutional monarchs and are expected to consult other bishops and the representatives of clergy and laity before taking any decision.

Besides these Churches there are other members of the Orthodox Federation which, because of their limited numbers, or comparatively recent origin, still depend on other Churches, and although they also enjoy degrees of autonomy, they are not yet entirely self-sufficient in their administration. Such are the Churches of Finland, in Japan, China and Korea, and the Orthodox Churches in North and South America, South Africa, Australia and Western Europe.

As a description of the internal organization of an autocephalous Orthodox Church, the present constitution of the Bulgarian Church is here included.[3]

This Church is divided into eleven dioceses, each presided over by a bishop with the title of Metropolitan. A diocese is subdivided into smaller units called vicariates, composed of parishes. The supreme legislative authority in the Bulgarian Church belongs to the National Council, composed of all bishops and the elected representatives of clergy and laity. Current Church administration in its religious aspects is delegated to the Synod of bishops alone. The Patriarch or presiding bishop is elected by the National Council from three candidates selected by the Synod. A candidate must be a bishop with at least five years' previous experience in administrating a diocese and one not less than fifty years of age. The successful candidate must obtain two-thirds of the votes. He is elected for life and becomes a permanent president of the Synod.

Besides the Synod, the Bulgarian Church has another supreme administrative organ dealing with the financial and practical affairs of the Church, consisting of two clergy and two laymen. They are elected by the National Council for four years. The Patriarch presides over the session of this supreme ecclesiastical soviet. The diocesan administration is in the hands of a Metropolitan in consultation with a diocesan council, which has four elected members, two clerics and two lay. A Metropolitan is chosen by a special electoral college consisting of an equal number of clergy and laity. The list of candidates is drawn by the Synod and from it two persons must be elected. The Synod has the final choice of one of these. An elected Metropolitan retains his title and diocese for life.

The parochial clergy are elected by their parishioners. Parish councils, composed of four to six members, assist the clergy in their administration of a parish.

The constitution of the Bulgarian Church reveals the main principles of ecclesiastical organization of Eastern Christians. Its structure is hierarchical and at the same time democratic. Bishops, parochial clergy and representatives of the laity all have their specific responsibilities and functions. Church leaders are elected, not nominated. It is a self-governing body, but on all major issues, especially those connected with doctrine and worship, the Bulgarian Church acts in agreement with other autocephalous Churches, adhering strictly to the general tradition of Eastern Orthodoxy.

The constitution of other Orthodox Churches follow the same pattern, but under different political conditions they often have to modify their ecclesiastical laws and adapt themselves to the temper of secular governments.

The approximate numerical strength of Eastern Christians today is as follows:

(a) The fourteen autocephalous Churches of the Byzantine Orthodox:
   1. The Ecumenical Patriarchate of Constantinople:

Greeks in Constantinople	80,000
Greeks outside Turkey	500,000

2. The Patriarchate of Alexandria	150,000
3. The Patriarchate of Antioch	280,000
4. The Patriarchate of Jerusalem	50,000
5. The Patriarchate of Moscow, which includes the Churches of the Ukraine, White Russia, Galicia (ex-Uniates), Lithuania, Latvia, Estonia and Carpato-Russia (probably)	100,000,000
6. The Patriarchate of Yugoslavia	9,500,000
7. The Patriarchate of Rumania (including the ex-Uniates of Transylvania)	15,000,000
8. The Patriarchate of Bulgaria (since 1946)	6,000,000
9. The Catholicate of Georgia	3,000,000
10. The Church of Greece	8,500,000
11. The Church of Cyprus	400,000
12. The Church of Albania	250,000
13. The Church of Poland	350,000
14. The Church of Czechoslovakia	150,000
To them must be added the Church of Sinai	300

(b) The four Autonomous Churches:

1. The Church of Finland	75,000
2. The Church in Japan	40,000
3. The Church in China	20,000
4. The Church in Hungary	40,000

(c) The five Churches being organized:

1. The Churches in North and South America and Alaska	3,000,000
2. The Church in Australia	75,000
3. The Church of the Ukrainians in USA and Canada	100,000
4. The Church in Korea	15,000
5. The Russian Church in exile under the Metropolitan Anastasy	50,000

Altogether there are 150,000,000 Orthodox of the Byzantine rite. Besides these there are 21,000,000 Oriental Orthodox comprising 4,000 Armenians, 2,000,000 Copts, 14,000,000 Ethiopians, 1,000,000 Orthodox Indians and 80,000 Jacobites in Syria and Lebanon. There are in addition some 5,000,000 Uniates and some 5,000,000 Old Believers in Russia; in all, some 180,000,000 Christians form the Eastern wing of contemporary Christendom.

CHAPTER EIGHT

THE FAITH AND DOCTRINE OF THE ORTHODOX CHURCH

The significance of doctrine in the East—The authority of the Church in the East—The Holy Scripture and Church tradition—The Communion of Saints—Canonization of Saints among the Byzantine Orthodox—The Mother of God—Prayers for the departed—The Eucharistic doctrine

WHATEVER THEIR nationality or culture, all Eastern Christians feel they are members of one community, and do not doubt their religious experience is the same. A strong sense of uninterrupted continuity makes them conscious of close kinship with the saints, martyrs and teachers of all ages. In spite of this, they feel separate from the Christian West. Both Roman Catholicism and Protestantism seem alien and defective. In the past a static conception of the Church encouraged both East and West to interpret differences in teaching, worship and customs as wilful, and therefore heretical departures from the Apostolic tradition.

There is at present a marked revision of this intransigent attitude: Christians have recognized that the Church is subject to growth and change within a context of many non-theological elements such as national temperament, political, social and economic conditions. A chief cause of the difference between East and West lies in the fact that Byzantine Orthodoxy grew up in the setting of Greek speech and culture and that the Roman ecclesiastical and doctrinal system sprang from the Latin mentality. In striving towards universal uniformity as a guarantee of truth, Christians failed to realize that the message of the Gospel can reach people only through their own language. God speaks to all men, but each one hears that voice in his own tongue. Every language is a powerful medium, both shaping and shaped by the outlook and personality of its users, and carrying in its vocabulary and grammar, the collective experience of innumerable generations—a distinct philosophy of life. Certain ideas clearly expressed in one language cannot be conveyed at all in another. Some notions change their meaning when translated by seemingly equivalent words.

Latin, with its logical precision, its concision, is ideal for formulating and dogmatizing. In Greek, with its much richer vocabulary and more complex grammar, finer shades of meaning can be expressed, but its subtleties may confuse. Greek is the language of philosophers and dialecticians, of men who enjoy intellectual speculations. It is essential to remember that even the same words like Catholic and Orthodox acquired different meanings in the context of Greek and Latin. The word Catholic, as used in the West, means universal. It brings out the idea of unity and even uniformity. The Catholic Church is a body obeying one head, and adhering to the same ritual and language. *Catholon* in Greek has a much wider range: integrity, wholeness, harmony of diverse parts; it is opposed to every form of onesidedness, sectarianism, exclusiveness. The Catholic Church signifies for the Orthodox a community distinguished by unity in freedom and creating out of many races and nations the family of the redeemed. The Slavonic text of the creed renders the word Catholic by the word *Soborny*, from the verb *sobirat*, to gather together. The Catholic Church is the 'gathered' Church, offering to each member opportunities for self expression and welcoming his special contribution. Catholicity has always been associated in the East with the use of the vernacular in worship, in the West with Latin as the universal tongue of the one Church.

It is significant that the Roman Catholics refer to the Church always in the singular in their liturgy. The Orthodox pray in their litanies 'for the peace and good estate of the Holy Churches of God', using the plural. For them the Catholic Church consists of many self-governing communities united in faith but independent in their administration.

Similarly the word Orthodox in the West is understood as 'correct' or 'generally approved' and is applied especially to doctrine. In Greek *doxa* stands for both teaching and worship. In Slavonic Orthodoxy is rendered by the word *Pravoslavie*, meaning 'true glory'. When a Russian, Serb or Bulgarian calls himself an Orthodox Christian he means he belongs to the community which praises and glorifies God in the right spirit. Orthodoxy in the East represents a balance between teaching and worship, prophecy and sacrament, faith and works.

An equally significant difference is associated with the Western term 'sacrament', and Eastern *mysterion*. 'Sacrament' has legal associations: it can be valid or invalid. The very term encourages its users to produce clear logical definitions of the character of each sacrament and of the benefits derived from taking part in them. The correct form of administration has also acquired primary importance.

The word *mysterion* (*tainstvo* in Slavonic) underlines the mystical element, that side of the divine-human encounter which eludes rational analysis, and regenerates soul and body without disclosing the *modus operandi*.

Even the Latin word *corpus* (body) is not identical with the Greek word *soma*, which can only be used of a living organism. *Corpus* can also be applied to inanimate objects and institutions. When the East associates the word 'body' with the Church, it thinks in terms of a living community created by the action of the Holy Spirit. The West adds the idea of the Church as an institution, either legally established or voluntarily promoted by the joint efforts of its members. The difference in the use of this key-word has had far-reaching practical consequences. The West has always tended to organize the Church along political lines; the absolute monarchy of Rome clashes with the republican independence of many Protestant sects. The East sees the Church as a Eucharistic fellowship, whose structure has no parallel in any secular association.

The study of these linguistic divergencies and of their impact on the doctrinal development is still in its preliminary stage. A considerable contribution to it has, however, been made by the Russian theologians in exile. Their participation in Ecumenical work has led to important discoveries especially as to the difference in Eastern and Western approaches to the relation between community and individual and between matter and spirit.

The West, starting from the individual, sees the community as the outcome of a collective desire to live and act together. For the East the community comes first and the individual is seen as a part of the whole. Matter and spirit are clearly distinguished in the West and at times even opposed to each other. For the East matter is spirit-bearing. The theology of both halves of Christendom has been coloured by these fundamental convictions and this to a large extent contributed to the disruption of their initial fellowship.

Before analysing the concrete instances of their disagreements it is necessary to point out the underlying unity of the Christian East and West. They accept the same scriptures as the authoritative source of their teaching; the entire East and the largest section of the West jointly confess faith in Jesus Christ as Incarnate Lord and Saviour, and worship One God in three Persons, the Trinity; the vast majority use the Nicene creed as the best summary of their common belief.* They both regard the sacraments, especially Baptism and the Eucharist, as indispensable parts of the Christian ordinance and teach that man survives his physical death.

This unanimity in essentials throws into relief their lack of unity concerning those theological statements wherein the Western individualism and the corporate spirit of the East are expressed. The first

---

* The only difference in the creed is the *Filioque* clause added to the original text by the West in the seventh century. See page 89 *et seq.*

divergency deserving attention affects the place of doctrine in the life of the community.

The significance of doctrine in the East

For the Orthodox the Church is primarily a worshipping community. Its main task is to praise the Creator and to teach its members to glorify Him in the right spirit. The very word Orthodoxy, so loved by Eastern Christians, exalts this function of the Church. This emphasis on worship in turn affects the importance assigned to different types of doctrinal definitions. They belong to three classes, dogma, theologumena and theological opinions.

The Eastern Christians consider that nothing which has not some direct bearing upon divine worship need be dogmatically defined. The confession of faith is for them a part of doxology. Dogmas safeguard the trinitarian vision of God and the truth of the Incarnation and are enshrined in the Creed and in the dogmatic definitions of the Ecumenical Councils. There is a marked difference here between East and West. The Western doctrinal systems include such items as the constitution of the Church, the nature of man, of sin and grace, and the ways of salvation. All these problems are, for Eastern Christians, in the sphere governed by theologumena, by the statements made by venerated teachers of the Church, and accepted by others; they have not, however, the same authority as dogma. But even theologumena do not provide the Orthodox with answers to all the doctrinal problems, many of which are open to free theological opinion where direct opposition arises at times among Church members. An instance of this is the much debated question of the status of Western Christians and the character of the sacraments administered by the heterodox confessions. On these points the Orthodox Church has reached no unanimous decision, whilst veneration of the Holy Theotokos, although not defined dogmatically, is sanctioned by the universally accepted theologumena about her unique position in the economy of salvation.

It is in the sphere of theologumena and theological opinion that East and West usually part company. Among other problems they also disagree as to the seat of Church authority, the comparative merits of scripture and tradition, and as to the Latin dogma of Transubstantiation in the Eucharist.

The authority of the Church in the East

In the East the authority of the Church is diffused among its members. In the West it has a definite source, the Pope, the Bible, the Articles of

Religion. The difference between these two views was well expressed in an exchange of letters between Pius IX (1841–1878) and the Eastern Patriarchs. In 1848 a reply to the Papal Encyclical, signed by thirty-one Eastern bishops, including three Patriarchs, was sent to Rome. They declared:

'The Pope is greatly mistaken in supposing that we consider the ecclesiastical hierarchy to be the guardian of dogma. The case is quite different. The unvarying constancy and the unerring truth of Christian dogma does not depend upon any of the hierarchical orders; it is guarded by the totality of the people of God, which is the body of Christ.'[1]

This answer deals with one of the major controversies of Christian history, the prerogative of the Roman see. The Pope, who had always been the senior bishop, has become to Latin Christians the final judge on all questions of doctrine and morals. The non-Roman West has rejected his authority altogether and transferred it to the inspired text of the Bible or to the official teaching of the individual confessions. The East has never fully grasped the implications of this essentially Western dispute, for it has adhered to a conception of authority in which there is no place for special sources of infallibility. Father Sergy Bulgakov, an eminent Russian divine, stated the Orthodox teaching in this way:

'Does any member of the Church possess of himself infallibility in his judgment of dogma? No, he does not; every member of the Church is liable to error, or rather to the introduction of his own personal limitations in his dogmatic studies.'[2]

Bulgakov explains this attitude by saying that for the Christian East neither the hierarchy nor the councils are organs of infallibility:

'Only the Church in its identity with itself can testify to the truth. It is the Church which agrees or not, with the council. There are not, and there cannot be, external forms established beforehand for the testimony of the Church about itself.'[3]

This type of corporate authority does not contradict the hierarchical structure of the Eastern Churches. The bishops and the priests have their clearly defined sacerdotal functions and are also responsible for the day to day ecclesiastical administration and for maintaining sound

Christian teaching. Local and general councils and synods are periodically convoked but none can claim infallibility. Their decisions require endorsement by the whole community if they are to be recognized as the voice of the One Holy Catholic and Apostolic Church.

The Holy Scripture and Church tradition

Trust in perpetual guidance by the Holy Spirit is the source of Orthodox reliance upon tradition. It implies fidelity to the past, for the Holy Spirit has taught the truth to the bygone generations of Church members who bequeathed their heritage to their successors; but it also means readiness to go forward, to experiment, to engage in new adventures. Professor G. Florovsky defines the tradition thus:

'Loyalty to tradition means not only concord with the past but in a certain sense freedom from the past. Tradition is not only a protecting, conservative principle, it is primarily the principle of growth and regeneration . . . tradition is the constant abiding of the Spirit, and not only the memory of words. Tradition is a charismatic, not an historical principle.'[4]

The Holy tradition does not compete with the Holy Scriptures, but both contain the same truth, for they have the same author, the Holy Spirit, who inspired the writers and compilers of books of the Bible and opened the minds of Church members to a true understanding of the Word of God.

Eastern Christians firmly believe that the Church has always been, and always will be protected by divine power and that so long as Christians remain within the Eucharistic fellowship they will be able to distinguish truth from error. This stress on mutual love as an indispensable condition of communion with the Holy Spirit explains the Orthodox attitude to the Saints.

The Communion of Saints

Every Christian is called to perfection, and is capable of revealing the image of God hidden in him. Only a few, however, become so transformed during their earthly life through willing co-operation with divine grace that they can be recognized as saints by other Christians. Their charity, wisdom and charismatic gifts of healing and prophecy are of immense assistance to other less advanced members of the Church. These, the saints, are the bearers of the authentic tradition, for it is not learning or ecclesiastical honours, but purity of heart and mind that makes a Christian capable of hearing the authentic voice of the Holy Spirit.

Eastern Christians, in both public and private prayers, ask the saints to pray for them and they pray for the saints. This uninterrupted communion with the victorious representatives of past generations, which begins with the Old Testament patriarchs and prophets, and includes the apostles, the eye-witnesses of the Incarnation, the martyrs, teachers and holy men and women of all nations throughout the centuries, makes Eastern Christians deeply rooted in Orthodoxy and offers them protection from heresy and schism. They test novel teachings or practices by considering how they harmonize with the lives and faith of the saints. All that might separate Christians from fellowship with the saints is rejected, all that can enrich it is welcomed.

The question is sometimes raised whether this devotion to the saints might divert attention from the worship of God; whether it might create an opinion that the saints can help better than God can.

The Orthodox do not regard the saints as mediators, but as teachers and friends who pray with them and assist them in their spiritual ascent. Jesus Christ during His earthly ministry was surrounded by disciples who did not prevent others from meeting Him, but on the contrary helped newcomers to find the Master. In the same manner fellowship with the saints facilitates communion with God, for their Christlike character brings others nearer to the divine source of life and light. All mankind is involved in the process of deification and the saints are those who, having advanced nearer to the ultimate goal, can uplift the rest.

Canonization of Saints among the Byzantine Orthodox
The names of those who rejoice in fellowship with their Creator are known only to God. The Church on earth remembers few of the saints, mostly those who struck their contemporaries' imagination and whom in consequence their fellow Christians gratefully and lovingly remember. Canonization of a saint is recognition by responsible Church leaders that such a remembered Christian, in his life and teaching, accords with other saints and may therefore be invoked in public prayers, and his acts and opinions used as an example for imitation by others. Canonization in the Orthodox Church begins locally. Its first requisite is continuous and increasing love and veneration for such an outstanding Christian by members of his community. The next step is reached when the hierarchy of a local church undertakes to examine all records left by the holy man or woman, and if these prove satisfactory, then the last part of the act is performed and canonization is announced and other

autocephalous churches are informed. This considered judgment of the Church is essential, for sometimes people of exceptional spiritual gifts, but not necessarily of sound moral life and Orthodox faith, attract admiration and can mislead their followers. The Holy Spirit not only illuminates the holy men and women, but also reveals who are the chosen vassals of His Grace to other members of the Church.

The Mother of God

Among the saints a unique place is reserved for the Mother of God—the Virgin Mary. The long process of purification and enlightenment of the Jewish race so vividly described in the Old Testament reached its culmination in the Theotokos. In her the faith and heroism of many generations of the Chosen People found fulfilment. She accepted with humility the challenge of the Annunciation. During the lifetime of her Son she kept in the background, but she presided over the assembly of apostles on the day of Pentecost, when the new period in the history of mankind was inaugurated by the descent of the Holy Spirit. 'Warm veneration of the Theotokos is the soul of Orthodox piety,' writes Fr Bulgakov.[5] Her name is constantly invoked in both liturgical and personal prayers, she is loved, not only as the Mother of Christ, but also as the Mother of mankind, for she embraces in her charity the entire human family, of which her Son is the sole Redeemer.

Her ikons can be seen everywhere, the hymns and prayers addressed to her are universally used, but the Christian East refrains from dogmatizing on her behalf and here again a difference is revealed between the Latin and the Byzantine traditions, for the Christian East has not included the recent Marian pronouncements of Rome among its dogmas.

The prayers for the departed

The Christian West has been inclined to speculate about the destiny of the departed. Roman Catholics have elaborated doctrines which imply that Christians, after death, pass through an intermediary state of purification before they can come into the divine presence. Many Protestants have rejected this teaching and believe that bliss or torment awaits each man after his death, and no further alteration in his condition is possible.

Eastern Christians have never been attracted to these clear-cut answers to the mystery of death. Their underlying conviction is that the end of physical existence closes only one stage in human ascent towards God, and that the seeds of good and evil sown on earth continue to bring forth fruit long after the death of the individual. The final reckoning can be made only at the end of history. So even the blessed do not reach their full glory immediately after death and those who failed to learn how to love in freedom are not deprived of the possibility of improvement in their position through the compassion of their friends. So the Orthodox Church prays for all the departed, both saints and sinners, trusting in the power of mutual love and forgiveness. It is reluctant to subscribe to the Roman doctrine of Purgatory as a place of pain and expiation, for it believes that a merciful God washes away the transgressions of all who sincerely repent and have been reconciled to the Church.

The Eucharistic doctrine

The final point of doctrinal difference is connected with the Eucharist. The Roman West has defined the form, matter, effect and ordinary ministry of each sacrament. Concerning the Eucharist it has elaborated the doctrine of Transubstantiation, which explains the change in the Eucharistic elements in terms of Aristotelian philosophy which distinguishes the substance of every material object from its external manifestation, such as colour, weight and smell. The Roman Church teaches that at the Eucharist the substance of bread and wine is replaced by the substance of Christ's Body and Blood, but that to our senses their appearance remains unaltered and the Eucharistic gifts continue to look and taste as bread and wine.

Most Protestants, in opposition to Rome, have formulated their own Eucharistic doctrines, such as Consubstantiation, according to which the communicant, while receiving bread and wine, partakes simultaneously of the Body and Blood of Christ.

The Orthodox do not share this desire for precision in approaching the mystery of the Holy Communion. They ask God to change the bread and wine into the Body and Blood of the Saviour, but are reluctant to define either the character or the exact moment of this change.

The increased importance given to the Eucharist which is noticeable in all confessions today, has extended their understanding of its meaning and purpose, and has mitigated the bitterness of the controversies that have raged in the past around the sacrament of unity and love. East and West are today much nearer to each other in sacramental theology and in practice, than at the time of their separation.

Such are some of the doctrinal differences between the Eastern and Western Christians. Their roots go deep down into their corporate experience and psychology. Western man has always been more confident than his Eastern counterpart in the power of human reason to penetrate into the mystery of life, and to define with precision the relations between Creator and creation. Hence the labours of Western divines in constructing elaborate theological systems, aiming at providing authoritative answers to a number of questions raised by inquiring minds. Hence also the usual distinction between the trained theologians and the laity who are supposed to accept without question the statements of their teachers.

The entire theology of the West is more rational, more abstract and more authoritarian than that of the East. The East stresses the transformation of the whole human being, of his restoration to the original prototype and the enlightenment of mind and heart which accompanies man's rebirth in Christ through the action of the Holy Spirit. This transfiguration brings men into new and more personal fellowship with the Triune God, but however intimate their communion, the divine essence remains impenetrable to the human mind, since the Eastern emphasis on apophatic or negative theology, insists that we can only say that God is beyond all our definitions and speculations.

This, however, does not exclude the Eastern desire to understand the nature of man, of the world which surrounds him and of the ways leading to his deification; but all these speculations have no claims to final authority, and therefore the Byzantine Churches have always refused to identify Orthodoxy with any one teacher, system of theology or institution, the path chosen by Rome, by Oriental Christians such as Nestorians and Jacobites, and by conservative Protestants. Orthodox theology, therefore, is experimental, rooted in the Eucharistic worship, linked organically with prayers and asceticism, and consequently close to the heart and mind of all Christians. A sharp line of demarcation between trained theologians and lay people has never existed in the East. The Orthodox consider that the real distinction lies between those members of the Church who grow in holiness and wisdom, and those who remain absorbed in self, and are therefore incapable of sharing fully the life of grace offered to the faithful of the Christian community.

This difference in approach is significant, and its consequences can be traced in the social and devotional life of Eastern and Western Christians. It does not destroy, however, the unity of their faith in Christ and the acceptance of the universal truth of his message.

In the past these disagreements among Christians were exploited by controversialists, and antagonisms were encouraged, whilst the possession of substantial common ground was seldom recognized. Today an

increasing number of Christians begin to realize that the distinct confessions can be seen not only as rival systems, but also as complementary
approaches to the same religion, and that the true progress of
Christianity depends not on the suppression of diverse traditions by any
one of them, but upon the willingness of the divided members of the
Church to enter into fruitful collaboration and friendly discussions with
one another.

CHAPTER NINE

WORSHIP AND SACRAMENTS IN THE
CHRISTIAN EAST

Holy Communion—The Sacraments of the Eastern Christians—Baptism—Confirmation—Confession—Holy Unction—Ordination—Marriage—Other sacramental rites—Offices of the Eastern Church—The Liturgical Books used by the Eastern Christians—Some reasons for the difference between Eastern and Western approaches to Christian worship

EASTERN CHRISTIAN worship differs considerably from that of the Christian West. The architecture of the churches, their interior decoration, the shape of the liturgy, the position of the clergy and the conduct of the laity are all features dissimilar in East and West.

Churches in the East are usually small, and are either round or built in the form of a Greek cross. The most distinctive feature is the *Ikonostasis*, a solid screen with three doors, dividing the eastern end from the rest of the building. Behind the central, or 'Royal' door is the altar, called the 'Throne', which is only visible when this door is open (Plate 59). When during the service the doors are closed the clergy are not visible to the congregation. The laity participates in the service by supporting the prayers said by the priests and deacons, with reverent gestures, bows and frequent use of the Sign of the Cross. Sometimes they join in the singing, but usually the choir represents them. The services are dramatic, vocal and colourful, processions are formed and the clergy come in and go out through the doors of the screen, magnificent vestments are worn, incense is constantly used, children, even infants in their mother's arms are communicated with adults: Eastern worship lacks the precision and restraint of the West, but conveys a powerful impression of the reality of the divine presence and stimulates mystical union between God and man.

The ritual of the Eastern Churches is the product of a long and complex evolution; yet it is much nearer the services of the early Christians than is the case in the West, and for this reason may be described as more primitive or archaic. Orthodox worship has three channels of expression: the chief one is the sacrament of Holy Communion (alternatively described as the Eucharist, the Mass, the Divine Liturgy or the Lord's Supper), the second one is the administration of other sacraments, the number and the purpose of which are differently defined by the Orthodox and the West, and, finally, various types of public offices,

238

not sacramental, consisting of reading the Holy Scriptures and singing hymns and psalms.

Holy Communion

Eastern Christians usually refer to their Communion Service by the Greek word *Eucharist* (Thanksgiving). This most sacred act of Christian worship commemorates the Last Supper which Jesus Christ shared with His disciples on the night of His betrayal by Judas. The evening meal which preceded the culminating events of Christ's mission was not an ordinary supper, but a ritualistic feast in which the Jews remembered *in East,* their miraculous deliverance from bondage in Egypt. The Eucharist therefore, links His blessing of the bread and wine with the mighty deeds of God, who led his people into the Promised Land.

All Eastern liturgies faithfully adhere to this two-fold character of the service, although differing considerably in detail. Most scholars distinguish four main types: (i) The Western Syrian or Jacobite; (ii) The Eastern Syrian or Chaldean; (iii) The Coptic and Ethiopian; (iv) The Byzantine and Armenian. Each of these groups includes several rites. Altogether nearly one hundred versions of the Communion Service are still used by Eastern Christians. Yet in spite of this all Eastern Eucharists follow the same basic pattern differing in several important points from the parallel development which in the West culminated in the Roman Mass. For example, the Eastern Eucharist is celebrated at the altar which is partially concealed from the congregation by a screen or veil. It may be presided over by a number of priests and requires a deacon to act as link between the congregation and the ceremonies at the altar. The laity play a vital part in the services which are always vocal. The liturgy begins with preparation of the bread and wine on a special table, and these elements are transferred to the altar in the course of a solemn procession. The Holy Spirit is invoked on the holy gifts and on the congregation during a prayer called *Epiclesis* (invocation). The lay people are communicated in both kinds, usually by intinction from the chalice. These are features common to all Oriental rites.

The central part of the service, called *Anaphora* (offering, sacrifice), is also similar throughout the East. It begins with the *Preface* or prologue, in which God is thanked for the creation of man. Then comes the *Sanctus* (angelic praise to the Lord and Master of the Universe) which is followed by the *Anamnesis* or commemoration of the works of Christ, His cross, His tomb, His resurrection and ascension. The *Anamnesis* includes the words 'take, eat; this is my Body', and 'drink ye all of this', spoken by Him at the Last Supper. The *Anamnesis* is completed by the *Epiclesis*, after which comes the Intercession, or Great Prayer for all, living and dead, summed up in the 'Our Father'. The *Anaphora* ends with the elevation of the Host, the fraction of the elements and communion.

The prayer of intercession is the least stabilized part of the Eastern Eucharistic Canon. In the Alexandrian rite of St Mark it comes before the *Sanctus*; in the Chaldean version is precedes the *Epiclesis*; in the Byzantine tradition it follows the *Epiclesis*.

All the four main groups of the Eastern liturgies represent one or another ancient local tradition. The Western Syrian or Jacobite rite follows the Antiochian pattern which took its present shape in the fourth century. It is now used only by the Monophysites or those Eastern Christians who still refuse to accept the Chalcedonian Council of four hundred and fifty-one. Their ecclesiastical centre is in the city of Homs in Syria, but their largest numbers are in the Kerala Province of South India. The Jacobite rite is more primitive than the Byzantine. Its liturgical language is Syriac and the liturgy is named after St James the Apostle. The chief part of the Eucharist (the *Anaphora*), which has only two different versions of prayer in the Byzantine ritual, has almost seventy alternatives among the Jacobites, all associated with the names of apostles or well-known saints, though few were composed by those to whom they are now ascribed. The most common among these *Anaphores* are assigned to St John the Evangelist, the Twelve Apostles, St Mark, St Cyril, St Eustathius and St Clement. The celebrant may select any of the seventy *Anaphores*, but that of St Eustathius is one of the shortest and is more frequently used. An important characteristic of this Syrian rite is a reading of the Old Testament as well as the lesson taken from the New Testament, an ancient custom become obsolete among other Eastern Christians.

The Eastern Syrians or Chaldeans are now a small remnant of the Church of the Persian Empire. They have three liturgies, the most often practised being the Eucharist of the Apostles which goes back to the origins of the Christian community in Persia. The liturgy of St Theodore is sung on Sundays from Advent till Palm Sunday. The liturgy of Nestorius is celebrated only five times a year, on the Feast of Epiphany, on the day of St John the Baptist, on the feast of the Doctors of the Greek Church, on Maundy Thursday, and on Wednesday and Thursday during the fast of the Nenevites commemorating the episode described in the Book of Jonah (III, 5, 10), and observed only by the Chaldeans. Their liturgical language is Eastern Syriac, although their vernacular is Arabic.

The Copts of Egypt also have three Eucharistic rites, the most ancient, that of St Clement, being celebrated only once a year on the Friday in Passion Week. This liturgy is derived from an original Alexandrian tradition associated with St Mark the Evangelist, founder of the Church in Egypt. Two other rites, of St Gregory and St Basil, resemble the Byzantine order. The first is used on three occasions only, Christmas Day, Epiphany and Easter Sunday. The second covers the rest of the year. The liturgical language is still ancient Coptic.

The Ethiopians have seventeen different liturgies, all derived from the Coptic rite, but representing a much greater variety of *Anaphores* than those used in Egypt. The liturgical language of the Ethiopian Church is ghiez. It remained the spoken language till the seventeenth century, but has been since replaced by Amharic, and is no longer understood by the worshippers.

The Byzantine Church has four liturgies: of St John Chrysostom which is the usual service; of St Basil the Great, celebrated only ten times a year, on the eves of Christmas and Epiphany, St Basil's Day (1st January), five Sundays in Lent, and Thursday and Saturday in Holy Week; the liturgy of St Gregory of Rome (the presanctifical) is celebrated on Wednesdays and Fridays in Lent, and finally, the liturgy of St James the Apostle, used only on rare occasions. These services are translated into many languages in accordance with local needs.

The Armenian Church is unique among Eastern Churches in having only one rite. It combines two Byzantine liturgies (of St Chrysostom and St James) and is known under the name of St Gregory the Illuminator. Its liturgical language is classical Armenian which differs considerably from the spoken tongue.

Numerically the largest body of the Eastern Christians makes the Eucharistic offerings according to the rite associated with St John Chrysostom, Archbishop of Constantinople. This service has achieved greater cohesion and balance than most Eastern versions of the Holy Communion and is typical of Orthodox worship. It commemorates in dramatic form the life, death, resurrection and ascension of Jesus Christ. It is divided into three parts: the *Prothesis* (or preparation of the bread and wine), the liturgy of the Catechumens, and the liturgy of the Faithful. During the *Prothesis*, the priest, assisted by a deacon and servers, cuts the bread for the Eucharistic offering and puts it on the paten. He pours wine into the chalice and mixes water with it. These actions are accompanied by prayers to associate them with Christ's sacrifice on the cross and His final victory. Symbolically the *Prothesis*, which takes place behind the screen and remains unseen by the congregation, represents the hidden years of the Incarnate life which Jesus spent at home, unknown to the world, before He started on His mission.

In the Russian Church lay members bring lists of names to the service —people for whom they require special prayers to be said. These are given to the priest, together with small round loaves, and during the *Prothesis* he reads the names, taking a portion from each loaf sent up and putting them on the paten. In Greece, bread, wine and olive oil are offered by the congregation from their own fields, vineyards and olive groves.

The second part of the liturgy, called the liturgy of the Catechumens, begins with the solemn exclamation of the celebrant, 'Blessed be the Kingdom of the Father and of the Son and of the Holy Ghost'. The Eucharist is an action which proclaims the coming of the Kingdom of God, and at the same time actualizes its hidden presence. The gathered believers in the Incarnation are already part of the Messianic realm and are at the same time the agents willing to extend it over the world. The liturgy of the Catechumens commemorates Christ's teaching and healing ministry. Its main theme is the proclamation of His message. The Book of the four Gospels is brought in a procession and presented to the congregation whilst the Beatitudes are usually sung or recited. They are the essence of the New Testament and remind hearers that communion with God is achieved only by a change of heart, and not by the observance of external rules.

The reading of the Holy Scriptures follows this procession, after which a sermon is usually preached and prayers are said which cover the spiritual and material needs of the congregation. The clergy and people pray together for the sick, the suffering and the departed. In early centuries the Catechumens (those who desired to join the Church but were not yet baptized) left the service at this juncture, and only the Chrismated (i.e. baptized and confirmed) members remained for the last and most sacred part of the Eucharist.

The liturgy of the Faithful opens with another procession, during which the celebrant and his assistants transfer the bread and wine from the table used for the *Prothesis* to the altar (the 'Throne'). Meanwhile, the cherubic hymn is sung: 'We, that in a mystery figure forth the Cherubim, sing now the thrice holy hymns to the life-quickening Trinity; let us lay aside all the cares of this life.' Many Christians associate this procession with Christ's going to Jerusalem for the last time to His crucifixion.

The Nicene Creed is recited after this procession, followed by an ancient Jewish dialogue repeated by the priest and people, which Christ used at the Last Supper with His disciples. The priest says 'Let us lift up our hearts', and the people answer 'We lift them up unto the Lord'. The priest then says 'Let us give thanks unto the Lord', and the congregation respond 'It is meet and right so to worship the Father, the Son and the Holy Ghost, the Trinity consubstantial and undivided'. This last response links the Old Testament with the New.

This dialogue is followed by the main prayer of the Eucharist (*Anaphora*) in which the priest thanks God for all the benefits bestowed by Him upon his creation, and gradually comes to the greatest of all of these, the Incarnation of His Son. The celebrant remembers the Last Supper and repeats Christ's commandment: 'Take, eat; this is my Body, which is broken for you for the remission of sins; drink ye all of this; this is my Blood of the New Testament, which is shed for you and for many for the remission of sins.' The congregation confirms these two injunctions by saying 'Amen'. These so-called words of institution are brought to their consummation by invocation of the Holy Spirit. The clergy and people jointly ask the Heavenly Paraclete to descend upon the gathered Church and to bless and hallow the gifts of bread and wine offered by the congregation, and to change them into the blessed Body and precious Blood of Christ. This prayer (*Epiclesis*) is one of the most solemn and distinctive features of all Eastern rites. After it the congregation sings or recites the Lord's Prayer, and then the communion begins. The clergy first partake of the bread and the wine behind the closed doors of the screen. Then these are opened wide and the chalice containing both elements is brought to the people with the words: 'With the fear of God, with faith and love, draw near.' This culminating point of the whole service is identified in the minds of Eastern Christians with Christ's resurrection. They communicate in the belief that they share the risen life of their Saviour.

The service ends when the congregation, blessed with the chalice (to signify Christ's Ascension), have the remaining unconsecrated bread (the *Antidoron*) distributed among them. This last act of the Eucharistic offering unites all present into one family, whether they were communicants or not.

Such are the main outlines of the liturgy of St John Chrysostom. In its present form it dates from the eighth century, but incorporates older elements which go back to the first centuries of Christian history. The Eucharist, therefore, is a sacred link with past generations who have worshipped God in the same spirit and followed the same ritual from time immemorial. It also unites different nations and people who form the Orthodox community today. The service is the same everywhere, but the language, music and customs vary considerably. In a big cathedral the service may be long and elaborate. In a small rural church it may be reduced to a bare minimum; but it never loses its distinctive characteristics. It represents the same mixture of solemnity and homeliness, of awe-inspiring mystery and childlike confidence in divine love and forgiveness.

Some Christians order their worship in such a way that it consists primarily of pleading the sacrifice of the Cross. Others stress the element of instruction; but for Eastern Christians the Eucharist is the gate to Heaven. It carries them into a world beyond space and time, with its peace, beauty and holiness, and offers them a taste of eternal life in their earthly existence. The following quotations may help the reader to enter into the atmosphere of Eastern Eucharistic worship. They are taken from the description of the Orthodox service by an Englishwoman, Miss C. E. Padwick.

'You enter the church and you have no fixed position. You are a transient comer, free to move, free to prostrate yourself when the Spirit moves you, without causing any remark. You are there perhaps for only part of a long service, and this is the picture of the true relationship of our little spasmodic acts of attention and the eternal worship for ever offered in the heavens. Before you the church is divided into two by the *ikonostasis*. Beyond that screen the heavenly mysteries are enacted. The Royal Doors at once reveal and conceal the actions of that other world. From the screen look down on you the faces of human fellow-worshippers, true fellow-worshippers with us, but now lifted out of our transiency, the Saints, the elder brethren who are with Christ. And the pictures of these precursors are ranged under the Figure of the Crucified who makes one the whole family in heaven and earth. The screen with the message of the Incarnation does not reach to the roof of the church. There above it in apse or dome are more unearthly figures, solemn, still; against a background perhaps of pure gold, all teasing details omitted as though they looked out from a passionless eternity. High above all is the figure of Christ the almighty ruler of the ages, Lord not of the human world but of all worlds. Below Him are the angels, prophets and men in a wonderful order ranged in a timeless act of worship. Beneath such a roof and behind such a screen the drama of the Eucharist is enacted. The service sets forth indeed the Lord's death from the standpoint of His heavenly triumph, ever remembering that the Lamb of God is slain from the foundation of the world and yet remains the source of eternal life. At the breaking of the bread the priest is to say "Broken and distributed is the Lamb of God, Son of the Father, who is broken but not divided, ever eaten and never consumed, and who sanctifies those who participate".

'In Van Eyck's great altar-piece at Ghent the Heavenly Lamb is seen surrounded with His people, kings, bishops, knights, merchants, hermits and the rest; and to all flows out the living stream of His heavenly Grace. In the Orthodox liturgy the picture is reality. To the Heavenly Lamb, enthroned and central, prayer is made for all sorts and conditions of men now on earth, for kings and rulers, for travellers and sufferers, and for the city and the congregation there present; and a memorial is made of those who worship with us beyond the veil, Saints mentioned by name or in the company of all the departed whose memory we celebrate.'[1]

This description of Eastern worship conveys the importance of the outer setting for the full impact of its Eucharistic rite. Its inner content, however, is not conditioned by architecture or by ikons; it makes direct appeal to every worshipper.

The Communion service is understood in the East primarily as a corporate meal, and like all meals it reminds men of the interdependence of the whole creation. Men need to eat and to drink like all other animals and plants, and not only for the maintenance of their well-being, but also for their creative activities. So the Eucharistic feast teaches men that material elements of food can be transformed by them into higher forms of energy such as prayer, thought and charity. Thus the universe is able to address its creator as 'Our Father' through the mind of worshipping men.

Nicholas Cabasilas, an Eastern theologian of the fourteenth century, called attention to the 'human' character of the food consumed at the Eucharist.[2] Jesus Christ ordered His disciples to eat bread and drink wine, and by doing so He sanctified the whole process of civilization, for these two products require long preparation and much labour. They are the result of careful study and observation of nature combined with technical inventiveness. In Christian worship man comes to meet his Creator, not empty-handed. It is not enough for him to praise His Maker; he is ordered to appear before Him with the fruits of the earth transformed and uplifted by his work.

There are religions which despise matter, and which call their followers to forget as far as possible the physical universe, and to lose sight of it in spiritual contemplation. Christianity teaches differently. Man is responsible for the rest of creation, and the Eucharist is a constant reminder of his duty to transform nature and to make it a better channel for activities of the spirit.

It is no accident that a scientific civilization, which tries not only to understand the structure of the cosmos but also to use this knowledge for the benefit of mankind, has arisen among nations trained in Eucharistic worship. It was in this unique service that men began to see the physical universe as a friend instead of fearing and despising it. They learned also the sacredness and dignity of every type of labour, including manual work, which has been considered as degrading both by the classical civilization and by the non-Christian religions of the East.

There is yet another lesson contained in the Eucharist, that of the interdependence of all human beings. At each communion service the celebrant and communicants are not alone in having an honoured place, but also those who have sown the seed, gathered the harvest, ground the corn, baked the bread and transported it. Likewise all who have tended the vines, crushed the grapes and made them into wine; who have worked in the mines and forged the metal of which the sacred vessels are made; who have printed the books and made the vestments of the priests; who have painted the ikons, composed the hymns and provided music for them; and finally all who have built the temple of God and contributed to its beauty and glory.

This universality of the Eucharist is emphasized by the invitations to come and eat and drink, addressed to all believers in the Incarnation. A meal may be a demonstration of unity and friendship, but it can also be used as a means of separation. Many religions stress this by forbidding their followers to share their food with those who belong to other castes or to the other sex. There are large sections of mankind where men and women do not eat together; where social distinctions are standardized by segregation at meals. Christianity cuts across all these barriers. The Eucharist is offered to all; the only condition imposed is the faith of the participant. His race, class and origin are brushed aside as irrelevant, for all men bear the divine image and according to Christian teaching are the children of God. It is significant that the practical application of this belief in the essential unity of all human beings, as exemplified by the rise of democracy, has taken place first among those nations which incorporated the Eucharist in their regular worship.

Such are some of the cultural and sociological consequences of the communion service. Its religious message reveals the essence of the New Covenant. By offering the bread of the mystical Body of Christ and by blessing the sacred cup, Christians enter into the most intimate organic unity with God and with one another. They greet the author of the Universe as their friend and collaborator, who offers his companionship to all who believe in His Incarnate Son. This experience of perfect communion between the believer and the Divine Logos is powerfully expressed by St Simeon the New Theologian, one of the great mystical writers of the Byzantine Church (*d.* 1033).

'Thou hast vouchsafed me, O Lord, that this corruptible temple, my human flesh, should be united to Thy holy flesh, that my blood should be mingled with Thine, and henceforth I am Thy transparent and translucent member. I am transported out of myself. I see myself such as I am to become. Fearful and at the same time ashamed of myself I venerate Thee and tremble before Thee.'[3]

Such is the power and the significance of the Holy Communion, yet the Eucharist has nothing magical about it. Those who are renewed and strengthened by it retain their freedom, and many fail to benefit from it altogether. Their unfaithfulness and carelessness deprives them of the gift they have received and bars them from its regenerating influence. Nevertheless the impact of the Eucharistic worship can be traced to all spheres of life in Christian countries. The nations brought up in its atmosphere have produced art, science, economic and social orders which bear the imprint of their Eucharistic experience. Christianity can be defined as the religion of those who meet each other and their Creator at the Eucharistic meal. All other sacraments and services of the Church are subordinate to this central act of Christian worship.

The Sacraments of the Eastern Christians

The sacraments are corporate liturgical actions by which Christians invoke divine blessings upon certain material objects like bread, wine, water and oil, or upon people being married or set apart for some special service. Eastern Christians call the sacraments 'Mysteries', and interpret them as twofold movements between God and man. The word 'mystery' emphasizes the divine part which transforms and purifies.

The teaching and practice of the East, while distinct from that of the West, is nevertheless not opposed to it. Western Christianity defines and classifies the sacraments more precisely and in greater detail than the Eastern Church. The early Christians took it for granted that the Church was endowed with the power and authority to bestow sacramental grace upon its members, but the number of the sacraments remained undefined. The process of differentiation started in the West. In the thirteenth century the schoolmen selected seven sacraments as having been ordained by Christ Himself. The form, matter and purpose for each were fixed, and these seven were elevated above other sacramental actions. The East did not participate in this, and so avoided being committed to a certain artificiality of scholastic classification which tried to find the proper 'matter' and 'form' for all seven sacraments in the Holy Scriptures. For instance, the handing of the chalice by the bishop to the priest was considered as the 'matter' of Ordination, though it was in reality a later custom of the West, unknown in the Early Church. Reaction against this excessive formalism soon followed.

In the fourteenth century Wycliffe (d. 1384) challenged the sacramental doctrine so formulated. His protest was taken up by John Hus (d. 1415) and by his Bohemian supporters. The reformers of the sixteenth century, Martin Luther (d. 1546), John Calvin (d. 1564) and Ulrich Zwingli (d. 1531), were also strongly opposed to the Roman teaching, and elaborated their own systems along the lines first adumbrated by the Latin divines, and brought the scholastic teaching to its logical conclusion.

Only two sacraments out of the seven, Baptism and Holy Communion, were retained by the Protestants as necessary for salvation and as explicitly ordered by Jesus Christ. Their purpose and character was expounded in a novel way and the mode of their administration variously revised. This new theory and practice has since become the main barrier separating the two halves of Western Christendom, and so far has made reconciliation impossible.

Other Protestants like the Quakers and the Salvation Army for instance went still further in their denunciation of the Roman tradition, and abrogated all the sacraments, reducing Christian worship to vocal or silent prayer.

At first the East took no part in this classification and reduction of the number of the 'Mysteries'. It used the seven sacraments sanctioned by the Roman Church, but also treated as sacraments the Blessing of the Water on the feast of Epiphany, the taking of vows by a monk or nun, the consecration of a church, the anointing of a monarch, and the recognition as brethren of Christians willing to unite themselves by this sacred bond with each other.* Eastern Christians continue the practice of the Early Church which regarded many manifestations of its liturgical life as sacramental.

In the seventeenth century Orthodox theology was, however, exposed to the repercussions of the Western sacramental controversy. It was a period of decline in scholarship among the Eastern Christians.

* The Sacrament of Brotherhood is used only in the Serbian Church.

The Mohammedan yoke made regular training of the clergy in their native lands impossible, and a number of men, educated in Roman Catholic and Protestant countries, borrowed ideas current in the West. The term 'seven sacraments' was accepted, and certain other definitions copied from the Roman system were uncritically absorbed and incorporated into the manuals of theology.

However, the use of the word *Mysterion* protected the Orthodox from the desire of some of their leaders to imitate the West more closely and rationalize further the divine-human encounter. The sacramental practice of the East has therefore remained richer and less formalized than that of the West, and has retained many features which link it with the life and faith of the Early Church.

Baptism

Initiation into the Christian community in the East, as in the West, is by Baptism. The Orthodox practice is three-fold immersion, using the traditional formula: 'The servant of God (name) is baptized in the name of the Father, the Son and the Holy Ghost.' This signifies the death of a sinner and his resurrection and redemption as a new Christian. In the case of an adult, Baptism is preceded by the recitation of the Nicene creed and by renunciation of the powers of evil. In the baptism of infants two sponsors on behalf of the child confess the Orthodox faith and accept in his name the offer of new life in the fellowship of the Church.

There are two features in the Eastern rite which distinguish it from that of the West. In the West the celebrant says 'I baptize'; in the East the formula used is 'The servant of God is baptized', thus stressing the corporate character of this act of initiation in which the Church receives the new member into its sacred fold. The baptizer in the East acts on behalf of the whole body, and not on his own sacerdotal authority. The second distinctive feature of the Eastern rite is the belief in its cosmic significance. This conviction is expressed in the prayer of consecration of the water, which precedes the threefold immersion. The grace of the Holy Spirit is invoked upon it in the following words:

'Great art Thou O Lord, and marvellous are Thy works, and there is no word which sufficeth to hymn Thy wonders. Before Thee tremble all the powers endowed with intelligence. The sun singeth with Thee, the moon glorifieth Thee, the stars meet together in Thy presence, the light obeyeth Thee, the water springs are subject unto Thee. Wherefore O King, who lovest mankind, come Thou now and sanctify this water by the indwelling of the Holy Spirit, and grant unto it the grace of redemption and the blessing of Jordan. Make it the fountain of incorruption, the gift of sanctification, the remission of sins and the remedy of infirmities.'

This prayer implies that every baptism not only adds another member to the Universal Church, but also extends the domain of the manifest Kingdom of the Holy Trinity. The sanctification of water as part of nature is a step in the gradual redemption of all life on earth, a process which, however, depends on man's willingness to co-operate with his Creator.

3 Confirmation

The corporate and cosmic interpretation of Baptism is extended by the manner of administering Confirmation (or Holy Chrismation), which in the East follows immediately upon Baptism. Although the priest anoints the new Christian, the sacrament is episcopal as in the West, for the Chrism, or holy oil, must have been consecrated by a gathering of bishops presided over by the senior hierarch of the autocephalous Church. Such consecration takes place during Lent, and is a lengthy and solemn ceremony. Each time, the newly-prepared Chrism is added to the old, and thus an uninterrupted supply of the sacred oil is preserved. Whenever the priest anoints with this Chrism he conveys the blessing of the united episcopate of all times. The words pronounced by the priest as he anoints the different parts of the body: 'The seal of the gift of the Holy Spirit' are the same used by the Jews at circumcision, and thus link the old with the new Israel.

Confirmation is differently understood by East and West. For the Orthodox, Chrismation is not the renewal of baptismal vows, but lay ordination, by which the Christian receives a special grace, in his capacity of layman, to participate in the administration of all other sacraments. These are corporate actions, and both ordained ministers and Chrismated lay people are essential for their proper celebration.

The consecration of the Chrism by the head of each national Church emphasizes the ecumenical character of Confirmation. It is a sacrament of Christian unity, for as all Church members are anointed with the same Chrism, so they are brought into fellowship of the same body. Chrismation is the sacrament of Pentecost. On that day the Theotokos and the apostles received the gift of the Holy Spirit, which brought their personal uniqueness into full light. Similarly the Holy Chrism

250

bestows on every member of the Church the power to make his own creative contribution to the life of the community in a spirit of perfect freedom, and to develop those abilities and interests which distinguish him from the rest of mankind. It marks the acceptance of individual responsibility in the fellowship of the Church.

The important consequence of Eastern practice is that children from their infancy are accepted as communicants under parental responsibility. Modern psychology recognizes the profound impact which good or bad influences make upon the first years of life, and the fact that the children of Orthodox parents share in the Eucharist from infancy binds them more strongly to the Church than in some other denominations.

Confession

The Orthodox practice of Confession is based on three convictions: (a) that men are morally answerable for their actions and that their conscience can be trained; (b) that they are all responsible for each other, for their thoughts, intentions and deeds are intricately interwoven with those of their neighbours; (c) that sincere reconciliation with men secures divine forgiveness, which effectively and permanently removes the stain of sin.

The Eastern form of Confession is the expression of the age-long experience of the Orthodox Church in dealing with repentant sinners. Its aim is to restore in the penitent the trust in divine love and forgiveness, by reconciling him to the community he has harmed by the evil that is in him. This reconciliation is achieved by helping him to see his wrong actions in a new light, and to assist him in his resolution to alter his conduct and repair the damage already done.

It is not easy for the individual to estimate the gravity of his behaviour. Often he judges his serious offences lightly, and provides excuses which seem to him to be wholly satisfactory, while he experiences disproportionate shame and guilt for lesser offences. Confession aims at helping a Christian to achieve a more balanced evaluation of his actions.

The form of the sacrament differs in the Orthodox Church from the Western usage, where the priest occupies the seat of judgment and the penitent kneels beside him when he confesses his sins. In the East the penitent stands in front of a small desk on which the Book of the Gospels and the Cross are placed. The priest does not sit, but stands by his side. After introductory prayers, the confessor addresses the penitent and says to him:

'Behold my spiritual son, Christ standeth here invisibly and receiveth thy confession. Wherefore be not ashamed, neither be afraid, and conceal nothing . . . so shalt thou have pardon from our Lord Jesus Christ. Lo, His holy image is before us, and I am but a witness bearing testimony before Him of all things which thou hast to say to me.'

The priest of the Orthodox Church is not a judge, but a physician helping the penitent to recover his spiritual health. By articulating his misdeeds the penitent achieves two important results; he objectifies his wrong actions and thus detaches them from his inner self. At the same time he receives the necessary medicine for his fight against his afflictions in the form of sacramental grace and the wise advice of the priest.

There is little formalism in Eastern confession, and most confessors have their own way of approaching it. Some ask questions to facilitate self-disclosure. Others refrain from questioning. Some encourage the penitent by telling him how others have committed the same and even graver transgressions, yet have recovered moral integrity and health; an experienced confessor can also bring home to a self-satisfied or careless Christian that actions he thinks unimportant and excusable are serious offences that might undermine his moral strength. Some priests confine confession to prayers in which they solicit divine forgiveness and assure the penitent that the All Merciful and All Loving God is ready to wash away the stain of sin from all who are willing to alter their conduct and have reconciled themselves with their fellow men. The Confession concludes with the following petition:

'Our Lord and God, merciful, gracious and long-suffering . . . forgive now O Lord this Thy servant (name); grant him the assurance of repentance, pardon and remission of his sins, and absolve him from all his offences, voluntary and involuntary; reconcile and unite him to Thy Holy Church, through Jesus Christ Our Lord.'

This last petition has a special significance. A sincere confession not only releases a penitent from the burden of his sins, but also establishes a closer and happier fellowship between him and the other members of the Church. Loneliness and mistrust of others is one of the inevitable consequences of sin. Repentance restores man to unity with God and his neighbour.

The last act of confession is the absolution pronounced by the priest. The Russian Church borrowed its present form from the West in the seventeenth century and the confessor says:

'May our Lord and God Jesus Christ, through the grace and bounties of his love towards mankind, forgive thee (name) all thy transgressions. And I, an unworthy priest, through the power given unto me by Him do forgive and absolve thee from all thy sins.'*

The use of the pronoun 'I' is foreign to the Orthodox tradition and the Greek and other Oriental Churches do not employ it.

The frequency of confession is left to the discretion of individuals. Among Russians confession is considered to be an integral part of every preparation for communion; in other Eastern Churches it is regarded as indispensable only in the case of a serious moral fall. In some Churches, only priests selected for this purpose by their bishops are authorized to hear confessions; in other parts of Eastern Christendom every priest is expected to act as a confessor.

5 Holy Unction

In the Orthodox Church anointing with holy oil is regularly practised and greatly valued. This sacrament is used in cases of bodily and mental illness, and by those seeking renewal and purification. In most cases the priest is invited to the sick person's house and administers the sacrament there, but recently its application has been extended, and in many Russian parishes this sacrament is offered during Lent to all members of the congregation who desire to avail themselves of its healing powers. In other Churches pilgrims to the holy shrines receive this special blessing.

The service consists of seven lessons dealing with the healing ministry of Christ. Each of these readings is followed by anointing. Usually several, preferably seven, priests take part in this service. The underlying idea of the sacrament is the interdependence of man's physical and spiritual natures. Some physical infirmities affect morality, and sins and transgressions can leave their marks on the body.

While the Sacrament of Penance heals the mental side of men, Holy Unction does the same for their bodies. The administration of this sacrament by several priests emphasizes that in this case the healing power belongs to the Church and not to an individual. The Eastern Christians recognize and highly esteem the gift of healing possessed by some exceptional persons, but in Holy Unction every priest is called to help suffering Christians and to alleviate their bodily infirmities together with the moral weakness resulting from them.

* A Greek and Russian form of absolution can be found in *A Manual of Eastern Orthodox Prayers*, London 1945, pp. 51 and 59.

6 *Ordination*

The corporate spirit of Eastern Christianity finds expression in the manner in which bishops, priests and deacons are consecrated. The West has been split on this vital point since the Reformation. Some of the Western confessions, Roman Catholics, Old Catholics and Anglicans, insist that the ordination of clergy can be lawfully performed only by bishops in the Apostolic succession. The Protestants repudiate this, and stress the inner call to the ministry. They consider the laying on of hands as merely a confirmation of this call which may be performed by any authorized representatives of a given confession.

The Eastern practice differs from both the Western forms. It combines elements which are separately emphasized in the practice of other Churches. In the East the ordinand is first brought into the congregation gathered for celebration of the Holy Eucharist. The two subdeacons then ask the assembly to sanction the ordination, and the unanimous approval, first of the lay people and afterwards of the clergy, who say *Axious* ('He is worthy to be ordained') is taken as an expression of divine approbation.

Then the candidate kneels before the bishop, who lays his hands on his head, and in the name of the whole Church sanctions the choice made by the local congregation.

Eastern Christians believe that the Holy Spirit speaks through the body of church members who are at unity among themselves. Every local Church is a living cell in the universal organism and has power to act on behalf of the whole body, but on condition that it remains in concord with the rest. The role of the bishop in the East is that of a witness, who testifies that the local congregation has retained its bond of unity with the Catholic Church. The Apostolic succession is a sign that successive generations enjoy mutual love and remain in fellowship with all believers in the Incarnation.

7 *Marriage*

The sacrament of marriage is known as 'crowning' in the Eastern Church. This is a solemn blessing by the Church of man and woman, that their new life together may be one of unity and concord, after the pattern of Christ's union with his Church.

The service combines some features of Ordination with those of the Eucharist. The bride and bridegroom are solemnly conducted by the priest to the middle of the church, where the crowning takes place in symbolic representation of the union between Christ the King and His Bride, the Holy Church. The priest blesses them three times, with the words 'O Lord our God, crown them with glory and honour'. Crowns are then placed upon their heads, and are worn till the end of the service. After the reading of the Epistle (Ephesians v, 20–23), and the Gospel (John ii, 1–12) and the recitation of the Lord's Prayer, the bride and bridegroom drink wine from the same cup in token of their new unity. The priest then takes them by the hand and leads them three times round the lectern, while the choir sings the hymns sung at the Ordination service. The similarity of the rites of Ordination and Marriage in the East expresses the belief that the clergy ought to live in unity and love with the community delivered to their charge.

The solemnity of this service emphasizes the sanctity of married life, and the connection between the mystery of human love and the love of God for His creation. Nevertheless the Eastern Churches of the Byzantine tradition allow divorce and even remarriage. This practice does not seem to the Orthodox incompatible with their high esteem for marriage. They believe that in marriage two people enter into an organic relation, so close that it is not dissolved even by death. It follows from this that, in its ideal, marriage can never be repeated, but this high standard cannot be imposed upon every Christian, for there are numerous causes which may deprive married couples of the experience of true love and unity. Some, for instance, find it difficult to remain single after the death of husband or wife; the married life of others may be ruined by prolonged absence, insanity, imprisonment for life, or unfaithfulness. In all these cases the Church, as a loving mother, condescends to the frailty of her children and gives her blessing to a second marriage. This service, however, is different from the glorious crowning; it contains a clearly penitential note, for those who enter upon a second marriage have failed to preserve the fidelity to their first intention. The priest says the following prayer:

'O Lord Jesus Christ . . . cleanse the iniquities of Thy servants because they, being unable to bear the heat and burden of the day and the hot desires of the flesh, are now entering into the bond of second marriage, as Thou didst render lawful by Thy chosen vessel, the apostle Paul saying "For the sake of us humble sinners, it is better to marry in the Lord than to burn".'

The penitential rite of second marriage is used both for the widowed and for the divorced. In order to make it clear that second marriage is tolerated, not approved, the Church requires that both priests and deacons shall only marry once, and candidates for Holy Orders may not choose widows or divorcees for their wives. If they feel they must

255

marry again, and this is often a real problem for clergy whose wives die while their children are still young, they are not condemned by the Church, but they are no longer allowed to exercise their priestly functions, though they often continue to work for the Church as readers or choir-masters.

Other sacramental rites

Besides these major sacraments the Orthodox Prayer Books contain more than forty other rites and sacramental blessings, which cover all the needs and tasks of human life. The Church invokes the grace of the Holy Spirit upon both sacred and secular objects, such as churches, ikons, houses, fields, animals and plants. Some of these ceremonies, like the great Blessing of the Water on the day of Epiphany (the feast of Christ's baptism in the Eastern Church) are sacramental in the full sense of the word; others are no more than blessings bestowed either by the priest or by lay-people.

The Orthodox believe that the Church has power to sanctify and purify all life, both matter and spirit, and that wherever and whenever she operates through the sacramental actions of her members, the matter receives the grace of the Holy Spirit and becomes the vehicle of His life-giving and saving influence.

Offices of the Eastern Church

For the Orthodox Church the sacraments represent the high marks of men's communion and collaboration with the Creator. Besides these corporate liturgical actions their Church offers also numerous other occasions for praise and prayers.

Eight of these services are regularly used and are arranged throughout day and night at equal intervals. For liturgical purposes the Christian East adheres to the old Roman system of counting time. The night is divided into twelve hours, from sunset or 6 p.m. The day begins at sunrise or 6 a.m. The round of offices begins with Vespers sung at 6 p.m.; Compline follows at 9 p.m.; Midnight Service (Nocturn) at 12; the First Hour (Prime) at 6 a.m.; Matins at 7 a.m.; the Third Hour (Terce) at 9 a.m.; the Sixth Hour (Sext) at 12 noon; the Ninth Hour (None) at 3 p.m. These services are recited separately in religious communities and provide frequent opportunities for worship. In parish churches the offices are grouped together in two main services, one held in the morning, the other in the evening. The liturgical material for these offices is rich in content and of various origins. The Old Testament psalms are widely used and supply a foundation for all the services.

Readings from the Old and New Testaments also have an important place in Eastern worship, but the greatest part consists of metrical hymns and prayers composed at different periods and in different lands of Eastern Christendom. Most of these religious poems are Byzantine. One of the leading Western experts on Eastern worship, Cardinal Pitra (1812–89) wrote:

'Nowhere has poetry received from the Church a fuller appreciation and encouragement than in the Greek lands of Homer. While it is evident that this great monument of hymnography could not have been created by a single effort, it is nonetheless difficult to follow the various stages of its development through the centuries. One realizes there have been successive creations, stages superimposed upon unfathomable depths, and many generations of poets, known and unknown.'[4]

The greatest Orthodox hymnographers were St Ephraim the Syrian (d. 378) and his disciple, Roman the Melode, who came from Syria to Constantinople. Roman popularized the art of religious poetry in the capital, and was followed by a number of Byzantine poets, Anatolius (d. 458), Sergius (d. 638) (both the Patriarchs of Constantinople) and George the Deacon (seventh century). The later hymnographers include Andrew of Crete (d. 720) the author of a magnificent penitential poem recited every Lent.[5] In the eighth century Cosmas, Bishop of Maium (d. 743) and St John of Damascus (d. 749) enriched the worship of the Eastern Church. In the following centuries valuable additions were also made by Joseph the Hymnographer (d. 983), the Emperor Leo the Philosopher (886–912) and St Theodor the Studite (d. 826), an ardent defender of ikons.

Several women also contributed to this religious poetry. The best known was a nun called Cassia (ninth century), author of one of the most moving hymns of the Orthodox Church, which describes the washing of Christ's feet by a harlot. This hymn is sung on Tuesday and Wednesday in Holy Week. Most of this elaborate poetry, however, was bequeathed to the Orthodox Church by anonymous writers. Only a proportion of this rich hymnography is incorporated in the printed service books and used regularly. The rest exists in manuscript and is only available to experts.

The language of Eastern poetry is ornate and contains a profusion of epithets in which the Oriental imagination luxuriates. It has many points in common with the shining colours of mosaics, for it exhibits the same combination of rich artistry with adherence to the strict code

R   257

of convention characteristic of Byzantine art.

The current services of the Orthodox Church conform to a complex system of cycles. The first is the seven days of the week, each with its own theme, reflected in the prayers. Sunday is the day of the Resurrection; Monday commemorates the angelic hosts; Tuesday St John the Baptist and the Prophets; Wednesday and Friday, Christ's Passion; Thursday, the apostles, St Nicholas and all the saints; Saturday, all the departed, especially martyrs.

The second cycle is based on the eight musical modes, each of which has its own set of hymns. A new mode is introduced on Saturday night and dominates the offices for the rest of the week. This cycle covers a period of eight weeks, after which the first mode is used again.

The third cycle is that of the year. Each day commemorates its own saints and the important events of Christian history; when the service is constructed hymns can be chosen from several themes in the service books for the day. These cycles provide an ever-changing and seldom repeated pattern of hymns and prayers. The task of composing the daily office requires expert knowledge and there is a special book, *Typicon*, of rules and advice.

There are two periods in the year when the rhythm of the service is changed, Lent and Easter. The music, the prayers and even the structure of each office is altered. The Lenten services are long and penitential, accompanied by kneeling and prostration. Easter, celebrated with a joyful sense of victory, contrasts sharply with the Lenten austerity. Orthodox do not kneel during the six weeks that follow Easter, and the music and hymns reflect the triumphant rising of the Saviour from the grave.

The Russian Church celebrates Easter Matins at midnight, and the special atmosphere of jubilation created on that occasion has no parallel in the experience of other Christians. To be present at this service is to realize why the Orthodox Church is sometimes described as the Church of the Resurrection (Plates 56 and 57).

Another characteristic of the Christian East is the close connection between Church prayers and family life. Many services are sung by a priest and his assistant, either in church or at home, at the request of his parishioners. Some are thanksgiving for God's blessing; others are requests for divine help, prayers for the sick, for a person starting upon a journey or commencing new work, for children going to school and for the departed. They cover all aspects of life with all its joys and sorrows. Frequently after a public service in a parish church an occasional office is sung and a small congregation is formed for this purpose while the majority of worshippers go home.

Russian Christians are particularly attached to their patron saints in whose names they are baptized. On the day of the commemoration of his saint a Russian is congratulated by his friends, and he often asks the priest to celebrate a special service on that occasion.

The Liturgical Books used by the Eastern Christians

The Bible provides the main material for all services of the Eastern Church. Besides the Bible and the above mentioned *Typicon*, Eastern Christians use the following office books for their corporate and private worship:

The *Horologion* which includes the unchangeable parts of all services, and the prayers assigned to each day of the week. This is a small volume which serves as scaffolding for the construction of public worship.

The *Octoekhos*, consisting of two parts in which the hymns of the eight modes are incorporated.

The *Menaia* which consist of twelve big volumes presenting hymns required for the daily commemorations.

The *Triodion*, the book of Lenten services.

The *Pentikostarion*, covering the season of Easter.

In addition there are two other volumes essential for the conduct of Easter worship:

The *Litourgion*, required by priests and deacons. It contains the prayers and litanies recited by them during the celebration of the Eucharist, Matins and Vespers.

The *Euchologion*, also used mainly by the clergy. It contains the forms of administration of all the other sacraments and also the prayers required for occasional services.

The *manuals of prayers*, designed for lay people. They include morning and evening devotions, the office of preparation before Holy Communion, the prayers of thanksgiving after it, the Akathist hymns addressed to Christ, to His mother and to the Saints, and other occasional prayers.

Some of these manuals have in addition a list of daily Bible lessons and the calendar of the Saints.

Some reasons for the difference between Eastern and Western approaches to Christian worship

The differences between Eastern and Western architecture, services and sacraments are theological, psychological and temperamental. As stated above, the Western Christian puts the individual above the community, while the East instinctively acts in the opposite way. The West sharply separates matter and spirit and tends to oppose what the East regards as indissolubly bound, bringing matter into the most sacred acts of communion with God.

Christianity is the religion of the Incarnation, of union between heaven and earth, time and eternity, God and man. Its main affirmation is that divine and human can be made one without losing their identity. This is achieved, not because God and the world are the same, but because God is the creator, the world is His creation, and the Creator is the absolute Master of His own work. He loves it, and desires the most intimate fellowship with beings endowed by Him with the power of free choice.

The Christian East and West stand in complete agreement with one another as far as these fundamental convictions are concerned. They teach that man, as the crown of creation, is called to act as a link between God and the world, and, moreover, that he is capable of promoting or retarding concord and co-operation between the Divine and creaturely wills. Eastern and Western Christians, however, begin to part company when they attempt to define with greater precision the role assigned to each human being in this divine-human encounter.

For Western Christians, the ray of divine light touching the earth illuminates above all the unique value and high responsibility of each man and woman made in the image of God. A reborn person is, for them, the corner-stone of the new order. The Christian Church is a fellowship of individuals called to live the Christian life together. This body is distinct from the rest of the world; it stands in opposition to temporal kingdoms, and proclaims the supreme power of the Spirit over matter and flesh. The redemption itself is conceived in the West as man's liberation from earthly bondage, and Church history is interpreted as a never-ceasing struggle between the Kingdom of God and the kingdoms of this world. Every moment of time must be redeemed by being so filled with meaning that it is joined to the realm of unchanging values and so made part of Eternity.

In the East a man is seen primarily as a member of a community. Those who live in peace and love among themselves become the mirror of the Holy Trinity, the reflection of the heavenly light. Man grows into a person when he realizes his interdependence with his fellow members in the Body of Christ. The Church is divine grace operating among the redeemed; Christians are those who have responded freely to the call from above; they are separated from the world only in the sense of coming together to form its sacred heart. Through the Church God

260

brings about the regeneration not only of men but of all nature. Spirit and matter are two manifestations of the same reality, and when they are sanctified and made the temple of indwelling grace then the past, present and future join together, and time stops its flow as it merges with the ocean of eternal life and light.

These distinctions, subtle though they may appear, have deeply influenced the presentation of Christian faith in West and East, and have consequently affected worship, culture, and even political conditions among these nations. This fact can be illustrated by examples taken from religious art, customs and liturgical traditions. For example, the flame-shaped cupolas of the Russian churches with their bright colours proclaim the regenerating power given to the Christian community. They announce the coming transfiguration of the universe, and they preach that even now the earth is changed into paradise whenever the Eucharist is celebrated and divine grace received through men's corporate action (plates 11–12).

The austerer architecture of Western churches symbolizes the conflict between two hostile realms; even while asserting that Christian forces cannot be defeated, the battlements of the grey walls remind members of Christ's army that the struggle is hard, the enemy strong, and victory not to be obtained without effort, suffering and sacrifice. This militant aspect of Western Christianity is, however, mellowed by another message, beautifully expressed in the lofty and serene spires, which tell of man's longing to leave this earth behind, with all its turmoil and temptations, to be liberated from all material concerns, to reach the celestial regions of sinlessness and peace.

The interior decoration of Eastern and Western churches is also eloquent of these two interpretations of Christianity. The Orthodox temples represent heaven and earth joined together in glorious union. The sanctuary divided from the rest of the building by the screen is heaven with its holiness and mystery; it is always there, yet inaccessible to sinful man so long as he remains in his isolation; therefore the doors leading into the sanctuary are closed except during the service. They are wide open however when Christians are gathered together in obedience to Christ's commandment, and in faith, love and fear, begin to celebrate the Eucharist. Then heaven illuminates the earth, and God meets His creation.

The screen, with the figures of the Incarnate Lord, His Mother, and the saints painted thereon, expresses the conviction that man both divides and unites the heavenly and the earthly kingdoms. The Royal Doors, with their pictures of the Annunciation and of the four Evangelists, declare that Christ alone is the door leading to communion with the Holy Trinity.

The interior of Western churches corresponds to the teaching that man must be continuously assisted from above in order to make progress along the right path. The altar and the pulpit supply mystical and intellectual sustenance distributed by the Shepherd to His flock. The pews, occupying the nave, organize and also detach members of the congregation, helping them to concentrate on their personal decision, thus stressing the responsibility of each Christian soldier of the Church Militant. This individualistic approach to religion is also revealed in the way in which Western and especially Protestant services are arranged. They are generally led by one individual, usually the ordained minister, on behalf of other individuals, and ideally they are so conducted as to be followed easily by everyone. They are well-timed, with a clearly marked climax, and the congregation has a full share in singing psalms and hymns and in prayers, and great importance is placed on listening with undivided attention to the Word of God and to the sermon.

The freedom and spontaneity of Eastern Christians springs from their conviction that they are all members of one great family composed of the living and the departed, and that the power of death only partially interrupts the fellowship of its members and is unable to rob them of their fundamental unity. Whenever the Church of God is gathered together in an act of worship, it is the saints and the faithful departed who lead the prayers of the congregation, while the Christians on earth intermittently join their great company in its never-ceasing praise. The strong corporate sense of the Christian East makes it easy for members of the Church to treat their participation in worship as a sharing in the life of the whole body.

They come to the liturgy as guests to a banquet, at which the saints have the place of honour. This attitude explains the presence of so many ikons. By these visible signs, the Christian wants to be reminded of his invisible hosts, and his first act when he comes into church is to salute them by offering a lighted candle, as a symbol of love and remembrance of his forefathers. This act is often followed by reverently kissing the ikon. The customs correspond to the ancient Christian salutation of the Kiss of Peace, which is still exchanged by the Orthodox at the Easter Night service, and by the clergy at every celebration of the Eucharist.

In contrast to his Western brother, keenly aware of his duty to worship God, the Orthodox stresses the privilege of joining the glorious company of saints when he goes to church. He knows that whether he stays for minutes or for hours, he makes but an inadequate contribution to the never-ceasing worship of the whole Church of Christ. All in the congregation are equally unworthy of being present yet all are equally welcomed by their loving Father and those elder brothers and sisters who have already entered into the joy of eternal life. It is this sense of being a member of a family that engenders the informality of individual behaviour. Prince and beggar, rich and poor, respected citizen and outcast, all have their place at this feast and no one can claim a position of authority and honour, since that belongs only to the saints. The warmth, joyfulness and family spirit of Eastern worship are among its great achievements, and they derive from the corporate approach to the liturgical services.

Pursuing these comparisons, one may say that the different attitudes to matter and spirit explain the opposed tendencies in the evolution of Eastern and Western sacramental teaching and practice. In the West the tendency has been to minimize the material aspect in administering the sacraments; in the East that element has been extended as widely as possible; in the West, for example, Baptism by sprinkling has replaced the solemn rite of the blessing of water and the threefold immersion, still practised in the East. The Baptist denomination is nearly unique in insisting on immersion, but does not ascribe any importance to the water itself, and regards inner conversion as the essential part of the rite.

The same development took place in the treatment of bread and wine at the Eucharist. The Roman doctrine of Transubstantiation, according to which only the visible sign of bread and wine are retained, whilst their substances are radically altered, and so to speak consumed by the divine fire, reduces the material aspect of the sacrament to a minimum. Bread is accordingly represented by a thin wafer, and wine is withdrawn from the communion of lay people.

Among some Protestants the communion service has received a strictly spiritual interpretation as the act of Union between Christ and the soul of the believer. The bread and wine are relegated to the fringe of the service, and are no longer consecrated and venerated as the vehicles of divine grace, merely regarded as reminders of the Last Supper. Their importance is minimized to such an extent that the wine in many denominations is replaced by a non-fermented juice. The belief that the highest form of worship ought to aim at being 'purely spiritual' and devoid of all material association finds fullest expression in the Quaker community, which dispenses with all material elements in its services.

In the East the bread and wine of the Eucharist are approached with awe and devotion. The full leavened bread is used and red wine warmed by the addition of hot water is offered to the communicants. More bread, this time unconsecrated, is distributed at the end of each service to all members of the congregation.

On many occasions other fruits and food are sanctified in the Church and eaten there. The sacramental blessings are bestowed by the Eastern Church upon other animate and inanimate objects. The Church is ready to touch with its transforming hand all that is essential to men and related to their daily life and labour.

The desire and ability to worship, like the urge to create, is innate in all human beings. The history of mankind displays an infinite variety of forms and objects and purposes of worship, and all these expressions, different as they are, reveal awareness that man is neither the beginning nor the end of the cosmic evolution, but a link in a chain, both ends of which escape his knowledge.

From the dawn of history men have worshipped the power which pulsates in the universe, and manifest in the heat and light emanating from the sun, in a stone's solidity, in the steady growth of a tree, in the beauty and strength of an animal, in the skill of man's hands, or the quickness of his brain. Men have adored that inexhaustible energy, that *élan vital*, and identified it with the creator of the Universe, their Lord and Master.

Some religious teachers and reformers refused however to follow the well-trodden path of other creeds. They have taught that the world of the senses is only a transient illusion projected by men themselves, that the realm of the spirit is diametrically opposed to the material world and that man can find himself only by liberating his being from all earthly concerns. These two different visions of man's part in the cosmos have continued to exercise their influence within the Christian community and have affected the evolution of its worship and lent it variety.

The austere, whitewashed chapel of the Puritans, devoid of artistic adornment, and the lavishly over-decorated Baroque temples represent extreme interpretations of the same religion.

The Orthodox have built their liturgical services on the article of their creed, that the Triune God is the omnipotent Maker of Heaven and Earth and of all things visible and invisible, and that men are intimately linked to the rest of creation. Eastern worship, therefore, involves the entire man, together with all nature, his body and soul, his mind and his feelings, his moral behaviour, his artistic creativity, and the fruits of his labour.

Man, with his will and reason, can choose to worship God or himself, but matter has no such freedom; it follows the line traced by human will. Yet matter is grace-bearing and once it is brought into contact with the divine power, it becomes Holy and sacred to men. This is the underlying conviction of Eastern Christians which shapes their sacramental practice; it may seem materialistic and superstitious to those who believe that spirit is the only channel of communion between God and Man. The Eastern Christians treat as holy not only the sacramental Bread and Wine of the Eucharist, the Water of Baptism, the Chrism and the Oil used for Chrismation and anointing, but also the vessels required for these sacraments, the book of the four Gospels, kept on the throne (or the altar) as the symbol of Christ's presence, the vestments of the priest and the Cross with which he blesses the people. Ikons are similarly venerated for they represent the Incarnate Lord, His All Holy Mother, and the saints. All is holy in the holy temple, and everything dedicated to God is set apart by divine grace and is transformed by it.

Liturgical worship is the source of inspiration for the Eastern Christians. It appeals to all the senses. The worshipper's eyes behold the beauty of the sacred paintings, his ears hear the songs, the incense surrounds him with its aromatic fumes, his palate enjoys the blessed fruits of the earth, his body glorifies his creator by symbolic gestures, his spirit rises in adoration of his Heavenly Father. The entire man is supported and uplifted by an atmosphere of worship created by the joint efforts of the congregation, united and inspired by their faith and love, and by the fellowship of the Holy Spirit.

Not all Eastern Christians make full use of orthodox worship, but nonetheless the majority benefit from the purifying and regenerating grace offered in the sacraments and services of their Church.

CHAPTER TEN

THE CHURCH IN THE LIFE OF EASTERN CHRISTIANS

The Church and the child—The Church and the laity—The last rites—Advanced training in spiritual life—The Orthodox Church and ethical and social problems

THE INFLUENCE of the Church has deeply penetrated the personal, social and national life of Eastern peoples. It has helped and guided them in their labours, their sorrows, and their joys, yet the Church has never imposed its authority and is regarded, not as a master, but as a loving mother and protector. It is not identified with the clergy; but with the community of the redeemed. 'Christianity is a new life with and in Christ, guided by the Holy Spirit.'[1] It attunes men to the mind of their Creator and makes them collaborators with Him.

This all prevailing and yet not dominating role of Eastern Orthodoxy contrasts with the paternal authority of the Roman Church which controls the thoughts of its members, directing their actions and assisting them with the detailed instructions on all major moral and intellectual problems of their life. The Orthodox have a profound organic link with their Church but the help and inspiration the Church gives them is mainly derived from their participation in its worship which transforms and purifies their hearts and minds.

In the Roman West the Church is often presented as a militant force, called to bring the world into obedience to Christ the King. Those who join its ranks are promised eternal life. Man, however, in his natural state is incapable of enjoying the beatific vision which he lost in the Garden of Eden. He needs supernatural grace, which Christ placed at the disposal of the Church through His sacrifice on the Cross. The Church alone has therefore the power to open the gates of Heaven for it controls all means of salvation. The emphasis on jurisdiction, discipline and on the special prerogatives assigned to the clergy are all characteristics of Roman Catholicism arising out of these fundamental convictions. Protestants agree on the fallen state of human nature, but differ from Rome by stressing justification by faith alone as the only sure way of salvation.

The East regards sin as only a temporary malady which hurts man but does not annihilate his God-like image. The divine love manifested

266

through the Incarnation has made it possible for men to restore their filial relations with the Father and reach holiness and purity. The grace of the sacraments, the life of ascetic self-control, of charity and prayer can cure men of their inner discord which hinders their spiritual growth, fills them with enmity, destroys their harmony with the rest of creation and causes suffering, disease and physical death. The Church has power to deal with these distortions of humanity, but the Orthodox believe that it can help only those who, of their own free will, accepting the truth of the Gospel, join its fellowship and receive divine grace through its sacraments. To be a Christian means for the Orthodox to merge one's own life with that of the whole body of believers and to be thus regenerated. On the one hand the Church is cosmic, beyond the control of its members, a free gift from above; on the other hand its destiny is delivered into the hands of sinful men, and it suffers from their bigotry, narrow-mindedness and lack of understanding. It is the organ of the Holy Spirit and His august voice is heard in the midst of the congregation, but both worthy and unworthy are included in its ranks and often those who appear the least important are made the bearers of divine message and the keepers of the apostolic tradition. Such a conception of the Church explains some seeming contradictions: ritualism of the Orthodox is not accompanied by clericalism. Conservatism does not mean loss of freedom. Eastern Christianity is not a rigid and authoritarian religion for it manifests itself more in worship and sacraments than in catechisms and confessional statements. In order to understand the role of the Church in the East, one must observe the home life and daily behaviour of its members, for it is in these spheres that Christianity operates in their midst.

Each national Church in the East has its own customs, which at times differ considerably from each other. In this chapter Russian customs are described as an example of contemporary Orthodoxy.

The Church and the child

The first contact between an orthodox and the Church takes place on the day of his birth. The priest visits the parents' home, blesses the child and recites certain prayers. On the eighth day he calls on the parents again and names the child. Every Russian Christian receives the name of a saint, who remains for the rest of his life his patron and protector. Some parents name their child after the saint on whose day he was born, others make their choice on other grounds.

The prayer read by the priest on this occasion contains the following petition:

'Grant, O Lord, that this thy new-born servant (name), may ever keep thy Holy Name unrenounced, that he may frequent thy Holy Church, and be benefited by thy life-giving sacrament, and having lived according to thy commandments, he may receive the bliss of the elect in thy eternal kingdom.'

Baptism and Chrismation administered together introduce the infant to the fullness of sacramental life. Regular participation in Holy Communion offers Orthodox children a possibility of spiritual growth which can be of great value in later life. Exalting and purifying memories of childhood and youthful experience at sacrament often lead to a return to the Church after a period of apostasy.

The first confession, usually at the age of seven, provides an opportunity for the parents and the parish priest to instruct the child. By that time he usually knows by heart such prayers as 'Our Father' and 'Hail Mary'. He is acquainted with the Nicene Creed and has some idea of moral responsibility. After his first confession he is a communicant in his own right and is expected to fast and confess his sins before receiving the Holy Sacrament. The dramatic and symbolic character of Orthodox worship, the frequent processions, the use of incense and the diverse activities of clergy and laity attract children's attention and make it easier for them to participate in liturgical services than in rites which lay greater stress on an intellectual approach to religion. There are also domestic customs associated with different seasons of the Christian year, often distinguished by special food. Christmas Eve and Epiphany have their own symbolic dishes, as has the week before Lent with its pancakes (as in the West). Lenten diet is confined to vegetables; all animal food, including milk and eggs is excluded. Lent, with this complete transformation of meals, emphasizes the supreme significance of the events commemorated by the Church, which continue to affect the life of mankind today. The great feast of Christ's resurrection is also reflected in a dramatic way in the customs of a Christian home. The Paschal table is dominated for the whole week by the *paskha* and the *kulich** surrounded by coloured eggs,† a sight not seen again until the next Easter. The rich variety of custom and ritual still in use among the Eastern Christians, the presence of ikons in their homes, before which family prayers are said, are edifying not only for children, but for adults too, who are reminded

* A pyramid made of sweet cream-cheese and a round spicy cake.
† The coloured eggs remind the Christians of a miracle associated with Mary Magdalene in whose hands an egg turned red in proof of the Resurrection.

they belong to a Christian community, united by its belief in the Incarnation.*

The Church and the laity

The most important gift that the Orthodox Church offers to all its members is the Eucharist. Through participation in this mystery an Eastern Christian feels himself renewed, strengthened and enabled to share in redemption. It is the principal morning service but frequency of communion varies considerably from one national Church to another and even from one parish to the next. In general the deep awe with which the act of communion is regarded has led to its infrequency. In some Churches, such as the Serbian, total abstention from animal food for at least a week is expected before each communion, which is therefore restricted to special occasions. In other Churches the stress on purification makes confession to the priest, and general reconciliation with one's neighbours, essential to the act of communion. There is, however, a growing tendency towards more frequent partaking of the sacrament but most Eastern Christians still receive it only three or four times a year and some only once—before Easter. Attendance at the Eucharist without communicating is therefore the usual practice of Eastern Christians who consider that participation in this mystery by prayer is uplifting and purifying. At the end of the service each member of the congregation receives a piece of bread blessed but not consecrated, and this is accepted as a sharing in the great service.

Next in importance to the Eucharist comes confession, and whether resorted to frequently, or only once a year, it brings home to every member of the Church his moral responsibility, not only for his outward conduct, but also for his inner state, his thoughts, desires, aspirations. Confession has a morally educative value and also provides release from tensions and anxieties. The practice of confession is based on a conviction that the inner disharmony in man which in the language of Christian tradition is called sin, can be effectively dealt with if the penitent recognizes responsibility for his wrong thoughts and actions, acknowledges that by committing them he not only harms himself, but also adversely affects other members of the community, and seeks a remedy in divine forgiveness.

The Orthodox adhere to the teaching of the Gospel: 'If you forgive men their trespasses your heavenly Father will also forgive you.'[2] In accordance with this promise a Russian starts his confession by asking pardon of all those to whom he is closely connected. Then, a reconciled

* The meaning of ikons is discussed in Chapter IX.

member of the community, he goes to church, where he confesses his sins in the presence of a priest, who is not a judge but a witness. Most Russian priests acquire experience in confession which helps them meet their parishioners' spiritual needs. Some reveal special gifts for the administration of this sacrament and these pastors hear confession from a much wider circle than their own flock. Every member of the Church is free to choose his own confessor.

Other sacraments and services of the Orthodox Church are grouped round the Eucharist. The usual preparation is Evening Song and Matins which in the Russian Church are combined and celebrated on Saturday night and on the eve of festivals. This service is called the All Night Vigil and if not curtailed it lasts from sunset till sunrise; as practised still, in some monasteries. In a parish church, however, it is usually shortened to two hours or an hour-and-a-half. The Vigil is popular among Russians for the beauty of its music, its moving ceremonies and the poetry of its hymns and prayers. Many of these are taken from the Bible, but others are the works of Byzantine poets.

The Orthodox are also taught to pray every morning and evening at home, and a selection of prayers recommended for this purpose is found in special manuals. These were originally composed by masters in the art of prayer and help the less advanced. The prayer books for the laity also contain the office of preparation for Holy Communion and the thanksgiving after it.[3] These prayers are a great bond of unity, for they have been regularly used by many generations. Some of these home prayers deal with special needs, like illness, or blessing for a journey or starting a new responsibility or work. In some families its members join each other in these prayers. Especially before setting out on a voyage a corporate act of worship is customary. After sitting some time in silence and recollection, blessing is given to the travellers.

These personal requirements and problems of Church members are also the subject of numerous occasional services, which can be celebrated either in Churches or in homes on the initiative of lay people. In these cases the priest is invited to preside over them and his presence brings the blessing and assistance of the whole Church to each of its individual members. These occasional services are private and public at the same time, for any other Christian may join them if he wishes. Many of these services commemorate the departed, for remembrance in prayers of those who are no longer on earth is considered the most adequate expression of love for them.

The last rites

The last rites of the Church form an impressive part of Eastern worship. The Orthodox Church neither minimizes the tragedy of death nor is overcome by its destructive power. It prepares its members to face it with hope and faith, but also with full awareness of their responsibility for what they have done on earth. Eastern Christians ask God in the Litany to grant them 'a Christian end to their life, painless, peaceful and unashamed, and a good answer before the dreadful judgment seat of Christ'. The last confession followed by Holy Communion is regarded as the best preparation for a new existence. Whenever possible the priest is also invited to recite special prayers during the passing over of a Christian.[4] Normally the body of the departed remains in the house for two or three days. During that time the psalter is read by his relatives and friends and short services called *Panihida* are held. The burial service contains a deeply moving reflection upon the transient nature of earthly life. One of its canticles says:

'I weep and mourn when I look upon death, and when I see our beauty, created according to the image of God, laid in the grave, formless, shapeless and without glory. What is this mystery that is our lot? Why are we given to corruption and yoked together with death?'

The service culminates in a farewell to the departed during which the congregation sings:

'Come O brethren, let us give the last kiss to the dead and render thanks to God, for our friend has gone from his kinsfolk and rests in the tomb and he has no longer a care for the things of vanity and of our much-toiling flesh. Where are we now his relatives and friends? Lo, we have parted from him to whom Lord, we pray, give eternal rest.'

To this prayer a choir responds in the name of the departed himself:

'I lie voiceless and deprived of breath. Beholding me, bewail me, for yesterday I spake with you and suddenly on me came the dread hour of death. Come all that love me and kiss me, for never shall I converse with you again. For I depart unto the Judge before whom king and servant, rich and poor, stand together; for each according to his deeds is glorified or ashamed. I beg you all pray to Christ our God for me that for my sins I be not bidden unto the place of torments, but be granted the light of life.' (Plate 54.)

The concluding prayer asks God 'to place the soul of His departed servant in the tabernacle of the just to give him rest in the bosom of Abraham and number him with the righteous'.

The burial service ends with the singing of 'Everlasting Remembrance'; for the Church, in her loving solicitude for all her children, remembers them all in her prayers, trusting that this bond of love is of real assistance to those who have entered into another life.

Such are the rites and the sacraments which the Orthodox Church places at the disposal of all. To those who desire further training in the art of Christian living more is offered.

Advanced training in spiritual life

The monastic communities have played, and still play a great part in the life of the Eastern Christians. The offices of the Orthodox Church originated in monasteries, and there too the method of confession and of spiritual vigilance was developed. Most of the literature on prayer and self-examination used by the Orthodox laity is the work of great Eastern ascetics. Religious communities in the East do not belong to various orders. Every monastery is a self-governing unit, and follows its own rules, all of which, however, have much in common. Most Eastern monks are not in holy orders and frequently the communities maintain themselves by the manual labour of their members. In agricultural districts monks and nuns cultivate their lands in the same manner as the peasants. Some communities however have more specialized activities such as caring for orphans, painting ikons (Plate 49) and printing books.

Monasteries and convents keep their doors open to anyone in need of spiritual or material assistance. Most of them offer free hospitality for three nights to all visitors. A Christian who wants to make a more careful preparation for his communion, or to live in retreat, may use a monastery for this purpose. In many cases he will find an experienced confessor there, who will give the penitent his undivided attention. Such a period of spiritual concentration, fasting and prayer is especially popular among the Russians and is called *govenie* (an untranslatable term). Many dedicate at least one week every year to this purpose. Before the communist revolution several monasteries in Russia, for example Valaam of Solovki, welcomed temporary inmates. A person who wanted to participate in the prayer life of a religious community and be trained in ascetic discipline could join these monasteries for two or three years and then return to his usual occupation. Many Orthodox are familiar with ascetic literature and follow its advice and instructions.

Special popularity is enjoyed by the five volumes of *Dobrotolubie* (*Love of the Beautiful*) containing extracts from the writings of the Church Fathers on the art of prayer.[5] A short prayer called 'Jesus Prayer' consisting of a petition 'O, Lord Jesus Christ, Son of God, have mercy upon me, a sinner', repeated at frequent intervals is recommended by spiritual advisors as the foundation of the prayer life.

An important place in the Eastern Church belongs to Athos, the Holy Mount, which since the tenth century has been exclusively reserved for monks (Plates 47, 48, 49, 50, 51 and 52). This beautiful peninsula in Greece is divided among twenty monasteries each of which is a self-governing body. Greeks, Russians, Serbians, Bulgarians and Rumanians have their own houses there. Many contain great treasures of Christian art and important manuscripts. For several centuries no woman has been allowed on Mount Athos, a unique monastic republic, and a remnant of the Byzantine world surviving into the twentieth century.

Besides the main monasteries the Holy Mount has many ascetics who live in small communities or by themselves. Some dwell in such inaccessible spots that they can be reached only by ladders. Their food is supplied to them in a basket hanging over precipitous rocks.

The Orthodox Church and ethical and social problems

The Eastern Church is often described as other-worldly and little concerned with the material and social sides of life. Its outlook is presented as typified by the monks of Mount Athos who withdrew from the world with its complex problems and find peace and contentment in timeless contemplation. Such a picture of the Eastern Church fails to take into account a deep sense of interdependence of all beings common to the Orthodox and their realization that man's salvation takes place within and not without the community.

The ethical and social outlook of the Eastern Christians is the outcome of their Eucharistic experience. The Orthodox Communion service stresses the corporate character of this sacred meal. Reconciliation, mutual forgiveness, the recognition that everyone is responsible for each other are underlined by its ritual. Before the recitation of the creed the celebrant calls on people 'Let us love one another that with one accord we may confess'. These words mean that charity is indispensable for a proper confession of Orthodox faith, therefore during the singing of the creed the celebrants give the kiss of peace to each other and say 'Christ is in the midst of us'. In the Oriental churches, among the Copts, Armenians and Jacobites, the kiss of peace is exchanged also among lay people, but among the Byzantine Orthodox it is practised only once a year, at Easter.

This emphasis on reconciliation and forgiveness is also expressed in a hymn sung during Eastern Matins:

'This is the day of Resurrection: Brethren, let us embrace one another and forgive those who hate us and thus being illuminated by the feast let us exclaim: Christ is risen from the dead, trampling down death by death and upon those in the tombs bestowing life.'

This constant reminder that a Christian is a man living at peace and unity with his neighbour creates moral solidarity among the Orthodox and contributes to open hospitality and readiness to share material resources with the needy which are some of the characteristics of Eastern Christians. Private charity does not exclude however other better organized expressions of social concerns, and hospitals, orphanages, homes for the old and destitute have always been generously endowed by the Orthodox. Sometimes these institutions are attached to religious communities, sometimes they are independent.

The political conditions like the Turkish yoke often interfered with the social, educational and philanthropic activities of the Orthodox, but these unfavourable factors could never stop them altogether. Since the middle of the nineteenth century several leading members of the Russian Church have given much thought to the social responsibilities of the Christians. The great pioneers in this field were the Slavophils and their writings contain much important material on this subject. In the twentieth century a number of outstanding Russian economists and philosophers made further substantial contributions to this side of Christian thought and action. In contemporary Greece the same problems also attracted much interest and several societies have been formed with this purpose in view. Yet it is essential to recognize that there is some marked distinction between the Eastern and Western approach to moral and social questions.

For the Orthodox the Church is not a militant force led by its clergy which judges the world from outside and calls it to repentance, but is conceived as a leaven which gradually transforms the life of mankind from inside by changing the hearts and minds of its members. The Church in the East is identified with all its members not only with its clergy and theologians; the national and Christian communities are seen as intimately connected with each other. This is both the strength and the weakness of Eastern Christianity. The Orthodox Church is not indifferent to social or political conditions, but is not inclined to preach on these subjects or to make public pronouncements; it prefers to work behind the scenes, for its members are better equipped to offer passive resistance to the non-Christian policy of their rulers than to oppose them openly.

The same misunderstanding accompanies the Western attitude to Eastern asceticism. For the Orthodox, the monastic profession and asceticism in general does not imply a rejection of Christian responsibility for the state of the secular world, but on the contrary, a special training for harder and more advanced struggle against evil. But if some of the Western incriminations of the Orthodox in social indifference are based on a biased approach to Eastern Christianity it is also right to mention in this context certain weaknesses of the Christian East affecting unfavourably its Church life. These failures of the Orthodox are usually the reverse sides of their achievements. Their strong communal sense tends to identify the Church and the nation to such an extent that religious concerns become subordinate to national interests and ambitions; the Orthodox belief in the gradual transformation of society encourages submission to the dictates of the state and provides little encouragement to an individual stand in the defence of moral principles and social justice. The great love for the Eucharist tempts the Orthodox to concentrate all their attention on beauty of worship at the cost of other sides of Church life, but these defects of the Eastern Christians, serious as they are at times, have never been able to deprive them of their commitment to a view on life firmly based on the teaching of the Gospels. The Orthodox recognize that their personal and social conduct must be inspired by the belief in the Incarnation, which reveals to men the goodness and blessedness of the earth and the capacity of matter to be a vehicle of divine power. The profound appreciation of beauty and glory of the creation leads to the insistence that Christian worship ought to include the best that artists can produce.

Art plays a vital role in the life of the Orthodox East.

CHAPTER ELEVEN

THE SACRED ART OF THE CHRISTIAN EAST

The meaning of ikons and frescoes for the Orthodox—Subject matter of ikons and frescoes—The ikons of the Church feasts—Doctrinal ikons—The contemporary revival of art in the Christian East—Stages in the evolution of Byzantine Art—The schools of Russian ikon painters—The Eastern and Western artistic traditions

TO PRAISE and bless the Creator is the sublime purpose of the Church in the eyes of the Christian East. Not only the spiritual side of man but also his physical frame is involved in this act of adoration, for the entire creation participates in the timeless liturgy. This feeling for the corporate and cosmic character of Christianity is expressed in the place of honour assigned to art in the East.

A Roman Catholic may be described as a disciplined member of a universal society, a Protestant as a man who has committed himself to the religion contained in the Bible. An Orthodox worships God as an artist, for he brings to the throne of his Lord and Master the works of his creative imagination. The colours and designs of the ikons, the sound of the sacred songs, the domes and arches of the buildings dedicated to the celebration of the divine mystery, are not merely a useful stimulus for the Christian East; they form an integral and indispensable part of worship, for man is called upon to humanize the material world, and one of the means at his disposal is the transfiguring power of art.

To a person trained in the Western tradition, Eastern Christian art looks remote and enigmatic. Its proper appreciation requires familiarity with the outlook of those who have created and admired its masterpieces. This chapter attempts an interpretation of the significance of art for the East, especially of its sacred pictures, or ikons, which have always been objects of special love and veneration among the Orthodox.

The meaning of ikons and frescoes for the Orthodox

There is nothing exactly similar in the experience of Western Christians to the place which ikons occupy in the life of the Christian East. The sacred pictures are not merely suitable decorations for the centres of worship; they are not even regarded as a means of visual instruction. To the Orthodox, they reveal the ultimate purpose of creation: to be the temple of the Holy Spirit; and they manifest the reality of that process of tansfiguration of the cosmos which began on the day of Pentecost and which is gradually extending to all sides of earthly life. At home, or on a journey, in hours of danger or in happy moments, an Orthodox wishes to see ikons, to gaze through these windows into the world beyond time and space and be reassured that his earthly pilgrimage is only the beginning of another and fuller life.

Ikons are prayers enshrined in painted wood, they are sanctified by Church blessing and in return assist worshippers in their aspiration to heavenly realm by actualizing the divine presence. Thus, ikons differ from religious paintings by the symbolic treatment of subjects, by their special technique of design and colouring, and above all by the change in their substance through the love and transforming prayer of those who made them and those who venerate them.

Subject matter of ikons and frescoes

Ikons and frescoes can be divided according to subject into three groups:
1. Portraits of the Incarnate Logos, of His Mother and of the saints.
2. Pictorial representations of Christian festivals and episodes from the lives of the saints.
3. Symbolic illustrations of Christian doctrine and theological concepts.

The portrait ikons are the most popular and widespread. They remind the beholder of the person represented, but in a unique way, for they contain both a call and a message. The fore-runners of these Byzantine ikons are the Egyptian funeral portraits. The persons commemorated in these striking pictures wanted to be remembered by the living when they left this familiar world for an unknown and disembodied existence. They wished to retain their link with friends and relations and remain in their memory and prayers. Accordingly, the departed was represented in the prime of life, young, handsome, attractive, with large, wide-open eyes, the intention being so to impress the minds of the living with his bodily form as to escape (at least partially) the total oblivion of death (Plate 16).

The early Christian ikons and mosaics followed the same convention. The saints whom they represented also looked straight into the eyes of their beholders and desired to remain operative in the lives of their fellow Christians. As an example of an uninterrupted tradition the Russian ikon of St Parasceva, painted in Novgorod in the fifteenth century, may be cited (Plate 17). Almost sixteen hundred years separate it from an Egyptian portrait. One was created in the hot African desert, the other in the marshy damp of the Russian north. Climate, race, religion, social and economic conditions are in sharp contrast, but these two paintings belong to the same school, for both express the similar underlying conviction that men have found in art an effective weapon in their struggle against total annihilation. This ikon, together with the Byzantine mosaic of St Demetrius (sixth century) (Plate 29), despite their affinity with the Egyptian portrait reveal also a substantial difference between the Christian and pagan representations of departed people for several important differences were introduced. For instance, the shape of the face was altered. Sensual exuberance was discarded by making the mouth smaller, and the nose thinner and longer. The spiritual nature of man was emphasized; the expression of the eyes was also changed. They were no longer the anxious eyes of a person looking with longing on the world dear to him which he was reluctant to leave. On the contrary, the eyes of the saints testified to the peace and contentment of one who has reached his Father's home. The saints called Christians to follow in their footsteps, to attain the same promised land (Plate 30). They wanted also to be remembered, but with a different purpose in view.

The ikons forcibly remind the Orthodox of the reality of God's kingdom. They represent victorious saints whose changed faces and bodies reveal the side of human personality capable of sharing the divine life. By gazing at such pictures a Christian experiences a fellowship with the saints; he is helped by their example and strengthened in his resolve to progress along their path.

The language of the portrait ikons is always purposefully restrained, though it is also eloquent and convincing. Those who can follow its symbolism receive help, inspiration and deeper understanding of man's complex nature. The ikons sometimes appear stiff and impersonal to Western eyes, the bodies of the saints seem attenuated and ascetic, over-stressing the superiority of the spiritual over the physical nature. However, not all the ikons are stern. Some express tenderness, compassion and love, virtues which man shares with the Creator. Eastern Christians do not despise the body. Even less do they regard it as an obstacle to communion with the divine, but they believe it needs purification and regeneration, and the ikons are a confirmation of this belief. This victory over the flesh is expressed through the eyes which reflect the eternal bliss experienced by those who have established harmony with their Creator.

The religious and redeeming influence of these images of Christ and of His saints reaches its climax in the setting of the interior decorations of Orthodox Churches.

Cecil Stewart described the role of sacred pictures in the following passage:

'The pictures seem to be arranged in a way which instils a feeling of direct relationship between the viewer and the pictures . . . each personality is represented facing one, so that one stands, as it were, within the congregation of saints. Byzantine art, in fact, puts one in the picture. Thus is achieved a spatial dynamic relationship across the volume of the church. The beholder belongs within the artistic envelope, and is linked visually with the heavenly host. He observes and is observed.'[1]

This close interdependence between the worshipper and the ikons explains the preference of Eastern Christians for circular buildings and the need for a dome to complete the vision of the Church underlying Orthodox liturgy. This liturgy is conceived as a corporate action, and the building itself is an image of the cosmos. The cupola represents the heavenly vault and contains the picture of Christ Pantokrator—the ruler and redeemer of the universe (Plates 23 and 24). He is surrounded by angels and archangels who serve Him and execute His commands. The remaining part of the ceiling and walls are decorated with episodes illustrating the redemption of the world, and with pictures of the saints who not only look at the worshippers but also converse with one another and form their own sacred circle. In the eastern apse, the most significant place after the dome, stands the Virgin Mother, the link between the Creator and creation. The Mother of God is the mother of all mankind, the friend and protectress of all members of the Church. The whole story of the Incarnation is depicted on the walls of an Orthodox Church. It begins with the Old Testament patriarchs and prophets; a special place of honour is accorded to Joachim and Anna, Simeon and John the Baptist. Then come the apostles and the evangelists, the martyrs, doctors and teachers, and finally the rest of the saints, drawn from all nations and all epochs, from the time when Abraham heard and responded to the divine call until our own days when other men and women have accepted the message of the Gospels, and have directed their lives towards the same ultimate goal (Plates 14 and 15).

The Basilica of St Apollinare Nuovo in Ravenna also conveys the reality of the communion of saints, but its artists employed another method; they covered the long walls with mosaics depicting the procession of the martyrs all moving with one accord towards the altar, and the worshipper is carried along with the saints in the same spirit of timeless adoration (Plate 19).

The ikons of the Church feasts
The mystical and theological strain is also present in the ikons illus-

trating biblical scenes or the lives of the saints. Those depicting passages from the Gospels stress the approach to the New Testament that is so powerfully expressed in Orthodox worship, namely that the life of the Incarnate Lord breaks through the barrier of time and takes place in an eternal present. The hymns and prayers of the Orthodox Church commemorating Christ's nativity, baptism, transfiguration, death and resurrection usually begin with the words: 'Today Christ is born', or 'today He has risen from the dead'. This present does not make history less important; on the contrary, the Orthodox Church can use the word 'today' with such confidence because it believes that all the great and decisive events of the Gospel are historical facts, and that there was a day when each event took place; but their significance is such that their effects are still operative.

The other aspect of Orthodox worship, the viewing of history in the light of its theological and mystical implications, also finds full expression in the ikons. Their masters are never satisfied with a mere factual account but add theological commentaries. The ikon of the Nativity illustrates all these points (Plate 39). This ikon is composed of several scenes linked by the imagery of Christmas hymns. Its symbolism is that of the Creator of the Universe entering history as a newborn babe, and the little helpless figure in swaddling clothes of white represents the complete submission of Christ to the physical conditions governing the human race. Yet He remains Lord of Creation, receiving homage at the solemn hour of His appearance on earth. The angels sing praises to the infant Redeemer; the Magi and the shepherds bring their gifts; the sky salutes Him with the star; the earth provides Him with the cave; the animals watch Him in silent wonder; and we humans offer Him one of us, the Virgin Mother, the sacred personal link between the Creator and creation. The lower scenes underline the scandal of the Incarnation and the incredulity with which men confront their Saviour. The right-hand scene shows the washing of the infant by the midwife and her assistant. It tells us that Christ was born like any other child. The scene on the left portrays Joseph, who, having observed the washing of the infant, is once again assailed by doubts as to the virginity of his spouse. He is tempted by the devil, who suggests that if the infant were truly divine He would not have been born in the human way. The mother Mary is in the centre, and from her reclining position looks at Joseph as if trying to overcome his doubts and temptations.

The ikon of the Annunciation represents the humility, obedience and sense of responsibility shown by the Virgin Mary. She is a free agent, but upon her answer depends the destiny of mankind. She is seated on

King David's throne, for she is one of his daughters, though called to a far greater glory—to become the mother of the eternal king. Her perfect humility preserves her from the vanity and pride of earthly rulers. She accepts the Annunciation as a call to suffering and service. The buildings which form the background of the scene are deliberately unrealistic, for the ikon painter is not an archaeologist trying to reproduce a Palestinian house of the first century. The veil hanging over the head of the Virgin is the conventional indication that the scene is an interior one and here again the ikon uses its own symbolic language which can be easily misunderstood (Plates 37 and 38).

The early Italian painters who followed the Byzantine tradition were obviously misled by this symbol, and, as Plate 38 illustrates, Duccio painted a ceiling in realistic fashion and added the veil almost certainly without realizing its original purpose.

The ikon of the Entombment is remarkable for its rhythm (Plate 41). Here again, the Creator of the world is seen as a helpless victim submitting to hostile forces. There is a striking parallel between the body of the Infant Christ and that of the Saviour killed by the hands of His own creatures; but not all men were murderers. A few lamented His death, and the raised hands of Mary Magdalene vibrate with the pain and sorrow of her heart pierced by love, and she is not alone in her grief. The hills are shadowed sorrowfully, and their strange shape lifts the lamentation of this woman into a cosmic accompaniment. Here, again, the symbolism of the picture was missed by Italian imitators. A similar well known painting by Duccio is excellent, but its artist obviously failed to connect the movement of the hands with the vibrating outlines of the hills.

The doctrinal ikons

The language of symbolism so widely used in the ikons commemorating the feasts of the Church reaches its most elaborate form in the doctrinal ikons.

One of their finest examples is Andrey Rublev's *Holy Trinity* (Plate 43) painted *c.* 1411. Its subject is the visit of three strangers to Abraham, in the course of which they announced the birth of a son to him and Sarah. The biblical narrative (Genesis xviii, 1–16) is unique, for it uses both singular and plural in speaking of the strangers. They are described as three men, but Abraham addressed them as 'My Lord'. This peculiarity of language encouraged the biblical commentators to see in this episode the first revelation of the trinitarian nature of the Creator, and the three messengers became the visible symbol of the Triune God.

Rublev followed this ancient tradition; his ikon is a supreme example of perfect blending of theology and art, for all unnecessary details are omitted, and the theological ideas are used in a most natural way in the structure of the picture. It produces an impression of profound harmony and peace. Three angels sit round the table in an atmosphere which vibrates with the self-sacrificing love of the Incarnation. This is indicated by the chalice which occupies the centre of the picture, with the right hand of each angel pointing to it. The angels themselves are engaged in a silent discourse with each other. The presiding angel addresses himself to his companion on his right hand, who looks at the angel sitting opposite to him.* The latter's gently inclined head indicates the response to the central figure. His green mantle is the traditional colour of the Holy Spirit. All three angels are graceful and spiritual. They are gentle but not effeminate; devotional without being sentimental. Each is absorbed in his own thought, but they share their concern with each other. The theme of their corporate meditation is Christ's life, death and resurrection. The table of Holy Communion is shaped like a

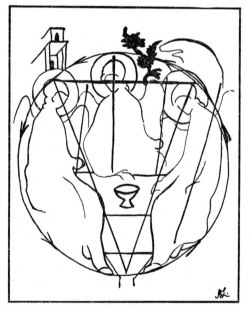

Diagram of Andrey Rublev's *Holy Trinity*, showing the main outline of this pictorial exposition of the Trinitarian doctrine.

* There are two different interpretations of the angels' positions in Rublev's *Holy Trinity* V. Lazarev (*Early Russian Icons*, Unesco publication, p. 27) identifies the central Angel with Jesus Christ and the Angel on the right side with God the Father. Such a scheme is supported by the dress of the central Angel which is the same as that of Christ on other Rublev Ikons. Besides Rublev's predecessors treated the central Angel as the Redeemer and two others as Mercy and Justice and it is arguable that Rublev followed in their steps. Other commentators

chalice, and the chalice itself, with the slain Lamb of God in it, is the subject of their contemplation.

Rublev was not only a creative artist, he was also a thinker and a theologian. He expressed his belief in the trinitarian God, the source of all life, in appropriate symbols which he skilfully incorporated in his scene. The doctrine of God as three in one is stated by a circle enclosing a triangle. His God is a living God, and so the circle is not static, but moving from right to left. The posture of the head of the central angel and the forms of the other two messengers puts this circle in motion.

According to Rublev the inner life of the Holy Trinity is focused in the Holy Communion by means of which the three persons share their life and love with creation. The Eucharistic sacrifice is inseparable from the Cross and this symbol of Christian faith is also included in the picture through the gentle elevation of the central Angel's head above two others. The earth, the scene of the Incarnation, is represented by the traditional square placed at the foot of the table for in the language of the Middle Ages the earth was described as having four corners. It rests on the green waters of the ocean which cover the lower part of the triangle. Above the right hand angel rises the temple of the Church. The timeless heavenly Jerusalem indicates the end of history, whilst the green tree* symbolizing the Garden of Eden, speaks of its beginning. It is linked with the angel—Holy Spirit, the giver of all life and the sustainer of the cosmos.

Here Rublev follows the pattern set forth by the Bible which starts its narrative with the garden and concludes it with the city, and he adds to it the Cross which he places between the two points. This elaborate symbolism does not overload the picture, it deepens its message and makes it intelligible to worshippers.

Rublev's Holy Trinity is so melodious and so rhythmical that it can be compared to a symphony. Its main theme, the circle, is repeated in the nimbus of each angel and again in the circles of their hair; while the second theme, the triangle, is not only the basis of the whole composition but also appears in the floor space under the table and in the shape of the chalice.

on Rublev's Ikon identify the central Angel with God the Father who sends His only begotten Son into the world and receives into His fold the Holy Spirit. Such a thesis is maintained by V. Zander, *Les Implications Sociales de la Doctrine de la Trinité*, Paris, 1936, p. 6, and by Paul Evdokimov, *L'Orthodoxie*, Paris, 1959, p. 235–36. These authors base their argument on the inner consistency of their theological interpretation and on the obvious centrality and seniority of the presiding Angel. It seems that Rublev, as some other great masters, surpassed the conventions of his time and discovered an artistic form better suited to his purpose than the symbols with which he was provided by tradition.
  * The tree represents also the Oak of Mambre and the Temple, Abraham's dwelling.

The originality and depth of Rublev's intuition, however, finds its most powerful expression in his colour scheme. Each angel has his own distinct posture and colouring, yet they are not separate from each other, they are indissolubly united with one another, through the interplay of blue, purple and green. The inner tunics of the angels on either side are blue, so is the mantle of the presiding angel. But his purple is reflected in the outer garment of the right-hand angel, and the Holy Spirit angel besides blue also has his green cloak. The colours blend together and thus reveal the unity and distinction of each person of the Holy Trinity. The ethereal transparency of the colours is unique. The ikon seems to be illuminated from within.

Robert Byron, one of the first western art critics, who saw the ikon after its restoration, wrote: 'The view was a revelation; before me was the greatest masterpiece ever produced by a Slav painter, a work of unprecedented invention, to which nothing in art that I could think of offered any sort of parallel. It was not that I saw a greater painting than any I had seen before, but simply that here was one which differed, in its greatness, more than I had thought possible from the accepted canons of greatness.'[2] He added: 'The reddish mauves, the pale slate, the leaf-green . . . shimmer like hills over a desert in the evening.'[3]

It is the masterpiece of Russian ikonography. Rublev dedicated his ikon to the memory of St Sergius of Radonezh, the founder of the Monastery of the Holy Trinity and his beloved teacher: it was the tribute of the most outstanding artist of the Russian Middle Ages to the great saint of his Church.

This language of symbols and colours was widely used in Russia, until its original culture decayed in the eighteenth century. Before their encounter with the West, Russians found it more congenial to express their ideas in the painting of ikons than in writing theological treatises. These theological and mystical ikons were their original contribution to the religious art of the Christian East, for the Greeks, though they laid much the same stress on the spiritual and inner essence of the portrait ikons and reached high perfection in the doctrinal interpretations of the Biblical and historical themes, never developed the speculative ikons, which attracted the special attention of the Russian Christians.

One of the Russian popular ikon subjects was Divine Wisdom (*Hagia Sophia*) which dealt with the relation between the Creator and the Cosmos. Divine wisdom is mentioned in several Old Testament books, and also in the New Testament in I Cor. i, 24–30. As early as the third century St Hippolytus of Rome elaborated the connection between the Incarnate Logos and the Divine Wisdom and Justinian's dedication of the cathedral in the capital of the Empire to *Hagia Sophia* proved the importance which the theological concept acquired in Byzantine Times.

The Russians inherited the same tradition, and the cathedrals in Kiev and Novgorod built in the eleventh century were also dedicated to the Divine Wisdon. At first the Russians followed the Byzantines in identifying Divine Wisdom with the second person of the Holy Trinity. But later a new interpretation was developed and the ikons painted in the sixteenth and seventeenth centuries expressed a cosmic approach to Divine Wisdom. In these ikons *Hagia Sophia* is represented as an angel seated on the throne, showing that the world was created in Wisdom. The Theotokos and St John the Baptist standing on either side of the angel proclaim the fulfilments in terms of humanity or the plan of creation conceived by the Holy Trinity before the world began. The complex colours of these and similar ikons further emphasize the interplay between the mind of the Creator and mankind's response to His call to perfection.

The Russian ikons of the sixteenth and seventeenth centuries covered many theological and devotional subjects, such as 'The Fatherhood or God', 'The Word of God', 'God rested on the seventh day', 'Our Father' and 'In this rejoiceth every creature'. As an example of these devotional ikons, 'the Only Begotten Son' is reproduced in Plate 44. It illustrates a hymn dating from the sixth century, probably composed by Severus, the anti-Chalcedonian Patriarch of Antioch (*d.* 538), which is sung at every Communion Service in the churches that follow the Byzantine tradition.*

The text of the hymn is:

'The only-begotten Son and Word of God, who being immortal was yet pleased for our salvation to be incarnate of His Holy Mother Mary and Virgin, and while remaining unchanged, has become man; save us, O Christ our God, who hast endured the Cross and death by death undone, who with the Father and the Holy Spirit, being one in Trinity, is glorified with them.'

Each scene of the ikon represents one of the verses of the hymn. In the centre the Theotokos laments the death of Christ to whom she gave birth. In the left lower corner the Cross of Christ illustrates the words 'who has endured the Cross'. In the right corner, death riding on the lion expresses the words 'and death by death undone'.

---

* It is a paradox that the hymn is sung by those Christians who repudiate its author for his refusal to acknowledge the Council of Chalcedon.

Even more striking in its imagery is the sixteenth century ikon called *The Vision of St Peter, the Patriarch of Alexandria.* It illustrates the text: 'I saw my Lord Jesus Christ as a youth of twelve years. He was wrapped in a white shirt torn apart from top to bottom, and he told me, "Arius tore my dress; receive him not into communion".' (Plate 45.)

The popularity of these theological and devotional ikons demonstrates that in Russia, before its Westernization, the ikons served as books, instructing the members of the Church and giving them a firmer grasp of its history and doctrine.

The contemporary revival of art in the Christian East

Such is the message of the ikons and their place in the devotional life of the Orthodox. They have always played an important religious role, but their renewed artistic appreciation is a comparatively recent development, for during the eighteenth and nineteenth centuries there was a considerable decline in Eastern art and in many places the ikons were replaced by second-rate imitations of Western religious painting.

There were several reasons, material, aesthetic and psychological, for this degeneration of Eastern sacred art. The material factor was important; most of the masterpieces of Eastern Christian art were until recently either difficult of access, or had been disfigured and altered. Many too were in the possession of the Mohammedans who covered the frescoes and mosaics with plaster and even preferred to erase them altogether when the opportunity for such barbarism arose. But even when the old sacred paintings were not wantonly destroyed by Islam, the original colouring and design of the famous ikons and frescoes were usually obscured.

The ikons were highly revered by the Orthodox and were therefore frequently repainted and restored. After each restoration they were re-varnished, and as they gradually darkened the dull browns and greens came to predominate and the original glorious colours were lost. By the eighteenth century no one realized that beneath the many layers of dark paint were concealed the superb paintings of the great medieval ikonographers. Even such masterpieces as Rublev's *Holy Trinity* were no longer recognizable, and the Russian art critics of the nineteenth century regarded the admiration of their ancestors for this ikon as a proof of their deplorable lack of artistic appreciation. In 1904 the first attempt was made at cleaning Rublev's painting but its importance was only partially revealed. Such a famous authority as Nikodim Pavlovich Kondakov (1844–1925) was still under the impression that it was 'not even the best copy of Rublev's ikon'.[4] It was only when the restoration was completed years later that the full significance of this painting was established.

During the last two or three decades the technique for restoring the ikons to their original state has greatly improved and systematic cleaning is now carried out in several special institutes in Russia and other countries.

The frescoes too nowadays attract much interest and study. Many of them have been disfigured by later additions, and the so-called renovations of the nineteenth century were usually undertaken by those who had no idea of the real character of Byzantine art. Unwittingly they destroyed, or seriously damaged, the great masterpieces by transforming them into mediocre imitations of Western pictures. Such mishandling has at last been stopped.

At the same time the improvement in communications has made it possible for lovers of art to visit the famous sites such as Hosios Lukas in Stiris, near Delphi, or the churches built on the tops of fantastic cliffs in Thrace, called Meteora (Plate 53) or the cave churches recently discovered in Cappadocia. Even a few years ago these outstanding monuments of Eastern art were inaccessible, but now they are within easy reach of ordinary tourists.

These material discoveries were external accompaniments of an inward change in the minds of art lovers. As long as a painting was believed to perform its proper function by reproducing as closely as possible the physical universe without attempting its interpretation or transfiguration, Byzantine art was bound to remain a closed book. The French Impressionists challenged this well-established conviction, and they were followed by many still more daring innovators. The general result of this revolution was a readiness to appreciate new ideas, to recognize the possibility of different approaches to art and to admit the appeal of the language of symbols. In the light of this new outlook the Orthodox ikons no longer appear primitive and barbaric. Only after Christian art had been liberated from a fixed interpretation of beauty did the vast and enchanting world of the Byzantine mosaics, Serbian frescoes and Russian ikons become accessible. The Eastern forms and colourings could at last be appreciated, and through this recognition their theological message also became more intelligible.

The reading of the doctrinal language of the ikons remains, however, the least advanced aspect of the gradual discovery of Eastern Christian art. The difficulty here is threefold. First, the ikon painters took for granted a knowledge of certain special symbols which are now no longer commonly recognized, but without this knowledge the ikon stories can never be fully understood.

Secondly, the ikons form an integral part of Orthodox worship and many of their themes illustrate Orthodox hymns and prayers. An ikon makes its full impact only when it is contemplated within its context.

Finally, the ikons are inspired by the vision of a transfigured and redeemed universe, the inner heart of Eastern Orthodoxy. Their purpose is neither to entertain, nor to give aesthetic satisfaction, but to proclaim the reality of the reconciliation between the creation and the Triune Creator, and thereby strengthen worshippers in their resolution to work and pray for fulfilment of the Divine Kingdom. A familiarity with Orthodox theology is therefore a further condition of a proper understanding of Eastern Christian art. An important contribution in this sphere was made by the leaders of the Russian religious renaissance of the twentieth century and one of its pioneers, Prince Eugene Trubetskoy (1863–1920) published in 1916 a remarkable book called *Philosophy in Colour* which was the first to open to the Westernized Russians the hitherto unexplored world of the medieval ikons. His example was followed by L. Uspensky, P. Evdokimov and others whose writings acquainted a wider circle of readers with the theology that inspires Russian religious art.

Stages in the evolution of Byzantine art

A further obstacle that often hinders the appreciation of Eastern Christian Art is lack of information about its main stages of evolution. In spite of its conservatism, its history is far from being an uneventful record of uniformity. Although there are still sharp disagreements among the experts on points of detail, considerable progress has lately been achieved in the classification of the principal schools of Byzantine painting and mosaics.

The Christian Art of the East had separate origins in a number of the big cities. Alexandria, Antioch, Ephesus each had its own tradition, influenced by the local pagan art. Gradually, however, Constantinople became the main focus of artistic activity and most of the surviving examples of early Eastern Christian art belong to the Constantinopolitan school in that their creators either lived or were trained in the capital of the Empire. So long as Italy remained part of the Byzantine State, its art retained many Eastern characteristics and Rome, Ravenna and Venice contain magnificent examples of Byzantine mosaics. The Constantinopolitan tradition had a glorious but chequered history. Three times it reached a high peak of development, and until the end it displayed vitality and superb artistic craftsmanship and genuine inspiration.

The first flowering started in the fourth and lasted until the seventh century and was centred in Justinian's reign (527–65) when the greatest monument of Byzantine architecture, St Sophia of Constantinople, was built (Plates 1 and 2). The Queen city of the East no longer contains any mosaics or frescoes dating from this period, but Rome, Ravenna, Salonica and Sinai have preserved examples of this early Byzantine art. The Church of St George in Salonica has remarkable mosaics; they are in a fragmentary state, but enough survives to show that they were of outstanding quality and they may be as early as the reign of Theodosius the Great (379–95). The largest number of early Christian mosaics are in Ravenna and although the work of provincial artists they belong to the Imperial style of the capital. The Mausoleum of Galla Placidia, dated *c.* 446, is the earliest of Ravenna monuments (Plate 3). San Vitale (Plates 20 and 21), Sant' Apollinare Nuovo (Plate 19) and Sant' Apollinare in Classe all belong to the middle of the sixth century. The mosaics of Cosmas and Damian in Rome are close in time and style to those of the Ravenna churches (Plate 30), and one of the most impressive of all is the transfiguration of Christ in the monastery of St Catherine of Mount Sinai (sixth century).

The Mosaics of churches at Chiti and Lythrangomi, both in Cyprus, also date from the pre-Iconoclastic period. So did the magnificent Church of the Assumption at Nicaea wantonly destroyed by the Turks in 1920. One of the latest monuments of this period is St Demetrius Church of Salonica. It belongs to the sixth and seventh centuries and contains several votive panels representing the saint and the donors (Plate 29). These mosaics combine excellent portraiture with the vision of a celestial, unchangeable world; the sacred figures seem to belong simultaneously to the divine and terrestial spheres.

The art of that first period has several common features. The figures are monumental; movements are restrained; the divine glory illuminates the scene and the saints although retaining individual characteristics are part of the eternal unchanging world. The artists who created these masterpieces saw the earth as incorporated into the divine realm, and their angels formed a link between time and eternity. The traditional presentation of the Incarnate Logos was not yet fixed, and sometimes Jesus Christ was represented as a beardless youth (Plate 22). Later, however, a more mature figure with a beard and long hair shows the victory of the Oriental school over the Roman one which had depicted Christ as an athletic youth rather than an Eastern sage (Plates 23 and 24).

The first period of Byzantine art was abruptly terminated by the Iconoclastic movement (725–843). By the orders of the Iconoclast Emperors sacred pictures were systematically destroyed all over the Eastern half of the Empire. Advancing Islam did the same in the lands it conquered. The damage done to Christian art was irreparable. The end of Iconoclasm in 843 opened the second period of Byzantine artistic expansion which coincided with the ascendancy of the Macedonian Dynasty (867–1056) and covered the second part of the ninth and the tenth and eleventh centuries. The artistic and religious revival of that time was vigorous and inspired by a desire to repair the devastation of the Iconoclasts. The artists intended restoration, but they gradually moved away from the ideas of the previous epoch.

The new stage was marked by an increasing introduction of movement into the composition of the scenes. The style remained monumental but the excessive rigidity and unearthly solemnity was no longer maintained. This can best be seen in the ecstasy of the apostles watching Christ's Ascension in the dome of St Sophia in Salonica (ninth century) (Plate 25). The Apostles seem to be uplifted in the air and almost dancing. The artists of the Macedonian period used more ornate, Oriental draperies and in general the celestial world was represented as following the same elaborate ceremonial as that evolved by the Byzantine court. The Emperor was regarded as Christ's representative on earth, and his palace as the replica of the Heavenly abode. The majesty of an earthly monarch was a reflection of the intangible mystical glory of the Divine Kingdom.

Several recently discovered mosaics at St Sophia in Constantinople illustrate well this outlook which saw the Empire and the Church hand in hand working for the glory of Orthodoxy—the pictures of Leo VI (886–912) prostrating himself at Christ's feet (Plate 27), and of Christ seated between the Empress Zoë (1028–57) and her second husband, Constantine IX Monomachius (1042–55) (Plate 28). The mosaics of Nea Moni on the Island of Chios (1042), of the monastic churches of Hosios Lukas near Delphi and of Daphni, near Athens (1100), all date from the same epoch. The Pantocrator Christ looks down from the dome of Daphni, majestic and forbidding (Plate 24). He is the autocrat, the Master and the Ruler of the Universe, and under Him is the Emperor, His earthly projection, anointed by God to protect and govern the redeemed mankind.

In this period of Byzantine glory its artistic influence expanded far outside the borders of the Empire. The mosaics of St Sophia in Kiev, the frescoes of St Sophia in Ohrid, and later the mosaics in Sicily—

Cefalu, the Capella Palatina and Monte Reale (Plates 4 and 23)—were all created by artists trained in Constantinople.

This brilliant epoch of Byzantine political history ended tragically in the twelfth century which saw a rapid decline of the Empire. But this collapse was not followed by artistic degeneration. On the contrary it was accompanied by a creative reorientation of its art, and some of the greatest achievements of the Constantinopolitan school date from the twelfth century. Christ, His mother and the saints lose their remoteness, something of their previous majesty is also no longer there. They become more human, more loving, more understanding. These warmer emotions of tenderness and sorrowful compassion are revealed in the ikon of Our Lady of Vladimir, painted in Constantinople and brought to Russia (c. 1150), which is one of the masterpieces of the school that flourished in the capital of the Empire (Plate 33).

Robert Byron, who saw it in Moscow after it had been cleaned and restored, wrote in 1933:

'It is one of the very few paintings in which an ecclesiastical formula has been made the vehicle . . . of as profound and touching a humanity as art has ever been able to express . . . the emotion is simple enough: a mother caresses the child whose cheek is pressed to hers and whose pale gentle fingers fondle her neck. . . . In those grave whiteless eyes and sad small mouth live the eternal sorrows and joys and the whole destiny of man. Such a picture can bring tears to the eye and peace to the soul. I have known no other picture so able.'[5]

The same manifestation of discovered humanism can be seen in a small church in Nerezi, near Scoplje in Macedonia, painted by an unknown Greek artist, in 1164.

The greatest surviving picture of this period of transition is the *Deisis** in the Southern Gallery of St Sophia in Constantinople. It was probably placed there at the end of the twelfth century. This mosaic can be classed among the best of the world. Christ is represented not as the severe judge, but as the Redeemer, strong but compassionate, wise and understanding at the same time. The eyes of His Mother reveal the depth of her love, while St John the Baptist expresses grief and penitence for the sins of mankind (Plate 26).

The sack of Constantinople by the Crusaders in 1204 temporarily arrested the development of Byzantine art and its last great period coincided with the Empire's dying agony in the fourteenth and fifteenth

* *Deisis* is Christ represented between His Mother and St John the Baptist.

centuries. The Church of Kahrieh Djami, decorated in 1305 (Plate 32), the churches of Mistras in the Peloponnese, the last stronghold of Greek independence, were the creative peaks of that era, and this last stage of Byzantine art preceded and anticipated many of the achievements of the Italian Renaissance of the fifteenth century.

The suffering experienced by the Orthodox Christians, the sense of approaching final catastrophe, made the art of this epoch vibrate with the full gamut of human feeling. Joy, sorrow, hope and fear are all reflected in the murals of the last churches built in Byzantium. Yet it was not a pessimistic and defeatist art, for the background upon which all these intense emotions were projected remained the same as in the age of the Byzantine glory, the faith in the Incarnation and the trust in the ultimate victory of good over evil.

At this time when the artistic genius of Byzantium reached its maturity the material basis for its expansion was rapidly shrinking. The great Imperial foundations were no longer there, the mosaics were still excellent, but they were expensive and increasingly replaced by frescoes. The Churches were built on a smaller scale, but they gained in the intimacy and cohesion of their decorations.

After the fall of Constantinople in 1453 the Greek artists continued to work under the Turkish yoke. The Macedonian and Cretan schools survived right down to the seventeenth century but the creative impulse was arrested. No outstanding masters appeared, although a number of them retained the skill of the established tradition. The hidden potentialities of Byzantine art were demonstrated by El Greco—Dominicos Theotocopoulos (1541–1614)—a native of Crete and one of the greatest painters of all time. Although he learned much from Italy, his technique and spirituality sharply contrasted with Western outlook, and he left a hiatus only bridged much later in the nineteenth century by the French Impressionists.[6] His uniqueness shows how different the evolution of Western art would have been if the Turks had not destroyed Byzantium and its artistic and cultural tradition.

A special chapter in the history of Eastern art was written in Serbia. In the course of the thirteenth and fourteenth centuries the Serbian kings and nobles built and endowed a number of monasteries such as Žica and Studenica (Plate 7), Mileševo, Peč and Sapočani (all thirteenth century), and Dečani and Gračanica (Plate 8) (fourteenth century). Most of them were adorned with magnificent frescoes, in which Byzantine art was blended with more Western influences and motives. But Serbian art, as well as the art of other Balkan countries after its most promising beginning, came to a halt under the oppressive domination of the Ottomans. The only country where the artistic development was able to proceed was Russia, and it was there that ikon painting developed and acquired a distinct character of its own.

The schools of Russian ikon painters

It used to be customary to distinguish five main schools of Russian painting. The Kievan or Russo-Byzantine school of the eleventh and twelfth centuries, the Novgorod school (twelfth–fourteenth centuries), the early Moscow school (fifteenth century), the Stroganov school (sixteenth century) and the later Moscow school of the seventeenth century.

This traditional classification of Russian ikons, however, needs considerable revision, for their more systematic restoration has revealed a much greater variety of regional characteristics than hitherto suspected, and it has also demonstrated the arbitrariness of certain previously maintained divisions. Many Iconographers from Novgorod, for instance, worked in Moscow. Many Moscow artists were invited to decorate churches in other parts of the country and in meeting and working with the local painters created new colour schemes and designs.

The proper study of Russian ikon painting is only beginning. The vast collections of ikons now gathered in Russian State galleries have not yet been properly examined. Until this has been done, the classification of Russian ikons according to the schools at present recognized cannot be considered as anything more than a preliminary attempt. Nevertheless, the main stages of Russian history have left their marks on the evolution of this greatest artistic achievement of the Russian Middle Ages and the usual division into periods can be helpful.

Few ikons from the pre-Tatar period have survived the disaster of the Mongol invasion, but they display outstanding qualities like the Angel of the Annunciation painted in Novgorod in the twelfth century (Plate 34). These early Russian ikons closely resemble the Byzantine originals and probably were the works of Greek masters or of their pupils.

The next stage in Russian ikon painting was reached in Novgorod and Pskov, two city republics, which alone escaped Mongolian destruction. The fourteenth century was the period of their political expansion and also of their artistic maturity. The Novgorod artists preferred simple subjects which did not require much commentary and explanation. Their palette was distinguished by pure colours and bold contrasts. Their direct appeal and vigour reflect the mentality and zest of the citizens of Novgorod, those daring merchant adventurers, who acquired large possessions in north-eastern Russia.

At the end of the fourteenth century the artistic Renaissance started under the Paleologues, reached Russia in the person of an outstanding master, Theophanes the Greek. He decorated several churches in Novgorod in an outspoken expressionist style and then in about 1395 moved to Moscow and thus linked the two main centres of Russian art.

The fifteenth century was the golden age of Russian ikon painting, the age of Andrey Rublev (1370–1430), Master Dionisy (1440–1508), Prokhorof Gorodets and Daniel the Black. The rhythm of composition, the harmony and luminosity of colour, the depth of theological and mystical intuition and warm humanism, give these ikons an unrepeatable perfection. They manifest the belief of their authors in the achieved reconciliation between God and his Creation. Love for suffering mankind and firm trust in Divine compassion inspire and illuminate these great masterpieces of Russian art (Plate 43). The fifteenth and the first part of the sixteenth centuries were the period of Russia's national revival when the Russians regained their political freedom and with optimism started the rebuilding of their cultural and religious life on the spiritual foundation laid down by St Sergius and his numerous disciples.

The consolidation of Moscow's political power in the middle of the sixteenth century, the suppression of local autonomy, the increasing pressure from autocracy, were reflected in the altered character of the ikon style. The school associated with the Stroganov family, the merchant princes, who controlled vast lands in the Urals, dominated the later-sixteenth and early-seventeenth centuries. Prokopy Chirin, Istom and Nikifor Savins were the best known artists of that period. Their works are distinguished by intricate details, by over-emphasis on decorative motifs. A love for miniature, the preference for highly sophisticated compositions superseded the balanced and direct appeal of the previous classical period (Plates 36, 44–46).

The second half of the seventeenth century, which corresponded with the end of Russia's political isolation, brought about the Westernization of Russian ikons. Simon Ushakov (1626–86) who imitated Western masters was an able artist, but he lost the understanding of the essence of the ikons when he moved towards the religious paintings of the West. To this last fifth period in the evolution of Russian visual art belongs the prodigious expansion in frescoes in the northern commercial cities, Rostov, Kostroma, Vologda. Romanovo-Borisoglebsk. Their citizens completed with each other in building new churches and in lavishly decorating them. Yaroslavl alone erected twenty-nine churches in the second part of the seventeenth century.

The reforms of Peter the Great (1699–1725) inflicted the death blow upon Russian sacred art. The inrush of Western ideas was overwhelming, and imitation of Italian, French and Dutch painting became the fashion. Ikon painters lost their artistic prestige and were degraded to the level of artisans. Revival began only on the eve of the Communist revolution and the effects of renewed appreciation of iconography are most marked among the Russian emigrants, who have produced several outstanding ikon painters.

The Russian ikons did not depart from the Byzantine original, but they introduced their own interpretation of the sacred art. Its special features are ably described by Otto Demus:

'In Russian ikon paintings Byzantine dogma became prayers and representation became legend. Clearly told stories with no romantic morals, asceticism without martyrdom, saints without devils, light without shadow, vision without mystic veiling—these are the new features which emerge in ever clearer form.'[7]

The Eastern and Western artistic traditions

In concluding this chapter on Eastern Christian art an important distinction between the art of the East and of the West must be emphasized. The Christian East has not experienced those turning points and opposing tendencies which characterize the evolution of art in the West. There is nothing in its history comparable to Romanesque, Gothic, Renaissance or Baroque. From the very first, Eastern Christian art discovered the dome, the perfect embodiment of its fundamental theological convictions. The Orthodox Churches proclaim that the Universe is the creation of one Omnipotent God who is the undisputed Master of all things visible and invisible, and at the same time the Saviour and Judge of mankind. This vision of the unity and harmony of the cosmos, and the centrality of the act of redemption was first realized architecturally in the sixth century cupola of *Hagia Sophia* in Constantinople. Since then its innumerable variations have been reproduced all over the East and today it remains the most adequate type of building for Eastern worship. In the thirteenth and fourteenth centuries it gave birth to the exquisite churches of Serbia (Plates 7 and 8); in the sixteenth and seventeenth centuries it branched out into the original architecture of northern Russia (Plates 11 and 12). The mosaics of the fifth and sixth century and the ikons of the twentieth century belong to the same tradition which is still alive and creative (Plate 18). Byzantine paintings are essentially Christian; their main theme remains constant; but within their broad outlines the creative genius of an artist can find ample scope for originality. This observation is equally applicable to architecture, but the frescoes, mosaics and ikons have especially achieved a happy mean between the stability of well-established code and the originality of the individual artist. This sacred art of the East points out the historicity of the Christian religion, and also emphasizes the timeless all-embracing nature of its message.

Byzantine art seemed in the past lifeless as long as the unrestrained liberty of the artist was regarded as the indispensable condition of true inspiration, yet it is possible to be creative and free within a tradition which claims to have seen the true light, and which offers firm guidance to its artists as to the ultimate purpose of life. This goal, as accepted by the Christian East, lies outside the confines of earthly experience, the final object being communion with the Triune God who surpasses all man's conceptions of truth, beauty and goodness. This awe-inspiring idea makes Eastern Christian art progressive and dynamic, for the vision is infinite and the greatest achievements are nothing compared to the glory of the Divine realm; yet even minor works may share in the dignity and authority of revealed truth if they receive their inspiration from the same source of Christian orthodoxy.

CONCLUSION
THE CHRISTIAN EAST AND THE
CONTEMPORARY WORLD

THE HISTORY of the Christian East presents a complex and variegated picture: the Church of the martyrs struggling for survival; the Church of the Ecumenical Councils absorbed in doctrinal disputes and torn asunder by fratricidal struggle; the Church engaged in rivalry with Rome and attacked by the Crusaders; the Church oppressed by the Turks and molested by the Mongols; the Church in its Russian branch claiming universal leadership in the art of Christian living; and the contemporary Church challenged by militant atheists. Such are the different stages in the evolution of Eastern Christendom and yet they reveal a remarkable inner unity. Eastern Christendom during two thousand years has remained a distinct community. It is a response to Christ's person and teaching from those who feel at home in the Hellenistic philosophical and artistic tradition. Certain fundamental intuitions and convictions divide Orthodox from Western interpretations of Christianity, such as the stress on the corporate and cosmic aspects of redemption, the vivid sense of communion with the departed, the rejection of the legalistic and rational approach to religion. These differences have estranged Rome and Constantinople. A firm belief on each side in its own superiority made co-operation impossible, and East and West attempted to build up their ecclesiastical systems without consulting each other.

The resulting one-sided and biased approach to religion seriously affected both, and many of the most flagrant defects in Eastern and Western Church life can be traced to the fatal rift between them.

The limitations of confessional Christianity have become more apparent in our time than ever before, for the rise of a universal scientific civilization has swept away many old barriers and brought nations and cultures much nearer to each other. The paradox of the present situation is that although belief in the Incarnation was the major force in the rise of our present social and economic order, the far reaching changes that same technological civilization has brought about have contributed to the decline of Christianity.

The Eucharistic experience gave birth to modern science for it profoundly transformed men's attitude to matter. The Church in its

297

sacraments taught that the physical world is good and real and that man has been appointed by the Creator to be its responsible master. The Eucharistic meal, which introduces the participants into the intimate circle of Christ's friends, gives Christians confidence in their ability to comprehend the mind of the Incarnate Logos and to share in his plans for the redemption and transfiguration of the universe. Christianity liberated its followers from the fatalism of heathen religions and delivered them from fear of the unknown which had haunted men since the dawn of history.

The process of the Christian education of mankind has been far from simple. At first the new religion was accepted only by a handful of disciples; after conversion of the Greco-Roman world, Christianity was greatly stimulated by the remarkable achievements of classical civilization, but also seriously handicapped by the finality and self-assurance of its philosophical outlook which became so closely associated with the Church as to shape its doctrinal system and ecclesiastical organization. The deep-seated pessimism of Hellenism contributed to the Byzantine Church's failure to realize the material consequences of the Incarnation, and to discover the scientific approach to life. This task, therefore, fell upon the nations which appeared on the scene of Christian history towards the end of the first millennium. They were barbarians, and training them in the rudiments of Christianity took a long time. Medieval culture was artistically vigorous and original but intellectually one-sided and its interpretation of the meaning of the Incarnation failed to take into account many essential characteristics of the Christian view of man and the world.

The Renaissance and Humanism of the sixteenth century enlarged Christian horizons but also confused the picture by uncritical absorption of much classical paganism. The Reformation stimulated and at the same time weakened the Christians of the West and provoked the growth of rationalism and secularism, which took many Christian convictions for granted without recognizing that their optimistic belief in progress and in the perfectibility of human nature rest on the facts of the Incarnation.

The scientific civilization of today is a child of mixed marriage, one of its parents the Christian belief that man is called by God to take an active part in the management of the earth, the other a wilful assertion that he is his own master responsible to no one for his actions. Spectacular scientific discoveries have created such self-confidence and pride in these achievements that the original cause of their inspiration—man's stewardship—has been lost sight of, and the existence of a connecting link between man's desire to understand the working of the universe and his recognition of his sonship to its author is no longer realized.

Man found freedom, optimism and superior knowledge in the fellowship of the Church, but these gifts opened to him the means of tyrannizing over his neighbours, of ruthless exploitation of animals, plants and all earth's resources on a scale unimaginable in the past.

The Church foresaw the possibility of this abuse of power, for it has always known that man is torn by the opposing desires to serve and love his neighbour and to make himself the centre of the universe. Modern civilization presents two crucial problems of history with new urgency; the creation of a political order that could safeguard the freedom of the individual whilst making him a disciplined and responsible member of a universal society, and the wise and generous distribution of the gifts of the earth for the benefit of all.

On the right solution of these two tasks depends the immediate future of mankind. Both of them in their present form arose within the community of Christian nations and can be properly dealt with only in the context of Christian belief in the unity of the human family and its filial relationship with the Creator of the universe. The Gospels teach that man's brotherhood is based on acceptance of the fatherhood of God; that man can become his own master only when he acknowledges the existence of his Heavenly Judge, that he can feel truly at home on earth only when he realizes that his personal existence is not confined to life in time and space. Men are called to transform the world, to make it the temple of the Holy Spirit. All men's activities contribute to this transfiguration. By eating and drinking men spiritualize matter, by weaving, by building, by creating works of art, by inventing machines that extend the operation of their bodies, they enlarge their senses and increase their mastery over the physical universe; men change the face of the earth and humanize it.

These achievements are not in the province of individual efforts, but are the result of the co-operative thinking and harmonious collaboration of many minds and hands. Only Christianity can provide the ultimate goal of such endeavours with its assurance that victory over discord, sin and death is included in the scheme of creation and is not wishful thinking. The Christian nations have built a scientific civilization and introduced it to the rest of mankind, but many of their members have lost confidence in the truth of their religion and are uncertain of the ultimate purpose of their labour. This crisis affects the Christian East and West equally. The difficulty of solving the social and scientific problems of today is aggravated by the traditional difference in emphasis between West and East; both sides seem unable to lead men on the road of Christian progress because in their present state of non-co-operation they cannot give a satisfactory answer to the practical problems of contemporary life.

Moreover, one may even say that the type of civilization now regarded as Christian suffers from the defects of its excessively Western outlook. In all stages, beginning from a Roman source, with its legalism, passing through medieval scholasticism, the Renaissance and the Reformation to the rationalism and individualism of today, it has remained self-sufficient and self-enclosed, looking down on its Eastern partner. Compared to the stormy and invigorating history of the Christian West during the past five hundred years, the Christian East seems to Westerners to have been plunged in moral and intellectual stupor, its development arrested, its creative power exhausted.

While the Christian West was re-examining the foundations of its faith and imposing its dominion on the rest of the world, the Christian East was suffering under the oppression of the Asiatic invaders and was not able to be engaged in similar adventure. Today they stand side by side, each with special contributions. The West offers its readiness to experiment, its keenness in the search for truth, and in the defence of individual freedom; the East has its trust in the guidance of the Holy Spirit, its uninterrupted tradition of teaching and worship and its faithfulness to the corporate wisdom of past generations.

Only together can they solve the problems of contemporary mankind. No balanced system of Christian doctrine, no effective action is possible without the reintegration of Christendom. Christianity is a universal religion, and no single branch of the Christian community, however powerful, can present its message convincingly in isolation from the rest. Sectarianism is the greatest enemy of Christian progress and its cure is reconciliation between the Christian East and West. Their separation was the major catastrophe in Christian history, their reunion is likely to be one of its greatest triumphs.

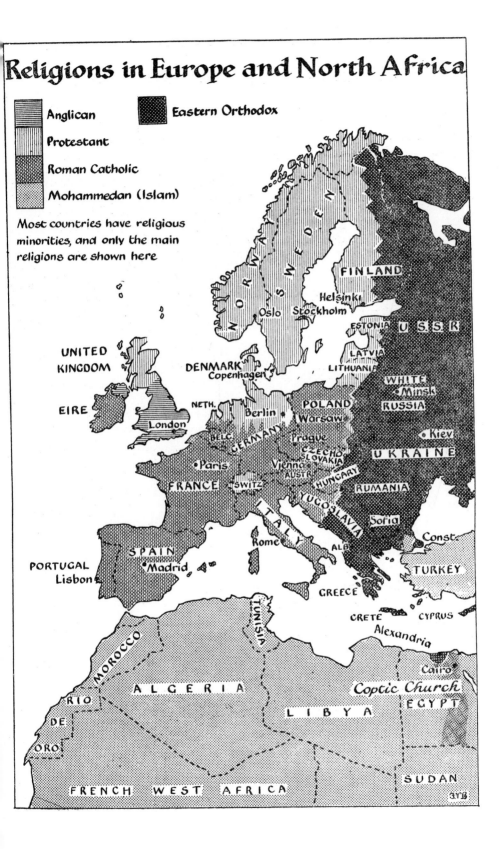

Religions in Europe and North Africa

Anglican

Protestant

Roman Catholic

Mohammedan (Islam)

Eastern Orthodox

Most countries have religious minorities, and only the main religions are shown here

NORWAY
SWEDEN
FINLAND
Oslo
Stockholm
Helsinki
ESTONIA
LATVIA
LITHUANIA
U.S.S.R.
WHITE
RUSSIA
Minsk
UNITED KINGDOM
DENMARK
Copenhagen
EIRE
NETH.
Berlin
London
BELG.
GERMANY
Paris
FRANCE
SWITZ.
POLAND
Warsaw
Prague
CZECHO-SLOVAKIA
Vienna
AUSTR.
HUNGARY
Kiev
UKRAINE
RUMANIA
YUGOSLAVIA
Sofia
ITALY
Rome
ALB.
SPAIN
Madrid
GREECE
Const.
TURKEY
CYPRUS
PORTUGAL
Lisbon
CRETE
Alexandria
TUNISIA
MOROCCO
RIO
DE
ORO
ALGERIA
Cairo
Coptic Church
EGYPT
LIBYA
FRENCH WEST AFRICA
SUDAN

Religions in Europe and Asia

Autonomous Churches

Autocephalous Churches (Patriarchates)

◆ Ecumenical Patriarchate of Constantinople

Byzantine Orthodox

Oriental Orthodox Church

Islam (heretical deviation of Oriental Orthodox Church)

FINLAND
Helsinki
ESTONIA
LATVIA
LITHUANIA
Vilna
POLAND
Warsaw
CZECH
Budapest
RUMANIA
Belgrade
Bucharest
BULGARIA
Sofia
ALBANIA
GREECE
Athens
CYPRUS

UNION OF SOVIET SOCIALIST REPUBLICS

Moscow
WHITE RUSSIA
Minsk
Kiev
UKRAINE

Constantinople
GEORGIA
Tbilisi
Echmiadzin
Ankara
ARMENIA
TURKEY
Antioch
SYRIA
Baghdad
IRAQ
Jerusalem
Alexandria
Cairo
Coptic Church
EGYPT
Sinai
LIBYA
SAUDI ARABIA
Mecca
CHAD
SUDAN
ERITREA
ADEN
Addis Ababa
ETHIOPIA
CENTRAL AFR REP
SOMALIA

Tehran
IRAN
AFGHANISTAN
PAKISTAN
CHINA
Buddhism
INDIA
Hinduism
OMAN
KERALA

J.V.B.

NOTES

CHAPTER I: THE CHURCH IN THE EAST DURING THE STRUGGLE FOR SURVIVAL

1. Acts ii, 4.
2. Pliny the Younger, *Letters*, 10, 97, 1.
3. Marcus Aurelius, *Meditations*, 11, 3, 2.
4. *St Cyprian ad Donatum*, 83.
5. Ibid., 84.
6. St Ignatius, *Epistle to the Romans*, iv, 1.
7. *Martyrdom of Polycarp*, 2.
8. Eusebius, *Prep. Evang.* IX, viii, Fig. 9, p. 165.
9. *Vita Plotinus* V, 1–15.
10. Ibid., LX, 32–39.
11. Clement, *Prot.* II.
12. Ibid., X.
13. Clement, *Strom.* VII, vii, 49.
14. Migne, *Patrologia Graeca*, XV, 174.
15. Ibid., 85.
16. Quoted by Eusebius, *Ecc. Hist.*, VI, xix, 5–9.

CHAPTER II: THE ECUMENICAL COUNCILS AND THE ORIENTAL SCHISM

1. Eusebius, *Ecc. Hist.*, X, v. 4.
2. *Cod. Theod.*, IX, viii, 1 (April 4, 326)
3. Ibid., III, xvi, 1 (331).
4. Ibid., I, xxvii, 1.
5. Eusebius, *Vita Const.*, IV, xxiv.
6. Acts xv, 9.
7. Eusebius, *Vita Const.*, III, x.
8. Ibid., III, xii.
9. Ibid., III, xv.
10. Acts, xv, 28.
11. Eusebius, *Vita Const.*, III, xx.
12. Mark, xiii, 32; John, xiv, 28.
13. Eusebius, *Ecc. Hist.*, II, xxiv.
14. Gregory, *Oratio*, xxix, 19–20.
15. Ibid., xlii, 27.
16. *Cod. Theod.*, XVI, v, 11. 1213 (383–84).
17. Gregory, *Oratio de Deitate Filli*, 4.
18. Mansi., *Sacrorum conciliorumi collectio*, Tom, VI, col. 839 and 89.
19. Math., xix, 21.

CHAPTER III: THE CHRISTIAN EAST BETWEEN ISLAM AND THE CRUSADES

1. Migne, *P.G.*, XCIV, col. 763–766.
2. F. Dvornik, *The Photian Schism* (Cambridge 1948), Epilogue.
3. Oto Bihalji Merin, *Fresken und Ikonen in Serbien und Makedonien* (Munich 1958); and S. Stewart, *Serbian Legacy* (London, 1959).

CHAPTER IV: THE MONGOL INVASION AND THE FALL OF BYZANTIUM

1. C. Dawson, *The Mongol Mission* (London, 1955), 73–6.
2. W. Wigram, *The Assyrians and their neighbours* (London, 1929), 136.

CHAPTER V: THE CENTURIES OF ISOLATION AND OPPRESSION

1. Dan., ii, 36–49.
2. E. Denisoff, *Maxim le Grecque et l'Occident* (Paris, 1943).

CHAPTER VI: THE PERIOD OF INTELLECTUAL STIRRING AND NATIONAL
LIBERATION

1. Dobbie Bateman, *St Serafim of Sarov* (London, 1936), 54.
2. N. Zernov, *Three Russian Prophets* (London, 1944), 53.
3. Khomiakov, *Works*, II, 69 (in Russian, 1886).
4. N. Zernov, *Three Russian Prophets* (London, 1944), 58
5. Dostoevsky, *Journal of an Author* No. 50 (1873).
6. N. Zernov, *Three Russian Prophets* (London, 1944), 106.
7. Soloviev, *War, Progress and the End of History: Three Discussions* (London, 1915).

CHAPTER VII: THE TIME OF TESTING AND TRIAL

1. Will Graham, *Kandinsky* (London, 1959).
2. F. Heyer, *Die Orthodoxe Kirche in der Ukraine von 1917 bis 1945* (Köln, 1953), 206.
3. L. Cholakov, 'The Contemporary Organization of the Orthodox Bulgarian Church',
Revue Internationale de Droit Comparé (New York, 1957).

CHAPTER VIII: THE FAITH AND DOCTRINE OF THE ORTHODOX CHURCH

1. N. Birkbeck, *Russia and the English Church* (London, 1895), 94.
2. S. Bulgakov, *The Orthodox Church* (London, 1935), 67.
3. Ibid., 88–89.
4. *The Church of God* edited by E. Mascall (London, 1934), 64–65.
5. S. Bulgakov, *The Orthodox Church* (London, 1935), 137.

CHAPTER IX: WORSHIP AND SACRAMENTS IN THE CHRISTIAN EAST

1. C. E. Padwick, *Aspects of Holy Communion* (Cairo, 1934).
2. Nicholas Cabasilas, *Explication de la Divine Liturgie* (Paris, 1944).
3. St Simeon, *La Vie Spirituelle* (Volume XXVII, Number 3), 309–11.
4. Pitra, *Hymnographie de l'Eglise Grecque* (Rome, 1867), 33.
5. English translation published by Fellowship of St Alban and St Sergius (London, 1958).

CHAPTER X: THE CHURCH IN THE LIFE OF EASTERN CHRISTIANS

1. S. Bulgakov, *The Orthodox Church* (London, 1935), 9.
2. Math., vi, 14.
3. *A Manual of Eastern Orthodox Prayers*, English translations (SPCK, London, 1945).
4. I. Hapgood, *Service Book of the Orthodox Church* (New York, 1922), 360–7.
5. *Writings from the Philokalia*, translated into English by E. Kadloubovsky (London, 1951);
and *The Way of a Pilgrim*, translated by R. M. French (London, 1954).

CHAPTER XI: THE SACRED ART OF THE CHRISTIAN EAST

1. C. Stewart, *Serbian Legacy* (London, 1959), 44.
2. R. Byron, *First Russia, then Tibet* (London, 1933), 117.
3. Ibid., 115.
4. N. P. Kondakov, *The Russian Icon* (Oxford, 1927), 68.
5. R. Byron, *First Russia, then Tibet* (London, 1933), 124.
6. R. Byron, *The Birth of Western Painting* (London, 1930), 59, 219.
7. *Early Russian Icons*, UNESCO, 11.

BIBLIOGRAPHY

The purpose of the select bibliography is to help the reader to pursue further studies of various aspects of Eastern Christianity referred to in this book. No complete bibliography has been attempted, but many works included in this list contain an up-to-date bibliography of their own subjects. The French and German books are mentioned only as exceptions in cases where no corresponding literature in English is available; magazine articles are not included. Except where otherwise stated, the books are all published in London.

CHAPTER I

Preliminary Remarks. The original sources for the study of the early period of Eastern Christianity can be found in several collections of their English translations. *Ancient Christian Writers* edited by J. Quastlin and J. Plumpe, 26 vols. 1950–59. *Ante-Nicene Christian Library* ed. by A. Roberts and J. Donaldson, 24 vols. 1867–72. *Cambridge Patristic Texts*, 11 vols. 1899–1927. *Library of Christian Classics*, 12 vols. 1953–58. *Library of the Fathers of the Catholic Church anterior to the divisions of East and West*, 48 vols. 1839–85. *Nicene and post-Nicene Fathers* edited by P. Schaff 1886–88, 1st series 14 vols. and 2nd series 14 vols. The last series continues the English translation of the most important ecclesiastical historians of antiquity, such as Eusebius of Caesarea, Socrates Scholasticus, Sozamen, Theodoret, Jerome, Rufinus and the decrees of the first seven Ecumenical Councils. There are also translations of Christian literature by diverse authors 1920–50. Series I. Greek Fathers of the Church; Series III. Liturgical Texts; Series IV. Oriental writing; Series VI. Selected passages. Those who desire to read the Christian literature in the original Greek or Latin may consult Migne, *Patrologiae Cursus Completus*, consisting of 390 volumes.

General Histories of the Early Church. *Atlas of the Early Christian World* by F. van der Meer, London 1958, gives a vivid picture of the monuments and art of the Early Church, and also includes excellent maps. P. Carrington, *The Early Christian Church*, 2 vols., 1957, an up-to-date and readable introduction to the history of the Early Church. A shorter work is by J. Wand, *A History of the Early Church*, London 1949. More scholarly and detailed information can be obtained from: H. Lietzman, *History of the Early Church*, 4 vols., 1937–51. B. Kidd, *A History of the Early Church*, 3 vols., Oxford 1922. L. Duchesne, *The Early History of the Church*, 3 vols., 1909–14, is one of the best books on this subject. Those readers who desire to acquaint themselves with the earlier Church histories are recommended to read Eusebius, the *Ecclesiastical History*, translated by H. J. Lawler, London 1928, which is one of the most important sources of information dating from the fourth century, but containing many quotations from earlier works, most of which have not survived. Josephæs, *The Jewish War*, translated by J. Williamson, 1959, gives a vivid contemporary description of Judea from 170 BC till AD 75. The question of the number of Jews martyred is discussed in Klausner, *Jésus de Nazareth*, Paris, p. 242.

The relation between Judaism and Christianity. C. Dodd, *Apostolic Preaching and its development*, 1936. G. H. C. MacGregor and A. C. Purdy, *Jew and Greek tutors to Christ*, Edinburgh 1959. It contains a good bibliography and also includes a chapter on the significance of the Dead Sea Scrolls, discovered between 1947 and 1956, which threw a new light on the origins of the Christian community. The best books on the Scrolls are: Millar Burrows, *The Dead Sea Scrolls*, 1955, Yigael Yadin, *The Message of the Scrolls*, 1957.

Christianity and Hellenism. Out of a large number of works dedicated to this subject, only a few can be mentioned here: C. Cochrane, *Christianity and Classical Culture*, New York 1957, C. Dodd, *The Bible and the Greeks*, 1935, E. Hatch, *The Influence of Greek ideas on Christianity*, 1959, M. Leistner, *Christianity and Pagan Culture*, 1951.

The Early Organization of the Church. J. Weiss, *Earliest Christianity* (AD 30–150), 2 vols., 1959. The flight of the Christians to Pella is described by Eusebius, *Eccles. Hist.* III, 5, 3. S. Brandon, *The Fall of Jerusalem and the Christian Church* (1957) considers the destruction of

Jerusalem as the decisive date when the Christian community finally broke away from Judaism. The hostility of the leaders of Judaism to Christ's disciples led to the martyrdom of St Stephen (Acts vi, 9–vii, 60) and St James (Acts xii, 1–2). This first persecution is described by Eusebius ii, 23, and Josephus, *The Jewish War* xx, 3, 1, 199. Hegesippus iv, Ch. 22, gives another version of the same martyrdom. Reasons for the persecution and the martyrs' conduct, see D. Attwater, *Martyrs* (1958) and H. Workman, *The Martyrs of the Early Church*, 1913. Marcus Aurelius, *Meditations*, II, 3, 2. St Cyprian. See E. Benson, *Cyprian, his life, his times, his work*. St Cyprian's own writings are in Ante-Nicene Christian Library, vols. 1 and 2, 1869.

Gnosticism. S. Angus, *The Mystery Religions and Christianity*, 1925. F. C. Burkitt, *The Church and Gnosis*, Cambridge 1932. R. Grant, *Gnosticism and Early Christianity* (New York 1959) contains the most recent Bibliography. R. Wilson, *The Gnostic Problem*, 1958.

Montanism. There is no book in English on this subject, but reference to Montanism can be found in all manuals of Church History. The best study of this movement is in French, P. de Labrielle, *La Crise Montaniste*, Paris 1913.

Tertullian. His works in the *Ante-Nicene Christian Library*, vols. I–III. The best books about him are in German: B. Nister, *Tertullian Sein Personlichkeit und sein Schicksal*, 1950, and H. Karp, *Schrift und Geist bei Tertullian*, 1955.

Paul of Samosata. There are two books in French about this heretical Bishop of Antioch. C. Bardy, *Paul de Samosate*, Paris 1923. H. de Reidmatten, *Les Actes du Procès de Paul de Samosate Paradosis*, 6, 1952.

The Formation of the New Testament. There is a good book by this title by H. F. D. Sparks, 1952.

The Origin of the Episcopate. This problem has attracted considerable attention from Church historians. C. Gore, *The Church and the Ministry*, 1936. E. Hatch, *The Organization of the Early Church*, 1882. K. Kirk, *The Apostolic Ministry*, 1946. J. Lightfoot, *The Christian Ministry*. B. Streeter, *The Primitive Church*, 1929, an original and provocative treatment of this controversial problem.

The St Ignatius Epistles can be found in many English translations. The most recent in vol. I of the *Library of Christian Classics*, Philadelphia 1953. A vivid portrait of St Ignatius is given by R. Payne, *The Holy Fire*, New York 1957. The martyrdom of St Polycarp in vol. I of the *Library of Christian Classics*, Philadelphia 1953.

Clement and Origen. The literature about these two leading Alexandrian theologians is extensive. The second volume of the *Library of Christian Classics* (1954) contains some of their writings. More information about their contribution to Christian apologetics can be found in: R. Hanson, *Origen's Doctrine of Tradition*, 1951; R. Cadou, *Origen*, St Louis 1941; V. Osborn, *The Philosophy of Clement of Alexandria*, 1957; R. Tollington, *Clement of Alexandria*, 1914; G. Butterworth, *Clement of Alexandria*, Harvard Univ. Press, 1953; E. de Faye, *Origen and his work*, 1926; An older, but excellent book is C. Bigg, *The Christian Platonists in Alexandria*, Oxford 1913; St Gregory Thaumaturgus, *Addresses to Origen*, Translations of Christian Literature, Series I, vol. 8, 1920.

CHAPTER II

Preliminary remarks. Original sources: Byzantine Church historians Eusebius, Socrates, Sozomen, Theodoret, Evagrius (see page 305).

The decrees of Ecumenical Councils. Hefele et de Clercq, *Histoires des Conciles d'après les documents originaux*. 11 vols. (English translation of the first three volumes only.) The writings of the Church Fathers in Migne and in various translations into English, French and German. (see page 365).

General Histories of the Church (see page 305).

Histories of the Eastern Churches. B. J. Kidd, *The Churches of Eastern Christendom from 451 to the present time, 1928*, gives a factual account without bias. W. Adeney, *The Greek and Eastern Churches*, Edinburgh 1908 (with Protestant bias). Two Roman Catholic authors present their versions of Eastern Christianity: D. Attwater, *The Christian Churches of the East*, 2 vols, 1947–48; A. Fortescue, *The Eastern Orthodox Church*, 1939. A useful addition to the study of Eastern Christianity is: R. Longford-James, *A Dictionary of the Eastern Orthodox Church*, 1923.

Special points raised in Chapter II. Constantine's conversion is discussed in the following special studies: A. Alfoldi, *The Conversion of Constantine and Pagan Rome*, 1948; W. Baynes, *Constantine the Great and the Christian Church*, 1930 (one of the best); S. Greenslade, *Church and State from Constantine to Theodosius*, 1954; A. Jones, *Constantine and the Conversion of Europe*, 1952; H. Mattingly, *Christianity in the Roman Empire*, 1955; E. Woodward, *Christianity and Nationalism in the Roman Empire*, 1916.

The importance and frequency of North African Councils is fully revealed by St Cyprian in his correspondence.

Council of Nicaea. A special study of this Council is A. Burn, *The Council of Nicaea*, 1925.

Arianism. H. Gwatkin, *Studies of Arianism*, Camb. 1900, and all general Church historians. For the study of the creeds see J. Kelly, *Early Christian Creeds*, 1950.

St Athanasius and Arianism. *Selected works of St Athanasius* tr. by A. Robinson, 1892, also *Library of Christian Classics*, vol. III, also R. Bush, *St Athanasius*, 1888. L. H. Hough, *Athanasius the Hero*, New York 1906. The latest work is by E. Schwartz, *Zur Geschichte des Athanasius*, 1959. The accusations against Athanasius are described by Sozomen, II, 21, 25. St Athanasius, *Life of St Anthony. Ancient Christian Writers*, vol. 10.

The Donatist scheme. W. Frend, *The Donatist Church*, Oxford 1952. G. G. Willis, *St Augustine and the Donatisr Controversy*, 1950. For the Monophysite Schism, W. Wigram, *The Separation of the Monophysites*, 1923.

The Cappadocian Fathers. Their original works are published in the *Library of Christian Classics*, vol. III, and in other collections of Patristic writings. W. Clark, *The Ascetic Works of St Basil*, London 1925. J. Daniélou, *Platonisme et Théologie Mystique*, Paris 1944. W. Wolker, *Gregor von Nyssa*, 1956. J. Srawley, *The Catechetical Oration of St Gregory of Nyssa*, 1917. J. Plaigneux, *St Grégoire de Nazianze*, Paris 1951. Socrates, I, 23. St Gregory of Nyssa left a moving description of his beloved sister in his *Vita St Macrinae*. E. Morison, *St Basil and his Rule, a study in early monasticism*. Oxford 1912.

St John Chrysostom. An excellent up-to-date biography of St John is by Donald Attwater, 1959, and a monumental work on his life and time is in two volumes by Dom Chrysostom Baur, *Der Heilige Johannes Chrysostomus und seine Zeit*. Munich 1929–30. English translation 1959–60 includes bibliography. There are also B. Vandenberghe, *John of the Golden Mouth*, 1958, and *St John Chrysostom and St Olympias*, 1959. St John Chrysostom, *Homilies on the Status. Library of the Fathers*, vol. 9, 1842.

Nestorius and the Nestorian schism. This has attracted the attention of many historians. Nestorius's surviving work *The Bazaar of Heracleides* was translated by Driver and L. Hodgson, 1923. The defence of his position is made by J. Bethune-Baker, *Nestorius and his Teaching*, 1908. F. Loofs, *Nestorius and his place in the history of Christian doctrine*, 1914. A. Vine, *The Bazaar of Heracleides*, 1948. There is a Roman Catholic repudiation of Nestorius by M. Jugie, *Nestorius et la controverse Nestorienne*, 1912.

St Cyril of Alexandria. W. Burghardt, *The Image of God in man according to Cyril of Alexandria*,

1951. A. Kerrigan, *St Cyril of Alexandria, interpreter of the Old Testament*, 1952. J. Liebert, *La Doctrine Christologique de St Cyrille d'Alexandrie*, 1951.

Chalcedonian Council. J. MacArthur, *Chalcedon*, 1931. R. Sellars, *The Council of Chalcedon*, 1953, (The latest study). Justinian and his time. J. W. Holmes, *The age of Justinian and Theodore*, 2 vols., 1905 and 1907. C. Diehl, *Figures Byzantines*, 2 vols., Paris 1906 and 1908, *Justinian*, Paris, *Theodora Impératrice de Byzanée*, Paris. A. A. Vasiliev, *Justin the First*. An introduction to the epoch of Justinian, Camb., Mass. 1950.

Severus of Antioch. Collection of Letters, *Patrologia Orientales*, Syrian section. *Vie de Sévère*, trans. by M. Kugener. A collection of letters, trans. by E. Brooks. *Les Homiliae Cathédrales de Sévère d'Antioche*, vols. I–X, trans. by diverse scholars. J. Lebon, *Le Monophysisme Sévèrien*, Paris 1909.

The Armenians. 'I have understood they were the first to embrace Christianity', Sozomen, II, 8. The best study of the Armenian Churches is by M. Ormanian, *The Church of the Armenians*, which includes the description of the origin of Armenian Christianity. Armenian Alphabet, see Korium. The life of Mashtots translated into French by W. Langlois, *Histoire Arménienne*, vol. II. R. Grousset, *Histoire de l'Arménie*, Paris 1947. K. Sarkissian, *Armenian Christian Literature (a brief introduction)* 1960. A short but useful study.

The Georgian Church. T. Dowling, *Sketches of Georgian Church History*, 1912. D. Lang, *Lives of Georgian Saints*, 1956. S. Malan, *A short history of the Georgian Church*, 1866. Bibliography: J. Kurst, *Littérature Georgienne Chrétienne*, Paris 1934.

The Conversion of Ethiopia. This is narrated by several ancient Church historians: Rufinus, *Hist. Ecc.*, I, 9; Socrates, *Hist. Ecc.*, I, 15; Theodoret, *Hist Ecc.*, I, 22; Sozomen, II, 23. The best introduction to the origins and present state of the Church is H. M. Hyatt, *The Church of Abyssinia*, 1928. There are also three smaller books: D. O'Hanlon, *Features of the Abyssinian Church*, 1946; J. Spencer Triningham, *The Christian Church and Missions in Ethiopia*, 1950; O'Leary, *The Ethiopian Church*, 1936.

India and Ceylon. St Thomas's missionary work in India is contained in Acts of Judas-Thomas, composed in Mesopotamia, and containing a mixture of legends and history. The detailed analysis of the Church's origin in India is given by A. Mingana. His account of the early spread of Christianity in India can be found in the *Bulletin of the John Rylands' Library*, Manchester 1926. Eusebius, *Hist. Ecc.*, V, 10, refers to the Indian Church. The first book about the Indian Church published in England was M. Geddes's *History of the Church of Malabar*, 1694. The best modern works are Cardinal E. Tisserant, *Eastern Christianity in India*, 1957, and L. W. Brown, *The Indian Christians of St Thomas*, Cambridge 1956. Both include full bibliographies. Other recent books: F. Keay, *A History of the Syrian Church in India*, Madras 1951. E. Philip, *The Indian Church of St Thomas*, Kottayam 1950. N. Zernov, *The Christian East*, Delhi 1957.

The Origins of Monasticism. General works: Owen Chadwick, *John Cassian, a study of primitive monasticism*, Camb. 1950; J. Smith, *The rise of Christian monasticism*, 1892; J. Hannay, *The spirit and origin of Christian monasticism*, 1903; K. Heussi, *Der Ursprung des Monchtums*, 1936; Dom J. M. Bess, *Les moines d'Orient antérieur au Concile de Chalcédoine*, Paris 1900. Special works on Egyptian monasticism and the Desert Fathers: E. White, *The History of Monasteries of Nitria and of Scete*, N.Y. 1932; P. Raschlot, *Doctrine ascétique des premiers maîtres Egyptiens de IV siècle*, Paris 1931; W. MacKean, *Christian Monasticism in Egypt*, 1920; Helen Waddell, *The Desert Fathers*, 1936; J. Bremond, *Les Pères du Desert*, Paris 1927. A vivid contemporary description of the Desert Fathers is contained in Palladius, *The Lausiac History*, tr. by W. Clarke, 1918, also C. Buttle, *The Lausiac History of Palladius*, 2 vols, Camb. 1898–1904. One of the most important manuals of Eastern asceticism is available in English translation: St John Climacus (579–649), *The Ladder of Divine Ascent*, tr. by L. Moore, 1959. T. Lefort, *Les Vies Coptes de St Pachome*, Louvain 1943. R. Genier, *Vie de St Euthyme le grand*, Paris 1909. H. Delahaye, *Les Saints Stylites*, Brussels 1923. E. F. Morison, *St Basil and his rule*, 1912. W. K. L. Clark, *St Basil*

308

the Great, a study of monasticism, Camb. 1913. Mount Athos. Kirsopp Lake, *The early days of monasticism on Mount Athos*, Oxford 1909.

The Church of the Persian Empire. All ancient Church histories, Socrates, Sozomen, Theodoret and Evagrius describe the trials and martyrdom of Christians in the Persian Empire. Special studies: A. Vine, *The Nestorian Church*, 1937; W. Wigram, *The Assyrians and their neighbours*, 1929; Maclean and Browne, *The Catholicos of the East and his people*, 1892; Browne, *The Eclipse of Christianity in Asia*, Camb. 1933. One of the older, but still useful, books is by J. La Court, *Le Christianisme dans l'Empire Perse*, Paris 1904.

Rome and the Christian East. This subject is one of the major points of controversy and is discussed in all works on early Church history, such as Kidd, Harnack, Robertson, Duchesne, Lietzman, Gwatkin and others. Special studies of this subject by Roman Catholics are: P. Batiffol, *L'Eglise Naissante*, Paris 1922; *Le Siège Apostolique*, Paris 1924; *La Paix Constantienne*, Paris 1914. Duchesne, *The Churches separated from Rome*, 1907. E. Jaspar, *Geschichte des Papstums*, a monumental work. W. Bright, *The Roman See in the Early Church*, 1896. F. Puller, *Primitive Saints and the See of Rome*, 1915. Jalland, *Leo and his time*, 1941; An Anglican Church historian, supporting Papal claims, is S. H. Scott, *The Eastern Church and the Papacy*, 1928.

CHAPTER III

Patriarch Sergius (610–38). His exceptionally important role in Byzantine history is discussed by A. Toynbee in *A Study of History*, vol. IV, p. 333, *et seq*. The detailed account of the reign of Heraclius with the full bibliography in G. Ostrogorsky, *History of the Byzantine Empire*, pp. 79–110, Oxford 1956.

Maxim the Confessor. English translation of his works: *The Ascetic Life* and the *Four Centuries of Charity* in *Ancient Christian Writers*, vol. 21. Other studies of St Maxim include: H. Balthasar, *Liturgie Cosmique, Maxim le Confesseur. Collection Théologie*, vol. II. L. Hausherr, *Philautie. De la tendresse pour soi à la charité selon St Maxim le Confesseur*, Paris 1952. P. Sherwood, *The earlier Ambigua of St Maxim the Confessor and his refutation of Origenism*, 1954. Studia Anselmiana 36.

Maronites. F. Dib, *L'Eglise Maronite jusqu'à la fin du Moyen Age*, refers to original sources. D. Attwater, *The Catholic Eastern Churches*, 1935, pp. 180–195, includes a short bibliography.

Zoroastrianism. R. C. Zaehner, *The Teaching of the Magi*, 1956. *Zurvan, A Zoroastrian Dilemma*, Oxford 1955.

Islam. The best source of general information is the *Shorter Encyclopaedia of Islam*, edited by H. Gibb and J. Kramers. Leyden 1953. Mohammed's personality is analysed by Tor Andrae, *Mohammed, the man and his faith*, 1936. W. Watt, *Mohammed at Mecca*, Oxford 1953, and *Mohammed at Medina*, Oxrord 1956. A Butler, *The Arab Conquest of Egypt*, Oxford 1909. The Koran translated and interpreted by A. J. Arbery, 2 vols, 1955.

The Appeal of Islam. H. Gibb, *Modern Trends in Islam*, Chicago 1947. W. Cantwell Smith, *Islam in Modern History*, Princeton 1957. A. Arberry, *The Call of the Minarets, Revelation and Reason in Islam*, 1957. T. W. Arnold, *The Preaching of Islam*, 1913, *The Legacy of Islam*, Oxford 1931. A. Wensinek, *The Muslim Creed*, Camb. 1932. A. P. Tritton, *Muslim Theology*, 1947. R. Levy, *The Social Structure of Islam*, Camb. 1957. Dvornik, *The Circus parties in Byzantium* in *Byzantine-Metabyzantium*, New York, vol. I. At the time of the spectacular advance of Islam its supporters and its oppenents treated each other as professing together a religion based on the Biblical Revelations. See A. Vasiliev, *Byzantium and Islam*, and Baynes and Moss, *Byzantium*, Oxford 1948, p. 309. The rapid expansion of Islamic civilization and its subsequent decline and long stagnation is liable to diverse interpretations. One of the important factors for its initial flowering was the political unification of the Mediterranean world by Arab conquest, and the considerable religious and intellectual tolerance displayed at first by the new masters. The majority of the conquered population was then still Christian and the intellectual and artistic stimulus came from the Greek classical and Christian sources.

H. Gibb says: 'Islamic culture was pegged to that stage at which the Arabic scientists had developed the concepts and methods taken over from the Greek.' (*The Influence of Islamic Culture on Medieval Europe*, Manchester 1955, p. 94.) T. Arnold says: 'Muslim medicine and science was derived from Greek sources.' (*Muslim Civilization during the Abbasid period*, The Camb. Med. Hist. 1927, vol. IV, pp. 297–8.) 'The learned men were mostly Christians or Jews bearing Arabic names.' Ibid, p. 314. 'The Christian family of Bucht-Yishu produced no less than seven generations of distinguished physicians.' Ibid, p. 315. The political and economic decline of the Middle East started when the gradual suffocation of the Christian religion and consolidation of Islamic Orthodoxy prevented further development of cultural and intellectual life in the lands conquered by Islam. Such is the opinion of T. Arnold: 'The Muslim political theory contained no principle of growth to provide for the development of self-governing institutions; no attempt had been made to widen the basis of government or train the subjects in co-operation with the state.' (T. W. Arnold, op cit., pp. 279–80). The remarkable artistic achievement of early Islamic civilization was also mainly due to the great cultured wealth which the Arabs found in the lands of the Byzantine Empire. 'In a word the cultural development of the Arabs was mostly due to foreign activities and foreign materials.' (N. Baynes, *Byzantium*, Oxford 1948, p. 315.)

Iconoclasm. E. Martin, *A History of the Iconoclastic controversy* (1930) is a general introduction to this subject. It contains a bibliography. See also: F. Bevan, *Holy Images*, 1940; C. Clerc, *Les Théories relatives au cultes des Images chez les auteurs Grecs*, Paris 1915; A. Grabar, *L'Iconoclasme Byzantine, Dossier Archéologique*, 1958. A more specialized study is P. Alexander, *The Patriarch Nicephorus of Constantinople*, 1958. It contains an up-to-date bibliography. Leo III's legislation is discussed by Ostrogorsky, *History of the Byzantine state*, pp. 140–2.

Charlemagne and Byzantium. *Libri Carolini* condemned equally the Iconoclastic Council of 753 and the second Nicene Council of 787. The aim of this Frankish attack on the Orthodox Church was to prove that Byzantium embraced heresy, and therefore ceased to be the universal Christian state. This was further confirmed by the Frankfurt Synod of 794 which condemned as heretical the veneration of ikons as formulated by the Nicene Council of 787. In spite of it the legates of Pope Adrian I (772–95) subscribed to the decisions of both Synods, Byzantine and Frankish. See Ostrogorsky, op cit., p. 164.

Mohammed and Charlemagne. Special study by J. H. Pirenne, *Mohammed and Charlemagne*. 1939.

Filioque controversy. The detailed account of it is in A. Vacant and E. Mongenot, *Dictionnaire de Théologie Catholique*, vol. V, Paris 1913, pp. 2309–51. The last Western point of resistance to this innovation was the Sorbonne, where the original version of the Creed continued to be recited until the middle of the thirteenth century. See also G. Every, *The Byzantine Patriarchate*, 1947, p. 150, Footnote 1. The current Eastern Orthodox, Anglican and Roman Catholic points of view on this subject can be found in the *Eastern Churches Quarterly*, supplementary issue, vol. VII, 1948, *Concerning the Holy Spirit*.

The conversion of the Slavs. The principal authority on this subject is F. Dvornik who has published several monumental works. *Les Slaves, Byzance et Rome, IX siècle*, Paris 1926; *Les Légendes de Constantin et de Méthodie*, Prague 1933; *The Making of Central and Eastern Europe*, 1949; M. Spinka, *A History of Christianity in the Balkans*, Illinois 1933.

The Photian schism. An exhaustive study of the schism is made by: F. Dvornik, *The Photian Schism*, Camb. 1948. It contains a complete bibliography both of original sources, pp. 459–73, including more than 500 titles, and a list of the recent books on this subject, pp. 474–87. A useful book also is G. Every's *The Byzantine Patriarchate*, 1947.

Byzantine shortcomings and achievements. A popular book on this subject is by René Guerdan. *Byzantium, its triumphs and tragedy*, 1956. G. Ostrogorsky, *History of the Byzantine State*, Oxford 1956. (A scholarly work.) Two excellent general surveys are by N. Baynes and H. Moss, *Byzantium*, Oxford 1948, and by S. Runciman, *Byzantine Civilization*, 1948. For further reading, consult: Charles Diehl, J. Bury, A. Vasiliev and Gibbon. (Biased but excellent prose.) Some of the causes of the Byzantine decline are discussed by A. Toynbee in *A Study of History*, vol. IV, p. 320 *et seq*. See also J. M. Hussey, *Church and Learning in the Byzantine Empire* (867–1185), 1937.

The Schism between Rome and Constantinople. One of the latest and best works is: S. Runciman, *The Eastern Schism*, a study of the Papacy and the Eastern Churches during the ninth and twelfth centuries. Oxford 1955. It contains an up-to-date bibliography. An older work by L. Brehier, *La Schism Orientale du XI siècle*, Paris 1899. A Roman Catholic view is stated by M. Jujie, *Le Schism Byzantin*, Paris 1941. Jules Gay, *L'Italie Méridionale et l'Empire Byzantin*, Paris 1904. A. Michel, *Humbert and Kerullarios*, 2 vols, Padeborn 1924–30.

The Crusaders. The literature about the Crusaders is extensive, but S. Runciman's *History of the Crusades*, 3 vols., Cambridge 1951–54 is not only one of the more recent studies of this movement, but also the one which pays special attention to the effect which it had upon relations between the Eastern and Western Churches. A full bibliography is included in each volume.

The Slavonic speaking churches. S. Runciman. *A History of the First Bulgarian Empire*, 1930. *The Life of St Sava* by Bishop Nikolai Velimirovich, Libertyville, Illinois, 1951.

Serbian art. Oto Behalji Mern, *Fresken und Ikonen in Serbien und Macedonia*, Munich 1958. C. Stewart, *Serbian Legacy*, 1959.

Russia's conversion to Christianity. Original sources: S. H. Cross, *The Russian Primary Chronicle*, Harvard Univ. Press, 1930. R. Michell and N. Forbes, *The Chronicle of Novgorod* (*1016–1471*), 1914. N. Zernov, *The Slavonic Review*, London, Nov. 1953, April 1954.

General Histories of the Russian Church. W. Frere, *Some Links in the Chain of the Russian Church*, 1945. N. Zernov, *The Russians and their Church*, 1945. R. Korper, *The Candlelight Kingdom*, New York, 1955. B. Grunwald, *Boris and Gleb, Saints of Russia*, 1956. St Theodosius of Kiev. His Life in G. Fedotov, *A Treasury of Russian Spirituality*, 1950, pp. 11–49. *Vladimir's Testament* in A. Stanley's *Lectures on the History of the Eastern Church*, 1862. The outlook of the Early Russian Christians is discussed by G. Fedotov in *The Russian Religious Mind*, Harvard 1946.

CHAPTER IV

The Mongols. The most comprehensive study in English is still an old work, H. Hawarth, *History of the Mongols*, 4 vols., 1876–88. A vividly written, but a lighter book is M. Prawdin, *The Mongol Empire*, 1940. The best studies of the Mongols are in French by H. Grousset, *L'Empire Mongol*, 1941, and *L'Empire des Steppes*, 1939. Genghis Khan—Timuchin's biographies. R. Fox, *Genghis Khan*, New York 1936. F. Grenard, *Genghis Khan*, Paris 1936. R. Grousset, *Le Conquérant du Monde*, Paris 1944. H. Lamb, *Genghis Khan, The Emperor of all Men*, New York 1927. H. Martin, *The Rise of Genghis Khan*, Baltimore 1950. B. Vladimirtzov, *Genghis Khan*, Berlin 1922. E. G. Browne, *The Eclipse of Christianity in Asia*, Camb. 1933. Russia under the Mongols, G. Vernadsky, *The Mongols and Russia*, Yale 1953, includes a good bibliography. St Sergius of Radonezh. N. Zernov, *St Sergius, Builder of Russia*, 1939. This includes an English translation of the Saint's life.

The Church in China. J. Foster, *The Church of the T'ang Dynasty*, 1946. A. C. Moule, *Christians in China before 1550*, 1930.

The Mongols and Christian Europe. The translation of the relevant documents and diaries is given by C. Dowson, *The Mongol Mission*, 1955, a book of a first-class importance. S. Runciman, *A History of the Crusades*. Vol. III also gives much useful information. W. Wigram, *The Assyrians and their Neighbours*, 1929, p. 136. S. Runciman, *The Sicilian Vespers*, Camb. 1958.

The Florentine Council. A comprehensive study of the Council based on a careful examination of the original sources by I. Gill, *The Council of Florence*, Camb. 1959, with full bibliography.

The last years of the Byzantine Empire. Alice Gardner, *The Lescarides of Nicaea*, 1912. W. Miller, *Trebizond, the Last Greek Empire*, 1926. O. Halecki, *The Crusade of Varna*, New York 1943. T. Longman, *L'Empire Latin de Constantinople*, Paris 1949.

St Gregory Palamas. There are three books in French, all by Jean Meyendorff: *Triades pour la défénse des Saints Hesychastes*, Louvain 1959. *Introduction a L'Etude de Grégoire Palamas*, Paris 1959, and a more popular book, *St Grégoire Palamas et la Mystique Orthodox*, Paris 1959.

Nicholas Cabasilas. Two of his books are translated. *The commentary on the Divine Liturgy*, 1960, *La Vie en Jésus Christ*, Amay sur Meuse 1934. The best book about him is Myrrha Lot Borodine, *Un Maître de la Spiritualité Byzantine*, Nicholas Cabasilas, Paris 1958.

The Fall of Constantinople. E. Pears, *The Destruction of the Greek Empire* and *The Story of the Capture of Constantinople by the Turks*, 1903. H. Russack, *Byzanz and Stambul—Sagen und Legenden*, Berlin 1941.

CHAPTER V

The Ottoman Empire. D. Vaughan, *Europe and the Turk*, Liverpool 1954. M. Koprulai, *Les Origines de l'Empire Ottoman*, Paris 1939. F. Hasluck, *Christianity and Islam under the Sultans*, 2 vols, Oxford 1929.

The Orthodox Church and the Reformers. John Covel, *Some Accounts of the Present Greek Church with Reflections on their Present Doctrines and Discipline*, Cambridge 1722. E. Benz, *Wittenberg und Byzanz*, Marburg Lahn 1949. P. Renandin, *Luthériens et Grecs Orthodoxes*, Paris 1903.

Cyril Lukaris. Germanos, *Metropolitan of Thyaterira, Kyrillos Lukaris*, 1951. R. Schlier, *Der Patriarch Kyrill Lukaris*, Warburg 1927. A. Mettetal, *Etudes historiques sur Cyrille Lucar*, Strasburg 1869.

The Russian Church. N. Zernov, *Moscow the Third Rome*, 1927. Hildegard Schaeder, *Moscow des Dritte Rom*, Hamburg 1929, Darmstadt 1957. Krupnitzkij, *Die Theorie des Dritten Rome*, 1952. E. Sarkisyanz, *Russland und der Missianismus des Orients*, Tubingen 1955. Kennet Medlin, *Moscow and East Rome*, Neuchatel 1959. Alexander Soloviev, *Holy Russia*, The Hague 1959. A detailed description of the Russian Christian customs is contained in a book called *Domostroy* (sixteenth century). It remained the manual of Christian conduct up to the time of Peter's Reforms in the eighteenth century.

Two tendencies in Russian Spirituality. St Nil of Sorsk's writings are translated by G. Fedovov, *A Treasure of Russian Spirituality*, pp. 85–136. E. Behr Sigel, *Prière et Sainteté dans l'Eglise Russe*, Paris 1950. I. Smolitsch, *Die Altrussische Monchtum*, Wurzburg 1940. I. Smolitsch, *Leben und Lehre der Startzen*, Koln 1952. E. Denisoff, *Maxim le Grec et l'Occident*, Paris 1943.

Ivan the Terrible. The original source for the study of his reign and outlook is *The correspondence between Prince A. Kurbusky and Tsar Ivan of Russia* (1564–79) ed. by J. Fennell, Camb. 1955, and Dr Giles Fletcher, which gives an eye-witness description of Russia in the sixteenth century. *The Treatise of the Russe Commonwealth* which is included in the collection of the Hakluyt Society, 1856, shows Russia at the close of the sixteenth century. Romanticized Biographies: K. Waliszewski, *Ivan the Terrible*, 1904; S. Graham, *The Life of Ivan the Terrible*; R. Wipper, *Ivan Grozny*, Moscow 1947 (in English), a study by a well-known Soviet historian.

The Schism in the Russian Church. W. Palmer, *The Tsar and the Patriarch*, 6 vols., is the most detailed study of the conflict (1871–76). N. Zernov, *The Russians and their Church*, 1945. The Union of Brest-Litovsk, A. Amman, *Ostslavische Kirchengeschichte*, Wien 1950. T. Pelesz, *Geschichte der Union der Ruthenischen Kirche, mit. Rom*, 2 vols., Wurzburg-Wien 1881. E. Likovski, *Die Ruthenich-Romische Kirchenvereinigung genant Union zu Brest*, Freiburg i.B. 1904.

Avvacum. Avvacum wrote his own life story which has been translated by J. Harrison, *The Life of Archpriest Avvacum*, 1924. This book is of utmost importance for the understanding of the Russian outlook in the seventeenth century. An excellent study of Avvacum and of his period is P. Pascal, *Avvacum et le début de Rascol*, Paris 1938.

Peter the Great. A popularly written biography of the Tsar-Reformer is by S. Graham, *Peter the Great*, 1929. A scholarly summary of his reign is by B. H. Sumner, *Peter the Great and the Emergence of Russia*, 1950. E. Schuyler, *Peter the Great*, vols I and II, 1884.

The Non-Jurors and the Orthodox Church. G. Williams, *The Orthodox Church of the East in the Eighteenth Century*, being the correspondence between the Eastern Patriarchs and the Non-Juring Bishops, 1868.

Catherine the Great. Gladys Thomson, *Catherine the Great and the Expansion of Russia*, 1947. A. Bruckner, *Katherine die Zweite*. G. Gooch, *Catherine the Great*, 1959. W. Reddaway, *Documents of Catherine the Great*, Camb. 1931.

St Tikhon of Zadonsk. Nadejda Gorodestsky, *St Tikhon Zadonsky, Inspirer of Dostoevsky*, 1951. G. Fedotov, *A Treasury of Russian Spirituality* contains some of St Tikhon's writings, pp. 186–241.

The Christian East and Rome in the sixteenth, seventeenth and eighteenth centuries. D. Attwater, *The Catholic Eastern Churches*, 1935, a comprehensive account of all Eastern Christians who have accepted the Papal universal jurisdiction. A. Fortescue, *The Uniate Eastern Churches*, 1923, includes a bibliography, also T. Jalland, *The Church and the Papacy*, 1944.

CHAPTER VI

Russian Bible Society. R. Pinkerton, *Extracts from letters on his tour in Russia*, 1817. R. Pinkerton, *Russia or Miscellaneous Observations, etc.*, 1833. E. Henderson, *Bible Researches and Travels in Russia*, 1825. R. Paterson and E. Henderson, *Extracts from Letters during their respective tours through the Eastern Provinces of Russia*, 1817. J. Paterson, *The Book for Every Land. Reminiscences of Labour and Adventure in the Work for Bible Circulation in North Europe and Russia*, 1858. B. Seebolm (ed.), *Memoirs of the Life and Gospel Labours of Stephen Grillet*, 2 vols., Philadelphia 1862. E. Benz, *Die Abendlandische Sendung des Ostlich Orthodoxen Kirche im Zeitalter der Heiligen Allianz*, Mainz 1950.

Russian Sects. A. Heard, *The Russian Church and Russian Dissent*, 1887. F. Conybeare, *Russian Dissenters*, Cambridge, Mass. 1921. S. Bolshakov, *Russian Nonconformity*, Philadelphia 1950.

St Seraphim of Sarov. A. Dobbie Bateman, *St Seraphim of Sarov*, London 1936. J. de Beausobre, *The Flame in the Snow* (a romanticized life of Seraphim) 1945. G. Fedotov, *A Treasury of Russian Spirituality*. Translation of St Seraphim's discourse with his disciple Motovilov, pp. 246–79.

Optina Pustin. J. de Beausobre, *Russian Letters of Direction*, 1944, contains Makary's correspondence with his followers. M. Rouet de Journel, *Monachisme et Monastères Russes*, Paris 1952.

Metropolitan Philaret. *Select Sermons and Short Biography of the late Metropolitan of Moscow*. 1873. Philaret, *Choix de Sermons*, 3 vols., Paris 1866. Exposition of differences between Eastern and Western Churches, R. Pinkerton, *Russia*, 1833, pp. 39–54. Philaret. Catechism in its English translation in R. Blackmore, *The Doctrine of the Russian Church*, Aberdeen 1845.

Russian Missionary Work. E. Smirnov, *Russian Orthodox Missions*, London 1903. S. Bolshakov, *The Foreign Missions of the Russian Orthodox Church*, London 1943. A. Spiridon, *Mes Missions à Sibérie*, Paris 1950, a Diary of a Russian Missionary of the nineteenth century. Dr J. Glazik, *Die Islam Mission der Russische Orthodoxen Kirche*, Munster 1959 (Excellent bibliography). K. Latourette, *A History of Expansion of Christianity*, 1954, vol. VI, p. 379, estimates the number of the Japanese Orthodox Christians at 32,000 in 1912 and 41,000 in 1940.

The Slavophils. N. Zernov, *Three Russian Prophets*, 1943. S. Bolshakov, *The Doctrine of the Unity of the Church in the works of Khomiakov*, 1946. N. Riasanovsky, *Russia and the West in the Teaching of the Slavophils*, Camb., Mass. 1952. A. Khomiakov, *The Church is One*, 1945 (One of the most important theological works of Khomiakov). His correspondence with W. Palmer is found in J. Birbeck, *Russia and the English Church*, 1895. W. Palmer's visit to Russia in 1840–41 is described in *Notes of a Visit to the Russian Church*, 1882, ed. by J. Newman. Khomiakov's theological works are available in French: *L'Eglise Latine et Protestantisme au point de vue de l'Eglise d'Orient*, Lausanne 1872. The best study of his life and thought is also in French. A. Gratieux, *A. Khomiakov*, 2 vols, Paris 1939, and in Abbé Pierre Baron, *Un Théologien laic Orthodox Russe au XIX siècle, Alexis Stepanovich Khomiakov*, 1940.

The Westernisers. E. Carr, *The Romantic Exiles*, 1933. E. Lampert, *Studies in Rebellion*, 1957.

The Liberation of the Balkan Christians from the yoke of Islam. There is no special book dealing with the religious aspects of this movement. The factual account of the Greek liberation is given by C. Woodhouse, *The Greek War of Independence*, 1952. H. Temperley, *History of Serbia*, 1917. L. Ranke, *The History of Servia and the Servian Revolution*, 1853. W. Petrovich, *Serbia, Her People, History and Aspirations*, 1915. R. W. Seton-Watson, *The Emancipation of South-Eastern Europe*, 1923. *A History of the Rumanians*, Camb. 1934.

Petar Niegosh. J. Wiles, *The Mountain Wreath of P. P. Niegosh*, 1930. This book contains the translation of Negosh's poem and his biography.

The Church in Greece. Fr Matthopoulos. Seraphim Papakosta, *Eusebius Matthopoulos*, 1939. *The Trial of Apostolas Makrakis*, Chicago 1954.

Eastern Orthodoxy in Austria-Hungary. M. Dampier, *The Orthodox Church in Austria-Hungary*, 1905. W. Seton Watson's books contain much valuable information about various national groups in the Austrian Empire.

Russian Intelligentsia and the Empire. R. Hare, *Pioneers of Russian Social Thought*: Studies of non-Marxian formation in nineteenth century Russia and of its partial revival in the Soviet Union, 1951. E. Lampert, *Studies in Rebellion*, 1957.

Dostoevsky. Literature about Dostoevsky is enormous. All his works are available in English, including *The Diary of a Writer*, tr. by B. Brasov, 2 vols, N.Y. 1942, which contains much material about Dostoevsky's religious views. This aspect of his works is discussed by N. Berdiaev, *Dostoevsky*, 1934; L. Zander, *Dostoevsky*, 1948; N. Zernov, *Three Russian Prophets*, 1944. A bibliography about Dostoevsky is in *The Making of a Novelist*, 1950, by E. Simmons.

V. Soloviev. *A Soloviev Anthology* by S. Frank, 1950, provides an excellent introduction to his writings. Soloviev's works in English translation are: *War and Progress and the end of History*, 1915; *The Justification of Good*, 1918; *God, Man and the Church*, 1938; *Plato*, 1935; *The Meaning of Love*, 1946; *Lectures on God-Manhood*, 1948; *Russia and the Universal Church*, 1948. Books about Soloviev are: N. Zernov, *Three Russian Prophets*, 1944. E. Munzer, *Soloviev, Prophet of Russian-Western Unity*, New York 1956. M. d'Herbigny, *Vladimir Soloviev, a Russian*, Newman 1918. L. Kobilinski-Ellis, *Monarchia Sancti Petri*, Mainz-Wiesbaden 1929. D. Stremoukhoff, *Vladimir Soloviev et son oeuvre messianique*, Paris 1935.

CHAPTER VII

For the Russian writers and poets of the twentieth century see D. Mirsky, *Contemporary Russian Literature*, Vol. II (1881–1925), 1926. D. Merezkhovsky's novels and essays are available in English, French and German translations. V. Rozanov is less known. Only one of his books has been translated into English. *Solitaria*, tr. by S. S. Koteliansky, 1927. Nikolay Roerich's main works in English: *Spells of Russia*, 1920. *Himalaya*, New York 1926. *Altai-Himalaya, A Travel Diary*, 1930. *Himalaya—Abode of Light*, Bombay 1947. Vasily Kandinsky, see Will

Graham Kandinsky, 1959. Kandinsky's own books, *Uber der geistige in der Kunst*, 1959. *Regard sur le passé*, Paris 1946.

Russian Religious Renaissance of the Twentieth Century. There is no book in English dealing with this return to the Orthodox Church of Russian Intellectuals, but the works of several prominent writers of this period have been translated into English including: S. Bulgakov, *N. Berdiaev* and *S. Frank*. Bulgakov, *Divine Wisdom*, 1936, *Du Verbe Incarno*, Paris 1943, *Le Paraclet*, Paris 1947, *The Orthodox Church*, 1935, *The Vatican Dogma*, 1959, *Die Tragoedie der Philosophie*, Darmstadt 1927. Berdiaev, *Freedom and the Spirit*, 1935, *The Russian Revolution*, 1931, *Solitude and Society*, 1937, *The Destiny of Man*, 1939, *Spirit and Reality*, 1939, *Slavery and Freedom*, 1944, *The Russian Idea*, 1948, *Towards a New Epoch*, 1949. Books about Berdiaev are: D. Lawrie, *Rebellious Prophet*, 1960; M. Spinka, *Nicholas Berdyaev*, Philadelphia 1949; E. Lampert, *Nicholas Berdyaev*, 1945. S. Frank, *God with us*, 1948.

The Russian Church on the Eve of the Revolution. J. Curtis, *Church and State in Russia* (1900–17), New York 1940.

Fr John of Kronstadt. E. E. Goulaeff Sergieff, *John Ilytch*, 1897. C. Bickersteth, *Father John, Thoughts and Counsels*, 1899. G. Fedotov, *A Treasury of Russian Spirituality*, pp. 350–416.

Contemporary Orthodox Churches of the Balkans. Serafim Papakosta, *Eusebius Matthopoulos*, 1939. M. Constantinides, *Life and Work in the Diocese of Athens*. A lively description of the Church of Greece after the Second World War is given by P. Hammond, *The Waters of Arah*, 1956. Other books: M. Loughborough, *Rumanian Pilgrimage*, 1939. M. Beza, *The Rumanian Church*, 1943. R. French, *Serbian Church Life*, 1942.

The Russian Church and Communism. M. Spinka, *The Church and the Russian Revolution*, New York, 1927. M. Spinka, *The Church in the Soviet Union*, New York, 1956. P. Anderson, *People, Church and State in Modern Russia*, New York 1944. J. Curtis, *The Russian Church and the Soviet State* (1917–50), Boston 1953. G. Fedotov, *The Russian Church since the Revolution*, New York 1928. N. Timashev, *Religion in the Soviet Union*, New York 1942. G. McEoin, *The Communist War on Religion*, New York 1951. K. Rose, *Drei Patriarchen von Moscow*, Berlin 1952. N. Berdiaev, *The Origin of Russian Communism*, 1937. A view of pro-Communist American is reflected in J. Hecker, *Religion under the Soviets*, New York 1927, also his *Religion and Communism*, 1938. *The truth about religion in Russia*, 1944, reflects the description of the conflict as presented by the Moscow Patriarchate and authorized by the Soviet Government. For the present state of the Russian Church see *Russian Orthodox Bishops in the Soviet Union (1941–53)*, by W. Alexeev, New York 1954.

Among a number of the books written by the exiled Russian theologians and translated into the Western language, the most important are: N. Lossky, *History of Russian Philosophy*, 1952; *Freedom of Will*, 1932; *Value and Existence*, 1935. V. Zenkovsky, *The History of Russian Philosophy*, 2 vols, 1953; *Das Bild von Menschen in der Ostkirche*, Stuttgart 1951. V. Lossky, *The Mystical Theology of the Eastern Church*, 1957; L. Zander, *Vision and Action*, 1952. P. Evdokimov, *L'Orthodoxie*, Paris 1959; *La femme et le Salut du Monde*, Paris 1958. G. Fedotov, *The Russian Religious Mind*, Harvard 1946. G. Florovsky, *The Eastern Orthodox Church and the Ecumenical Movement*, 1950. V. Weidle, *The Dilemma of the Arts*, 1948, and *Russia, Absent and Present*, 1952.

The Orthodox Church and the Ecumenical Movement. R. Rouse and Stephen Neill, *A History of the Ecumenical Movement*, 1954, contains two contributions on this subject. G. Florovsky, *The Orthodox Church and the Ecumenical Movement prior to 1910*, pp. 171–221. N. Zernov, *The Eastern Church and the Ecumenical Movement in the twentieth century*, pp. 645–77, both articles include bibliography. A Makrakis, *Orthodox-Protestant Debate*, Chicago 1949 and *A Scriptural refutation of the Pope's primacy*, Chicago 1952, represent the most outspoken anti-Western point of view. The same attitude is to be found in the books of a convert to Orthodoxy. J. Overbeck, *Die Providentielle Stellung des Orthodoxen Russland und sein Beruf Zar Wiederherstellung des rechtglaubigen Katolische Korche des Abendlandens*, Hall 1869. J. Overbeck, *Die Wiedervereinigung des morgen und abend landischen Kirchen*, Hall 1871. Another convert from Rome to the Eastern Church was W. Guettee (1816–1892). *Souvenires d'un Prêtre roman devenu prêtre orthodoxe*, Paris 1889, also his *Exposition de la doctrine de l'Eglise Catholique Orthodoxe*, Paris 1884. A positive attitude towards Eastern and Western reconciliation is expressed in L. Zander, *Vision and Action*, 1952. N. Zernov, *The Reintegration of the Church*, 1952. The relations between Eastern and Western Christians are also reflected in the following books: S. Bulgakov, *The Vatican Dogma*, 1959; N. Zernov, *Orthodox Encounter*, 1961; L. Zander, *Western Orthodoxy*, 1960; E. Mastroyiannopoulos, *Nostalgia for Orthodoxy*, Athens 1959. D. Lawrie, *St Sergius in Paris*, The Orthodox Theological Institute, 1954. The Fellowship of St Albans and St Sergius publishes a magazine in English, *Sobornost*. Information about its work and other publications can be obtained from St Basil House, 52 Ladbroke Grove, London, W11.

The relations between the Anglican and the Orthodox Church. Much valuable material is contained in *Annual Reports of the Eastern Churches Association* from 1893–1909, also occasional papers of the *Eastern Church Association*, I–XVII, 1863–75, New Series I–X, 1902–04, also the *Annual Reports of Eastern Orthodox Churches Union*, 1–11, 1906–35. The magazine, *The Christian East* (1220–38, 1950–54). Between 1908–14 Anglican and Orthodox Church Union published a magazine *Eirene*.

P. Shaw, *The Early Tractarians and the Eastern Churches*, 1930, and *American Contacts with the Eastern Churches* (1820–70), Chicago 1939. Ch. Androustos, *The Validity of English Ordination from an Orthodox-Catholic point of view*, 1909. J. Douglas, *The Relations of the Anglican Church with the Eastern Orthodox*, 1921. A. Riley, *Birkbeck and the Russian Church*, 1917. Chrysostom Papadopoulos, *The Validity of Anglican Orders*, 1931. E. Hardy, *Orthodox Statements on Anglican Orders*, New York 1946. W. Vissert t'Hooft, *Anglo-Catholicism and Orthodoxy*. D. Chitty, *Orthodoxy and the Conversion of England* 1947. H. Hodges, *Anglicanism and Orthodoxy—A Study of Dialectical Churchmanship*, 1957. An older, but still useful book is W. Palmer *Dissertations on Subjects Relating to the Orthodox or Eastern Catholic Communion*, 1853. The most recent discussion between the Russian and Anglican theologians is reported by the Archbishop of York in *Anglo-Russia Theological Conference (Moscow, July 1956)*, 1957.

Père. Couturies. M. Villain, *L'Abbé Paul Couturies*, Paris 1957. D. Allchin, *L'Abbé Paul Couturies*, 1959.

CHAPTER VIII

Faith and Doctrine of the Orthodox Church. S. Bulgakov, *The Orthodox Church*, 1935, is the best book on the subject. The author is one of the great theologians of the Russian Church. His book is authoritative without being pedantic. S. Zankov, *The Eastern Orthodox Church*, 1929. R. French, *The Eastern Orthodox Church*, 1951. Another introduction to the study of the Eastern Christians, which describes them by comparing their faith and worship with the Christian West is by N. Zernov, *The Church of the Eastern Christians*, 1942. F. Gavin, *Some aspects of contemporary Greek Orthodox Thought*, 1936, an important book for trained theologians. It consists of detailed study of contemporary Greek theological writings. *The Holy Catechism of Nicolas Bulgaris* faithfully translated from the original Greek by W. E. Daniel, 1893, introduces the reader to the type of instruction which was given to the Orthodox in the seventeenth century. The catechisms of the Russian Church and a number of other doctrinal statements are found in: R. Blackmore, *The Doctrine of the Russian Church*, Aberdeen 1844; W. Palmer, *Dissertations on subjects relating to the Orthodox or Eastern Catholic Communion*, 1853. Also Melchisedec, *The Orthodox Doctrine of the Apostolic Eastern Church*, 1857. A very different book giving the present interpretation of Eastern Orthodoxy is *The Mystical Theology of the Eastern Church*, 1957, by V. Lossky. Three symposiums to which both the Eastern Orthodox and Anglican theologians have contributed are: *The Church of God*, ed. by E. Mascall, 1934; *The Mother of God*, ed. by E. Mascall, 1949; *The Angel of Light and the Powers of Darkness*, 1954. The best book in French is P. Evdokimov, *L'Orthodoxie*, Paris, 1959, and in German: K. Friz, *Die Stimme des Ostkirche*, Stuttgart 1950; E. Benz, *Geist und Leben der Ostkirche*, Hamburg 1957; Fr Heiler, *Urkirche und Ostkirche*, Munchen 1937; J. Tyciak, *Wege Ostlicher Theologie*, Bonn 1946; R. Klostermann, *Probleme der Ostkirche*, Goteburg 1955. Besides the dogmatic decrees of the seven Ecumenical Councils the Orthodox Church also accepts the decisions of the nine ancient local Councils, and of the four Synods which met in Constantinople in 861, 879, 1341 and 1351. The last two dealt with the question of divine energy as formulated by St Gregory Palamas. The Orthodox also recognize several other doctrinal statements like the confession of faith of St Gregory Thaumaturgus, St Athanasius and St John of Damascus, but they have not the same significance as the Nicene Creed. Still less is the authority of controversial doctrinal statement issued in the seventeenth century, such as the confession of faith of Peter Mogila or that of Dositheus, Patriarch of Jerusalem, approved by the local Synod in 1672. These documents served some useful purpose in their own time, but lacked the restraint and balance of the accepted Creed.

CHAPTER IX

The Worship and Sacraments of the Christian East. Only a small proportion of the service books used by the Eastern Christians is available in English translation. The translation of the Communion service is the most important. The English text of the Byzantine liturgies of St John Chrysostom and of St Basil the Great exists in several translations. One of the more recent ones was published by SPCK in London 1939, under the title *The Orthodox Liturgy*. The Coptic Morning Service for the Lord's Day was translated by John, Marquis of Bute, London 1908. The Armenian Liturgy was published by Cope & Fenwick, 1907. Other services of the Byzantine rite have been translated by I. Hapgood, *The Service Book of the Holy Orthodox Catholic Apostolic Church*, New York 1922. The English of this useful book does not do justice to the original and has been generally considered to be unsatisfactory. Other English translations include: *The Coptic Offices*, translated by R. Wooley, Madras 1930. *The Great Canon*, a poem of St Andrew of Crete, translated by D. Chitty, 1957. *The Liturgies of St Mark, James, Clement and the Church of Malabar*, by the Rev J. Neale, London 1869. *The Syrian Daily Offices*, translated by A. MacLean, 1894. *The Akathistos Hymn*, translated by V. McNabb, 1947. *The Manual of Eastern Orthodox Prayers*, 1945, contains morning and evening prayers, widely used for daily devotions by the Russian Orthodox, and the Rite of Confession. Those readers who desire to make a more specialized study of the Eastern Liturgies can find a useful bibliography and good treatment of this subject in F. Brightman, *The Eastern and Western Liturgies*, Oxford 1956. S. Salaville, *Eastern Liturgies*, London 1938. A. King, *The Rites of Eastern Christendom*, 2 vols, Roma 1947–48. R. Janin, *Eglises Orientales and Rites Orientaux*, Paris 1955. E. Mercenier, *La Prière des Eglises de Rite Byzantim*, 3 vols. N. Cabasilas, *A Commentary on the Divine Liturgy*, 1960. A description of Orthodox services as they used to be given in the Russian secondary schools is found in *Our Mother Church, Her Worship and Offices*, by E. Zvegintsev, 1948. N. Gogol, *Meditation on the Divine Liturgy*, 1961.

CHAPTER X

The Church in the life of the Eastern Christians. An old but useful book giving a vivid picture of Russian life is by H. C. Romanoff, *Sketches of the Greco-Russian Church*, 1869. Russian Church life in the twentieth century before the Communist Revolution is well described by S. Graham, *The Way of Martha and Mary*, 1914, and *With the Russian Pilgrims to Jerusalem*, 1914. The Greek Church life after the Second World War is presented by P. Hammond in his book, *The Waters of Marah*, 1956. Other popular books dealing with the life and customs of various national Churches of the East are: N. Arseniev, *Holy Moscow* (religious and spiritual life of Russia in the nineteenth century), 1940. M. Loughborough, *Rumanian Pilgrimage*, 1939. R. French, *Serbian Church Life*, 1942. A. Abrahamian, *The Church and Faith of Armenia*, 1920. D. O'Hanlon, *Features of the Abyssinian Church*, 1946. Surmad, Bait Mar Shimum, *Assyrian Church Customs*, 1920. A unique place in this devotional literature is held by the two anonymous writings, *The Way of a Pilgrim*, and *The Pilgrim continues his way*, translated by R. French, 1934. It is a diary of a Russian pilgrim describing his adventures in search of holy men and women in Russia, in the middle of the nineteenth century. The mystical tradition of the Eastern Church is revealed in two valuable books written by a monk of the Eastern Church: *Orthodox Spirituality*, 1943, and *On the Invocation of the Name of Jesus*, 1950.

Mount Athos. Many books have been published about Mount Athos and its monastic republic. The most important among these works is the study of one of the Holy Elders, Staretz Silouan (1866–1938), written by his disciple Archimandrite Sofrony, *The Undistorted Image*, 1958. Other books about Mount Athos are more descriptive: A. Riley, *Athos or the Mount of the Monks*, 1887. R. Byron, *The Station*, 1949. R. Dawkins, *The Monks of Mount Athos*, 1936. F. Hasluck, *Athos*, 1924. S. Loch, *Athos the Holy Mountain*, 1957. The author is a Scotsman who lived for twenty-five years in the vicinity of the Holy Mountain. P. Sherard, *Athos: The Mountain of Silence*, Oxford 1960. This has excellent coloured photographs. A Greek description of Athos is Constantin Cavernos's *Anchored in God*, Athens 1959. An earlier book describing Eastern monasteries in the middle of the nineteenth century is by R. Curzon, *Visits to Monasteries and the Levant*, 1840. A similar book is by O. Parry, *Six Months in a Syrian Monastery*, 1895. An account of a stay at Mardin with the Jacobite Patriarch Mar Ignatius Peter III. A later description of the same part of the world is given by H. Luke, *Prophets, Priests and Patriarchs (Palestine and Syria)*, 1927.

CHAPTER XI

The Sacred Art of the Christian East. There has lately been a steady stream of publications dealing with the art of the Christian East, and only the most important and most recent works on this subject can be given here. Two classical works are O. Dalton, *Byzantine Art and Archeology*, Oxford 1911, and N. Kondakov *The Russian Ikon*, Oxford 1927. A book of primary importance is R. Byron and D. Talbot Rice, *The Birth of Western Painting*, 1930. It is the work of men who have revealed the importance of Byzantine Art for the contemporary world. The latest books on Orthodox ikons, mosaics and frescoes are: L. Ouspensky, *Essai sur La Théologie de l'Icone dans l'Eglise Orthodoxe*, Paris 1960. A. Grabar, *Byzantine Painting*, 1953. D. Talbot Rice, *The Beginning of Christian Art*, 1957. D. Talbot Rice, *The Art of Byzantium*, 1959. L. Ouspensky and V. Lossky, *The Meaning of Ikons*, 1952, gives not only artistic, but also theological explanations of the ikons. The best reproductions of ikons are in the Unesco World Series, *The Early Russian Ikons*.

Church Architecture. D. Buxton, *Russian Medieval Architecture*. C. Stewart, *Byzantine Legacy*, 1947. C. Stewart, *Serbian Legacy*, 1959. G. Hamilton, *The Art and Architecture of Russia*, 1954.

Conclusion

Christian East and West. The significance of the meeting between Christian East and West and some special contributions of Russian Orthodoxy are discussed in the following books: P. Sherrard, *The Greek East and the Latin West*, 1959. A philosophical approach to their contrast and similarity. W. Schubart, *Russia and the Western Man*, New York 1956. A work of great originality and penetration by a German Sociologist who perished during the Second World War. N. Gorodetsky, *The Humiliated Christ in Modern Russian Thought*, 1932. R. Korper, *The Candlelight Kingdom*. A Meeting with the Russian Church, New York 1955. N. Zernov, *Orthodox Encounter*, 1961.

INDEX